Musings of the Heart

365 Reflections on God's Word

Aaron E. Peters

First printed 2012
Musings of the Heart
Copyright © 2012 by Cephas Media Group
ISBN 978-0-9876954-0-6

All rights reserved. No part of this book may be reproduced or transmitted in any form or by any means without written permission from the publisher.

e-mail: publishing@cephasmediagroup.com

Scripture quotations are from
The Holy Bible, English Standard Version® (ESV®), copyright © 2001 by Crossway, a publishing ministry of Good News Publishers. Used by permission. All rights reserved.

&

The HOLY BIBLE, NEW INTERNATIONAL VERSION®.
Copyright © 1973, 1978, 1984 by International Bible Society.
Used by permission of Zondervan. All rights reserved.

To God be the glory.
Who has created minds to reason,
Eyes to see,
And hands to write.

ACKNOWLEDGMENTS

There are many to whom I would like to extend my thanks for their contribution towards the production of this book. To my father, who suggested that I should write these devotionals, and whose technical expertise I would be lost without. To my mother, for her steadfast commitment to be my editor, and whose honest yet constructive feedback has proven to be invaluable on more than one occasion. To my family and friends, who have never failed to show their support whether it be through their encouragement, their suggestions, or their willingness to share my writings with others. Finally I would like to extend my thanks to my online friends, whose comments on my writings and how Christ has been working in their lives through them, always remind me why I write and the focus I need to keep; so that God may be glorified and that He will carry out His work in the lives of others as well as mine.

Aaron E. Peters

FOREWORD

I am always looking around for younger people who know God and can articulate His truth clearly. One such young man is Aaron Peters. With wisdom and insight beyond his years, Aaron has skillfully written these daily devotionals, which point to Christ and lead us to greater dependence on Him in every facet of life. Though living in Canada, Aaron has had rich experience of serving God in India and parts of South East Asia (some of which come out in these pages).

Truth is never given to us as mere information, but to lead us into greater experience of God. To 'know God', which is how Jesus defined eternal life in John 17:3, is not to accumulate propositional truths about Him, but to experience Him, His presence, His guidance, His empowering, and His work of reproducing His character in our lives. These musings are with that in mind. They lead us to a sense of greater love for Christ, a fuller obedience to Christ, and a deeper dependence on Christ, who alone can make the Christian life workable and real.

Charles Price
Senior Pastor of The Peoples Church, Toronto
Host of Living Truth Television and Radio

January 1

STAY TRUE TO YOUR RESOLUTIONS!

"When you make a vow to God, do not delay in fulfilling it. He has no pleasure in fools; fulfill your vow." -Ecclesiastes 5:4 (NIV)

In the first days of the New Year it is a common practice to make resolutions. How many of us have promised ourselves to do something different about our behavior or our habits for the year ahead? Maybe we have decided to give up certain small pleasures to lead more healthy and active lifestyles. Perhaps we have set particular goals we hope to meet by the end of this year. Yet what often happens is that while we may hold true to the promises we made for the first few weeks, our commitment begins to waver as time goes on. Come mid-year we would have forgotten all about our resolutions and when reminded we say to ourselves that we will get right on it; though with no real intention to do so.

Promises are not meant to be broken. Throughout Scripture God makes clear the seriousness and weight behind making commitments. In His dealings with us He always keeps His word. Never will He abandon His promises to us on a whim or out of frustration for it goes against His very nature as being steadfastly faithful and loving. While humanity continues to grieve Him with our reckless pursuit of sin, He has fulfilled His promise to Adam and Eve that the power of sin would be broken through the redemptive sacrifice of Christ. He stands as the only way by which we may be saved and restored from our wickedness, and God has no intention of withdrawing His free gift of salvation to us.

Likewise, as His children who have submitted ourselves to His Spirit and seek to conform ourselves to His likeness, we are to regard the practice of promise-making with much reverence. Whether we make them before God, before each other, or before ourselves, we are to ensure that they will be fulfilled no matter the cost. If we think we can handle such an adamant commitment to keeping our promises, we will be proven wrong by our own human failings. Only when we have allowed the Spirit of Christ to reside and work out His righteousness through us will He give us the strength and discipline to see through to our promises to the end. In doing so, we will be bearing witness to all who see that we serve a God who will always remain true to the assurances He gives us.

January 2

PEACE IN THE STORM

"You rule over the surging sea; when its waves mount up, you still them." -Psalm 89:9 (NIV)

Having a restless spirit is not a pleasant thing to be in possession of. When fear and anxiety grip our minds, we feel as if we are in a perpetual storm. A variety of things can trigger the emergence of this in our lives. Circumstances, people, disappointments, all these things can bring a dark cloud over our minds and bind us to despair. Though we yearn for peace and seek to find it, it always seems to elude us. No matter where we turn, our human sources fail to provide the serenity we long for. In our frustration we give up searching; allowing the storms of life to govern us and rob us of our joy under the false notion that peace is not something that we are meant to obtain.

We were not designed to handle worry and sorrow. That is why we are so eager to find relief from the anguish that torments us; looking for that strong foundation on which we can stand upon and find rest. But if our search is leading us to find solace and comfort in the impermanent things of this world, we will only find disappointment when we see that our troubled spirit still remains. Only through Christ, who has overcome the world and the suffering inherent in it, will we find the unshakable peace that we seek. Man was meant to live in a relationship with God under His love and faithful provision. When we have personally accepted Christ's redemptive sacrifice for our sins and have allowed His Spirit to reside in our hearts, He will fill us with His peace if we choose to take hold of it. The same God who has the power to control the storm is the same God who will put to rest our fears if we simply choose to submit all our cares and worries to Him. We will find true and lasting peace when we cling to Him knowing that He is greater than our sufferings and will restore us according to His perfect will for our lives.

January 3

WORKING TOWARD ONE PURPOSE

"There are different kinds of gifts, but the same Spirit. There are different kinds of service, but the same Lord. There are different kinds of working, but the same God works all of them in all men." -1 Corinthians 12:4-6 (NIV)

Occasionally I enjoy watching programs on how things are made. These programs take the viewer on a tour of a particular factory in which the subject of the episode is produced. Showcased are the different machines used on each step of the assembly process and the role they play.

What fascinates me is that while each task, if taken individually, may seem mundane and insignificant, the truth is that each one is integral to the completion of the final product. The designers have built every single machine in the factory with a specific purpose in mind and have placed them in a particular order to facilitate the production of everyday items such as crayons, cars, or computers. If even one of these machines were to be removed or malfunction, the finished product would not look or function as it was intended.

When God created us, He built within each of us unique characteristics. Allowing the Spirit of Christ to help us discern what these are and how they are meant to be used is part of figuring out the perfect plan God has for each one of us. Perhaps He has bestowed upon us the ability to teach, preach and encourage, or has given us the acumen to work through the complexities of administrative tasks. Maybe He has blessed us with an artistically talented mind, or one that is more inclined to philosophical or historical inquiry. Regardless of the abilities He has graciously given to us, they all have their place within His Church and within the wider plan of redemption He has for the entire world. We in our pride have no right to claim that our individual gifts have more or less validity and importance over those of another. Such attitudes do not stem from our obedience to Christ's Spirit in our lives for He cannot contradict Himself. Therefore He cannot diminish or discredit that which He is working out in the lives of others. Though Christ has called each one of us to serve in different ways according to our specific gifts, His final purpose is the same; to draw others into the hope and joy of being restored through Him. When we submit ourselves to Christ, we will be able to work together by His enabling in unity of purpose and spirit; bringing our individual gifts to the table so that He may use them for the furtherance of His Kingdom.

January 4

PREPARATION IS KEY

"Joshua told the people, 'Consecrate yourselves, for tomorrow the Lord will do amazing things among you.'" -Joshua 3:5 (NIV)

Track and field was one of the many events of which we had to be participants in school. One year I had signed up for a 400-meter run. I had never participated in one before but in my ignorance I thought that as long as I could run a lap around the school gym I would be fine. Falsely thinking that I would do well on the day of the race, I did not take my training seriously. Never did I practice outside the limited times we were allowed to train at school, nor was I mindful of what I ate. When I walked out onto that track that day to take my starting position I realized two things; this track was much bigger than the school gym, and I should not have snacked before the race. I ended up hobbling along the track into last place; with the most painful stomach cramp I have ever felt!

Joshua declared to the people that God will work wondrous things before their eyes. However they must first consecrate themselves today by living in obedience to God and seeking to pursue the righteousness He has called them to abide by as His chosen people. Often times we mistakenly think the reverse. We would like to believe that God will deliver on His victorious promises now. Only until He has proven Himself to be faithful will we live our lives in accordance with His perfect will. But if we have assumed such a view we will only find defeat; not by the hand of God, but by our own unwillingness to prepare our hearts and minds so as to receive His promises. When an athlete trains or a student studies, he is assured of victory because he has prepared himself for it. Likewise if we truly desire to see God perform His redemptive and restorative work in our lives, we must first submit ourselves to the Spirit of Christ residing in our hearts and allow His righteousness to flow from within us. In doing this today, we will find hope and victory tomorrow; resting confidently in the promise that He will bless those who seek Him first.

January 5

SEEING THE TRUTH

"No one from the east or the west or from the desert can exalt a man. But it is God who judges:" -Psalm 75:6-7a (NIV))

How easily do we bend to the opinions of others! While we may think that our beliefs about ourselves and the people we come in contact with are formed independent of any outside influence, often the opposite proves to be true. Can we point to moments in our lives where we have wrongly judged people because we believed the false rumors or prejudices of another? Conversely, what about those moments where we praised and idolized certain people because those around us did so? Yet upon further investigation we found that the figures of our adoration lived lifestyles that were depraved and detrimental. If we have placed our complete trust in the opinions of man, we will only find ourselves confused and disillusioned for such opinions often find their root in the fallibility of human wisdom. As a result of our fallen nature we are unable to correctly discern truth; inadvertently praising that which is actually evil and shunning that which is actually good.

Who then is the final arbiter of truth? It cannot be we in our imperfections, but One who is not bound by our failings. God is truth personified, and all that is good and pure derives from His perfect righteousness and love. In His omnipotence He sees what our limited vision cannot; the inner depths of each individual, human heart. While our minds can be easily deceived by the lies of wickedness, His eyes pierce through its deceptions. All of us are afflicted by sin and this has affected our judgment. But God did not want us to remain in such a state. In His love He sent His Son, Jesus Christ, so that through His death and resurrection we may be freed from the yoke of sin. When we have personally accepted Christ's redemptive sacrifice for us and have allowed His Spirit to work in our lives, He will open our eyes to the truth. Our opinions of ourselves will not be determined by what others think, but by the reality that we are cherished beings created in the image of God and lovingly redeemed by the work of Christ. Submitting ourselves to His Spirit residing within us we will also gain the wisdom of His righteousness; measuring the words and beliefs of others according to His perfect standards. Yet at the same time He will prompt and guide us in the proper use of this knowledge, not to condemn but to point to the hope of being restored through Him.

January 6

WHO ARE WE REALLY?

"But when you pray, go into your room, close the door and pray to your Father, who is unseen. Then your Father, who sees what is done in secret, will reward you." -Matthew 6:6 (NIV)

Often we live two lives. The first is lived out in the public realm; how we interact and behave when we are in the presence of other people. By this definition it includes everyone from our friends and those in authority over us, to even our own family members. The second is lived in the private realm. This includes what we think and believe in our individual hearts, and what we do and say when we feel that no one is watching. At times, these two lives can be completely different. What we may present to the world may not necessarily be who we really are. We may perhaps don a mask of piety and righteousness when we move in the public realm, yet go against these very things in the private realm. However, we are sadly mistaken if we think we can maintain a balancing act between these two lives. One will inevitably overpower the other, and it is much more difficult to maintain a façade than it is to act according to one's own nature.

What is Jesus trying to say in this verse? What does it mean to go into our rooms, close our doors, and pray? He is trying to make a very specific point. God tests our hearts. Though we may say the right things and be full of good deeds when the eyes of others are upon us, He sees right through our disguises. If our hearts are far away from Christ, and are without any intention to conform ourselves to Him, then our outward actions are insincere deceptions; reminding us of our own depravity. The private realm informs the public realm. When we allow the Spirit of Christ to carry out His redemptive work in our lives, we are given a new nature. Through Him our old sinful nature is broken and we are clothed by His righteousness. By surrendering every area of the private realm to Christ's refining work, He will manifest Himself in the public realm. In doing this God will reward us for our obedience to Him as we live within His perfect will and allow His love to overflow from within us; consuming ourselves and those we come into contact with.

January 7

HE IS WITH US!

"...the Lord will watch over your coming and going both now and forevermore." -Psalm 121:8 (NIV)

All of us are called to a journey in this life. Each journey is unique to the individual, and what may be one person's journey may not necessarily be the same for another. Yet our journeys are bound by several shared characteristics. There are times when we walk along the path with our heads held high, and times when the clouds of despair hang over us. Sometimes the journey may feel like an exciting adventure, or at other times a laborious ordeal. There are moments where we find ourselves standing at a crossroads, thoroughly confused and gripped by uncertainty, and there are moments where we stumble and fall. In light of these realities we ask ourselves where God is. Does He see us when we fall? Does He see us when we are overcome by fear and sorrow? Where is His wonderful master plan in the midst of all this, and will He truly fulfill His perfect will for our lives?

These questions are natural ones to ask when we feel overwhelmed by the complexities of life. But to allow these questions to distort the truth about God will lead us further down the road of despair and hopelessness. The unquestionable truth is that God does see! His eyes never leave us for a moment. What is more is that He not only sees, He cares! He takes delight in our joys and grieves with us in our times of distress. In His love He wants to guide us along the path He has called us to, and will always extend His hand when we find ourselves sprawled on the ground. The real question to be answered now is, will we take His hand? Will we allow Him to guide our steps and trust in His unfailing faithfulness? When we allow the Spirit of Christ to enter our hearts and submit ourselves to Him, He will direct us in the path we must go and carry us through whatever we may face. He will strengthen us when life seems arduous, defend us when life seems unfair, and restore our joy when it seems that it has been stripped away. Through Him we have hope; resting in the promise that He never breaks His word, and that He will be with us to the very end until we are united with Him in Heaven.

January 8

NOTHING'S IMPOSSIBLE, ONLY BELIEVE!

"Everything is possible for him who believes." -Mark 9:23b (NIV)

It is easy for us to become prisoners to discouragement. When our hopes and aspirations appear to be shattered, when we have reached the limit of our own human capabilities, we want to throw our hands up in the air in frustration and resign. Embracing a spirit of defeatism we are quick to say that it is impossible, that our miracle will not come, that we are not meant for great things, and that we are destined to live a miserable life of banality and sorrow. While we may recognize the bleak nature of this outlook, we say that it cannot be helped; allowing ourselves to become slaves to our circumstances and negativity. However, such a view clouds our minds to the fact that there is someone greater; someone that stands supreme above the world and wants to help us.

Nothing is difficult for God. Before the world began He existed. The vastness of the universe, and the laws it is governed by, is His handiwork. By His voice He is able to calm the raging sea and by His hand He is able to make time stand still. His power knows no boundaries and what may be insurmountable for us cannot stand before His omnipotence. When we enter into a relationship with Christ, accepting His redemptive sacrifice for us and allowing His Spirit to reside in our hearts, we are conquerors through Him. We have triumphed over sin and death with Him by identifying with His death and resurrection. Dwelling in the hope and knowledge that He is faithful and all-powerful, we can rest in the assurance that when we have reached our limit, He will prove to us that His strength is more than enough. Will we take that step of faith and take hold of the fact that nothing is impossible with Him? Putting aside our worries and our fears and submitting them to the Spirit of Christ, He will lift us out of despair; showing us that despite our seemingly impossible circumstances, He is able to and will work out all things together for good.

January 9

IN PERPETUAL HUNGER

"'The days are coming,' declares the Sovereign Lord, 'when I will send a famine through the land-not a famine of food or a thirst for water, but a famine of hearing the words of the Lord.'" -Amos 8:11 (NIV)

Usually I am not one prone to develop sudden cravings. But when they come, they hit me hard. A whole host of things have the potential to stoke my hunger. It could be a particular chocolate, pastry, drink, or even an entire dish! Like a flood these desires come over me and like a whirlwind I would scour the kitchen for anything that could satisfy my appetite. While most times I cannot quench my desires immediately, the day when I am finally in possession of the object of my longing is always sweet. That milky bar of chocolate is so much more delightful! That iced cappuccino is so much more refreshing! That juicy steak is so much more delectable! What bliss, what joy, when finally that feeling of fulfillment comes over you!

People under the conditions of famine define what it means to be starved. They yearn for that which will satisfy their hunger and will go to great lengths to see that it is met. Likewise God wants to create a famine in our lives. Not a desire for food and drink, but a desire to hear His Word. When we have allowed the Spirit of Christ to invade our hearts, He will give us that craving to hear from Him; to seek His face and glean from His infinite and unfailing wisdom. It is a famine that should not see an end, but kept in a perpetual state as to continue to kindle that desire for the things of God. The moment we find ourselves satisfied and content with our spiritual lives is the moment when the process of spiritual degeneration begins. When we ask God to keep us in that state of hunger, to allow Him to foster within us the desire to learn from Him, He will speak into our lives through His Word; challenging us and thereby molding us into His exhibits of His love and righteousness.

January 10

THE RIGHT INTERPERTATION

"For we do not preach ourselves, but Jesus Christ as Lord, and ourselves as your servants for Jesus' sake." -2 Corinthians 4:5 (NIV)

We like to be in authority. There is something about being the final word that appeals to our pride and lust for power. When people look to us for guidance or when we are given a forum to speak, it is tempting to promote our values and opinions as being the unquestionable truth. This is true even when the Scriptures are the focus of inquiry. Taking pride in our own wisdom, we declare that our own interpretations of the Word of God are superior to any other. But invariably what we have done is we have elevated ourselves above God and have placed our faith in our own fallible understanding. When we assert interpretations constructed by our sinful nature as being true, only our sin will be displayed, not the truth and righteousness of Christ.

Who are we to say that we can discern the mind of God through our flawed comprehension? What right do we have to alter the Word of God to fit our own desires and agendas? The Scriptures are His divine revelation to man, not man's revelation to other men. Should not He therefore be the sole arbiter of what is truth, and should not He be the only one to correctly interpret His own Word? When we truly allow the Spirit of Christ to dwell within our hearts and carry out His redemptive work in our lives, He will purge us of our sinful pride. By submitting our minds to Him and permitting Him to reveal His truth to us, we will gain the correct understanding of His Word and by His strength apply them in our lives. Humbling ourselves before Christ we will understand what it really means to proclaim the Word of God; to simply remain in obedience to Him as He speaks His truth and love through us, and draw others to the hope which comes by being one with Him.

January 11

LISTEN AROUND YOU!

"For lack of guidance a nation falls, but many advisers make victory sure." -Proverbs 11:14 (NIV)

Why do totalitarian states fail? The answer can actually be boiled down to one simple answer; one man runs the show. When a person is given or assumes absolute power, his will also gains unquestionable supremacy. Any opposition to the desires of the leader is placed under charges of subversion, real or imagined, and is summarily eliminated. With no external body to offer helpful critique and counsel without the fear of repercussions, it is necessary that the success of the nation be solely dependent on the leader's wisdom. However, no one can guarantee that the policies he enacts or the decisions he makes will be beneficial to the health of the nation and the wellbeing of its people. Therefore, with the absence of an accountability system, victory eludes the regime of the totalitarian ruler and decay is inevitable unless total change is set in motion.

God wants us to live in accordance with His wisdom. He does not desire this for His own sake, but for ours. So that we may not be ensnared by our folly, He wants to guide our steps and live in the freedom and security which comes from abiding in Him. Yet often God places people in our path so that through them He may speak His wisdom into our lives. When we ignore these voices in our pride and worship of our limited capacity to reason, we set ourselves on the path of destruction. But while we are to listen to what others have to say, their advice must be tested against the Word of God. Only when we have the Spirit of Christ residing in us, allowing His redemptive work in our lives to shatter our pride and draw ourselves closer to Him, will we be able to gain discernment. Armed with this we will know by the wisdom of Christ in us the advice which God wants us to hear, and the unsound counsel which should be ignored. Stubbornness in our flawed understanding will only lead to our defeat. But there is victory if we listen to the voice of God.

January 12

WHO IS YOUR KING?

"In those days Israel had no king; everyone did as he saw fit." - Judges 21:25 (NIV)

The book of Judges is certainly not for the faint of heart. Its pages account for one of the darkest times in Israel's history. Stories of war, bloodshed, wickedness, and tragedy abound, and testify to the extent of the chaos that engulfed the land. The only factor which kept Israel from descending into total anarchy was God's faithful and loving provision of the judges. Living in obedience to God, these judges defended the nation and upheld His righteousness for all to follow. Yet as the second chapter of the book attests, the majority of the people did not listen to them; choosing instead to live in disobedience to God's holy standards. It is no wonder therefore that the book, after describing the destructive and horrible consequences resulting from their obedience to sin, ends with the words, "In those days Israel had no king; everyone did as he saw fit."

When we refuse to enthrone Christ as the Lord of our lives, we take the first step towards a path which will ultimately lead to our degradation and ruin. While our sinful nature wants us to believe that the ideal state of existence is to live however we choose and place ourselves as the highest authority, this is a cruel deception. Though we may claim that we are free living outside of Christ, we are actually enslaving ourselves to our innate depravity and allowing it to consume every area of our lives. If we truly want to be saved from such a fate, our only hope is Christ. When we personally accept His redemptive sacrifice for us on the cross and enthrone Him as the King of our hearts, we will understand that life is not meant to be lived on our terms, but on His. By walking in obedience to Him, with His Spirit helping us to live in accordance with His righteousness, He will carry out His restorative work in our lives and the world around us. His purity and love will shine forth from us when we acknowledge Him as our one and only King.

January 13

WHOSE GIFT IS IT?

"Pharaoh said to Joseph, 'I had a dream, and no one can interpret it. But I have heard it said of you that when you hear a dream you can interpret it.' 'I cannot do it,' Joseph replied to Pharaoh, 'but God will give Pharaoh the answer he desires.'" -Genesis 41:15-16 (NIV)

Joseph had an incredible gift. The ability to correctly interpret dreams is definitely something to marvel at. This gift which Joseph had reached the ears of Pharaoh, who as ruler of ancient Egypt was the most powerful man on Earth. Though he had many under him who claimed to have the ability to interpret dreams, all of them failed to deliver on their claims. What an opportunity for Joseph to make a name for himself! Standing before a man of such stature, he had the perfect chance to advertise himself as the undisputed authority on dream interpretation. He could gain the prestige of being the man Pharaoh goes to whenever he is disturbed by a troubling vision. Yet, Joseph knew that his ability to interpret dreams was not through any capacity of his own. It was solely by the work of God in his life and he humbly acknowledged this fact before Pharaoh. For his humility, God rewarded Joseph by prompting Pharaoh to appoint him as prime minister over Egypt; giving him power and status that was subordinate only to Pharaoh himself.

All of us have gifts and abilities given to us by God. But what do we do with these gifts? Do we use it to boost our pride, our reputation amongst men? In our egocentric attitudes we wrongly attribute that which God has graciously bestowed upon us to our own human capabilities and determine that only we are able to discern their proper use. However, if we rely on our faulty wisdom tainted by our sinful nature to direct us, we cheat ourselves out of the vision God promises us for an inferior one. God knows us intimately well, and knows of the abilities He has given us. Shouldn't He therefore be the only one who can help us guide us in how to use them? When we cast aside our pride and humbly allow the Spirit of Christ to work in our lives, He will exalt us as we permit Him to use whatever we have for His restorative mission to the world. Our humility before Christ and our surrendering of our gifts to His perfect plan for our lives will take us to places we would have never imagined; leaving us in awe of His faithfulness and love.

January 14

OUR FAITHFUL CHAMPION

"...the Lord your God fights for you, just as he promised." -Joshua 23:10 (NIV)

Life can often feel like a battlefield. It has a way of sending wave after wave of challenges which need to be overcome. Perhaps it could be the everyday demands which we must face in our schools and workplaces. Maybe it is those obstacles and hurdles that stand between us and our hopes and dreams. It could even be our circumstances and situations themselves, and we work hard to see to their improvement. Yet there are times when we may feel that it is all an uphill battle. No matter how hard we try or how adamant our determination, we only see defeat around us. Naturally this can be a source of discouragement for us and in our frustration we may give up hope; wondering if victory is destined to elude us.

But how far this is from the truth! We do not fight alone for there is Someone who has overcome the sufferings of the world. When we have reached our limitations, Christ will perfect His strength in our weakness. He promises that whosoever calls upon His name shall find deliverance and restoration. Like reinforcements coming to relieve a besieged city, He will rush to our side and empower us in our darkest hour. Though the battles will still have to be fought, our victory is assured when we have acknowledged Him as Lord of our lives and allowed Him to work through us. By His enabling He will give us the vigor and endurance to fight the good fight when feel we cannot go on. Through our obedience to His perfect wisdom, He will guide our steps and give us discernment in how to handle our situations. When we have allowed Christ to fight for us, we can rest in the fact that nothing will be able to stand against us. As sure as the rising of the sun we will know that our trials will bow down to the light of Christ, and that no power on Earth can snatch away the hope we have of life through Him.

January 15

JOY IN THE PRESENT

"When God gives any man wealth and possessions, and enables him to enjoy them, to accept his lot and be happy in his work – this is a gift of God." -Ecclesiastes 5:19 (NIV)

We all have an ideal in our minds as to what our lives should be. Who doesn't dream of having wealth, fame, and success beyond their wildest imaginations? It is why we stand in awe of palatial mansions and royal residences while taking in all their lavish splendor. A part of us wishes that somehow the grandeur we behold could be ours too. But when contrast our ideals with our realities; it may not match with what we hope to have. Perhaps we do not have the mansion, the riches, and the status we desire. Reminded of this we may feel discouraged and frustrated we may wonder if there is anything good about our present circumstances. We long for that day when the material blessings we yearn for will rain down upon us; thinking that once they do, we will find lasting happiness.

There is nothing inherently wrong with seeking to better ourselves. God says in His Word that we are to pursue excellence wherever we are placed. But if we become obsessed with chasing after visions of material success, we blind ourselves to the blessings that we already have. The treasures of this world are destined to come to an end, but the joy and security we have in Christ will last into eternity. When we allow Christ to enter into our hearts and have made Him the centre of our lives, He will open our eyes to His loving provision all around us. No situation, however bleak, is devoid of hope and reason to be thankful for every day is a gift from God; a moment in time where He will reveal to us His faithfulness. Whatever our lot may be, we can find reasons to rejoice knowing that Christ is eternal and that as we remain in obedience to Him and trust His perfect will, we are storing up for ourselves heavenly treasures that will never perish.

January 16

DON'T BE LED ASTRAY!

"Dear children, keep yourselves from idols." -1 John 5:21 (NIV)

When we were children, there were things and practices which our parents told us to stay away from. A classic example of this is eating too much junk food. One day my mother bought a whole bag of cookies. Knowing my love for them she instructed me to not eat too many in one sitting. But in my childish folly I continued to devour them despite her repeated warnings. The next day I woke up with the most painful stomach ache I have ever experienced! It was in that moment that I learnt a very important lesson. I had a choice to listen to my mother and refrain from overeating. But because I chose to submit myself to my cravings, I allowed them to steer me away from the wise instruction of my mother; a decision which I had to pay the consequences for.

It is the same with idols in our lives. While an idol usually conjures up images of statues made of stone and wood, the definition of the term is much broader than that. In the eyes of God an idol is anything that draws us away from Him and living in obedience to His perfect will. Scripture tells us quite clearly that we are to keep ourselves away from them, and for good reason. Initially our idolatry may seem harmless and even enjoyable; just as how a child takes pleasure in his over-indulgence in sweets. However, we will soon realize that our idols have deceived us with their false promises of pleasure and that their sole purpose is to destroy us and our relationship with God. When we allow the Spirit of Christ to reside within us, He will not hesitate to reveal areas of our lives where we have erected idols that need to be cast aside. If we cling to these idols, we are only depriving ourselves of the restorative work He wants to conduct in our hearts. But if we submit ourselves to His Spirit and choose to abide in Him, we will find life and security that no idol on Earth can provide.

January 17

AN UNAVOIDABLE LIGHT

"If I rise on the wings of the dawn, if I settle on the far side of the sea, even there your hand will guide me, your right hand will hold me fast." -Psalm 139:9-10 (NIV)

Nowhere on Earth is there a place that is not warmed by the sun. People living in North America are exposed to the same ball of solar energy as those living in the islands of the Pacific Ocean. Wherever we travel we can always expect the sun to make its appearance for its rays encompass the entire world. This is true even in parts of the world where the sun does not seem to shine. For nearly six months anything north of the Arctic Circle is engulfed by total darkness. But that does not mean that the sun has somehow forgotten or abandoned the desolate region. In fact it reminds the people of its existence with six months of its light!

In the same manner we cannot escape the presence of God. He is omnipresent and no matter where we are, He is there with us. When we are at the heights of elation, He is there rejoicing with us. In the pits of despair, when all our hope and joy seems to have been extinguished, He is there to comfort us and bring healing to our soul. If we find ourselves lost in the deserts of our circumstances, confused and perplexed, He is there to strengthen us and guide our path. Christ has promised that He does not abandon those who call upon His name. No situation is beyond His restorative work and when we allow Him to intervene in our lives, enthroning Him as the sole Lord of our hearts, He will not fail in proving His faithfulness. If we choose to embrace and cling to Him, we will know that He is our ever-present help. When we abide in Him our hope will never be snuffed out for our trust is placed in the One who has plans to prosper us and who has emerged victorious over the world.

January 18

ALWAYS BE ALERT!

"So, if you think you are standing firm, be careful that you don't fall!" -1 Corinthians 10:12 (NIV)

The mark of a good guard is that he is ever vigilant. Whether he is keeping watch over a building or an entire city, he knows that lives and property are at risk if he slacks even for a moment in his duty. That is why falling asleep at one's post is such a serious matter. Though it may be tempting to rest their eyes, especially in those late hours of the night when all seems quiet, they cannot. If they fail to be alert, what they were charged with protecting could fall into the hands of lurking enemies or criminals. Destruction and sorrow follows negligence, and the guard which takes this seriously disciplines himself to be watchful. He does this so that he may be able to defend himself and the people he is responsible for from potential assailants.

It can be easy to become comfortable with our spiritual lives. When we find ourselves under the blessing of God and everything is going our way, the tendency is to allow ourselves to become lax in our obedience to Christ. We allow certain wrong attitudes, habits, and values to slip into our minds. But while we may attempt to justify our allowance of these things to permeate our minds by claiming that they are somehow harmless, we will soon be awakened to the unpleasant truth. Sin if tolerated will only continue to grow. Once it has made known to us the full gravity of its destructive nature, we will mourn our lack of vigilance. Like a guard clumsily aroused from his sleep in the midst of an invasion, we will be unprepared and overwhelmed by the onslaught of sin's arrows.

It does not have to be like this however, if we discipline ourselves in standing for the righteousness of Christ in the first place. When we allow the Spirit of Christ to reside within us and seek to remain in obedience to Him, He will give us strength and wisdom to discern what violates His holy standards. With this knowledge He will help us prevent sinful practices from establishing a foothold in our lives. By doing this we will find freedom and security in His righteousness; protecting both ourselves and others from the ravages of wickedness and bearing witness to the life that comes by being restored through Christ.

January 19

TENDING THE FLAME

"Do not be slothful in zeal, be fervent in spirit, serve the Lord."- Romans 12:11 (ESV)

Fire is valued for the warmth and comfort it provides. In those cool summer nights or frigid winter days, it is truly a blessing to be in front of a campfire or fireplace depending on the season. But fires are not eternal. They need to be maintained in order to survive. If we provide the fire with fuel, such as wood or paper, then we are assured of the continued heat that it will provide. However, if left alone any fire, be it a small candle or a raging inferno, will slowly die out simply because it does not have enough fuel to sustain itself. The life of a fire depends on what is there and what is done to keep it alive. A lack of these things will eventually make it cease to exist.

What vision, what desire, has God placed in our hearts? In many ways this is a flame we are called to tend. Initially we may have approached this task with vibrant passion and conviction. But perhaps the storms of life have dampened our enthusiasm and crushed our spirit. Confronted by such circumstances we may wonder if tending to our flame is a futile endeavor. However, when we give up on the vision God has given us, we have traded His wonderful plan for our lives for something inferior. Living in dissatisfaction and restlessness we want to rekindle that flame but are afraid of encountering disappointment again. Yet in Christ we are promised victory. He does not place visions in our hearts only to watch them fizzle out. When we allow Christ to enter our lives and remain obedient to Him, He will strengthen us and fuel the desires which He has given us. Though the rains may come to extinguish the flame, our zeal will continue to shine knowing that it is Christ who sustains us and who will see to the realization of His perfect will for us; encouraging not only ourselves but all who see the work of Christ in our lives.

January 20

A FEARLESS LOVE

"There is no fear in love. But perfect love drives out fear, because fear has to do with punishment. The one who fears is not made perfect in love." -1 John 4:18 (NIV)

There is an analogy used in psychological studies that attempts to explain the hesitation we may sometimes feel in forming relationships. Called the "hedgehog's dilemma" it compares us with hedgehogs seeking warmth from each other. Though the hedgehog wants the comfort and security of being close to other hedgehogs, it is afraid of the harm that will be caused by their quills. Consequently, as a result of this fear the hedgehog either gets insufficient warmth or avoids the others altogether. In the same manner we may wish to love and be in relationship with others, but are afraid of the possibility of getting hurt or hurting the people involved. Thus we become either virtual hermits, or our relationships never move beyond the superficial.

Such an attitude however, is not love. Rather it is selfish in the sense that we do not want to go through the perceived unpleasantness and inconvenience of actually loving someone. Love in its truest form is concerned about the other and disregards the self. This is clearly expressed in the love Christ has. Though He knew that His death was required to save humanity from our innate depravity He did not allow fear to trap Him. So great was His love for us that He endured the agonizing pain of the Cross for our sake, so that we may be redeemed from our bondage to sin. Likewise as children of Christ who seek to emulate Him, we are to love no matter the cost. The process may stretch us in more ways than one, and there may be times when we wonder if loving is worth the pain. But when we allow the Spirit of Christ in our hearts to outwardly display His love, we can take hope in the fact that His love works towards the restoration of the other. Just as how His love has freed us from sin, His love as it overflows through us will bring steady healing and life to all who come in contact with it. There is no fear in love for in Christ there is hope, and when we love without fear we will draw others into the joy of being in relationship with Him.

January 21

BEAT THE PRESSURE

"Who is going to harm you if you are eager to do good? But even if you should suffer for what is right, you are blessed. 'Do not fear what they fear; do not be frightened.'" -1 Peter 3:13-14 (NIV)

I was once told that nobody will punish you for doing what is right. However, as I became older and my awareness of history and the world around me grew, I realized that sometimes this is not true. In Germany during the Second World War, people who showed any compassion to the plight of their Jewish neighbors, and gave of themselves to shelter them during their persecution, were brutally punished by the Nazi regime. Today under tyrannical governments that have no respect for human life, there are those who suffer because of their struggle to defend fundamental human rights. Even in societies where justice and integrity are officially respected and promoted, people in power often bully or pressure others into doing that which is unethical and immoral. Under such intimidation it is easy to silence ourselves in proclaiming what is right, and though every fiber of our being wants to take a stand against such wickedness, we fail to do so because of our fear.

When we are called to be bearers of Christ's righteousness we are not guaranteed an easy task. What we are promised is that we will be mocked and persecuted for His name. But why? What drives people to be so opposed to Christ and those who proclaim Him by their words and actions? It is fear. When we allow the Spirit of Christ to invade our hearts and allow His righteousness to be made manifest in our lives, it acts as a light dispelling the darkness. God's holy standards expose the wickedness of men and naturally, those who bend to their innate depravity do not like this. They will do all they can to hide from the light and silence the voice of truth. However, when we have identified ourselves with Christ and seek to follow Him, we will not fear the light for it protects and vindicates those who dwell within it. Therefore we will not be afraid of allowing the righteousness of Christ to shine forth from our lives knowing that His truth will always triumph. Our obedience to Christ will ultimately serve towards the restoration of all who see Him through us; even those who stand against us.

January 22

SNAKES AND DOVES

"I am sending you out like sheep among wolves. Therefore be as shrewd as snakes and as innocent as doves." -Matthew 10:16 (NIV)

This was a verse which always baffled me. What is Jesus trying to say? To suggest that we are to be like doves, but at the same time like snakes, seems impossible. The two creatures are antithetical to each other! Doves are usually associated with gentleness and purity. They are commonly used as symbols of peace, and world leaders and organizations have often used this imagery to show their advocacy for the cause of peace. Snakes on the other hand do not have such noble connotations. They bite, poison, and kill. What is more is that they use their environment and stealth to ambush their prey. Indeed it is no surprise that they are associated with mercilessness and deceit. How are we to reconcile these two together in our lives?

We live in a fallen world. As a result of man's disobedience, sin has tainted human interaction. Often people will lie, cheat, and swindle to fulfill their selfish ambitions while trampling over others in the process. If we were to remain in a state of naïve innocence, we are susceptible to the designs of the unscrupulous. They will seek to take advantage of us and string us along into their trap; thereby allowing them to make us do things that will compromise ourselves and our witness for Christ. However, this does not mean that we are to resort to deception and intrigue in an effort to guard ourselves from those who seek to do us harm. Doing so would make a mockery of our call to stand of the righteousness of Christ in our lives.

To be as shrewd as a snake means to be aware, to be discerning, just as how a snake takes into account his surroundings and prey before he strikes. But as children of Christ we are to be unlike the snake in that it goes in for the kill. Rather we are to be like doves, pure in heart knowing that we bear Christ. When we allow His Spirit to carry out His restorative work in our lives, He will give us the wisdom and discernment to be mindful while at the same time allowing His love to overflow from within us. In doing this we will be able to walk blameless in the sight of Christ and of others as He draws them closer to Him.

January 23

AN UNDISTURBED PEACE

"And Elisha prayed, 'O Lord, open his eyes so he may see.' Then the Lord opened the servant's eyes, and he looked and saw the hills full of horses and chariots of fire all around Elisha." -2 Kings 6:17 (NIV)

The king of Israel was at war with the king of Aram. As the conflict between them raged on, news reached the king of Aram that the prophet Elisha was giving away their positions to the king of Israel. Naturally the king of Aram was not amused and ordered his army to encircle the city of Dothan where Elisha was staying. When Elisha's servant awoke that morning, he was horrified. Surrounded by soldiers on every side he felt that the hour of their death had come. Terrified he asked Elisha what they should do. Yet in stark contrast to his servant, Elisha remained calm and composed. He knew that victory would be theirs. Wanting to put his servant's mind at ease, Elisha prayed that God would allow his servant to see what he sees. What the eyes of his servant saw was the army of God ready to overwhelm their enemies. Striking the soldiers with blindness they became disoriented and God delivered the army of Aram into the hands of the king of Israel.

When we find ourselves in unpleasant situations, what is our first reaction? Most of us would react in a manner similar to Elisha's servant. Worried and afraid we look at the bleakness of our circumstances and ask ourselves how we will ever get through this in one piece. In these moments we wonder where God is. But the truth is that He is there with us in every situation. He has promised to never leave nor forsake those who call upon His name, and to stand by those who acknowledge Him with their hearts. The question is do we see Him? Are our eyes opened to His constant presence and loving hand in our lives? That was why Elisha was able to remain in undisturbed calm and confidence despite the seemingly hopeless situation around him. His eyes were opened to the reality that God was in their midst, and with Him as their defender, their deliverance is assured. Are we looking for peace? That unshakable peace which will never depart from us even in the midst of trying circumstances? When we allow the Spirit of Christ to reside in our hearts He will open our eyes to His omnipresence and faithfulness. We will find hope and serenity knowing that we are in His hands and that He works all things together for His good and perfect will for our lives.

January 24

THE KING WORTHY OF PRAISE

"For God is the King of all the earth; sing to him a psalm of praise." -Psalm 47:7 (NIV)

Monarchs often have many grand titles to add to their name. Some examples which come to mind are "the Magnificent", "the Defender", "the Conqueror", "the Thunderbolt", or the most common one, "the Great." I remember coming across letters from kings in which they included their name and their full title. Some of these titles would take up almost a quarter of page! Such titles describing the deeds, attributes, and greatness of a particular king have a specific purpose. They are meant to instill reverence and awe for the monarch in the minds of all who read and hear them. However, human fallibility has a tendency to render such titles to be superficial, and often the very same monarch who claims all these impressive attributes and qualities fails to live up to his name.

When we allow the Spirit of Christ to dwell within our hearts and seek to conform ourselves to His likeness, we are adopted into the royal family of God. As children of Christ, we have a King as our Heavenly Father. But God is no mere human king. Were we to put all the monarchs and leaders of the world together, even then they could not surpass the greatness that is God Himself. The dominion of God knows no end, for while a human king has restrictions over where he rules, God is the Creator of the entire universe. His Kingship spans the totality of the created order and into eternity. God is our true Defender, for while earthly leaders cannot be everywhere at once and fail in standing up for justice, He is omnipresent and will always defend those who stand for His truth and righteousness. God is our victorious Conqueror, for through Christ He overcame what no man could -sin and death- so that we may be redeemed from our depravity and have life through Him. What is beautiful is that unlike an earthly king He lives up to all His titles because He is not bound by human limitations. There is much to praise God about and when we allow Him to open our eyes to His work in our lives, we will be able to sing psalms of praise to Him with confidence knowing that He is worthy of every title attributed to Him.

January 25

ORIGINS IN PRESPECTIVE

"Nazareth! Can anything good come from there?'" Nathanael asked. 'Come and see,' said Philip." -John 1:46 (NIV)

Nazareth, in the days when it was under Roman rule, did not have a particularly good reputation. Not only was it a small town, but it was located in the region of Galilee. For centuries Israel had come under the influence of many powerful empires. These empires often attempted to forcibly assimilate the Jewish people into their own culture. But such polices had disastrous results and solidified in the Jews of the time resentment towards foreigners. Galilee lay between the major trade routes which connected Israel with the rest of the world. Through them foreign armies and cultures swept into Israel, and the people of the Galilee reflected this fact in their generally relaxed attitude towards those who were not Jewish. Viewed as a place of traitors and collaborators, Nathanael's response to Philip was to be expected. But when he saw Jesus at Philip's invitation, Nathanael recognized Him as the promised Messiah. The fact that Jesus was from Nazareth became irrelevant to him as he stood before the Savior of Mankind.

Our past can sometimes make us feel inadequate. Haunted by the memories of destructive lifestyles and terrible decisions, we wonder if Christ can ever really love and forgive us; if He can truly use us for His restorative plan for the world. Sometimes we may be the ones who look down upon others because of their past, their heritage, or their status. But why do we define ourselves and others by these distinctions? Indeed we are fed with messages claiming that our worth is dependent on who we know, what we have, and where we come from. Those who lack in these areas are subsequently deemed as not having worth.

But God stands in clear opposition to this view. Each and every one of us is precious in His sight for we have all been created in His image. This gives us a worth that far out measures any earthly standard, and though we are tainted by sin, Christ in His love works to save us from our slavery to wickedness. None are beyond the redemptive work of Christ for there is nothing that Christ cannot forgive. It is not in His will for any to perish, but to have everlasting life through Him. When we allow the Spirit of Christ to work in our lives, we will find confidence and security knowing that despite our past failings God is and will work out His purpose for our lives. Likewise, when we have Christ within our hearts and are seeking to conform to His likeness, we will find ourselves drawing away from judging others because of their past. Instead, with praise and awe, we will be quick to acknowledge the work of Christ in their lives and minister to others with our love and service knowing that they bear His image.

January 26

WHAT DO WE PRASIE?

"Like snow in summer or rain in harvest, honor is not fitting for a fool." -Proverbs 26:1 (NIV)

As a collective society, what do we value? What do we view as permissible, or at least tolerable? To answer this question, contemporary television shows and movies can give us important insight. For better or for worse, popular media often reflects or informs the shared worldview, beliefs, and morals of a culture. Next time we sit down to watch a series or a film, consider what is being portrayed through the dialogue and lifestyles of the characters. But more than simple observation consider how it is being portrayed. What are the reactions that these depictions want to elicit from us? Sympathy? Condemnation? Laughter? Admiration? Finally, what is our ultimate repose to what is being broadcast to us? Our answer to this question can often tell us what we subconsciously approve of and believe to be good.

Truth, however, is objective. God as the Creator of the universe has ordained certain laws and rules to remain in place over His creation. These remain true and binding regardless of the age and culture we live in. There is a specific reason as to the purpose of these laws. They exist so that the created order may be harmoniously maintained, and that we may be protected from the devastating consequences of disrupting that order. Imagine, for example, if snow arrived during the summer! The crops which we need to sustain us will not grow and there will be nothing to reap for the harvest. For this reason, winter and summer have their respective seasons so that we may survive. Likewise, God has set laws for human interaction that are founded upon His perfect wisdom and love. Those who deviate from His laws have succumbed to their own human folly and have exchanged His truth for a dangerous lie. When we give honor to their choices, either by our vocal or unsaid approval, we will find ourselves descending down with them a path that may seem initially harmless, but will eventually lead to our destruction. How can we avoid such a fate? Only when we have allowed Christ's Spirit to work in our hearts and mold our attitudes will we know what is worth honoring according to His perfect standards. We will be able to rest in the security and life which comes from living under His righteousness being worked out in our lives and allowing Him to refine us into the people we are meant to be.

January 27

WHAT IS THE REASON?

"The Spirit of the Sovereign Lord is on me, because the Lord has anointed me to proclaim good news to the poor. He has sent me to bind up the brokenhearted, to proclaim freedom for the captives and release from darkness for the prisoners, to proclaim the year of the Lord's favor and the day of vengeance of our God, to comfort all who mourn," -Isaiah 61:1-2 (NIV)

Why do we do what we do? Our actions always have a purpose behind them. We cannot divorce ourselves from the fact that behind whatever we do there is a motive which drives us. Then what is the reason that compels us to do good? Why are we concerned about the needs of others and seeing to their restoration and welfare? One reason we may give is that it feels good to do what is right and noble. But basing our actions on feeling can be quite problematic; especially considering that human feelings are fickle. When we grow weary and frustrated of doing what is admirable and helping others, will not our attitudes change? Will we be as willing and enthusiastic to serve those around us in love and with joy?

Our acts of goodwill, if our feelings are our prime motivator, are self-centered and self-congratulatory at best. As long as it makes us feel good about ourselves, we will continue to act in a benevolent manner. However, once our feelings change, our actions or lack of action will reflect this shift in our hearts. If we truly desire to consistently and genuinely act toward the benefit of others, our reason must not be found in our fallible emotions. When we allow the Spirit of Christ to enter our lives and seek to conform ourselves to His likeness, our desire to act in righteousness will not be dependent on our feelings, but what God desires for us and the world. He commands us to comfort all who mourn, to bring hope, to proclaim freedom and good news to the poor, and to work towards the healing of those who have been hurt. But there is more to this than a simple duty to God. If we leave it at this then it becomes a chore; dependant on our own action and subject to our feelings. In order to truly serve with a cheerful and selfless heart, we must allow Christ's Spirit to work out His love through us; permitting Him to use us in His restorative mission to the world.

January 28

TURNING OUR EARS

"For God does speak—now one way, now another— though man may not perceive it." -Job 33:14 (NIV)

When I was 12 years old I went to the gym with my cousin. Though I was not aware of this, there was an age limit and I was well under it. The moment I stepped into the room I heard a loud, booming voice. "Please step out of the gym!" I was taken aback. Looking for the source of the voice, I saw no one except my cousin, and turning around there was no one behind me. Thoroughly surprised and baffled I complied and waited outside. It was only later did I realize that there was a speaker and a security camera near the entrance of the gym. Clearly the voice was that of a security guard wanting to enforce the age restriction so that I, in my childish folly, would not misuse the equipment or get myself hurt.

Sometimes, in the face of trial or uncertainty, we wish that God would speak to us in a tangible way. We may feel that ideally it would be nice if God directed us from a loudspeaker; telling us to "Go here!" "Go there!" "Do this!" and "Stay away from that!" In most cases however, God does not do this. But that does not mean that He is not speaking to us. On the contrary He is always speaking to us; attempting to guide us according to His perfect wisdom and love so that we may find lasting security and joy in Him. The question is are we listening? Sin has corrupted our senses, and therefore our ears have been dulled to the voice of God. But when we allow the Spirit of Christ to reside in our hearts and seek to follow His will, He will tune our ears to His voice. We will begin to hear His voice through the Scriptures, and through the people and situations He brings along our path. As long as we remain close to Him, His voice will always remain audible, and will always seek to impart to us life as we allow His Spirit to lead and guide our steps.

January 29

MAINTAINING A LASTING IMPRESSION

"In everything set them an example by doing what is good...show integrity, seriousness and soundness of speech that cannot be condemned, so that those who oppose you may be ashamed because they have nothing bad to say about us." -Titus 2:7-8 (NIV)

First impressions are always important. How we are portrayed in the minds of others is often determined by the initial contact we make with them. Whether it is a job interview or meeting a new person for the first time, we are taught to put our best foot forward in an effort to present ourselves well. But as we become more familiar with others however, our true personalities begin to reveal themselves. We may take for granted that because the other person has achieved a certain level of friendship with us; we can take certain liberties around them without any consequences to our relationship with them. Yet so often we fall into this trap of unknowingly hurting others by our careless words and choices; even if we have not done so directly to them. By the time we realize the example we have been setting, the damage is done and we lament over our folly.

Living a blameless life never does harm. On the contrary it will ultimately serve to the benefit of ourselves and of others. Abiding in the righteousness of Christ leads not only to a restored relationship with God, but brings healing and life to human relationships as well. That is why it is imperative that in our interactions with others we do not use familiarity as a reason to justify our willingness to say or do that which is not in keeping with what is right and pure. Sin taints all that it touches and like a corrosive acid it will break the precious bonds which bind us to those we love. Wherever we are placed, in whatever context, we are to live in a manner that pleases Christ so that no one will have an excuse to condemn us of being unashamed hypocrites. But if we think we can do this on our own, we are mistaken and will find it to be an impossible task. It is only when we have allowed the Spirit of Christ to enter our lives and free us from our bondage to sin that we will be made righteous through Him. By submitting our thoughts and attitudes to His Spirit's refining work we will rest securely in the fact that when we walk blamelessly in Him, we are participants in His restorative mission to the world; with none able to justly condemn us.

January 30

LET OUR CHAMPION FIGHT!

"The Lord will fight for you, and you have only to be silent." - *Exodus 14:14 (ESV)*

We love to give advice. Whether it is asked of us or not, we do not mind at all sharing our opinions on what to do in a certain situation or when tackling a specific problem. It makes us feel clever and useful to know that we have a voice and are able to use it for the benefit of others. Of course there is nothing wrong in giving advice. A timely piece of counsel said with genuine humility and love can do wonders for its hearers and set them on the right path. However, sometimes we may condescendingly give advice to others because we do not have faith in them. Though they may know what they are doing, we may feel that they do not. Thus we compel ourselves to enlighten them so that they would fulfill our expectations; even at the expense of their irritation.

Often times we do the same thing with God. While we may declare with our mouths that we surrender our circumstances to the perfect wisdom and will of Christ, we may not do the same with our hearts. When we see that things are not going our way, we mistakenly take it as a sign that God is not doing His job and decide that it is up to us to pick up the pace. We then make our suggestions to God; arrogantly thinking that the Creator of the universe needs the aid of our fallible human wisdom. How quickly do we forget the faithfulness and love of God! He has promised us that when we call upon His name and submit our situations to Him, He will fight for us on our behalf; overcoming them so as to fulfill the wonderful plan He has in store for our lives. Trying to work through our situations on our own faulty understanding will only serve to hinder the realization of the work that Christ is doing for each and every one of us. But when we allow ourselves to truly trust in our Savior, giving our fears and apprehensions to Him, we can rest in calm and quiet peace knowing that we are in His hands and that He will always emerge victorious no matter the storms we may face.

January 31

WHO IS THE REAL CRIMINAL?

"You, therefore, have no excuse, you who pass judgment on someone else, for at whatever point you judge the other, you are condemning yourself, because you who pass judgment do the same things." -Romans 2:1 (NIV)

Crime has become something characteristic of life in this fallen world. In every society, in every culture, and in every age, we are made aware of the prevalence of criminal activity. Whether it is through historical documents, popular movies, or even today's news, we cannot escape the reality that deviance exists and will continue to exist as long as humans populate this world. Yet when we see images of thieves and murderers we become inflated by self-righteousness. Though we may acknowledge the depravity of their actions and look down upon them in disgust, we blind ourselves to our own innate wickedness. How many of us, in envy and jealousy, have desired to take that which was not ours to take? How many of us, in our rage, have wanted to act in violence toward another person? Sin according to Christ is not defined by sole outward action, but by the very thought, and under that definition we are all criminals.

To redeem us from our sinful nature, Christ came so that by His death and resurrection we may be free from the bondage of sin and clothed with His righteousness. But we often forget to put on these clothes which He has given us. While we may think that we are wearing these clothes and are standing up for the holy standards of Christ, we are actually naked if we have done so in a judgmental spirit. Usually we end up using our self-proclaimed righteousness as weapon to slander others and boost our own pride. Truly wearing the garments of purity Christ has given us means humbling ourselves knowing that while we were bound as sinners and still chose to indulge in sin, Christ has forgiven us in His love. Nothing will be able to snatch us from the love of God and He will continue to remain faithful to the redemptive work He wants to carry out in our lives. When we have submitted ourselves to Christ's Spirit and have allowed His righteousness to be made manifest in our lives, we will remain unapologetic in His view of sin while at the same time displaying His love. He will prompt us to remember that just as He has forgiven us of much, we are to show mercy and love by His enabling; drawing others into the hope of being restored by Him.

February 1

THE WAY HAS BEEN PROVIDED

"For we do not have a high priest who is unable to sympathize with our weaknesses, but we have one who has been tempted in every way, just as we are-yet was without sin." -Hebrews 4:15 (NIV)

Sin is a destructive parasite. While it may promise us fulfillment, bliss, and confidence, it does everything but. Once we have allowed it to enter our lives, it feasts on us; robbing us of our joy and dignity. We then find ourselves at the point where our sin makes us feel filthy and depraved. Knowing that we cannot live like this we seek to overcome our sin. But despite our most earnest of efforts to combat wickedness in our lives, the temptations that entice us into sin continue to plague us. One of the greatest lies that we could ever succumb to is that no one understands the temptations we face. Believing this lie we see no hope of deliverance. Thus we become paralyzed in a vicious cycle that continues to bind us to our sin.

The truth however, is that there is someone who understands! Christ knows the temptations we face. While He was on Earth, Christ became acquainted with the weaknesses that we are subject to as a result of our fallen bodies. But though He knew what we as fallible human beings must face, He was without sin; blameless and pure. He was God Incarnate, and therefore He cannot tolerate sin. Yet the whole reason for why He came down to Earth to experience what we experience was so that through His death and resurrection we may be free from sin. Christ, by what He has done for us, has provided us a way out; a single path through which we may enjoy the freedom which He has to offer. The cross of Christ bears testimony to the fact that God knows the struggles we face with our corrupt nature and in His love He has given us the hope and promise of being delivered from it. When we allow Christ to enter our hearts and submit ourselves to His redemptive work in our lives, He will break the chains which bind us to our sin; enabling us to rest in the joy of being restored through Him.

February 2

AN URGENT CALL

"Then he said to his disciples, "The harvest is plentiful but the workers are few."" -Matthew 9:37 (NIV)

I enjoy looking at military recruitment posters from the First and Second World Wars. Not only do they have great historical value, but they are also full of emotion. The purpose of these posters was to rally people to fight for the cause; and they employ many images to stir up their sentiments. Some depict strong, well-built soldiers or famous generals imploring the viewer to take up arms and join the struggle against the enemy. Others paint horrifying pictures of what would happen as a result of the viewer's unwillingness to do battle. In both cases, the goal is to instill a sense of urgency, and inspire people to contribute to the war effort. They also subtly promote the idea that somehow a person's individual participation could potentially turn the tide of the larger conflict at hand and lead to a brighter future for the world.

Christ is looking for people to be a part of His redemptive mission to the world. Though it may at times deny it, mankind is desperately searching for a Savior. Through His death and resurrection, humanity is promised victory over their sinful nature and given the hope of being restored by His work in their lives. But though the need for Christ's free gift of salvation is great, the numbers of those who are willing to be His witnesses through whom He works are few. When we have allowed the Spirit of Christ to enter our hearts and carry out His redeeming work in our lives, He will prompt us that this restoration we experience is not only for our benefit, but for all those around us. The fact without Christ, there is only death and slavery to sin will inspire us to share with others the hope and life we have through Him. The days are short and darkness threatens to engulf the world. Will we respond to Christ's call to combat this darkness by being bearers of His light?

February 3

STRENGTHENING EACH OTHER

"As iron sharpens iron, so one man sharpens another" -Proverbs 27:17 (NIV)

Friendship is a beautiful thing. God has designed us for human relationships and to be in the company of cherished friends does wonders for the soul. Whenever I have felt the chill of loneliness, He has faithfully provided people to lift my spirits with their warm companionship. Through them God has taught me of the blessing of helping one another in our hour of need, and of sharing our joys and sorrows with people whom we can trust and depend upon. Building each other up is what makes friendship so wonderful, and with God's help I seek to do this just as how others have done for me.

We live in a broken world. If we look carefully, we will see that there are many who are suffering and hurting. Something is clearly not right with this picture. It is for this reason that God has called us to come alongside others. He gives us opportunities to befriend people so that we may encourage them by showing His faithfulness and the restorative power of His love. But are we capable of displaying these things by our own efforts? We may for a time. However, human love and faithfulness has its limits and there will come a point when these limits will become glaringly apparent. It is only when we allow our hearts to be molded by the Spirit of Christ that we, by His enabling, can show His unfailing love and bring His healing to others. As we abide in Christ, He will train us in being an encouragement and blessing to others, painting for them a picture of what it is like to be in relationship with Him.

February 4

BRIDGING THE GAP

"If we confess our sins, he is faithful and just and will forgive us our sins and purify us from all unrighteousness." -1 John 1:9 (NIV)

Can you imagine life without guilt? It is an unpleasant feeling that we have all experienced, but one that is highly necessary in healthy amounts. If somehow the feeling of remorse was eliminated from our emotions, we would find ourselves in a very cruel world. Heinous crimes would be committed with impunity; giving no regard to the pain and misery of others. People would simply shrug their shoulders when they have been confronted with the hurtful nature of their actions. Guilt, when it is applied properly, tells us that what we have done is wrong and that it needs to be made right. This in turn can become the stepping stone to relationships being restored and can bring healing into the lives of others.

Sin has separated us from God. Our willful choice to act contrary to His holy standards has created a rift between us and Him. However, God does not want our relationship with Him to remain this way. For this reason He gave humanity Christ, so that through His death and resurrection we may be reconciled to Him. But in order for that process of reconciliation to begin, we first need to acknowledge that we have sinned before God and need His forgiveness. This is not an easy thing to do, for our human pride does not want to admit when we have done wrong. Our pride however, cannot stand against the truth for long. Once we have come to that point of humility, accepting the fact that we have been sinful in the eyes of God and wanting to make amends, Christ will always extend the hand of forgiveness. Through

Him our relationship with God is restored and He will cleanse us of our impurities. Admitting when we have been wrong and seeking forgiveness is the way to mend relationships. Just as how it is in our relationship with Christ, He will help us to model this relationship in our interactions with others; bearing witness to His righteousness and love to those around us.

February 5

NEVER GOING HUNGRY

"Then Jesus declared, 'I am the bread of life. He who comes to me will never go hungry, and he who believes in me will never be thirsty." - John 6:35 (NIV)

I enjoy going to buffets. To walk into a hall and find rows upon rows of different types of food is truly tantalizing. Going to one buffet in particular, I was hungrier than usual. As I gazed upon the array of color and was bombarded by the wide variety of beautiful smells, I immediately grabbed a plate and started serving. I ended up gorging myself until I could not even look at another plate of food! I thought that after that meal I would never eat again. But sure enough however my natural processes brought me to the point that by evening I felt my stomach growl. Despite how much I felt that the buffet I went to that afternoon satisfied me, it did not, and again I became hungry and in need of food.

All of us have that desire to find satisfaction. It is what drives us to achieve that state in our lives where we will have all that we will ever want, and rest in blissful contentment. But often we spend our lives chasing after things which will never be the cure for our lack of fulfillment. We think to ourselves that maybe we will find it in the accumulation of possessions, or in excelling in our careers, or maybe if we have the right relationships. In the end however, all these are only temporary. Once we have lost them, we again feel hungry, and again feel restlessness in our souls. Yet there is hope for relief from this cycle! The very fact that we have this constant desire for fulfillment and are always seeking it, indicates that we are destined to find it in an eternal source. Christ promises that through Him we will never suffer from a spirit of being in continuous want. By allowing the Spirit of Christ to work in our hearts and aligning ourselves to Him, our striving, our yearning to find satisfaction will cease as we find complete and eternal fulfillment in Him.

February 6

GOING TO THE SOURCE

"No wisdom, no understanding, no counsel can avail against the Lord." -Proverbs 21:30 (ESV)

In elementary school we had several rules. One rule in particular was that if we were doing an assignment in class and had a question, we were to ask three other people before asking the teacher herself. While this was meant to build teamwork, even then I knew of the possibility that all three of the people I asked could have been wrong. That is why I always made it a point to let the teacher have the final word when I needed to clear my doubts. Sometimes her answer was the same as that of the others I had asked. Sometimes it was completely different. Yet I knew that if I took my uncertainties to my teacher, I would always leave with the right answer and a better idea of what she is expecting from me as a student.

When stricken by doubt, to whom do we take these feelings to? In such moments we may try to seek the counsel of family and friends. If those avenues do not seem to work, we may attempt to find guidance in the many philosophies of this world. But has it ever occurred to us that the wisdom we can find in this world has the potential to be wrong? As a result of sin, human fallibility has corrupted even the most brilliant of minds. Though occasionally we may be able to discern sound advice and act upon it, there are times when we are simply unable to do so. However, if it is true wisdom we seek, why do we fail to ask God? He is the Creator of the Universe! Nothing is new to Him for He is all-knowing. When we allow Christ to carry out His redeeming work in our lives, He will restore our minds so that through His help we may be able to understand the beauty and love found in His perfect wisdom. Knowing this, He will become the standard by which all wisdom is measured, and we will be able to discern whether the counsel of the world is there to hinder us, or to keep us walking in the right path.

February 7

SWEAR BY NO NAME!

"Above all, my brothers, do not swear—not by heaven or by earth or by anything else. Let your 'Yes' be yes, and your 'No,' no, or you will be condemned." -James 5:12 (NIV)

We hear it all the time. Phrases and variants of these phrases such as, "I didn't do it, I swear to God!" or "Promise to God I will do it!" are so commonplace that we do not even stop to think about it. But why? Why must we swear by God, or by anything else for that matter, when explaining ourselves? Often times we do this to express our sincerity and truthfulness. By involving God we hope to prove and convince those around us that we are serious about what we are saying. Ironically however, such attempts often fail to prove that we are genuine. Many times when we swear by God that we will do something or are telling the truth, we do the exact opposite! Instead of showing our earnestness, it accentuates our hypocrisy; cheapening the name of God in the process.

God is the manifestation of truth. It is impossible for Him to deceive because it goes against His holy nature. Likewise as human beings created in His image, we are programmed to value the truth. That is why seek honesty in our interactions with each other. Honesty builds relationships and trust. However, because we have been corrupted by sin we have become horridly selfish creatures; willing to sacrifice the truth if it preserves our own interests. But this is not meant to be! God takes seriously anything done in His name. If we swear by Him while failing to honor with our lives the name we have sworn by, we will stand condemned as the verse indicates. We are designed to be sentinels for truth, not crooks who use deceit to cover up their real intentions. When we allow the Spirit of Christ to cleanse us of our sinful nature and place upon us His righteousness, He will train us and empower us to pursue that which is right and pure no matter what the cost. We will not need to swear by anything, for we will have nothing to hide as long as we submit ourselves to Christ; giving meaning to both our "yes" and our "no".

February 8

REVERING CHRIST THROUGH SERVICE

"Submit to one another out of reverence for Christ." -Ephesians 5:21 (NIV)

Human tendency is to argue and fight. Our sinful nature dictates that we should always have our way no matter the cost. If for some reason we do not get what we want, we will resort to whatever means necessary to have our desires met. But this worship of the self only leads to destruction. Not only will it taint and shatter our relationships with others, it will also degrade ourselves. The obsession to satisfy our wants will make us say things we would not usually say and do things that we would not usually do; even if it is at the expense of those around us. In the end, though we may think that we are expressing our freedom through such behavior, we have actually become slaves to our own depravity.

Pride and selfishness is what characterizes our corrupt nature. Therefore, according to this nature, acting in loving submission to others is regarded as a sign of weakness. However it is anything but. To serve does not imply a passive timidity, but a strength that comes from knowing that in Christ we find our worth and security. When we have allowed Christ to enter our hearts and carry out His redemptive work in our lives, He gives a new nature; one that is characterized by His humility and selfless love. By submitting ourselves to Christ, He will break the power that sin has over us to reveal the freedom and joy which comes by serving Him. If we seek to solely gratify ourselves, misery will be our only companion. But when we allow the love of Christ to overflow from within us, we will see how His love restores our lives and the lives of others. When we see people through the eyes of

Christ, we will see them as precious individuals created in the image of God. With this in mind we will love and serve others by Christ's enabling knowing that in doing so we respect and revere their Creator.

February 9

DON'T GO WITH THE FLOW!

"Do not follow the crowd in doing wrong...do not pervert justice by siding with the crowd," -Exodus 23:2 (NIV)

Why is it so easy for us to turn a blind eye when confronted by injustice? Why is it so tempting to side with those who do wrong? There are a variety of reasons to which we can attribute our willingness to do so. Though we may know that the crowd is clearly acting against all that is noble and pure, perhaps we may feel that we have much to lose if we stand against them. We may fear the loss of status, friends, privileges, all the comforts we cherish and treasure. Rationalizing our passivity we may argue that even if we raised our voice in opposition we would only be shut down and ignored. We then keep silent; tolerating evil in an effort to maintain a false sense of peace and security.

We would like to think that we can sit on the fence between what is right and what is wrong. Reality however does not permit us to adopt such a position. Whether we like it or not, we must choose which side to be on. We cannot openly support immorality while condemning it secretly and claim to be good. If anything, it actually accentuates our allegiance to sin. Quietly siding with the crowd when they challenge God's holy standards reveals our selfish, opportunistic nature in that we would only stand for His righteousness if it is convenient for us. But if we want to see true justice and integrity flourish, we must understand that it comes at a price. It means fighting against the crowd and proclaiming the righteousness of Christ no matter how many times we may be ridiculed, no matter how many times we may be scorned, and no matter what we may lose in the process. The wonderful fact is that we do not fight this battle alone. When we have allowed the Spirit of Christ to dwell within our hearts and seek to conform ourselves to Him, He will give us the boldness and strength to stand for what is right and true. He will always side with those who honor Him and resting in this promise our voice will rise above the crowd knowing that the truth of Christ will always emerge triumphant.

February 10

GREATER THAN ANYTHING

"'The Lord who delivered me from the paw of the lion and the paw of the bear will deliver me from the hand of this Philistine.' Saul said to David, 'Go, and the Lord be with you.'" -1 Samuel 17:37 (NIV)

Being a shepherd was not exactly an easy task. David knew this full well. Not only was it imperative for him to keep track of an often large flock and make sure they did not stray off into the wilderness, he had to protect them from all manner of ferocious animals. Lions and bears are dangerous to encounter even for the well-equipped. Imagine how much more it would be for a young shepherd with little amour and armed with only a wooden staff! Yet David was able to overcome them both; not by his strength, but by the power of the One who created the lion and the bear. It was God who protected David in the wilderness, and who prepared and strengthened him for all that he was to face. When given the opportunity to fight Goliath, David already knew the outcome. With God as his defender, David knew that the Philistine would not be able to stand a chance, and Israel would be saved.

Situations and people can often stir fear in our hearts. Standing before them we tremble, and allow ourselves to be bound to them. We say that it is impossible to change our circumstances, that any hope of victory is just a cruel illusion. How far this is from the truth! We fail to see that there is someone greater than the problems we face. Every part of God's creation is under His ultimate sovereignty. He is all-powerful and there is nothing which can stand against Him. What may seem insurmountable to us is easily conquerable for Him. In His love He wants to help us in our struggles. But what is our response? Will we place our faith in Him who is Master over all? When we allow Christ to restore our hearts and permit Him to set right our relationship with God, He will come to our aid; imparting His strength to us so that through Him we will be able to overcome all obstacles. By abiding with Him, we will be able to confidently say with David that though what we face may seem overwhelming, we serve a God who is greater and who will grant us victory when we call upon His name.

February 11

TESTING THE HEART

"The Lord does not look at the things man looks at. Man looks at the outward appearance, but the Lord looks at the heart." -1 Samuel 16:7 (NIV)

Human beings can be incredibly gullible at times. How easy it is for us to be fooled by outward appearances! Often we only see the external image of a person without seeing, or even considering the internal. There is a famous French play called "Tartuffe" written by a playwright in the 17th century named Moliere. It tells the tale of a seemingly pious priest who in actuality is a scoundrel. Though he tries to deceive one family in particular, and is successful with some of its members, other members are suspicious. These family members soon reveal the truth about him and expose his ruse. But the play makes an important point. Too often we judge others by what we see with our fallible eyes; not through the eyes of God who sees all.

All of us have been corrupted by sin. No matter how much we may try to use our material qualities or our displays of piety in order to convince others that we are good people, it means nothing if we have not made ourselves acceptable in God's sight. He knows every detail of our being and there is no area of our lives of which He is ignorant. We may succeed in deceiving others, and even deceiving ourselves. But before God, we wear who we really are on our sleeves. Until we deal with our innate depravity, it will continue to betray the façades we create. However, we cannot deal with our wicked nature by our own efforts or strength. It is only when our hearts have been transformed by the redemptive work of Christ will He make us acceptable in the sight of God. With

His Spirit molding and shaping our hearts, He will break the bonds which tie us to our sin; having nothing to hide before Him and before others so that He will carry out His perfect will for our lives.

February 12

KEEPING OUR EYES FOCUSED

"Let your eyes look straight ahead, fix your gaze directly before you." -Proverbs 4:25 (NIV)

I always used to wonder why horses often have shutters over their eyes when attached to a carriage. It is only when I worked with horses at a summer camp did I realize why. Horses are curious creatures. They enjoy taking in their surroundings. However, they also scare quite easily. By instinct the moment it senses danger it will run, and even the slightest unexpected movement can send it into a panic if the horse feels threatened. Imagine a horse riding through a city. With so many distractions around it, the horse will be looking all over the place. This would not only be problematic for the driver trying to steer it in the right direction, but should the horse witness something that would frighten it, there would be chaos everywhere. That is why the shutters are placed over its eyes; to make sure it stays on track and not be distracted by everything else around it.

Sometimes we are no different. In this fallen world there are many things which seek to attract our sinful nature. Though we may find such temptations appealing, they ultimately serve to divert us off course from the path God has called us to travel on. Only misery and destruction awaits us when we seek to chase after that which runs contrary to

God's holy standards. At other times, when God is leading us according to His perfect will, situations may come along our way that will instill fear and anxiety in our hearts. In our despair we may look for a place to escape to and, losing sight of the wonderful plan God has in store for us, make decisions that are actually harmful to us. That is why it is so important to keep our eyes focused on Christ. When we allow His Spirit to work in our hearts, permitting Him to perfect His righteousness in us and direct our steps, nothing will be able to distract us from following Him. With His hands making us fixate our eyes on Him, nothing else will matter; only the goal to live for Christ so that He may fulfill His excellent purposes for our lives.

February 13

A MESSAGE WORTH THE COST

"They stoned Paul and dragged him outside the city, thinking he was dead. But after the disciples had gathered around him, he got up and went back into the city. The next day he and Barnabas left for Derbe. They preached the good news in that city and won a large number of disciples. Then they returned to Lystra, Iconium and Antioch, strengthening the disciples and encouraging them to remain true to the faith." -Acts 14:19b-22b (NIV)

Paul was a man on the run. On his first missionary journey in what is now southern Turkey, he came across a city called Iconium. Stopping here to preach the message of Christ, he found many who were drawn to the hope which is available to them through Christ's redemptive work. But Paul also made enemies. There were some who did not like what Paul was saying and the religious leaders of the city sought to stone him to death. In response, Paul fled for his life. Yet the religious leaders did not let him go that easily. Hunting him down in a nearby city called Lystra, the religious leaders got a hold of Paul and brutally stoned him; leaving him for dead. Paul survived, but what is incredible is that he goes back! Despite the obvious threat to his life, Paul returns to proclaim what Christ has done for him, and what Christ can do for all who place their faith in Him.

All around the world today, Christians boldly practice and proclaim their faith despite threats of horrendous torture and death. But why? To many it seems ludicrously foolish. Why would anyone go to or stay in these dangerous places and risk their lives for the message of Christ? The reason is simple. It is too good of a message to keep to oneself. Through Christ's death and resurrection, man has the hope of being free from their bondage to sin. By His transformative work in our lives, no longer will we be bound to our depraved impulses. Instead Christ will restore us to the people He has destined us to be; those who uphold His righteousness and love so that we may live in harmony with Him and with each other. What is more is that by our faith in Christ, we are guaranteed eternal life with Him in Heaven, and the hope that one day Christ will return again to wipe every tear and set the world right. That is what drove Paul, and drives Christians today under persecution, to stare death in the eye for the sake of Christ. Only through Him there is freedom, hope, and life. Do we know this for ourselves? When we allow the Spirit of Christ to work in our hearts and conform ourselves to Him, the things of this world will be of no consequence to us. Our greatest joy will be to share His love and message of hope with others. In this task we will be assured of the fact that Christ will enable and empower us by His strength to be bearers of His light no matter what we may face.

February 14

BEYOND JUST WORDS

"Dear children, let us not love with words or tongue but with actions and in truth." -1 John 3:18 (NIV)

It is tragic when words become nothing more than meaningless utterances. Many make promises and commitments to stand up for justice, to display love in all circumstances, and to serve with willing hearts. However, when the time comes to put these words into practice few actually take up the challenge they have issued themselves. We quietly shrink away from opportunities to show our love, conjuring up a variety of excuses to dodge the responsibility we have to act upon what we have proclaimed. This reduces our words to mere empty talk. Often we fail to recognize that the weight of our declarations to love is dependent on our actions. Without actions to support these declarations, they become cruel and hypocritical statements for those who need to be shown compassion.

To truly love is not an easy task. It requires us to sacrifice our pride, our interests, our comforts, and our resources for the sake of the other. That is why it is incredibly easy to simply say that we will love because it does not require much of us. We can sit back in our self-satisfaction thinking that we are wonderful people for saying the right things. Yet Christ requires that we go far beyond the verbal if we claim to be His children. He did not come down to Earth so that He could merely declare to humanity that He loves them and will save them from their depravity. Rather, Christ made this tangible to us. Sacrificing Himself on the cross He performed an act of love that known no parallel in human history. Through His death and resurrection all who come to Him, regardless of their past, their race, their creed, their gender, their wealth, or the age in which they live, have the hope of being redeemed from their sinful nature and restored by His Spirit. When we allow Christ to mold our hearts and seek to imitate Him through His enabling, He will ensure that we display His love not just by or words, but the actions that accompany them.

February 15

THE TRUTH HEALS

"Therefore each of you must put off falsehood and speak truthfully to his neighbor, for we are all members of one body." -Ephesians 5:25 (NIV)

There is no such thing as a good lie. We have become comfortable with the idea that in some circumstances it is acceptable to not tell the truth. Not wanting to hurt those around us, we lie so that even though they may believe a fantasy, at least they are content and the peace is not disturbed. But we must truly question what our real intent is in lying to each other. Do we fear the truth and the consequences it has for us? Are we afraid of what may happen when we say what is right? Though we may try to justify our lies as being motivated out of concern for the other, they actually do more harm than good. Eventually the truth will always reveal itself, and our lies will be exposed as cowardly utterances that were said out of our self interest.

Lying tears relationships apart. Involved is a betrayal of trust which makes people feel cheated and trampled over. God knows this full well. That is why among His Ten Commandments God makes it clear that His people are not to bear false testimony against one another. But in our sinful state which is always concerned about ourselves and preserving our pride, telling the truth can be an undesirable task. However, when we allow the Spirit of Christ to enter our hearts, He will break the power that sin holds over us and bestow upon us His righteousness. With Him molding our minds and attitudes, we will understand that God is Truth and we will value His truth above all else. Though telling the truth may seem difficult, He will give us the strength and wisdom to do so when we allow Him to guide our words and actions. This may result in outcomes that we would otherwise not want. But He will remind and encourage us with the fact that His truth will ultimately bring healing and life both to ourselves and to those around us.

February 16

STILLING OUR FEARS

"You came near when I called you, and you said, 'Do not fear.'" - *Lamentations 3:57 (NIV)*

As a child everything seems so big. It is for this reason that in the eyes of a child, the world can be both filled with wonder and can be intimidating at the same time. In their limited understanding about the world around them, they can become easily frightened and afraid. I remember as a child that whenever I was scared there were two people I could count on. By calling my parents I knew that they would always come to my side, and comfort me. I would be able to rest easy knowing that without fail they will do whatever that is in their power to keep me safe and not give me cause for worry. Even today, though I have grown older, I know that they will come to my aid with their support, advice, and encouragement whenever I am in distress.

But there are times when not even human help will suffice. In moments like these there is only one person in whom we can find rest, and He is more than sufficient for us. Christ is described as our Mighty Fortress and Wonderful Counselor. He will never abandon those who call upon His name. When we allow His Spirit to enter into our hearts and seek to follow after Him, we can take assurance in the fact that He is leading us according to His perfect plan for our lives. Whenever storms come along our path and we have nowhere else to turn, we can take refuge in Christ and in His promises which are revealed through His Word. By placing our trust in Him and acknowledging that He is Lord over all, He will prove to us His faithfulness and fill us with His peace as He reveals the great purposes He has in mind for every one of us. In Christ we have hope that can never be taken away and can find comfort in the knowledge that He knows what He is doing and will always strengthen and encourage us when we call upon His name.

February 17

IN NEED OF GRACE

"The Pharisee stood up and prayed about himself: 'God, I thank you that I am not like other men-robbers, evildoers, adulterers-or even like this tax collector. I fast twice a week and give a tenth of all I get.' But the tax collector stood at a distance. He would not even look up to heaven, but beat his breast and said, 'God, have mercy on me, a sinner.'" -Luke 18:11-13 (NIV)

In Roman-occupied Judea, tax collectors had a notorious reputation. They were seen as swindlers who would cheat the people into paying large amounts of money that the state did not actually require. These tax collectors would give the mandatory amount demanded by the Roman government, and then pocket the remainder for themselves. Thus, the Pharisee had reason to condemn the tax collector of being a sinner. But if the tax collector is guilty of sin, then the Pharisee is just as guilty as him! In boasting in his own righteousness before God and his haughty derision for the tax collector, the Pharisee was blind to the fact that he was sinning right before God Himself! Pride had taken over the Pharisees' heart and Jesus says that it was the tax collector who, with humility admitted his sin before God and sought forgiveness, left with God's favor.

No one is perfect; not even ourselves. All men have fallen short of the glory of God. Though in our minds we may think that we are morally superior to those around us, the very fact that we have such thoughts shows how prideful we are. This then leads to the worship of ourselves instead of God; in our arrogance thinking that we can achieve moral and spiritual perfection without the help of God. But the truth is that in the eyes of the One who is the embodiment of holiness and perfection, none of us will be able to stand before Him and claim that they are righteous. However there is hope! God knows that we cannot match His holy standards by our own efforts. For this reason He sent Christ so that through His death and resurrection we may be made spotless and pure as He bestows upon us His righteousness. What right do we have then to claim that we are better than anyone else? All of us need God's grace everyday; a grace that He is always willing to give. When we have allowed Christ to enter our hearts He will correct our pride so that His love may overflow from within us. With humble hearts we will be able to bear witness to the work of Christ in our lives and draw others into the hope which is available through Him.

February 18

THE GOOD OLD DAYS ARE NOW!

"Do not say, 'Why were the old days better than these?' For it is not wise to ask such questions." -Ecclesiastes 7:10 (NIV)

When things go wrong in the world, it is tempting to become nostalgic about the past. We think back to years and ages gone by and feel that those days were the best in which to live. Conjuring up images in our minds of the happiness, prosperity, and simplicity of those times, we conclude that all our problems would be solved if we just returned to how it was in those days. Such a romanticizing of the past however only serves to blind us to the realities of the age we fantasize about. Pick any age in human history, in any country, and one will find that for every good aspect there was a darker side as well. That is why it is erroneous to say that one age was better than another. There is always evidence to show that it was not paradise.

Every day is a gift from God. This day, today, has been made by God and we rejoice in it because in His love and goodness, He has created each day so that we may experience His promises and faithfulness. To say that nothing good can come of these days is to show contempt for God who is the giver of life and who sustains every part of our being. According to His perfect will He has placed us in this point of time and in this location for a reason. Instead of complaining about the ills of this age, or this time in our lives, and pining for an idealized fantasy of the past, our question should be to ask God what His purpose for us is in our present circumstances. When we allow the Spirit of Christ to enter our hearts and permit ourselves to be guided by Him, He will slowly reveal to us the reason for which He has placed us where we are. His timing is always flawless and when we continue to trust in His wisdom, we will know this fact to be true as He fulfils His restorative work in our lives and in the lives of others. The solution to our present woes is not to return to a utopia which is the creation of our flawed understanding, but to make the most of our days by walking with Christ. In doing this we will find lasting joy and peace knowing that when we are guided by Him, He opens our eyes to the wonderful beauty of our present and the assured hope of our future with Him.

February 19

TAKING OUR GRIEF TO HIM

"For godly grief produces a repentance that leads to salvation without regret, whereas worldly grief produces death." -2 Corinthians 7:10 (ESV)

The First World War was unlike anything the world had ever seen. Never in the history of mankind was there such carnage and devastation; that too in a period of only four years! After the guns fell silent and peace began to settle, the prevailing attitude was one of grief and of a solemn commitment to the goal of eliminating all wars. The hope was that never again would such a horrid conflict visit the world. However, only two decades later the Second World War erupted; causing even more bloodshed and destruction than the first. Again there was a commitment to peace with the conclusion of the war in 1945. Yet since that year, thousands have died and continue to die on battlefields around the globe. Humanity has not learnt its lesson and it seems that too often it forgets its grief.

If we honestly look at ourselves and the world around us, we can rightly conclude that humanity is not perfect. Our inherent depravity is the source of much pain and misery; both to ourselves and to others. It destroys everything that comes under its corrosive touch and it leaves us with no peace. Confronted with the reality of our sin we grieve over the damage it causes. But soon our period of grieving ceases, and we repeat the cycle again; bending to sin, grieving, and feeling that peace is destined to elude us. Is there any way to break this cycle? The beautiful hope is that there is! Christ came to this world so that man may be freed from His sinful nature. When we believe in His death and resurrection and allow His Spirit to carry out His redemptive work within us, there is the firm assurance that when we confess our sins to Him, He forgives and cleanses us of our wickedness. By choosing daily to keep in step with His Spirit, He will clothe us with His righteousness and fill us with a peace that none can take away.

February 20

A BETTER ROUTE

" *When they came to the border of Mysia, they tried to enter Bithynia, but the Spirit of Jesus would not allow them to.*" -Acts 16:7 (NIV)

For as long as I can remember there was one place where I always wanted to go. Japan had captured my imagination and I became enamored by its history and culture. When three years ago I heard that my university was sending a team of students to Japan on a missions trip, I thought that finally the day had come! After years of waiting I would at long last be able to set foot on the land that I had only been able to experience through books and movies. Sadly, I did not make the team. Pleased with my application however, the missions committee offered me the chance to go on a mission trip to India. Thoroughly disappointed I asked God why. For what purpose did He present this window of opportunity, knowing how much I desired to go, only to shut it? Why did He want me to go to India; a country that I had been to several times before? It was with initial reluctance that I accepted the offer. But looking back on how God used that trip to help me grow spiritually and change my perspectives, I am glad that He had His way instead of mine.

Why does God close doors? It is a question that we all face at some point in our lives. Why do things simply not work out when we want them to? At times like these we question God and doubt whether He is truly loving and faithful. But if God says no to a certain avenue, that means He has something better in mind. During his second missionary journey, Paul wanted to go to Bithynia. Yet God worked in such a way as to prevent him from going. Was this because God was somehow being unfair? Not at all! God prevented Paul from going to Bithynia so that the way would be open for him to go to the city of Philippi. Through a vision, God told Paul that the people of Philippi needed the message of Christ and Paul went. The Philippian Christians would soon become Paul's loyal supporters in his ministry, and as his letter to them shows, Paul remembered them with much joy and fondness. Likewise, God always leads us according to His perfect plan for our lives. When we trust in Christ and allow Him to guide our steps, He will take us to places where we will be blessed, challenged, and strengthened in our walk with Him. By keeping in step with Him and surrendering our desires to His will, we will be able to watch with awe and wonder His work being carried out in our lives and in the lives of others. Eventually, God did bring me to Japan and He gave me one whole week of unhindered sightseeing! But not before He taught me that to walk His way is the most rewarding path I could ever take.

February 21

THROUGH THE EYES OF GOD

"For our light and momentary troubles are achieving for us an eternal glory that far outweighs them all." -2 Corinthians 4:17 (NIV)

Often times our problems simply need to be put into perspective. Take an ant for example. Due to its small size, the ant may see certain things as enormously large when to our eyes the very same things are actually of little consequence. What is for us a small patch of grass may be a vast forest for an ant; one that is never-ending and fraught with danger. Perhaps what may be a small mound of dirt to us might as well be for the ant a mountain that could rival Everest itself! Yet if the ant were to climb onto our fingers and see these things from our eyes, it will know that the obstacles they face are not as insurmountable as they seem and that overcoming them is not a faint hope.

In the same way we might face situations which to us may seem overwhelming and devoid of any assurance that they will pass. But when we see our circumstances through the eyes of God, our entire perspective will change. Though to us our struggles may seem impossible, nothing is impossible for Him who is Lord over all Creation. In light of His omnipotence and eternity, our troubles are nothing but minor bumps in the road He has called us to travel. When we have allowed the Spirit of Christ to enter into our hearts and have surrendered ourselves into His hands, He will strengthen us in our trials and open our eyes to see that through Him we have the final victory. While we live in a fallen world and are not exempt from suffering, Christ promises His children that we should trust in Him and His perfect wisdom, He will prove to us His faithfulness as He turns our mourning into dancing. Throughout the Scriptures He has taken the most miserable of situations and used them to fulfill His perfect will so that His children may find joy and hope in Him. Christ is able and willing to do the same for us and when we call upon His name we will rest knowing that His steadfast love will bring us a glory that will never fade and never be taken away.

February 22

NOTHING IS OURS

"Stop trusting in man, who has but a breath in his nostrils. Of what account is he?" -Isaiah 2:22 (NIV)

We like to think of ourselves as independent and powerful. As a result we often admire, even idolize, the abilities we as collective humanity possess. Looking at all the advances we have made in science and art, we say to ourselves that man is supreme and that we are the only authority we can trust. But not even the most powerful and intelligent of men can compare before God. In fact, it was Him who gave us the faculties to achieve what we boast about. Who gave us legs to travel and hands to build? Who gave us minds to invent marvelous things and create works of such artistic beauty? Who is it that gives us breath to sustain us? Was it not God who has created each and every one of us? Therefore, we cannot elevate man without looking like fools ourselves because God has enabled us to do everything we do!

When we place our trust in man, disappointment is inevitable. Eventually we will realize that man has his limitations and can never overcome his innate depravity. In whom then can we trust? Upon whom can we lean? Man was meant to live in a loving relationship with God. That is why throughout history and in all cultures, man is seeking Him. However, because of our fallen nature, man is looking for Him in all the wrong places. Yet despite our failings and our pride, God wants to restore our relationship with Him so that we may have everlasting life and peace. He does this through His Son, Jesus Christ. By His death and resurrection we are freed from our sin and are reconciled to our Creator. When we have allowed Christ to invade our hearts and have placed our trust in Him, He will open our eyes to see the world around us as it is. Looking through His eyes we will know that all have been corrupted by sin, but have the hope of being redeemed by the power of Christ. Knowing that in Christ we have an eternal confidence that cannot be stripped away, He will give us boldness to proclaim His Name so that all may be restored and have life through Him.

February 23

STOP THE FIGHT!

"You are still worldly. For since there is jealousy and quarreling among you, are you not worldly? Are you not acting like mere men?" -1 Corinthians 3:3 (NIV)

Human tendency is to quarrel and fight. Sometimes there are not even any logical reasons as to why we have certain arguments. Our ire and jealousy can be stoked by even the most insignificant and trivial of things. I have seen relationships torn apart and rivalries formed over disputes that were started over reasons that were petty and simply bizarre. It used to baffle me that people were so quick to form enemies out of people who were close friends.

However, understanding that we are all fallen creatures contaminated by sin places it into perspective. When sin is our master and we are under its yoke, it will make us to pick fights over matters that are of no consequence. Subsequently, and true to its nature, sin will destroy our relationships with others and distract us away from God.

Can we be free from such harmful attitudes? The answer is that indeed we can! However, it is not by any work of our own, but solely by the work of Christ in our lives. When we have allowed Christ to carry out His redemptive work in our hearts, He will break the power sin holds over us and clothe us with His righteousness. This new nature He has given us is at odds with the remnants of our old sinful nature. Having a quarrelsome and envious spirit is not part of the new nature Christ has bestowed upon us. He has called us as His children to something greater and which far surpasses the inconsequential matters of this world. When we have submitted our attitudes to Christ's refining work in our lives, He will fill us with His love and humility. By turning our eyes upon Jesus we will be able to see things and situations through His eyes and by His enabling respond in a manner which brings glory to God and restoration to those around us.

February 24

A CONSTANT REMINDER

"Do not let this Book of the Law depart from your mouth; meditate on it day and night, so that you may be careful to do everything written in it. Then you will be prosperous and successful." -Joshua 1:8 (NIV)

Repetition and practice is what helps maintain our skills. Athletes lead disciplined lives of training so that their abilities may stay sharp for the next competition. Students continuously pour over their notes and textbooks so that they may be prepared for their examinations. Failing to do these things will only prove to be detrimental and they will lose what they have gained because of a lack of concentrated practice. Even our ability to speak is not immune. If placed in a different linguistic setting from our native tongue, we have the potential to lose our first language if there are limited opportunities to use it. Our minds need to be constantly trained because we are prone to forget, and the only cure is to continue reminding ourselves of what we know.

Similarly, we need to constantly spend time in the God's Word. He knows that due to our fallen nature we are forgetful, and it is tempting for us to drift away from Him. That is why He implores us to always keep His Word at the forefront of our minds, write it on our hearts and to make it a practice to study it daily. Complacency is one step away from destruction and to be overconfident in our own faith and piety will eventually harm our walk with God. His Word is the path to life and when we have allowed Christ to enter our hearts and carry out His redemptive work, He will give us a desire to seek His face. Unless His Spirit is working within us, we cannot live up to what God expects of us or remember to keep His commandments. Only through His enabling and prompting will we be able to live according to His righteousness. The question before us is will we open our hearts and listen to His voice? When we do so and with obedience seek to align ourselves with Christ, we find an unshakable joy and security in Him and in His Truth.

February 25

HIS WILL, NOT OURS

"Father, if you are willing, take this cup from me; yet not my will, but yours be done." -Luke 22:42 (NIV)

Crucifixion was not a peaceful death by any stretch of the imagination. In fact it was arguably the most excruciating and humiliating form of execution invented by man. Rome would not use this method to carry out justice even for its own citizens regardless of who they were. It was reserved for those who could not boast of having Roman citizenship and who were deemed to be the irreversibly degenerate and depraved. No one wished to be crucified and even Jesus knew the pain and shame that it entailed. Yet what is remarkable is that even though Jesus wished that somehow God would prevent His violent death, He acknowledged that God's will was not up for debate. With humble obedience He went to the cross so that through His death and resurrection we may be free from sin and have life through Him.

Sometimes God will call us to do things that we really do not want to do, and go to places where we really do not want to go. We wrestle and argue with God, wishing that there was some other way. Such a reaction is indeed very human and normal. But if we allow such attitudes to take control over our minds, we harden ourselves against His will and in our stubbornness deprive ourselves of the incomparable blessings which come from being obedient to Him. God promises that His will is perfect and that it is always for good, never for evil. When we allow Christ to enter into our hearts and take reign over our lives, His Spirit will train and enable us to live in accordance with the will of God. By allowing Christ to deal with our stubborn and prideful attitudes, He will fill us with His humility and the understanding to know that when we are within His will, we will have life abundant; seeing His beautiful work carried out in our lives as well as in those around us.

February 26

THE RIGHT CAUSE

"Do not stand up for a bad cause…" -Ecclesiastes 8:3 (NIV)

We are taught to stand up for what we believe in. Admiring people who have stood by their principles no matter the cost, we feel inspired and compelled to do the same. Indeed there is nothing wrong with such spirited determination in and of itself. If there were, then we would be like leaves being blown by the wind; always under the whims of the powerful and those who intimidate us. It becomes a problem however when we have decided to stand behind a bad cause. In the marketplace of ideas there are a lot of ideologies, philosophies, and movements. Some of them we might find appealing and we may be drawn to them. But upon closer inspection they may prove themselves to be flawed, destructive, and even criminal.

How are we able to distinguish between a good cause and a bad one? If we try to discern this by our limited wisdom we may obtain a vague idea of what is worth defending, but not a full and complete understanding. Sin has tainted our perception and therefore our reason is imperfect. Only when the power of sin has been broken in our lives will our eyes be opened to the truth. But how can this be done. God wants to redeem us from our fallen state and He has done so through the death and resurrection of His Son, Jesus Christ. When we have allowed Christ to enter into our hearts He will purge us of our sin so that our minds may be able to grasp His truth. Through the Scriptures He has revealed to us His heart and when we understand the heart of God, allowing His wisdom to direct our minds, we will know that He is truth personified and worthy to be upheld. By constantly submitting ourselves to the restorative work His Spirit is doing in our lives, we will be able to see through the deceptions of the philosophies of this world and draw others into the hope and joy of personally knowing Christ as Lord and Savior.

February 27

HAVING TRUE WISDOM

"Who is wise and understanding among you? Let him show it…by deeds done in the humility that comes from wisdom." -James 3:13 (NIV)

Kings and rulers often like to style themselves as being wise. Indeed, it is part of legitimizing their right to rule. No one wants a foolish monarch to rule over them and if the competency of a monarch is cast into doubt, it could be serious problem for their continued reign. Thus, they go to great lengths to convince their subjects of their wisdom.

Through the titles and attributes they place upon themselves, rulers try to persuade the people that they are the right men for the job. But when given such power, human pride tends to take over and causes them to make foolish decisions. Their pride therefore, makes a mockery of their claims to wisdom; instead making them utter fools and proving that wisdom was not with them in the first place.

What does it mean to have wisdom? A truly wise person is not someone who flaunts his wisdom, but with humility knows who he is, and who it is that enables him to act. God is the real source of wisdom. It was by His wisdom that God created the world and gave it order. He assures us that when we seek to be guided by His flawless understanding, we will find life abundant and total fulfillment. But this can only come when we have submitted ourselves to His ultimate Lordship. Our human pride does not want to acknowledge this, and our refusal to do so ensures that we will continue to be slaves to our own folly. However, when we have allowed Christ to enter our hearts and restore us from our sin, He will purify us of our pride. We will know that it is He who gives us breath, who has given us the capacity to think, and who sustains every part of our being. By humbly permitting ourselves to be guided by His wisdom, we will be able to act in a manner that bears witness to God's righteousness and love; becoming wise only because it is Christ who has given us understanding and knowledge.

February 28

BEING THE INFLUENCER

"Do not be misled: 'Bad company corrupts good character.'" -1 Corinthians 15:33 (NIV)

Sometimes we place too much faith in our goodness. We would like to think that because we have achieved in our eyes a high standard of moral excellence, our character is unassailable. Due to this trust in our righteousness, we think that we are good people and will be unaffected by the kind of company we keep. We may even believe that we can be a positive influence on them if they are living in a manner that is not right. However, because of our sinful nature, we are tempted to follow the crowd in their sin instead of pulling others away from it. Slowly we will make compromise after compromise attempting to justify our friend's behavior. Soon we will find that our goodness was a weak shield against the lures of sin and that instead of setting a good example, we have adopted attitudes and lifestyles that are immoral and destructive.

We deceive ourselves if we think that we can remain pure by our own strength. If we have not anchored ourselves in Christ, no matter how confident we may feel about our integrity, we will be swept away by the crowd. The pressure to conform to the standards of the world around us is great. We want to feel loved and accepted and this desire is strong enough to lead us into choices and patterns of behavior that we thought would never be a problem for us. But when we have found our confidence in Christ, we will not find our worth in what other people think, but what God thinks of us as His precious children. Created in His image, we are immeasurably loved by God and nothing will be able to take that away from us. When we have allowed His Spirit to dwell within us, He will free us from our sin and enable us to walk in His righteousness; guiding us in the path which assures us abundant life. By holding the hand of Christ wherever we go and in whatever setting, we will be able to bear witness to those around us of the perfect work He is doing in our lives without becoming ensnared ourselves by the traps of this world.

February 29

A FOTRESS NOT EASILY OVERCOME

"Because you have made the Lord your dwelling place-the Most High, who is my refuge -no evil shall be allowed to befall you, no plague come near your tent." -Psalm 91:9-10 (ESV)

When I was visiting the city of Halifax in the Canadian Maritimes, I made it a point to visit the Citadel. It is a great example of fortress architecture. The defences follow a design known as the *trace italienne*, or simply the star fortress. Perfected in Europe, the star fortress design places the defenders behind its walls in a strong position to repel invaders. Owing to its planned geometrical complexity, the star fortress enables the defenders to fend off any attack from almost every conceivable angle. From a military standpoint they made great defensive installations and from an aesthetic standpoint they were often treated as works of art by their architects. To lay siege to such a monumental structure often proved to be an immensely difficult and costly task and were not overcome easily.

Likewise, God is our ever present strength in times of trouble. Sometimes it may seem as if we are being attacked on all sides with nowhere to turn to. We wonder if there is any place which we can run to and be assured of security and rest. But no matter how hard we may look here below, we will never be able to find such a place. The walls of the supposed fortresses of this world are prone to crumble under pressure and can only offer a mediocre defence against the tribulations we must endure in this fallen world. It is only when we have placed our ultimate trust in Christ that we will be able to find enduring strength and peace. When we have turned to Him and have allowed His Spirit to reside in our hearts, He will reveal to us His faithful protection over us. Though suffering and misery may be all around us, we can find confidence in the truth that in Christ we are protected on all sides. With Him as our refuge no evil will emerge victorious over us for He is insurmountable and able to use all things towards the fulfilment of His perfect will.

March 1

A LASTING JOY

"Do not grieve, for the joy of the Lord is your strength." - Nehemiah 8:10b (NIV)

Troubling circumstances can often rob us of our joy. Faced with situations that seem overwhelming and demanding, our hearts sink and any trace of peace we feel in our lives slowly vanishes. Like a toy being fought over between two children, we feel as if we are being pulled here and there about to reach the breaking point. In our despair we feel weak and powerless to confront and overcome the many obstacles that weigh heavy on our minds. We want to be free, we want to breathe that sigh of relief, and we search for that strength and joy which will carry us through. But no matter how hard we look or where we turn, nothing in this world can seem to provide what we yearn for; further heightening our misery.

But there is hope! Hope in the One who has conquered the world and its grief. God sent His Son, Jesus Christ, so that man may be set free from sin and be reconciled to Him. Through His death and resurrection, Christ has promised us with the hope of dwelling with Him in Heaven and has assured us that His Spirit will strengthen us through this life until the day we meet with Him face to face. In His omnipotence nothing is too great for God and we can find rest in the fact that His Spirit always works towards our benefit so that we may have life abundant. When we have allowed Christ's Spirit to enter into our hearts and have permitted Him to fulfill His perfect plan for our lives, we will find a lasting joy that transcends our circumstances and can never be taken away. This joy is rooted in the knowledge that Christ never forsakes those who call upon His Name, and that when we seek to align ourselves with Him, He will restore us when we are weary and will always emerge victorious over all that we may face.

March 2

IN HIS ARMS

"The eternal God is your refuge, and underneath are the everlasting arms." -Deuteronomy 33:27 (NIV)

Crocodiles have an odd way of carrying their young. When wanting to transport her children, a female crocodile would gather them up in a most unexpected place; her mouth! It truly seems like a dangerous place to be in, and in fact from the outside it almost looks as if the crocodile is devouring her babies. However, crocodiles are extremely protective of their offspring and would never wish any harm to come to them. The young crocodile knows that they are safe in the powerful jaws of their mother. Who would dare confront the full strength of such a great reptile; especially if they were protecting the nascent lives of their young? When the mother lets her children run free from her mouth, each and every one of them emerges in good condition.

Sometimes we may wonder if we are truly safe in the will of God. The path which he has called us to walk may be filled with trials and struggles of many kinds. When we are thrust into the midst of such moments, it is tempting to question whether this is our purpose; that God has placed us in such circumstances only to watch us suffer. But God is quite unlike what our circumstances might portray Him as. He is not malevolent or spiteful. While man in their fallen nature may use their power to inflict suffering on others, God is not bound by our human failings. He is perfect in goodness and love; assuring us in His Word that He has plans not to harm us, but to give us hope and a future. When we have placed our trust in His Son, Jesus Christ, and allow Him to carry out His redemptive work in our lives, we can rest in the knowledge that God uses our moments of darkness to prove His never-failing providence. He is victorious over the misery of this world because He is able to use our sufferings to strengthen our faith in Him so that He may perfect His righteousness in us. When we choose to trust in Him, we will be able to dwell in His powerful, everlasting arms knowing that He will always be our eternal refuge and will guide us on the path to life according to His plan for our lives.

March 3

LET US PREPARE!

"Therefore, since we have these promises, dear friends, let us purify ourselves from everything that contaminates body and spirit, perfecting holiness out of reverence for God." -2 Corinthians 7:1 (NIV)

If we knew that we were going to meet someone, what would we do? Certainly we would not meet them as if we had just gotten out of bed! We would take a bath, put on proper clothes to wear, and groom ourselves in such a way as to be presentable before them. What if they decided to visit our home? Would we leave it in a mess? Of course not! We would make sure that every room is spotlessly clean and carefully organized before our guest arrives. What do all of these actions show? They show how much we honor and respect our guest by preparing ourselves before he comes and treating them in a manner deserving of their friendship.

How much more should we do so before God! He is Lord and Creator of the Universe; perfect in holiness, justice, and love. Indeed He is worthy of our worship and reverence. For those to dwell in His presence, one has to be pure and blameless because in His holy nature God cannot tolerate sin. This is a problem for us because we all have been tainted by sin since we chose to go contrary to God's righteous standards. But God does not want to leave us like this; separated from Him and the life He brings to all who are in relationship with Him. In His love God sent down His Son, Jesus Christ, so that through His death and resurrection we are made pure by His Spirit residing within us and are reconciled to God. However, does this mean we are to take for granted this love which God has shown us? Not at all! God still requires us to live in a way worthy of His righteousness. The only difference is that we now have Christ who is more than able to help us live in accordance with God's standards. Are there areas in our lives which need to be subject to the refining work of Christ? When we have allowed His Spirit to purify us of our sin and continue to keep in step with Him, He will make us presentable before God; not because we have been made so as a result of our efforts, but solely through the power of Christ in us.

March 4

MAINTAINING YOUR HEALTH

"For physical training is of some value, but godliness has value for all things, holding promise for both the present life and the life to come."
-1 Timothy 4:8 (NIV)

We live in a very health conscious age. Studies are always being published on how eating certain foods or doing certain exercise regimens can benefit our physical well-being. Perhaps out of fear that we can lose our vitality and develop health problems, we are careful about what we eat and we make sure that we get plenty of exercise. Are these things wrong? Of course not! God has called us to be good stewards of our bodies He has given us. However, the unquestionable fact of life is that we are mortal and destined to face a physical death. One day, our physical bodies will become no more than bones buried in the ground, and we will come face to face with God Himself. When that moment comes, what will we say before Him?

God does not look at the external. Rather, His focus is on our hearts. Though our physical bodies may look healthy on the surface, God is not fooled and He sees the rotten state of our hearts as a result of being under the grip of sin. Due to His holy nature, God cannot tolerate sin and our sinful nature has caused us to be separated from Him. But God, in His love, does not want to see sin carry out its destructive work in our lives. He wants to restore us so that we may have life through being in relationship with Him. That is why He sent Jesus Christ so that by His death and resurrection, sin's hold over us may be broken and we are reconciled to God. When we allow Christ's Spirit to work in our lives and submit ourselves to Him, He will train us in His righteousness for the well-being of our souls. Remaining obedient to Christ and permitting Him to enable us to live according to His standards and perfect will, we will be strengthened to face our fallen world and shine for Him; knowing that we have the promise of joy and hope both in this life and into eternity.

March 5

HE IS THE MAIN FEATURE!

"He must increase, but I must decrease." -John 3:30 (ESV)

John's disciples heard that Jesus was attracting crowds and baptizing the people who came to Him. Distressed over the matter, they went directly to John and told him what they saw. John's answer to their concerns however, was one of humility and grace. While his disciples were more worried about losing numbers and therefore prominence to Jesus, John had it in perspective. He recognized that though Jesus was his cousin, He was first and foremost his Lord and Savior. John was not called to redeem the world; it was Christ. Rather, John's role was to call the people to repentance and prepare the way for Jesus' coming; and he fulfilled this role well. Now that Christ had come, all John had to do was sit back and watch; humbling himself and not allowing pride to get the better of him so that Christ may carry out His redemptive work in the world.

We do not want the spotlight taken from us. In our human pride we want to be the centre of attention; loved, revered, and adored by all who come into contact with us. But these things are temporary and when we are faced with the possibility of losing such a position, we will do anything to maintain it; even resorting to methods which are deceitful and corrupt. Consequently, our pride leads us to do things that will shatter our relationships with others, and lasting peace and joy will elude us. What is more is that pride, if we allow it to take root in our hearts, will tarnish our witness for Christ and prevent the work which He is doing in our lives. If we truly wish to be redeemed from our sin and bring glory to God, we must first acknowledge that it is not about us. We can do nothing on our own because it is God who gives us breath and the ability to do what we boast about. When we allow Christ to enter into our hearts and purge us of our pride, we will know our place before Him and He will arrange our priorities according to His perfect will; not ours. By humbling ourselves so that Christ may work in us, we will be able to see the wonder and blessings of living in obedience to Him as He unfolds His plan before our eyes.

March 6

SHINE LIKE STARS

"Do everything without complaining or arguing, so that you may become blameless and pure, children of God without fault in a crooked and depraved generation, in which you shine like stars in the universe" - Philippians 2:14-15 (NIV)

When I first traveled into the countryside, what struck me was the amount of stars. Illuminating the night sky in all their resplendent glory, it was a wonderful sight to behold for one who has spent his life in the city and I spent a good amount of time trying to pick out the constellations I remembered from reading books on astronomy. Due to pollution, urban dwellers can only see a handful of stars and perhaps one constellation. But because rural areas are not as affected by the scourge of pollution, I could see the lights of numerous stars shine in the darkness. However, the stars in the city have one thing in common; they are so bright that we can see their light despite the pollution which tries to obstruct them.

When everything seems to be going our way it is easy to be witnesses for Christ. We can love, serve, and say all the right things when all is well, but what about when it is not? People and circumstances can often arouse our anger and frustration; leading us to react in ways that are not befitting to a child of Christ. If we have allowed situations around us to take control over our thoughts and actions, we have become bound by them and have permitted them to obscure the work that Christ is doing in our lives. Admittedly, it is hard for us on our own efforts to live up to the standards God has called us to and He knows this full well. That is why He gave us His Son, so that when we have allowed Him to dwell within us and carry out His redemptive work in our lives, He will by His Spirit help us shine for Him in this dark world. Only when we have allowed Him to take reign over our attitudes and reactions will we be able to display His love and righteousness being manifested in us regardless of what we may be facing. The world is watching, and when we let Christ shine His light through us, He will make us shine like stars in the sky, bearing His hope and love to a world in despair.

March 7

A DESTRUCTIVE POISON

"For where jealousy and selfish ambition exist, there will be disorder and every vile practice." -James 3:16 (ESV)

Throughout history there are countless examples of political intrigue and assassination plots. In the vast majority of these cases the motivations are the same; jealousy and selfish ambition. It is human tendency to covet, to yearn after and seek to take something that does not belong to us. When such greed has taken over our hearts, we will go to any length to see that we obtain the object of our desire. That is why we see in the pages of human history, rival families squabbling over an earthly throne and leaders ousting leaders in an often highly violent fashion where every act of depravity and deceit is employed. What adds to this tragedy is that prolonged internal struggles for power ruins empires and kingdoms; rendering them ineffective and vulnerable to outside threats.

When we have allowed jealousy and an obsession over our selfish desires to gain a foothold in our hearts, nobody wins. Such attitudes only serve to degrade ourselves and destroy our relationships with others. The preacher Robert Schuller once said that, "Ambition without love is dangerous." If compassion is absent from us, we can guarantee that our envy and selfishness will cause destruction wherever we go and shatter our unity amongst each other. However, through Christ we can spare ourselves of this misery. When we have allowed His Spirit to enter in our hearts and carry out His redemptive work in our lives, He will fill us with His love. Christ will open our eyes to see ourselves and those around us as being created in the image of God and therefore precious in His sight. Our jealousy will be purged from us when we find our security and worth in Him, and rest in His faithful providence; enabling us by His Spirit to serve others and remain in harmony with God and with each other.

March 8

FINDING THE TIME

"For God alone, O my soul, wait in silence, for my hope is from him." -Psalm 62:5 (ESV)

Today as I was walking through the mall I came across an interesting product. Running late for an early morning appointment? Take "Cereal on the Go" with you; a curious little container in which you can pour your milk and cereal, and eat from it while you travel. But what was interesting about it was not what it does, but the statement which it made. We have become such a fast-paced culture that we cannot even carve out time so that we may sit down and enjoy the first meal of our day. So great is the demand to meet deadlines and go from here to there as quickly as possible that we end up having to multi-task almost everything we do. But if our minds are everywhere, we are actually nowhere, and this causes much stress and anxiety in our lives.

Sometimes we face this problem when it comes to spending time with God. In the midst of our busy lives we feel that we cannot possibly fit Him into our schedules. Even when we want Him to be involved in our lives, we find ourselves being so caught up in the affairs of this world that He becomes only a mere afterthought. But this is not meant to be. If it is true peace and strength we seek, we can only find it by spending time with Christ; who has created the day and given us breath. It is only sensible that we bring our day before Him. When we have allowed Christ to enter our hearts and seek to align ourselves with Him, He will teach us what it means to put Him first. By taking time to be in His presence through prayer and reading His Word, we will learn that when we wait on Him, He will strengthen and empower us for the day ahead. Placing our trust in Him first, we will be blessed as He proves His faithfulness to us; assuring us with the hope that through Him we are able to overcome.

March 9

A GUIDED ZEAL

"It is not good to have zeal without knowledge, nor to be hasty and miss the way." -Proverbs 19:2 (NIV)

There have been times where I have gotten so excited about something that I become absent minded and forgetful. Every week I volunteer at a nearby church with their youth program. Occasionally, after the program had ended, the leadership staff and I would go out for dinner and fellowship. On one such occasion, I knew that we were going to one of my favorite restaurants later that night and I was looking forward to it all week. But as I neared the office door of the youth pastor, I realized something. I forgot my house keys! Considering that my parents would be out that night, there would be no one to open the door for me when I returned from the dinner. There was still some time before my parents had to leave and turning an about face I walked back home and returned to the church with keys in hand; ready for the night ahead and the delicious dinner which was to follow.

Sometimes we can be like that in our zeal; forgetting knowledge in the process. There is nothing wrong with zeal in itself. In fact we are to allow zeal to consume us for the things of God and for His Son, Jesus Christ. However, blind zeal without Christ's direction and guidance can often get us into more trouble than we wish despite our good intentions. When we have allowed Christ to reside in our hearts and submit ourselves to His refining work in our hearts, He will give us the knowledge to channel our passion so that He may use it to fulfill His restorative work in our lives and in the lives of others. By permitting His Spirit to guide our minds, words, and steps, Christ will ensure that only He, in His perfect love and righteousness, will be displayed. The knowledge of Christ, what He has done for us and what He promises to do for all who come to Him, will serve to remind us what we must do with our zeal; submitting it to His Spirit so that He may use us as witnesses for Him wherever we are.

March 10

LIFTING OUR HEADS

"If then you have been raised with Christ, seek the things that are above, where Christ is, seated at the right hand of God. Set your minds on things that are above, not on things that are on earth." -Colossians 3:1-2 (ESV)

Often times when we see someone who appears to be not connected with reality, we describe them as having their "head in the clouds". Lost in their thoughts and lacking in practicality, we deem such people as being ineffective and perhaps a little bit bizarre. Of course it is important to be sensible; making full use of the minds God has given us and having an awareness of the world in which we live. However, we can gravitate to the other extreme of being too caught up in the things on Earth. Concerned over the material affairs of this world and being entangled in petty matters and conflicts, we lose sight of God and the path to life He has called us to walk on.

Life is more than the things which we buy and the wealth we hope to attain. It is more than the trivial arguments and rivalries we embroil ourselves with. A preoccupation with these things only fails to tilt our heads upward and deprives us of the blessings and joys of seeing through the eyes of Christ. When we have allowed Him to enter our hearts and carry out His redemptive work in our lives, He will break the power that sin has over us. Our innate depravity has tainted our senses; thereby distracting us away from God and enslaving us to sin. It is because of sin that we find ourselves obsessing over things that will only leads towards our own destruction. But when we have permitted the Spirit of Christ to work within us and seek to align ourselves with Him, He will correct our vision to see what truly matters in this life. He will give us discernment to know that only He is worth pursuing and will give us the desire to seek the heart of God. When we do this and turn our faces heavenward towards Christ, He will make us lights in this fallen world as He uses us for His restorative mission to His Creation.

March 11

IN NEED OF DIRECTION

"Whether you turn to the right or to the left, your ears will hear a voice behind you, saying, 'This is the way; walk in it.'" -Isaiah 30:21 (NIV)

Asking for directions in a city can sometimes get you nowhere. I remember moments when my friends and I would ask two different people how to get to a certain place, and we would get two completely different answers. When this happens, uncertainty sets in. We do not know if one is right, if both are wrong, or if both are right. Trying to figure this out can be frustrating and we wish that we had a built-in global positioning system that would tell us where to go and where to turn, or at the very least a map. But when we have neither of these, it is easy to feel confused and lost. We want to find the right path to our destination, but we do not know where to turn, and this can cause much anxiety and worry.

Often times, we may feel as if we are wandering through life in the same manner. Seeking direction and not knowing where to turn, we look to the sources in this world to help us when we are perplexed. It could be family, friends, mentors, or earthly philosophies. But it may be the case that all these voices tell us to go in different directions, adding to our confusion. We ask ourselves if there is anyone who can point to us the way; who can say to us that this is the right path in which we should go and give us confidence in that fact. The wonderful assurance is that there is! When we have allowed Christ to enter our hearts and have allowed His Spirit to work within us, He will guide and lead us according to His perfect wisdom. By keeping in step with Him, His Spirit will prompt us and direct us to His Word so that we may understand the path we must take. When we are within His will, we are safe and are promised that He has plans to prosper us and to give us hope. In this hope we will rest knowing that when God calls us to walk a certain way, it is for our benefit and He will prove His faithfulness to us as he works out His glorious purposes for our lives.

March 12

DON'T LAY LANDMINES!

"Do you see a man who is hasty in his words? There is more hope for a fool than for him."-Proverbs 29:20 (ESV)

Landmines are dangerous weapons. They are lethal in that they do not discriminate between friend or foe, or combatant or civilian. When an army decides to use landmines in a given area to combat enemy forces, they run the risk of harming innocent lives and even themselves! If a minefield is not properly marked anyone, even the very people who laid these weapons, can be vulnerable to its destructive power. They can sometimes be soldiers unwittingly walking to their deaths, or little children a step away from getting maimed or worse. There are organizations which seek the complete ban on the usage of landmines, and are actively involved in clearing battle-scarred nations of these tools of war so that they may not cause any more harm.

Our careless words often have the same effect. When we say things without thinking, we are essentially laying mines for both ourselves and others to step on. We make promises we cannot keep, and hurt the people we love and care about. The result is strained and broken relationships which bring us much pain and regret. Though these may not manifest themselves immediately, like a landmine in wait they will explode on us and others when we least expect it. But how can we control our tongues? Trying to keep a filter on our mouths can seem to be an impossible task. However, if we rely on our own efforts to keep reign over what we say, we are guaranteed an uphill struggle. Only when we have allowed Christ to work in our hearts and have adopted His righteousness will our mouths reflect His wisdom, love, and goodness. By permitting His Spirit to help us conform to Christ's likeness, He will be able to use our tongues to bring life and healing to those around us, and towards His restorative purposes for the world.

March 13

MUSIC IN THE AIR

"Speak to one another with psalms, hymns and spiritual songs. Sing and make music in your heart to the Lord." -Ephesians 5:19 (NIV)

When I was in southern India we travelled through a series of towns. What was remarkable however was that the streets of these towns were lined with large speakers! With the volume turned up to full blast, these speakers played a fusion of both traditional and modern music which made one want to get up and dance. Clearly the concept of noise pollution was non-existent! Yet it was a wonderful experience and it certainly contributed to the jovial atmosphere in the lively towns we passed through. The love for music is universal, and this is confirmed by the fact that every culture and nation has its own rich musical tradition. It would appear that humanity is programmed with a love for music and a source of great pleasure for many.

But this love for music has not come to us out of nowhere. It is ingrained in us by God Himself. God loves music, when it is directed in worship to His perfect goodness! Heaven is filled with angel choirs and orchestras declaring the glory of God and His handiwork. It is no wonder therefore, that we as humans created in the image of God, share this love with Him. However, God knows full well the power of music has to influence our minds and hearts. Each and every song has a message behind it. This message can either influence us for good or for evil. While we might claim that the messages within what we listen to do not affect us, they will slowly take reign over our thoughts and attitudes. If we sow sin in our lives by allowing it to plant itself in our thoughts, we will reap sin in our actions. How are we to avoid this? When we have allowed the Spirit of Christ to enter our hearts and carry out His redemptive work in our lives, He will train us in His righteousness. By allowing ourselves to be guided by His wisdom, He will help us discern the messages behind what we listen to so that we may be able to dwell upon what is pure and worthy of praise. In choosing this path we will find life as He leads us in the worship of who He is, and enables us to share the life we have in Him with others.

March 14

STILL IN PLACE

"He is before all things, and in him all things hold together." - *Colossians 1:17 (NIV)*

What is the most important part of a train? The most obvious answer would be the engine. Every car is connected to each other, which are all in turn ultimately connected to this essential part of the train. If the engine was somehow disconnected, the other cars would not be going anywhere. Their cargo would not arrive to where it is needed and their passengers would not be able to go where they intend to travel. Thus it falls to the engine, with its strength and power, which keeps the convoy moving together on time and leads it towards its destination. Without it, nothing will be accomplished, and chaos will set in as schedules fall apart and there is a scramble to set things right.

Sometimes in the direst of circumstances it may feel as if the engine has been detached from our train. Looking at the devastation which has happened in our lives, we feel as if our world has been unraveled. Dazed we remain at a standstill, wondering where do we go from here and how we will be ever able to pick up the pieces of what has been shattered. But the wonderful truth is that the train has not been derailed! God is still in control and the world is firmly in His loving hands. No tragedy is greater than Him and He is more than able to work all things together for His good and perfect purposes. He goes before us; preparing the way He wants us to travel so that we may be restored. But will we trust Him? Will we allow Him to lead us in our darkest hour? When we have allowed Christ to enter our hearts and permit His Spirit to direct us, we will rest in the assurance that in Him our hope will never be extinguished. With wonder we will see how He is able to make all things new, and stand firm in the knowledge that He holds everything in place.

March 15

WHAT ARE YOU A SLAVE TO?

"For whatever overcomes a person, to that he is enslaved."- 2 Peter 2:19b (ESV)

What does it mean to be addicted to something? Often we use the word to describe that we really like a particular food, hobby, or television show. But having an addiction goes beyond mere attraction and desire, having more sinister connotations. When we inwardly feel compelled to do something even though we do not want to, that is what addiction truly is. We may know that our sinful habits our destructive. We may know that no good ever comes out of them. Yet like one who has stepped into quicksand, it drags us against our will. If we give even an inch to sin, it will become a brutal taskmaster; demanding that we satisfy it with our wickedness even though we want escape.

But if we have grown weary to this addiction to sin, there is hope! God knows our torment when we are slaves to our depravity. He knows that this was never meant to be and He mourns the damage sin is doing to His creation and to us in particular who bear His image. That is why He wants to deliver us so that we may be restored and dwell in relationship with Him. He has given us this hope through His Son, Jesus Christ. When we have allowed Him to enter our hearts and submit every area of our lives to His redemptive work, He will break the chains that bind us to our sinful nature. By binding ourselves to Christ, He will allow His love and righteousness to consume us; overflowing from our hearts so that all may see the work which He is doing in us. To be slaves to sin is a slavery that will only bring us misery and grief. But to be a slave to Christ means that His goodness will overcome us; bringing us life, and a joy that we will be able to find in all circumstances and that will never be taken away.

March 16

RISING ABOVE THE STORM

"Hear my prayer, O Lord; listen to my cry for mercy. In the day of my trouble I will call to you, for you will answer me." -Psalm 86:6-7 (NIV)

It is an almost instinctive cry. When our world has been turned upside-down, and chaos and despair is all around us, our voices turn to God. Knowing that He has ultimate power when we are powerless, we ask for His aid; to help us in our misery and suffering. But sometimes it feels as if our cries are in vain. Despite our constant prayers it feels as if God is not listening. Our sufferings continue to haunt us and we begin to wonder where He is in the midst of our circumstances. We ask if He sees our pain and feels our hurts, or if He is blind and simply does not care. These thoughts can discourage us greatly. But if we allow them to consume us they will lead us away from the truth of who God really is.

God is love. It is in His very nature. Him creating us is an act of love in itself because we are made in His image and we are irreplaceable to Him. Yet we live in a fallen world, made so because of the entrance of sin. But does His seeming silence mean that He has turned His back on humanity because we have allowed sin to corrupt His creation? Not at all! It grieves Him to watch us suffer and He knows full well the hardship we endure here on Earth. That is why He is always at work, seeking to redeem us from sin and restore what has been destroyed. He has done this to Christ so that by His death and resurrection we are cleansed of our sin and have the hope of eternal life with Him. When we choose to trust in Him, He will prove His faithfulness to us for He is able and works all things together for good. In Him we will find joy in our sufferings as He lifts us up according to His perfect will, and assures of the day when He will wipe every tear from our eyes and will turn our mourning into dancing.

March 17

ANSWERING THE CALL

"Amos answered Amaziah, 'I was neither a prophet nor a prophet's son, but I was a shepherd, and I also took care of sycamore-fig trees. But the Lord took me from tending the flock and said to me, 'Go, prophesy to my people Israel.'." -Amos 7:14-15 (NIV)

Sometimes, we know exactly what we want to do with our lives. Based on our desires and what appears to be in our minds the logical fit for us, we move forward and chart the path that we feel is right. In this we develop a zone of comfort because we feel that we are in control of our destiny. But God's plans for our lives may not entirely agree with ours. In fact His plans could be in complete opposition to what we wish; taking us in a different direction than we imagined. When this happens, we stubbornly refuse to obey Him. We come up with excuses saying that we are incapable and are not suitable for the task God has called us to.

However, these excuses only serve to betray our unwillingness to leave our comfort zone and surrender ourselves to God and His perfect will.

If God has called us to something, He will provide us with all that we need. In His love, God does not abandon those who call upon His name and choose to walk with Him. Our perceived weaknesses and inaptitude means nothing, for God promises to be more than sufficient for us to carry out the task He wants us to accomplish. The question is will we trust Him? Will we like Amos leave our comfort zone to follow the will of God? His plan is never to harm us, but to prosper us and give us hope. When we allow Christ to reign in our hearts and seek to align our desires with His, He will guide us in the path we should go. By choosing to walk with Him and follow His voice, He will prove to us His faithfulness and He equips and sustains us; teaching us of the blessings and joy which comes by submitting our lives to His purposes.

March 18

FINDING PEACEFUL REST

"I will lie down and sleep in peace, for you alone, O Lord, make me dwell in safety." -Psalm 4:8 (NIV)

Sleep is a precious gift. Our mortal bodies are weak and therefore God has given us the provision of rest so that our bodies may be renewed and recharged. But how often do our anxieties rob us of this cherished blessing? When our fears and worries consume us, everything is thrown out of order. Our minds are deprived of calm. Our search for peace proves to be elusive. We long and yearn for the day when we can finally be free from this stress; when we can rest in our beds and have that peaceful sleep knowing that all is well. But no matter where we turn in this world, we cannot find it; and so we descend into grief and hopelessness.

No matter how desperate and miserable we may feel however, there is hope in God. He transcends the world and holds it in place. What is more is that He cares when we are suffering and hurting, and He wants us to dwell in serenity and security. Man was not designed to handle worry for we were meant to live in relationship with a God who lovingly provides for our every need. But because of our sinful nature, we have been separated from Him. For this reason God sent Jesus so that through believing in Him the relationship we shared with God may be restored. When we have allowed Christ's Spirit to enter our hearts and submit ourselves to Him, we will find the joy and peace we are looking for as He causes it to overflow from within us. With Him we will be able to rest securely knowing that He is greater than our circumstances and promises us that His perfect will is meant to prosper us; never to harm us. Clinging onto Him, He will restore our souls and give us a peace that is eternal and surpasses all understanding.

March 19

PERFORMING INNER MAINTENANCE

"All wrongdoing is sin," -1 John 5:17a (NIV)

I enjoy looking at machines from the Industrial Revolution. With the advent of steam power and the need for mass production, this period spanning from the 18th to the 19th centuries produced some of the most fascinating machines to have ever been invented. Indeed in some ways they form the foundation of modern technology today. Whenever I have the privilege of going to museums where they showcase these technological wonders, I always marvel at their complexity and order. Yet it is surprising that even the smallest factor can render such intricate machines to be inoperable. Things such as rust, or a rock caught in the cogs can damage the machine and hinder its productivity. Thus, it always needs to be well-maintained to run efficiently and smoothly.

Sometimes we try to justify the seemingly "small" sins we commit in our lives. Feeling that we are essentially good people, we see our lapses into what we deem to be minor sins as excusable and harmless. But the truth is that in the eyes of God, sin is sin regardless of what it is. Even what we see as small sins can be devastating to ourselves and our relationships with others. Like rust developing in a complex machine or a rock caught in between its cogs, it can prevent others from seeing the work that Christ is doing in our lives and would cause harm to ourselves as well. How can we prevent this from happening? We cannot do so through our own efforts, but solely through Christ. When we have allowed His Spirit to enter our hearts and carry out His redemptive work in our lives, He will help us by His enabling to maintain the righteousness He has given us as we surrender our lives to Him. In Christ we are able to live life in its fullest sense as He leads us away from our bondage to sin and into the freedom which comes from knowing Him as Lord and Savior. By cleansing us of anything that is not in keeping with His holy standards in our lives, He will shine through us as He pours out His love and goodness so that others may be drawn to Him.

March 20

A WORTHWHILE INVESTMENT

"Why spend money on what is not bread, and your labor on what does not satisfy? Listen, listen to me, and eat what is good, and your soul will delight in the richest of fare." -Isaiah 55:2 (NIV)

None of us would waste money on that which is of no benefit to us. We have been taught to conserve our energy and resources for something that is worthwhile and in our best interests in the long run. Whether it is what we eat or the career path we choose to take, we want to be wise in our decisions and make the right choice so that we may live healthy lives and that nothing be done in vain. But though we desire this, we often fall short of them. How often do we frivolously spend our time, money, and energy on that which is corrupt and depraved? How often do we worry and lose sleep obsessing over our careers and plans. Though we think that these will give us satisfaction, they only provide an illusory contentment that will give way to grief and misery.

There is only one way through which we can find true and lasting satisfaction. Man was designed for a relationship with God so that we may dwell in His eternal and unfailing love. However, because of our sinful nature gained as a result of Adam's disobedience against God, the relationship we formerly shared with Him has been severed. But God does not wish for it to be like this. For this reason He sent Jesus so that through His death and resurrection we may have the hope of being freed from our sin so that we may enter into a relationship with God and bear witness to His goodness. When we allow Christ's Spirit to enter our hearts and carry out His work of restoration in our lives, we will find joy and peace that nothing on this Earth can match. Investing all that we have by surrendering ourselves to Him, we will find it more than worthwhile as Christ fulfils His perfect will for our lives. He will prove to us His love and faithfulness and by His Spirit give us a lasting satisfaction that will remain constant regardless of our circumstances.

March 21

EXTINGUISHING A FIRE

"Refrain from anger and turn from wrath; do not fret—it leads only to evil." -Psalm 37:8 (NIV)

Anger can be a very destructive force. When our rage is unleashed, anyone and anything can be a target. Controlled by our fury we do things that we regret, and say things we do not mean; inflicting damage both upon ourselves and the relationships we share with others. Sometimes we say that we cannot help ourselves and that our anger is something that cannot be dealt with and changed. But the truth is that anger is like a fire, and a fire grows when it is fed. The more we allow things to feed our anger and irritation, the more our anger will develop into an inferno which will consume all in its path. When our ire has dimmed and we look upon the devastation we have caused, we hang our heads in shame and resolve to not descend into such anger again.

The problem is that we cannot remain true to such a resolution. No matter how hard we may try to search for inner peace and keep a reign on our anger by our own strength, there come moments when we lose all sense of calm and self-control. That is because our sinful nature renders any human attempt to control our rage useless and as long as this dominates in our lives our sinfulness will be expressed in our anger. However, there is hope! Our anger can be dealt with once Christ deals with our sinful nature. When we allow His Spirit to enter our hearts and carry out His redemptive work in our lives, He will cleanse us of our wickedness so that His righteousness may be made manifest in our lives. By surrendering our attitudes to His Spirit, He will douse the flames of our anger so that His love and peace may overflow from within us, bringing life and healing to all who bear witness to the work He is doing within our hearts.

March 22

UNDER HIS WINGS

"How precious is your steadfast love, O God! The children of mankind take refuge in the shadow of your wings." -Psalm 36:7 (ESV)

In general, birds are known to be monogamous, loyal, and caring creatures. I remember being given a poignant reminder of this fact while I was walking downtown. In the midst of the crowds of people going here and there absorbed in their lives, I heard the chirping of a little bird. As I moved closer to investigate, I saw the chirping bird hovering over another bird which was hurt and wounded. Shielding it with its wings, the bird was tending to the injuries of its companion; making sure that nothing would be able to harm it in its crippled state. But though I was given a picture of the love and devotion the birds often show to one another, I was also given a beautiful picture of a greater love that God shows to us.

Sometimes we feel as if we are alone in our grief. Though we suffer, the world seems to move on; not giving a single thought or care to our plight. This increases our misery even more, and we think about how cruel a world we live in. But there is hope in our darkness, and there is someone who cares far more than anyone on Earth ever could. Each and every one of us is precious in the eyes of God. We are created in His image and it pains Him to see us grieve and under the yoke of sin. For this reason He sent Christ, so that when we have allowed His Spirit to enter our hearts, He will redeem us from our bondage to sin so that He may work within us and assure us of the hope that we have life through Him. When we call upon His name, we can count on Him spreading His wings around us; protecting us as He brings healing and restoration to our lives. In Him we are never alone and by His Spirit we can put our confidence in the fact that God sees our need when no else will and will come alongside us to bring hope when all seems lost.

March 23

LOVE THAT IS INSEPARABLE

"For the sake of his great name the Lord will not reject his people, because the Lord was pleased to make you his own." -1 Samuel 12:22 (NIV)

Sometimes we may feel as if we are unlovable. Confronted by the depravity of our own sinful nature and lifestyle choices we wonder if we can even love ourselves; let alone by others around us. Perhaps we have told ourselves that there is no hope for us; that we are destined to live without ever feeling loved. We may even feel that not even God could love us. So far have we gone astray from His holy standards that we feel that we are beyond the love that God has assured to all. But the wonderful truth is that these are all lies; lies meant to pull us into despair and away from the joys that come from being with Christ.

God is perfect in His love. The love which God pours out as a result of His nature has no limits. Nothing will be able to ever separate us from the love of God. The fact that He has sent his Son, Jesus Christ, to die for us is proof of this love. God is holy, and because of our sinful nature He cannot tolerate anything that is impure. Thus, our relationship with Him has been severed. But He does not wish for us to be separate from Him. In His love He wants to restore, breaking the bonds which bind us to sin so that we may find freedom through Him and the life which He gives to us. When we have allowed Christ to enter our lives and have permitted His Spirit to carry out His redemptive work in our lives, we will know that He loves us whether we feel it or not. He will remain faithful to the work which He is doing in our lives for He wants and desires for us to be with Him. As being counted amongst the redeemed in Him, we will rest in the assurance that He wants to make us his own and that His doing so is an act of love that can find no equal.

March 24

A DOUBLE LIFE

"If we had forgotten the name of our God or spread out our hands to a foreign god, would not God have discovered it, since he knows the secrets of the heart?" -Psalm 44:20-21 (NIV)

It is fairly easy to tell when someone is being insincere. Somehow we are able to discern whether a person is saying something because they genuinely mean it, or if they are saying it simply to please or appease us. Things such as their tone of voice or their facial expressions can often be indicators as to the true intent behind their words. However, because our human understanding is flawed, even the most astute of minds can be deceived by those who are able to put on a good show. But while we may try and succeed to be thoroughly convincing to those around us in our claims and statements, our hearts could be far away from what our mouths confess. Though we may feel that our deception is flawless, there is One who cannot be fooled.

God is all-knowing. He has created us, and knows us better than we know even ourselves. Thus, He knows when we are simply paying lip-service to Him. He knows when our hearts have enthroned an idol that is not deserving of the primary place He should occupy in our lives. It is foolish for us then to think for a moment that we can successfully live a double-life before God for He knows our every thought and move before we even consider it! If anything we deceive ourselves into thinking that we can somehow convince God that we are sincere in our worship of Him when we are really not. God is very clear; no one can serve two masters. The question before us is whether we choose life with Him, or cling to our idols which lead us into despair and misery. When we allow the Spirit of Christ to enter our hearts and permit Him to carry out His redemptive work in our lives, we are assured that He will lead us according His perfect will so that we may find freedom in Him. Through the power of His Spirit in us, we are able to stand justified before God; not because of anything we can do, but because of what Christ has done and is doing in our lives.

March 25

FROM DARKNESS TO LIGHT

"I have come into the world as a light, so that no one who believes in me should stay in darkness." -John 12:46 (NIV)

Several years ago in the region where I live, there was a major blackout. For nearly 24 hours we were without electricity. When the lights in our home were suddenly shut off, I remember stumbling through pitch darkness trying to find anything that would illuminate the rooms of our home. Spending our evening and night by candlelight was a new and interesting experience. However it was clear that we all wanted our electricity back. Imagine our joy then when we came home to find out that the power had been restored! No longer did we have to go about the activities of the evening in darkness, but now we had bright lights to help us see and guide our steps.

Humanity continues to remain in darkness. Why is it that everywhere we turn we are reminded of our wickedness? It is because our eyes and minds have been tainted by our innate sinful nature. Man was meant to live in relationship with God. But because man chose to forsake Him and His knowledge, we have separated ourselves from God. Wanting to fill this void we have created in our hearts as a result of choosing to reject God, we look for that which will satisfy this need we have for Him. Yet in our search, sin has blinded us, and we stumble and fall into its clutches no matter where we look in this world. However, God sees our stumbling and does not wish for us to remain in such a state. That is why He sent His Son, Jesus Christ for us. Through His death His blood has washed us clean of our impurities once and for all, and by His resurrection we have the promise of being restored and renewed. When we have allowed Christ to enter our hearts and redeem us from our sinful nature, He will enter us as a light that dispels the darkness with which sin has blinded us. By His enabling we will be able to see clearly the way in which we should walk in fullness of life; allowing Him to make us lights for others as He shines His righteousness through us.

March 26

WHO IS OVERCOMING WHO?

"Do not be overcome by evil, but overcome evil with good." -Romans 12:21 (NIV)

Human behavior is tragically repetitive. It is repetitive because we use the exact same methods time and time again to deal with conflict. It is tragic because we often resort to such violent and vengeful means to somehow ensure in our minds that justice has been served. When someone strikes us, our instinctive response is to strike back and sometimes with even more malice. But if we do this, what is it that separates us from the one that has harmed us? Though we may think that we are justified in our reactions and that this gives us the moral high ground, we are no different from our enemies if we use the same underhanded and destructive methods they use. Instead of overcoming evil it has conquered us and made us its slave.

How then can we escape from this dilemma? As long as our sinful nature continues to hold sway over us, our concept of justice will be skewed and warped, and this will be reflected in our actions and reactions. The solution therefore lies in dealing with our innate depravity. But how can this be done? It is only through Christ, who entered this world so that humanity may be freed from their slavery to sin, that we have the hope of being restored. When we have acknowledged His death and resurrection for us and have allowed His Spirit to enter our hearts, He will give us wisdom and discernment as to how to live as His children. Through His righteousness being worked out through us, He will teach how to walk justly and to love mercy. In this we are able by His enabling to overcome the evils we may face with the light that He shines forth from us; bearing witness to the fact that we are new creations in Christ, holy and blameless before Him and before men.

March 27

BEING RENEWED IN STRENGTH

"The lions may grow weak and hungry, but those who seek the Lord lack no good thing." -Psalm 34:10 (NIV)

I am unable to count the number of times I have seen nature documentaries featuring lions. But every time I happen to watch such documentaries, I am always amazed by how they portray the lion's power and might. With the way they hunt and chase down their prey, it is no wonder they are often associated with the label, "king of the jungle." In fact, it should come as no surprise that with its regal appearance and strength, the lion has been adopted as a symbol for many kings and empires. However, even lions can grow hungry and lose their vigor. A weakened lion may not even pursue a nearby gazelle if he is sapped of his energy and his legs cannot give chase.

Sometimes we may feel as if we are in the same position. Weary of everything around us we sink into fatalistic hopelessness. Though we reminisce of those days where everything seemed to be going our way, we resign ourselves to a false view that we are powerless and have been defeated. But the wonderful truth is that in our weakness, Christ is able to make us strong. When we have allowed His Spirit to enter our hearts and seek after Him, He will renew and restore us. When our situations wear us down, we are able to take hope in the promise that we are able to surrender our burdens to the One who holds the universe in place, and whose grace is more than sufficient for us. By entrusting ourselves into His hands, He will prove Himself to be faithful; giving us His strength so that we may find total fulfillment in His provision. In Christ we have victory, a victory that can never be taken away nor can ever be eclipsed, for nothing will be able to stand against Him.

March 28

TO TRULY FORGIVE

"If your brother or sister sins against you, rebuke them; and if they repent, forgive them. Even if they sin against you seven times in a day and seven times come back to you saying "I repent," you must forgive them." -Luke 17:3-4 (NIV)

Forgiveness is not something which comes naturally for us. The resentments and grudges we hold, and our willingness to hold onto new ones, continues to remind us of this fact. When we have been slighted and hurt by someone else, it is easy to allow anger and bitterness to settle in. We might boast about our abilities to forgive, but we will always be reminded that our forgiveness has limits. The moment we declare an action to be unforgivable we have confessed to ourselves that we are unable to show that unconditional love and grace we are so keen to show off. We may be able to forgive the first time, and perhaps even the second. But our patience soon begins to wear thin, and we deem our offenders not worthy of our mercy.

Why choose forgiveness? When we are faced with injustice we want our enemies to feel retribution, not give them clemency. But if we allow our desire for revenge to fester, it will consume us. We will become prisoners of our anger, and we will soon find that in our thoughts, words, and actions, we will have fallen into sin. As children of Christ we forgive because we do not deserve it ourselves. All of us have sinned and fallen short of God's holy standards. Yet, in His unfailing love, God sent down His Son, Jesus Christ, so that through Him we may find forgiveness. When we accept this free gift of salvation and allow the Spirit of Christ to cleanse us of our sin, we are able to stand before God not because of anything we have done, but by the grace He has willingly shown us. If He does not withhold forgiveness from us no matter what we do, why should we refrain from doing so as His children? Only through allowing Christ's Spirit to perfect His love in us will we be able to truly extend the hand of forgiveness; in that finding freedom and life.

March 29

ALL THINGS WILL BE RESTORED

"Blessed are you who hunger now, for you will be satisfied. Blessed are you who weep now, for you will laugh." -Luke 6:21 (NIV)

There are times when circumstances seem as if they are nothing short of bleak. We look back on our hopes and dreams and compare them with our present realities. Perhaps we have not made it to the point where we would like to be in our lives. Maybe situations have come along our path, and these have pulled us into the depths of despair and sadness. In times like these it is hard to laugh or to find joy. It may even seem impossible to do so when all around us we see failure and misery. We cry out saying it is all hopeless. Those cherished times of celebration and merriment seem to be distant memories we cannot reclaim, and sorrow appears to be our only friend.

But there is hope! A hope that will never fade, and can never be taken away. It is not within the will of God that our suffering be permanent. Indeed it was never a part of His plan in the first place. This world is a fallen place, caused by man's deliberate choice to forsake Him. Yet despite this, God has not forsaken us. He is the restorer of all things and desires that we be brought back into relationship with Him. When we have allowed the Spirit of Christ to enter our hearts and have submitted every area of our lives to His redeeming work, we will be able to take assurance in the fact that He cares for all who call upon His name. We will find laughter again and find fulfillment knowing that in Christ we have victory over whatever may come our way. God is able to use our sufferings and sorrows to fulfill His perfect will, and He will do so with gladness when we choose to trust in Him and allow ourselves to be guided by His hands.

March 30

PRIDE COMES BEFORE A FALL

"The Lord detests all the proud of heart. Be sure of this: They will not go unpunished." -Proverbs 16:5 (NIV)

Arrogance is one of the most destructive and humiliating attitudes to have. By playing upon the ego of a person, it inflates man's perceptions about themselves and creates a fantasy of their abilities. Those who have succumbed to arrogance accept this lie and strut with haughty pride. Thinking that they are better than everyone else they lord their self-proclaimed superiority over others and look down upon those they deem inferior with contempt. But when the day comes when someone with humble confidence exposes the arrogant for who they really are, the same men who marched with pride are put to shame. They learn the hard way that there is no room for conceit and that the proud are sure to fall.

Do we have pride within our hearts? Sometimes we may think that we know better than God. Blind to our own folly we say to God that we do not need Him; that we are perfectly capable of living independent of Him and controlling our destinies. But such a pride has its cost. By forsaking the wisdom of God, our minds have become dulled and we are unable to see the folly of our choices. Thinking ourselves to be wise, the punishment we receive for our arrogance is that God allows us to go our way only to realize, after a painful reminder of the consequences of our actions, that we are fools. However, the beauty of this punishment is that there is hope if we choose to grasp it. God will never point and laugh when we have fallen. Rather, He wishes that all men come into relationship with Him so that they may find abundant life and lasting joy. When we allow Christ's Spirit to enter our hearts and surrender our pride to His infallible wisdom, we will find that being within God's perfect will is the best place to be.

March 31

WHERE IS OUR REFUGE?

"The high mountains belong to the wild goats; the crags are a refuge for the coneys." -Psalm 104:18 (NIV)

Mountains have forever served as natural fortresses for both animals and humans alike. Their tall peaks and rugged landscapes have created sanctuaries and strong defenses for those who look to them for shelter. Wild goats and coneys are safe from predators when they seek refuge in the hills. The advance of armies can be stopped and repelled by those resisting from the safety of mountain heights. Even with technological advancements in flight and travel, traversing a mountain range is a difficult task. To do so is a costly endeavor in more ways than one and that is why mountains are always looked upon as being a place where one is assured protection and security. They are near impregnable barriers which no one will be able to overcome easily.

Where do we run to when disaster strikes and when trial come along our way? Frightened and looking for sanctuary, we search everywhere for that place where we can find rest. But often times we turn to the wrong things in our pursuit.

Convinced that these can be our fortresses in times of trouble, they soon prove to be easy to crumble and fall. This leaves in disillusionment, and in our despair we cry out asking if there is any place where we can run to in our distress. But there is! God is all-powerful and eternal. Nothing will be able to shake Him or stop Him from carrying out His perfect will. When we have our relationship with Him restored by allowing Christ's Spirit to enter our hearts, we will be able to take refuge in Him knowing that in Him we have victory. Living under His providence and faithfulness we will know that even in the most desperate and darkest of moments, Christ always has the final word. He will preserve and protect us while using our sufferings to restore us and fulfill His great purposes for our lives. Will we trust Him with our lives today?

April 1

WORRIED BIRDS

"Look at the birds of the air; they do not sow or reap or store away in barns, and yet your heavenly Father feeds them. Are you not much more valuable than they?" -Matthew 6:26 (NIV)

Christians are perhaps the most worried of sorts. Ironic is it not? The very people who serve a God who promises to protect and provide for them even more than His loving care for the sparrow, are the most notorious for being anxious and troubled. Whenever trials come, the first response always seems to be "why?" Why did God allow this to happen? Why doesn't God provide for us now? Despair is a natural human response, and because we can never look above our circumstances and see the whole plan God has set for our lives, we often react to our present reality. God understands our short-sightedness and allows us to despair. Psalm 88 is prime evidence of that fact. It is perfectly understandable when troubles come to grieve, wail, and mourn for in reality, keeping a stiff upper lip is often hard to do.

At the same time however, Christians should take comfort in the fact that God never forsakes His people, and always has a beautiful plan for their lives. Although we can never see the whole plan, we can see bits of it in retrospect. God's faithfulness to His followers is often understood by His followers after the trial has passed. Suffering produces strength and faith in the believer. Should a believer hold the hand of God and trust Him in his present situation, not only would he have the strength to face greater challenges, but his faith in God's faithfulness will be strengthened simultaneously. Despair has its place no doubt, but clinging onto despair will only further entrench a person into helplessness and misery. Christ came to set humanity free from a lot of things. One of these things was worry. As long as the believer continues to place his trust and obedience in Christ, he can rest and find solace in his Savior's promises never to abandon and never to forsake, that the torturous night eventually gives way to the glorious day.

April 2

YEARNING THROUGH THE NIGHT

"My soul yearns for you in the night; in the morning my spirit longs for you. When your judgments come upon the earth, the people of the world learn righteousness." -Isaiah 26:9 (NIV)

I've often had sleepless nights. Not out of fear, but usually out of excitement. The promise of a much-anticipated trip or a reunion with an old friend whom I haven't seen in years is enough to keep me up at night tossing and turning in a futile attempt to make morning come faster. Do I have the same reaction when it comes to spending time with God? Rarely, if never, have I had a night when I was sleepless on account of being excited about reading the Bible. Does this mean that I should? Perhaps. But in His goodness, God has given man the gift of sleep to rest his mortal body. Man is but dust, and I am thankful that I serve a God who understands this well. Besides, I hardly think that God wants His message to be spread by insomniacs. How ineffective a witness that would be for the Christian!

But like all verses in the Bible this one raises a good point. How often do I rush through my morning not stopping to spend time in His Word? I would like to describe myself as someone who pursues righteousness, justice, and truth. But what good is this pursuit without consulting the perfect source from which all these things flow? Can man comprehend the standards God has placed on these qualities? To an extent perhaps, but as with anything man touches, even the purest of pursuits end up tainted by his sinful nature. It is only through reading God's Word that the Christian may understand such concepts in their purest form, and interact with them in a way that glorifies God and alleviates the suffering of the world. That alone should keep me up at night.

April 3

TOTAL DEPRAVITY, TOTAL SOLUTION

"Therefore he is able to save completely those who come to God through him, because he always lives to intercede for them." -Hebrews 7:25 (NIV)

One only needs to crack open a history book to see the depravity of man. Even the most noble of ideologies, the most benevolent of movements, fall prey to the corruptive force that is human nature. Throughout history, man has tried to wrestle with the problem of human depravity by proposing ideas and methods that would eventually take man to a perfect society where their corruption will cease to persist. However man, in his finite understanding, can and will continue to only come up with solutions that may address and solve part of the problem, but never the whole. The unfortunate result is that the part which was not dealt with festers and grows until it completely destroys every noble aspect of the movement or ideology. Why does this happen? The reason is that man constantly applies small bandages to gaping gashes. Man's depravity is total. It is inherent and affects every single person born into this world. It does not discriminate against race, gender, or socio-economic status. As long as human beings exist, depravity will exist.

What then is the solution? Total depravity deserves a total solution. Jesus' sacrifice on the cross had as its intent to deal with the root of human nature; its inherent wickedness. God knew that man could not save himself because all have fallen short of His standards. Since God is holy and just, He cannot tolerate sin and by His standards, all who sin face death. Yet, God in His love did not want to send His creation to such a fate and thus sent His Son to die in place of humanity. If an individual only believes that Christ came to die in order that the penalty of their sin may be satisfied, then they are completely forgiven. Christ's act of redemption through His death and burial is complete and final. It had to be so in order that each and every sinful desire of man would hold him back no more. Through an acceptance of this fact, man can be elevated out of his corruption. Not by his own hands, but by those of Christ working through him. Total depravity is a problem bigger than humanity itself, and it needs a person bigger than humanity and its depravity to solve it.

April 4

ON THE FLEETING WORLD

"For you know that it was not with perishable things such as silver or gold that you were redeemed from the empty way of life handed down to you from your forefathers, but with the precious blood of Christ, a lamb without blemish or defect." -1 Peter 1:18-19 (NIV)

Why do humans tend to focus on things that will pass away? Money, fame, success, relationships. When our time comes to die and be buried, will we be able to take these things with us? Naked we have come into this world and naked we will depart. Are these things evil in themselves? No, but once they become an obsession, a craving, not only does it become sin, but it becomes the source of much grief. How many people have all the money and wealth in the world, but are never satisfied? How many pursue fame and success, only to find emptiness? How many drift from relationship to relationship, yet never find happiness?

Humans feel that somehow the things of this world will make them complete. If only I get the contract, the degree, the right partner, then I will lack nothing. The sad reality is that this is not true. In this world, man will never be satisfied because everything in this world is fleeting, a chasing after the wind. One can lose money as quickly as they gained it. Fame and success may last during one's lifetime and may even persist after their death. However, time eventually erodes human greatness. Friends come and go, and even spouses die eventually. In this world, where everything seems to slip from our grasp if it hasn't already, what do we cling onto? He who calls upon the name of Christ will never thirst. Those who understand and believe in Christ's sacrifice and His resurrection, and have dedicated their lives to Him, will never be restless. They will always find satisfaction in His eternal love and grace, and comfort in the hope of a beautiful life in the hereafter.

April 5

HE WHO KNEELS BEFORE GOD CAN STAND BEFORE ANYTHING.

"It is written:" 'As surely as I live,' says the Lord, 'every knee will bow before me; every tongue will confess to God.' " -Romans 14:11 (NIV)

When I was traveling in India, I came across a church with a sign bearing these words. "He who kneels before God can stand before anything". It's a profound statement. There are times when I feel that life has overwhelmed me. Once I feel comfortable with the rhythm life is at, the tempo picks up speed and the rhythm becomes distorted; leaving me to struggle in an attempt to keep up. Sometimes life seems so confusing, to the point of absurdity, that I often wonder whether I am living in a dream. At times when I feel that life has left me lying on my back, I remember that I serve a God who is constant and unchanging in an often fluid and chaotic world, who stands above the world and keeps it in His hands.

What a great privilege I have, that this same God desires to guide me through the chaos of life. Realizing that the world is fallen He, in His compassion, wants to aid the suffering and redeem His Creation. All that He requires of me is to trust Him in humble submission. Truly I, in my imperfect state, cannot hope to make sense of my own life. I have tried and failed on more than one occasion. But a God who not only has ordained my days for me, but wants to reveal His plan for me should I allow Him to, is the most perfect and compassionate guide to help me sift through and make sense of the disorder that life seems to bring about. By kneeling to Him, I gain the strength and confidence that only He can provide, to brave any storm life seems to throw at me. This is why God allows suffering in the life of the Christian. So that we may grow stronger, both mentally and spiritually, and that we may come out more enlightened than before towards His ways.

April 6

BANDAGING OUR WOUNDS

"He heals the brokenhearted and binds up their wounds. -Psalm 147:3 (NIV)

When we are injured, our instinctive response is to cry out in pain. But though this response is to inform us that we are in pain, it also serves a distress call. Imagine if we were walking through a remote area and suddenly found ourselves on the ground in pain. Yet we were unable to cry out, thereby preventing anyone within audible range to take note of our predicament and come to our aid. That is why God has given us not only the blessing of pain to tell us that something is wrong, but the ability to cry out when we are wounded. When help finally comes, what a relief it is as people concerned about our welfare tend to us seeking to bring restoration and healing!

Life comes with both its joys and sorrows. When those moments of agony strike, where do we turn to when we feel shattered and broken? Often when we cry out for help in our despair, it seems that no one is listening, and those which do seem to never truly understand our misery. Tired of the indifference we face and half-hearted remedies we get, we wonder if there is anyone out there who can help us. But the wonderful truth is that there is! God knows our suffering and He knows the struggles and hardships we endure. It grieves Him to see us be slaves to such conditions. That is why He sent His Son, Jesus Christ. He came to restore humanity and free us from our afflictions. When we have allowed Christ's Spirit to dwell within us, He will bring life and healing to our souls. Through Him we will be able to partake in the hope of knowing that in Christ we have victory for He is faithful and greater than our circumstances. Nothing will be able to stop His perfect will for our lives and in His promises we will be able to find a lasting joy and peace that will sustain us despite all that we may undergo.

April 7

AN IMPORTANT RESPONSIBILITY

"The earth is the Lord's, and everything in it, the world, and all who live in it;" -Psalm 24:1 (NIV)

When we are entrusted with something delicate and precious, what do we do? Sensing the privileged responsibility that has been bestowed upon us, we ensure that the object in our keeping is well taken care of and preserved from damage or harm. We would certainly not treat it in a careless manner; tossing it here and there with reckless abandon. Doing so would greatly displease the one who has entrusted us with his treasured possessions. That is why we are taught to treat each other's things with respect, knowing that they do not belong to us and that we are to be good stewards of that which has been given to us. Our failure to do so requires that we explain ourselves to the one who has given us his trust.

Yet while we are so careful to take care of the possessions of others, how negligent are we in caring for that which belongs to God! As the Creator of the Universe, everything that His hands have formed are His precious treasures. This not only includes the Earth itself, but each and every one of us as human beings created in His image. Despite this however, we can often be cold and harsh in our treatment of others. But why? It is because of our sinful nature that our relationships with others have been tainted. When we have failed to place God at the center of our lives, sin will grab hold of us. By allowing sin to establish a foothold in our lives, it will not hesitate to trample over others to have its way. But this not only degrades the other person, it harms us and our relationship with God. When we have allowed Christ's Spirit to enter our hearts and perfect His righteousness in us, He will give us the wisdom to know that we have no right to treat others with contempt and cruelty for they bear His image. We will know that He has given us the relationships we have with others as opportunities to show His love as it overflows from within us.

April 8

THE RIGHT FOUNDATION

"Woe to him who builds a city with bloodshed and establishes a town by crime!" -Habakkuk 2:12 (NIV)

When an empire or state resorts to violence and corruption to maintain its hold on power, it will not last. Though the swift power of their repression may seem intimidating, there will come a day when their perceived invincibility will be exposed for the myth that it is. Not only will the victims of its oppression grow weary and fight for their liberty, but also those who are brave enough to support them and take up their cause. If the foundation of a regime is based upon bloodshed and tyranny, it will be swept away by those willing to stand for justice and truth at all costs. It serves as an assurance of hope to those who must bear with injustice, as well as a warning to those who perpetrate it.

In our lives as well this same principle applies. Each of our actions has consequences either for better or for worse. If we have allowed sin to form the basis of our lifestyles, our relationships, or our careers, we have set ourselves on a path that will lead to our destruction. We will feel the sting of regret when we realize our folly and we wish that we could go back in time and correct our mistakes. However, while we cannot change our past, there is hope for the future through

Christ. When we allow His Spirit to cleanse us of our sinful nature and permit Him to carry out His redemptive work in our lives, He will give us the wisdom to know that what we sow now we will reap in the future. By choosing to walk in His ways through His enabling, we will be able to rest in the assurance that as long as we keep in step with Him we will be laying a foundation that God will honor; bringing life and hope to ourselves as well as others.

April 9

NO DOUBLE STANDARDS

"...not domineering over those in your charge, but being examples to the flock." -1 Peter 5:3 (ESV)

It is interesting to see what power can do to a person. When a dictator assumes control over a nation, he makes certain demands upon his people. These demands usually involve the masses under his authority to conform to a certain ideal. Yet what often seems to be the case is that while the people are forced to realize this ideal, the man in charge either fails to live up to the ideal he has purported himself, or disregards it entirely. Somehow, the standard that he has laid out does not apply to the one making the rules. Thus, the people live under his tyranny and resentment sets in while the dictator enjoys the unscrupulous benefits of having absolute power.

Leadership is not supposed to be a tool of oppression. Indeed this model of leadership stems from the sinful desires of man, not from Christ. When in our roles as leaders we condemn others and force people to obey what we preach when we do not obey what we say ourselves, then we lead by the wisdom of man and not the wisdom of Christ. To lead as Jesus led is to do so by example, living blamelessly before God and others in love and humility. But to do this by our own strength is an impossible task. Human pride and sinfulness prevents us from practicing leadership the right way. That is why we need Christ. When we have allowed His Spirit to enter our hearts and seek to conform ourselves to the redemptive work He is doing in us, He will enable us to have the right attitude towards leadership. He will help us lead by example as we model His love and righteousness through His enabling. Does this mean that we will always get it right? On the contrary there will be times when we will stumble and fall. But when we are quick to humbly acknowledge our wrongs, God will honor that and He will be able to use our failings for His glory as He calls us to be lights to the world.

April 10

DON'T RUN AWAY!

"Let us not give up meeting together, as some are in the habit of doing, but let us encourage one another—and all the more as you see the Day approaching." -Hebrews 10:24-25 (NIV)

A lack of unity at a critical point has often decided the outcome of battles. The victorious army is the one which, despite the situation, maintains itself as a dedicated and cohesive fighting force. Its members do not simply run away or defect to the other side when confronted with danger or when it all seems like an uphill struggle. A loyal solider serves both the commanding officer placed over him, and his fellow comrades. He puts aside his personal conflicts with others so that they may fight together as one. The army which will lose however is the one where soldiers desert and fail to lend their aid when it is needed most. Such an army will never win if its members fail to rally together and fight so that they may carry out their mission.

Sometimes we may become discouraged when we see people around us who profess Christ with their mouths but not with their hearts. We wonder why they do not seem to get it, and the temptation is to wish that we would withdraw away from their hypocrisy and ignorance. But it is in these moments when Christ calls us to allow His truth to shine all the more. Being reclusive will not help anyone. Instead it deprives both ourselves and others of the opportunity to be blessed by the work of Christ. As His children, we are called to stand together in one spirit, serving each other just as how Christ serves us. When we allow His Spirit to enter our lives and seek to abide in Him, He will direct our steps and attitudes. Guided by His Spirit we will know that the days are short and that we cannot waste time arguing and drawing ourselves away from each other. Rather when His love is being made manifest in us, we will be able to love and help build up those around us so that we may be the people of hope and righteousness Christ has called us to be.

April 11

HE IS ALWAYS THERE!

"I call to God, and the Lord saves me. Evening, morning and noon I cry out in distress, and he hears my voice." -Psalm 55:16-17 (NIV)

Human beings cannot be in two places at once. This fact is exacerbated even more in the fast-paced culture we currently live in. As much as we would like others to be where we want them to be, this does not always happen. I remember moments when I travelled wanting to meet someone, hoping to catch them in their office, only to find that they were not there. I have also had times when I urgently needed to get something from the local convenience store only to find out that they had just closed. Of course this is all understandable. Whether it is because of unexpected events or simply a matter of needing rest, we cannot guarantee that the people we wish to see will always be there when we call, despite our wishes that it be otherwise.

But the wonderful truth about God is that He is there for us! No matter when we call upon Him or for whatever purpose, He promises in His Word that He listens to and answers those who come to Him. We are His precious children and He wants to hear from us and be a part of our lives. Just as how a loving and caring parent would rush to their children when they are in need, God does the same for us. What is more is that when we call upon God, we have the Lord of the Universe as our rock and fortress, against which no obstacles will be able to stand! When we have allowed Christ to enter our hearts so that by His blood He may cleanse us of our sin, we have entered through Him into a restored relationship with God. We become adopted into His family and are able to dwell in the faithful love and providence He will show to those who have chosen to abide in Him so that He may work out His perfect plan for us.

April 12

WE ARE HIS INVENTIONS

"Before I formed you in the womb I knew you, before you were born I set you apart; I appointed you as a prophet to the nations" -Jeremiah 1:5 (NIV)

I have always been fascinated by inventors and their inventions. Whether they are in the past, or even in the present day, inventors always have an idea of what he wants to make before he sits down to put it all together. His blueprints and notes reveal that his invention will be tailored for a specific purpose and work in a particular manner. What joy the inventor has when his creation, with all its gears and many components, works in the manner he intended and flawlessly executes its purpose. But should his invention encounter a glitch and does not function as he intended, he does not give up on it and throw it away. Rather he continues to perfect and refine it until it does what he wants it to do.

In the same manner, each one of us born into this world have been lovingly created and designed by God. All of us bear His image and He has made us with a specific plan in mind. The purposes He has for us are always to give us hope, never to harm us. Indeed He is love and He is just. Therefore, because of these truths about His character, He cannot and does not create people only to condemn them and watch them fall. However, it is in our own stubborn disobedience that we deprive ourselves of the perfect plan He has in store from us. Choosing to follow our own wisdom and understanding, we in our arrogance think that we know what is best for ourselves; only to painfully realize that we do not. But God does not give up on us. His love for us is so great that He wants to draw us to Himself so that we may have life through Him and live according to the wonderful plan He has for us. When we have allowed Christ to enter our hearts, cleansing us of our sin so that we may be reconciled to God, He will lead us in the path He has called us to follow. By humbly submitting ourselves to Him, we will be able to see the goodness and faithfulness of God as He works to fulfill our glorious destiny.

April 13

HIS UNSTOPPABLE PLAN

"I know that you can do all things; no plan of yours can be thwarted" -Job 42:2 (NIV)

One of my favorite cartoons growing up was "The Roadrunner Show". Each episode focused on a coyote named Wild E. Coyote, and his efforts to capture a fast and agile roadrunner. Some of the plans the determined coyote would come up with were quite elaborate and sometimes involved the most outlandish of inventions. Yet no matter how hard he tried and how careful he planned, something would always backfire on him with humorous results. So often has the hapless coyote failed in his quest that it is assumed that he will never be able to catch the roadrunner. Thus the viewer never has faith in the coyote that he will someday be able to claim his prize, and laughs at his attempts to do so.

In our lives we may often adopt a similar attitude. When we have faced discouragement and setbacks in our past, we wonder if God can truly fulfill His perfect plan for us. This is why it is so hard for us in our human understating to trust Him and surrender our ambitions and hopes into His hands.

But the wonderful truth is that God knows exactly what He is doing. Though we may not see the entire picture, God assures us through His Word that His plans for us are to give us hope and a future. Nothing will be able to stop Him from carrying out His desires for us because He is omnipotent and can never be overcome. When we choose to allow Christ to enter our hearts, surrendering every area of our lives to His redeeming work, we will know of the joys which come by knowing Him. As we allow Him to guide our steps and entrust our futures to Him, we will stand amazed as He proves to us His goodness and faithfulness in our lives; saying with confidence that He can do all things and nothing will be able to thwart His purposes for us.

April 14

THE DIVINE ARTIST

"Lift your eyes and look to the heavens: Who created all these? He who brings out the starry host one by one, and calls them each by name. Because of his great power and mighty strength, not one of them is missing." -Isaiah 40:26 (NIV)

While I was doing research for a term paper, I came across an interesting story. During the closing decade of the 18th century, when the French Revolution was in full swing in France, there was a concentrated effort to destroy religion and Christianity in particular. Entering a village in the countryside, a group of revolutionaries proclaimed to the people assembled that they would tear down everything that reminded them of God. To this one of the peasants spoke up and said, "Well then, tear down the stars!" For all their boasts of power, the revolutionaries could never eradicate Christianity and further attempts to stamp it out have proven to be futile. In the absence of Bibles and missionaries, God continues to make His presence known through His created order.

When we take a good look at creation and contemplate on its complexities, there is something so alluring and marvelous about it that to suggest it all somehow came about by chance is ludicrous. Do we say that a beautifully painted portrait was the result of accidental spills of color? Of course not, for we know that its strokes were drawn on the canvas by the careful hands of a painter. Likewise, the work of art that is His creation, bears testimony to God its artist, and this knowledge has been placed within us by Him. The question is what do we do with this knowledge? Do we use it to allow God to draw us closer to Him and His truth? Or do we reject this knowledge and live as we see fit. If we chose the latter, we will find ourselves feeling incomplete and lacking fulfillment while being slaves to our sinful nature. But when we choose the former and allow Him to lead us to Christ, we will find lasting joy and contentment as He, by His Spirit, frees us from our sin so that we may have life through Him and live victoriously in Him.

April 15

WE HAVE A SOUL!

"The Lord God formed the man from the dust of the ground and breathed into his nostrils the breath of life, and the man became a living being."-Genesis 2:7 (NIV)

There is something intimately beautiful in the way God created Adam. Taking the dust of the Earth He carefully molded and shaped the form Adam would take according to

His perfect wisdom; all in its harmonious perfection. He created our legs to walk, our hands to grasp, and our minds to think and reason. But the defining moment of this process would soon come. One could have all the physical qualities of existence, but still the most critical component as missing- life! As the crowning glory of His creation of man, God reached down and breathed life into his nostrils. The result was Adam, a body now with a vibrant soul lovingly given to Him by God and able to experience all that He has created.

Sometimes we ask the question whether our lives have meaning. Everyday seems to be just another day of existence, going through the motions of our lives but never truly living. This can frustrate us greatly and we wonder if there is something more to our existence; that we are not simply nameless bodies, or cogs in an enormous machine. But the wonderful truth is that each and every one of us is lovingly created by God and in Him destined for something great. When we have allowed Christ to enter our hearts He will breathe new life into us. No longer will we feel as bodies drifting through a dreary existence, but souls being led by God towards His glorious purpose for our lives. Entrusting ourselves to Him we will know what it means to live. Serving Him and allowing Him to guide our steps and see the world through His eyes, we will be filled with joyous awe and wonder as His love and righteousness is made manifest through us; bearing witness to the hope and life that is available to all who trust in Him.

April 16

LISTEN TO HIS CALL

"When the Lord saw that he had gone over to look, God called to him from within the bush, 'Moses! Moses!' And Moses said, 'Here I am.'" -Exodus 3:4 (NIV)

As Moses was out tending to the sheep and going about his daily routine, he noticed an unusual sight. In fact a burning bush in which the flames did not consume the plant would definitely be worth an investigation for anyone with a basic knowledge of the laws of nature. But as Moses drew closer, he realized that he was about to enter the presence of God. Calling out Moses' name, God was about to reveal His plan for the redemption of His people out of Egypt's tyranny and tell Moses of his role in that plan. At this point Moses did not know this. But regardless he approached God with humility and waiting to hear what God had to say to Him. Though Moses was first apprehensive when God told him the plans He had in store for him, Moses ultimately obeyed knowing that God would be with him each step of the way.

God is always calling out to us. Through situation and circumstances He seeks to bring our attention to Him so that He may reveal to us the perfect plans He has in store for us. Yet how often do we fail to listen? Content with our own little lives we do not want to acknowledge His call and in our human arrogance we think that we know better than Him; believing that only we know the best way to live our lives. However, when we adopt such an attitude, we deprive ourselves of the blessings of walking within the will of God. Forever we will live in our small little worlds and there will come a point when the feelings of living an unfulfilled existence will consume us. But it is never too late to claim the promises of God. What He requires is only a heart that is willing to be guided by Him. When we allow Christ to enter our lives and carry out His redemptive work, He will break us of our sinful pride so that He may give us life. In Him we have the assurance that as long as we keep in step with Him, He will fulfill a plan that accomplishes His fullest for our lives; giving us hope and confidence in His faithfulness and love for us.

April 17

WHY WE MUST LOVE

"From one man he made every nation of men, that they should inhabit the whole earth; and he determined the times set for them and the exact places where they should live." -Acts 17:26 (NIV)

Ethnic violence is still an ever present reality for many in the world. Even after the Holocaust, the civil rights movement in America, and the collapse of apartheid in South Africa, racial hatred continues to persist. The programs of one ethnic group to eliminate another, the bloody reprisals of the oppressed, together they form a cycle of bloodshed and injustice that is both tragic and horrifying. Faced with these issues, where do we begin to respond? We are all taught that racism in all its forms is wrong. But why is it wrong? Is it merely because it is a nasty and ignorant attitude to adopt, or is there a much deeper reason? To answer this question, one needs to look at humanity through the eyes of God.

Each and every one of us born into this world is created in the image of God. As an expression of His creativity, He has made us all unique; having varied physical characteristics and speaking different tongues. But these differences do not nullify the fact that before God we are all equal, both as cherished bearers of His image and as fallen creatures in need of His redemptive power. Like our forefather Adam, we have all chosen to rebel against Him and indulge in our sinful desires. This even includes turning against one another either in thought, word, or action, and in effect spitting upon those whom God has lovingly created. But God does not want us to be bound to our sin. He knows the destruction that it will cause both to ourselves and to the people around us. That is why He sent His Son, Jesus Christ so that all, regardless of who they are, may come to Him and be saved from their sin. If Christ has shown such impartial love, what right do we have to withhold it from others? When we have allowed Christ to enter our lives and seek to conform ourselves to Him, we will see with new eyes. Through Him we will understand that all men are precious in His sight, each of whom God has a specific plan for, and in need of His grace.

April 18

THE HEALING HEART

"A cheerful heart is good medicine, but a crushed spirit dries up the bones." -Proverbs 17:22 (NIV)

Joy is truly contagious. To see someone in cheerful spirits can often do wonders to dispel clouds of despair. I know of many times where God has used the exuberance of others to boost my spirits. Whether it has been through a friendly smile, a hearty laugh, or a pleasant conversation, God has been able to use these to lift me out of a crippling state of woe and bring life back into my soul. Through them He has taught me the value of having a heart of gladness so that it will infiltrate those around me and bring hope into the lives of those who need it. Like wildfire the joy in our hearts spreads to others and uplifts them in the process

But if our joy is dependent on our circumstances, then our joy is but a mere fleeting sentiment that comes and goes as it wishes. If the joy we spread from ourselves is temporary, then that which is spread to others is also short-lived. Human happiness quickly gives way to sorrow when situations turn grim and oscillating between delight and grief will soon leave us feeling unfulfilled. Where then can we find lasting joy? It is only when we have allowed Christ to dwell within us. By permitting Him to carry out His redemptive work in our lives, we will find lasting joy knowing that through Him our salvation is assured and nothing will be able to prevent Him from fulfilling His perfect plan for our lives. In this we will find a happiness that will never be taken away from us, for despite the situations we face, we have peace in the fact that God is bigger than our circumstances and that in Him we will emerge victorious. Celebrating His goodness and faithfulness we will be able to be bearers of His light to others; bringing healing and restoration to those in despair.

April 19

ADMITTING THE TRUTH

"Christ Jesus came into the world to save sinners-of whom I am the worst." -1 Timothy 1:15 (NIV)

In the days of the Ottoman Empire, when the Turks ruled over most of the Mediterranean and the Arab World, one of the sultans decided to invade the island of Malta. Over such a small island, the sultan was confident that he and his armies would emerge victorious. But Malta would prove to be a humiliating defeat for the sultan as the island's defenders put up an admirable resistance. Embarrassed by his defeat, the sultan attempted to eliminate any reminder of the campaign by having the official records state that "Malta does not exist". This very action however, instead of erasing the memory of the Malta debacle, shows the length to which the sultan was willing to go to in order to save his pride.

As humans our lack of humility seems to be innate. We do not like it when we are wrong and it causes us great discomfort to be honest with ourselves when we know that we have erred. Our pride tells us that we must always be seen in a light that glorifies ourselves and thus we make excuses for our behavior in an attempt to justify our attitudes and actions. However, we live hypocritical lives if we think that nothing is wrong with us when we know that we are sinful. Such a contradiction will soon destroy us and we will sink further into our depravity. How then can we be saved from such a fate? Half of the answer is to come to that point where we can be honest about ourselves and with humility admit that we are sinful creatures. The other half is to acknowledge that the love of Christ is greater than our sin. He came so that by His death and resurrection we are cleansed of our sin by His blood and lifted into newness of life with Him. When we allow Christ to enter our hearts and carry out His redemptive work in our lives, we will know that though we are amongst the worst of sinners, by the grace of Christ we are forgiven once and for all. Through His enabling we will be able to walk in His righteousness; finding true freedom in Him and bringing hope to others.

April 20

WHERE ARE OUR ROOTS?

"So then, just as you received Christ Jesus as Lord, continue to live in him, rooted and built up in him, strengthened in the faith as you were taught, and overflowing with thankfulness." -Colossians 2:6 (NIV)

We can draw several conclusions from seeing a beautiful tree. If it stands tall and firm, with lush green leaves and resplendent flowers, we can tell that not only does it get ample rain and sunlight, but its roots run deep into the ground. It will not be uprooted easily and it draws upon the abundance of groundwater to sustain itself. Compare this with a tree which is dead. There are no signs of life on its boughs and neither fruit nor leaves grow. Such a tree is barren and is easily uprooted when storms come its way for its roots are not anchored deeply to give it support against the winds. By its fruit and strength we can tell if a tree is either dead or alive.

In the same manner the way we live our lives is often an indicator of how deeply we have rooted ourselves in Christ. If the Christian faith is to us just a philosophy or a part of our culture, then we have not anchored our roots into Christ Himself. We will not find life through Him because we have chosen not to abide in Him. Thus, we will become like trees that are dead because we have not allowed Him to sustain us, and we will be easily pulled away from Him when trials come. But when we have allowed ourselves to be rooted firmly in Christ by permitting Him to reside in our hearts, He will bring about a transformative restoration in our lives so that we will reflect His righteousness and love. When we choose to remain in Him, rooting ourselves in His Word and allowing Him to apply His truths to our lives, the beauty of who He is will be revealed through our obedience to Him. In Him we will find life and hope, able to stand strong during times of distress and be bearers of His light to all around us.

April 21

FOLLOWING THE TRUTH

"And he continued, 'You have a fine way of setting aside the commands of God in order to observe your own traditions!'" -Mark 7:9 (NIV)

What is so appealing about tradition? It is surprising that even in a world of rapid technological advancement where what is new is advertised as being better, the idea of having traditions to hold onto remains strong. Traditions often have sentiments behind them. To go through the motions and rites of traditions preserved for countless years certainly has a sense of grandeur to it, and they come to form a part of our identity. But the problem with tradition is that it is often blindly followed. Soon what becomes the case is that people follow tradition not so much as a matter of it being right or wrong, but for the sole sake of clinging onto them regardless. Indeed history has shown that unimaginable atrocities have been committed in the name of upholding traditions that were never questioned even though they were clearly wrong.

Tradition, if it is not rooted in truth, can turn into a deceptive and destructive idol. Instead of being in obedience to Christ, we worship our traditions and allow them to turn us away from Him. Though we might mistake our upholding of tradition as religious zeal and piety, it in fact turns us into oppressors who have strayed far away from what Christ requires of His children. How then can we obey God? It is only when we have allowed Christ to dwell within us. By acknowledging Him as Lord and allowing Him to enter our hearts, He will refine us and open our eyes to see His truth. As long as we seek to keep in step with Him we will understand how we must walk as His children; training us in His righteousness and love. In this we will find that the only traditions worth clinging onto are not those rooted in human sentiment or wisdom, but those which have their roots in Christ alone and what He has revealed to us in His Word.

April 22

BETTER IN HIS PRESENCE

"Better is one day in your courts than a thousand elsewhere; I would rather be a doorkeeper in the house of my God than dwell in the tents of the wicked." -Psalm 84:10 (NIV)

What do we think of when we think of splendor? Perhaps our minds may conjure up images of opulent palaces and mansions with beautiful furniture and treasures inside. Maybe we might think of the celebrations and parties thrown by the rich and famous; full of guests dressed worthy of their affluence and banquet halls filled with the finest of foods. Yet none of these things can compare with being in the glorious presence of God. He is the King of Kings and the Lord of Lords. Whenever in Scripture God gives mortal men the privilege of seeing Heaven, they cannot describe its indescribable beauty. All the things of the Earth pale in comparison to God for while they are fleeting, He is eternal.

Yet how often do we desire the things of this Earth. In our blindness we elevate the material things of this world to the status of god. Though we may not admit it we may worship our wealth, our careers, or our relationships and place them on a platform that should only be reserved for God alone. We foolishly think that nothing can compare with being in the presence of these things and we think that we can find our security in them. However, we will become sorely disappointed when our treasures soon begin to wither and fade away. Where then can we find our confidence and hope? When we have allowed Christ to enter our lives and seek to abide in Him, we will find that being in His presence far outweighs anything the world can offer. Though the world may crumble around us, we can rest in the eternity of God, praising His faithfulness knowing that ultimate victory lies with Him.

April 23

TRUSTING HIS WISDOM

"If any of you lacks wisdom, you should ask God, who gives generously to all without finding fault, and it will be given to you." - James 1:5 (NIV)

Imagine yourself in a thick and foreboding forest with nothing but the clothes on your back. It would definitely be a frightening experience! Perhaps one of the greatest fears we have is the fear of the unknown. Without something to guide us and provide us with that sense of direction and security, we would walk aimlessly into unfamiliar territory. Lost and confused we become paralyzed by fear, constantly dreading where each step of ours will take us. Now compare this to if we were placed in the same forest but with a map, a compass, and even a GPS system. What a difference this would make! We would be able to walk confidently through that forest knowing that we are going in the right direction.

Sometimes life can feel like as if we are walking through a vast forest with nothing to aid us. In the face of uncertainty we become fearful of the future and wonder if we are going in the right direction or stepping into disaster. Nothing seems to make sense and in our frustration we cry out for help and guidance. But the wonderful truth is that our cries do not fall on deaf ears. God hears us when we call out to Him in our despair and He wants to help us. For each and every person on this Earth He has a perfect plan that He wants to have fulfilled in our lives; plans to give us hope and a future. When we have allowed Christ to reside within us and continue to submit ourselves to Him, He will give us wisdom and guide our steps towards the fulfillment of the great purposes He has for us. We will not fear uncertainty for when we are guided by God's flawless wisdom we can rest knowing that He is taking us along the path He wants us to go so that we may praise His faithfulness and love.

April 24

LET IT OVERFLOW!

"But let justice roll on like a river, righteousness like a never-failing stream!" -Amos 5:24 (NIV)

Water takes on the form of whatever contains it. If we were to pour water into a bottle, it will take the shape of the bottle. If we were to pour it into a bowl, it will take the shape of the bowl. This makes water, or any other liquid for that matter, a very malleable substance. Through technological innovation we have the power to divert rivers for irrigation and reap the agricultural benefits this would bring for us. We also have the ability to build dams which partially block the natural flow of water so that we may harness it to produce energy for ourselves. Such architectural feats are fascinating to learn about and it shows how through technology we can use the natural force of water to our advantage.

But how often do we attempt to pervert the course of justice and righteousness for our own benefit! How often is it that instead of justice rolling on like a river, it is diverted here and there so that the selfish interests of the unscrupulous may be persevered? How often is it that we have prevented ourselves from standing up for righteousness out of fear that we will be ridiculed or silenced? In a world where sin is promoted and a blind eye is turned to corruption, it can be hard to be the voice calling for integrity and purity. However, as children of Christ we are called to be bearers of His light wherever we go. When we have allowed Christ to enter our hearts and carry out His redemptive work in our lives, His righteousness and love will overflow from within us. He will give us the boldness and confidence to stand up for what is right and true so that others will see that we serve a God who is holy and just. What is stopping the flow of righteousness and justice in our lives? Only by surrendering these areas to Christ can we shine for Him in a world overtaken by darkness.

April 25

PROOF OF HIS LOVE

"No one has ever seen God; but if we love one another, God lives in us and his love is made complete in us." -1 John 4:12 (NIV)

How many of us have seen the wind? Try as I might I can never get a visible image of its form or grasp it in my hand. Yet I know that it exists because I can feel it and I can see what it does. I can see it as it gently carries autumn leaves into the sky. I can feel as it wraps me in its cooling touch on a hot summer day. I may not be able to physically see the wind, but I am confirmed of its existence because I see evidence of it at work. No one can logically say that the wind does not exist on the basis that we cannot tangibly see it because it is clear that its action bear testimony to its existence.

In the same manner no one can physically see God. If we were to stand before God, we would be blinded by His holiness. Our eyes, tainted by our sinful nature, cannot behold God in all His glory. But this does not mean He wants to remain aloof from humanity. Though each one of us has sinned against Him and as a result has severed our relationship with Him, He wants to restore us back into relationship with Him so that we may have life. When we have allowed Christ to enter our hearts and carry out His redemptive work in our lives, He will break the chains that bind us to our sin if we submit every area of our lives to Him. He will then fill us with His love and righteousness so that we may bear witness to the loving and holy God we serve. If we rely on human love in an attempt to show the love of Christ we will ultimately fail for human love is easily tainted by our sinful nature. It is only when we have made His love to be made manifest in us will we be able to be witnesses for Christ, allowing Him to reveal Himself to others through His love and draw them into the hope of having a restored relationship with God.

April 26

PERSISTENT IN PRAYER

"For this reason, since the day we heard about you, we have not stopped praying for you..." -Colossians 1:9 (NIV)

Have you ever left something unfinished? Perhaps it was a model kit or home project that seemed too difficult to complete. Maybe it was a hobby which we had an initial passion for, but soon grew wearisome as it became harder to do. Often times when we do not see immediate results, we become frustrated and give up on what we have invested our energies and resources towards. Yet how often do we turn around and complain why we are not good at this or that. Why can't we excel at that hobby or interest, or why can't we complete that project we had set our minds to. The answer is simple actually. We did not persevere. If we see our tasks through to the end, we will be able to complete what we started and would have gained valuable experience to help us become better at what we do.

In prayer as well we are often tempted to give up. Despite our most earnest and faithful prayers, we do not see the results we hope for. We question whether God is really there listening to our prayers, or if He is even there at all. Thus in our despair we give up and stop praying thinking it is all hopeless. But in our frustration we tend to overlook an important truth. No prayer directed to God falls on deaf ears. He is always listening and working out His perfect plan for our lives. Though we cannot see Him at work, He is there behind the scenes bringing together events in such a way as to fulfill His great purposes for us. But do we trust Him and His ability to lead us? Or is our unwillingness to continue our prayers a subtle declaration that we do not trust the Lord of the Universe to do what He has promised to do. When we have allowed Christ to enter our heart and carry out His work in our lives, we can rest in the assurance that He always answers prayer according to His flawless timing and will in order to fulfill His plan for us. All He requires is that we trust Him, being persistent in our prayers that we can see for ourselves His faithful providence and thereby strengthening our faith in Him.

April 27

LET HIM LIFT YOU

"He raises up the poor from the dust; he lifts the needy from the ash heap to make them sit with princes and inherit a seat of honor." -1 Samuel 2:8 (ESV)

I love a good "rags to riches" story. So many such tales abound not only in literature and movies, but continue to be made even now. I have read many stories of refugees, sometimes even being young orphaned children, leaving their devastated war-torn countries seeking a better life elsewhere. Making harrowing journeys across strange and unfamiliar lands they finally find sanctuary. But even here there are battles of different kinds. Overcoming language barriers and financial difficulties they work hard starting from nothing and eventually going on to lead successful lives doing what they are passionate about. To hear and read about their stories is truly inspiring and reminds me of how God uses all things for His good.

Sometimes we look at our circumstances and we wonder why we must endure them. Perhaps we are encountering struggles that seem insurmountable, or situations that seem unbearable. In our misery and frustration we cry out to God asking for what purpose has He brought us to this place in our lives. Indeed God understands these cries. He knows what it is like to suffer and He intimately knows our grief. However, He has also come to give us hope. His plans for us are never to harm us, but to give us life and hope for the future. In His love and power He is able to use our circumstances to fulfill His glorious purposes for our lives. But will we take hold of this truth for ourselves? Will we choose to trust in Him to lead us towards life? When we allow Christ to enter our hearts and allow Him to work in our lives, He assures us that He will guide us according to His perfect will as long as we keep in step with Him. With humility submitting ourselves to His wisdom and walking in obedience to Him in the situations He has placed us, we will be amazed as He proves His love and faithfulness to us.

April 28

IT HAD TO BE THIS WAY

"Father, if you are willing, take this cup from me; yet not my will, but yours be done." -Luke 22:42 (NIV)

Why did Jesus have to die? As we reflect on Good Friday and its meaning, our minds immediately turn to Him. We see images of Him being rejected, scorned, flogged, and finally executed by crucifixion, the most humiliating and excruciating of deaths. But why? Was there not another way to bring about the salvation of mankind? He was God so He could have certainly done so in a less painful and tragic manner. However, to understand why He endured the anguish of the Cross for us we must first understand man's relationship with God. It is only when we have grasped this fact that we are able to understand the significance of Christ's sacrifice for humanity and why it shows how much He loves us.

From the time Adam and Eve disobeyed God, man has been corrupted by sin. Even today we see evidence of the fallen nature of man all around us. Since God is holy He cannot tolerate sin. Thus the once intimate and close relationship we had with Him has been severed because of our deliberate choice to indulge in what is depraved. The penalty for sin is death according to the holy standards of God and when measured against His standards not one of us can honestly say that we are not guilty before Him. Yet God knows this full well and in His love He sent His Son, Jesus Christ, to die on our behalf. Christ voluntarily chose death to give us life. Through His blood shed for us on the cross, the penalty of our sin has been paid in full and we have the hope of living in a restored relationship with God. But will we take hold of Christ's sacrifice for us? Will we allow Him to carry out His redemptive work in our lives? When we have allowed Him to enter our hearts, His blood will cleanse us of all our sin. But this is only half the story and in the coming days there is much to follow.

April 29

BURIED WITH HIM

"We were therefore buried with him through baptism into death in order that, just as Christ was raised from the dead through the glory of the Father, we too may live a new life." -Romans 6:4 (NIV)

Rarely do we give a second thought to the burial of Jesus. In the wider Easter story the two main events are His death and resurrection. Yet when we come to the burial of Christ, how often do we treat it as a mundane detail of the story? On the surface there does not seem to be anything extraordinary about Jesus' burial and we think nothing of it; anticipating the glorious resurrection soon after. But nothing that God does is devoid of meaning. To understand the significance of Christ's burial is of prime importance in understanding the meaning behind His death and His resurrection. The burial is a key part of God's plan of redemption and how we are to view our personal salvation.

When we accept Christ as our Savior, we become like Him in His death, burial and resurrection. The sins of humanity were laid upon Him so that through His death the penalty for each and every one of our violations of God's holy standards is paid in full. By His blood we are forgiven and stand cleansed before God. However, Christ was buried to show that through Him our old nature of sin has passed away to make room for the new nature of righteousness that is bestowed upon us from God in Heaven. Have we truly become like Christ in His burial? Have we left behind our sinful nature, or do we continue to return to it? When something is dead and buried, it is dead and buried for good. True repentance in Christ is only when we have asked for the forgiveness of our sins and, by identifying with His burial, not returning to them again. Doing this we will find real freedom from our slavery to sin; living instead in the joys and blessings which come from having our new nature through Christ.

April 30

FREEDOM IN HIM

"...but the men said to them, 'Why do you look for the living among the dead? He is not here; he has risen!'" -Luke 24:5-6 (NIV)

At the centre of humanity is the resurrection. It is what believers in Christ on Easter have celebrated throughout the ages, and it is what continues to be celebrated around the world by those who proclaim Christ to be Lord. Without the resurrection, the redemptive mission of Christ loses its power and His sacrifice becomes irrelevant; bearing no transformative implications for our lives. While Christ died for our sins and we are forgiven and made right with God through His death, His sacrifice becomes a convenient excuse to continue living in sin if the story was just left at His crucifixion and burial. The purpose of Christ's coming was not simply to cleanse us of sin, but to give us life and freedom from it.

When Christ arose from the tomb, there was something markedly different about Him. His resurrection resulted in Him gaining two things; a new body and a new nature. This nature was characterized by the righteousness which comes from God and it shone forth for all to see. The old sinful nature was dead and buried, and God raised Jesus up to bring Him into newness of life and clothed with His holiness. But how does this relate to us? When we accept Christ and allow Him to come into our hearts, we become like Him in His resurrection. Through Him our old sinful nature has died and we are clothed by the righteousness which comes from God. Though we were once slaves to sin, we are now freed by becoming slaves of righteousness as we allow His Spirit to help us live according to the new nature He has given us.

Have we become dead to our sin and entered into new life with Christ? In doing this we will find freedom from the destructive consequences of sin and allow Christ to raise us up; unshackling us from our depravity so that we will find liberty, hope, and life eternal in Him.

May 1

AGAINST TYRANNY

"For freedom Christ has set us free; stand firm therefore, and do not submit again to a yoke of slavery." -Galatians 5:1 (ESV)

Why do humans return to their vomit? If there is one quality which proves the stupidity of humanity it is the fact that humans often regress into old and detrimental habits even if they know full well that there is a far better way to live life. When humans are faced with struggle when they want to pursue a lifestyle radically different from their previous one, suddenly their old way of life becomes more attractive; to the point where they forget the reason why they abandoned their previous lifestyle in the first place. This is seen especially with the case of the Israelites after they were delivered from Egypt by God's hand. Once the Israelites began to feel that their journey to the Promised Land was too hard, they began to dream of all the food and pleasures available in Egypt, even though they were under the whip of their Egyptian overlords! Ironically, the chains of slavery seemed to be more comfortable to them than the wings of freedom.

No one ever said that the Christian life would be easy. Neither did anyone say that it would be a free ride. Yet, many seem to think like this. Whenever the going gets tough, or a hard teaching comes across their path, they feel as though they can ignore it and continue to live in their old habits. After all, they are covered by their "heavenly insurance". However, whenever the Christian chooses sin, he chooses to voluntarily submit to slavery. Before salvation, he had no choice but slavery to sin for he never knew of freedom from sin. But once Christ liberated him from the shackles of sin, why should the Christian turn back to bondage and oppression? Doing so not only makes light of Christ's sacrifice on the cross, but also makes a mockery out of humanity. Truly, the irrationality of man is proven when they are presented with the joys of freedom but choose the suffering of tyranny instead. Christians must make a conscious effort to avoid sin and, whenever they struggle, to fall back on Christ their Redeemer instead of regressing back into old patterns. Be freed people! It's about time that we start living as freed people!

May 2

ETERNAL TREASURES

"Better is a poor man who walks in his integrity than a rich man who is crooked in his ways." -Proverbs 28:6 (ESV)

When the wicked seem to prosper and have it all together, we often wonder why this is the case. Why do the unscrupulous, despite their decadent lifestyles and questionable ethics seem to get fame, fortune, and success beyond their heart's content, whereas the honest and diligent end up with nothing but misery? In light of this reality, it often leads people to question whether God is blind to this injustice. However, He is not. The very fact that God does not include wealth in His requirements into Heaven, rather faith and obedience to Him and His Son, is indicative of the fact that material prosperity is immaterial to Him. For all the wealth they may have gained in this present life through deceit, the wicked will not prosper. If they are not punished in this life, they will be in the life hereafter. Money cannot buy you into Heaven and thankfully so. Otherwise, it would make Heaven a very corrupt place.

However, this does not necessarily mean that living a moral life would get one into Heaven either. No one can truly claim to live a pure life because all have sinned against God in some manner, be it in word, deed, or thought. The strict standards of God on what constitutes as sin contain no loopholes. Only through a relationship with Christ could man hope of entering into Heaven. But it comes at a price. Once we enter into a relationship with Christ, we are obligated to serve Him and follow His ways and standards. Since it is hard to let go of our sinful nature, we constantly need Christ to help us in our decision to choose integrity over dishonesty. Thus, for the Christian, he should not be concerned over the material pursuits of this world. He should not use underhanded methods to gain profit. Rather, should he pursue integrity with Christ as his Guide, he will be blessed even in his poverty and these blessings will be far more satisfying than those of an ill-earned material lifestyle. The comfort of eternal rewards in Heaven for his obedience of Christ should be enough of an impetus for the believer to pursue integrity and righteousness.

May 3

AN EYE FOR AND EYE

"Do not say, "I will repay evil"; wait for the Lord, and he will deliver you." -Proverbs 20:22 (ESV)

Humans love to take revenge. Whenever we feel wronged by someone else, the desire for revenge becomes an unquenchable thirst. How many times have we caught ourselves plotting ways to make the person who has slighted us suffer? Such emotions arise out of our sense of justice. It is natural to feel indignant when we have been unfairly mistreated and it is natural to seek redress. Likewise, it is natural to feel enraged by the injustice that seems to plague our world. These things break the heart of God as much as it breaks us; perhaps even more so because He is a just God who cannot bear the presence of injustice in His creation.

However, because of our fallen nature, our pursuit of justice can easily turn into revenge. It is at this point where we forget the other attributes which God has given us such as love, mercy, and compassion. All we want to see is the accused party suffering and squirming under our retribution. Is this attitude right? Often, revenge has an ironic way of making people commit the same acts done against them with as much force and malice. In the manner, the wronged party is no better than the accused. Justice, instead of pursuing the cause of fairness and impartiality, becomes increasingly subjective and unnecessarily harsh. This is why justice should be left to God. He, being by His nature just, is bound to be impartial and He sees that every man has been sinful and deserves death. No one is holier than the other. But in His love, He sent Himself to pay the penalty for sin so that justice may be served and that those who believe in Him may be restored. It is not humanity's place to take revenge because no man can claim to be a perfect judge. Therefore it is best to wait upon God and He will deal with the offender. He will vindicate the oppressed; there is no question about that. But it is important to remember that even the oppressor needs to hear the message of God's love, and this should be enough to compel the believer to act with mercy towards those who have hurt them.

May 4

BEHIND THE MASK

"Confess your sins to each other and pray for each other so that you may be healed. The prayer of a righteous man is powerful and effective."
-James 5:16 (NIV)

Why do we like to keep our problems to ourselves? We do so for a number of reasons. Our fear that being candid about our problems would result in the loss of our respect and reputation in the eyes of those around us is a dominant one. Another reason is that we are too prideful to admit that there is something wrong with us and we soldier on, denying that there are issues in our lives which need to be dealt with. Yet another reason for Christians especially is the false assumption that followers of Christ need to have their lives in a constant state of perfection and it is unthinkable that a true Christian should have problems in their lives. Such an attitude in particular is soundly debunked considering the fact that there is not a sinless person in the Bible save for Christ Himself. All of the characters in God's Word who are labeled "Heroes of the Faith" were broken and sinful people. Yet thankfully it was not their own efforts or deeds that made them righteous, but it was God's work through them which sanctified them and made them obedient to His purposes.

No one is perfect in this world. The sinful nature of mankind is its equalizer and thus no one can truly be justified in adopting a "holier-than-thou" attitude because in all likelihood, they have many issues in their lives which need to be dealt with. This should serve as a strong reminder for Christians to discard any inhibitions they may have about sharing their problems with each other and seeking guidance from those who are also on a journey with Christ. Since God, Jesus, and the Holy Spirit commune together as one, we as believers should adopt the same attitude if we want to follow Christ's example. We are one body, a community where if one person hurts, the rest of the body feels it as well. We should never feel that being open with our problems will make us weak or vulnerable. More often than not, when a believer shares his problems with another, he will find that the person he is sharing his problems with is also dealing with same issue. Thus they may counsel, strengthen, and pray for each other, contributing to the unity of the brotherhood of Christ and to the refinement of fellow followers of the Savior.

May 5

TAMING THE TONGUE

"Make the most of every opportunity. Let your conversation be always full of grace, seasoned with salt, so that you may know how to answer everyone." - *Colossians 4:5-6 (NIV)*

We often say stupid things. An off-color joke or a snide comment is sometimes more than enough to offend its listeners and clasp your hand over your mouth. It's hard to control what we say at times. When we are in the moment, we usually don't think of what we end up saying and by the time it comes out, it's already too late and the damage is done. Some might say that since we cannot control what we say, we should accept it; justifying that whatever we say, good or bad, is a genuine effort to be honest and "real". Such a view seems to imply that words don't matter compared to a person's heart when saying them. It's true that we need to be honest and open about our feelings and views on a subject, but it is equally true that words do matter, despite any sentiment that says the contrary. God gave man the wonderful gift of tact that enables one to deliver a sharp point without the unnecessary collateral damage to accompany it.

Taming the tongue is a hard thing to do. The book of James acknowledges this full well. It is an endeavor that truly requires discipline and a reliance on God to help one keep a close watch on the words he uses. We must always be aware that the words we use could either hurt or aid in our witness for Christ because we are His representatives on Earth. Thus we must always be sensitive to other people's sensibilities and not be an unnecessary stumbling block to those around us. In this light the old cliché rings true; "You attract more flies with honey than with vinegar".

May 6

SOMEBODY CALL A DOCTOR?

While Jesus was having dinner at Matthew's house, many tax collectors and "sinners" came and ate with him and his disciples. When the Pharisees saw this, they asked his disciples, "Why does your teacher eat with tax collectors and 'sinners'?" On hearing this, Jesus said, "It is not the healthy who need a doctor, but the sick." -Matthew 9:10-12 (NIV)

Wouldn't the Christian life be so easy if we were obliged to only serve those who we can tolerate? Those with whom we can easily get along with and enjoy their company? Although this would certainly be ideal, this is only fulfilling part of the Christian definition of service to others. Christ, by His example, demands that we serve everyone regardless of who they are. All of us are sinners and thus we all need to be restored by Christ and His redemptive work. Christians take on the role of the doctor, with the message of Christ as his medical expertise. But just as a doctor should be prepared to deal with minor health issues, he must also be prepared to deal with larger issues as well. A doctor cannot have any qualms about helping a patient because to have any would be a violation of the nature of his profession.

Looking at the group of disciples Jesus had illustrated this point well. Take for example Matthew the tax collector. Jesus would have had every reason to refuse to deal with his kind. Not only did tax collectors collect taxes from every Jew, including Jesus' own family in all likelihood, for their Roman oppressors, but many tax collectors would also amass their own personal wealth by helping themselves to some of the money collected from taxation. Or take for example Simon the Zealot. As he belonged to a group that murdered anyone who they deemed to be collaborators with the Roman occupiers, Jesus would have been abhorred by Simon's readiness to shed blood if need be. Yet he included such people to be His disciples. If Christ Himself wasn't picky on who needed to experience the love of God is his life, why should we as followers of Him?

May 7

THE PROBLEM OF SELFISHNESS

"Do not neglect to do good and to share what you have, for such sacrifices are pleasing to God." -Hebrews 13:16 (ESV)

If humanity was consistent in doing good to others and sharing what they have with those around them, all of the world's conflicts would be solved. However, this ideal is destined to remain an impossible reality because of man's sinful and selfish nature. We always want to horde and accumulate material things for ourselves. Sharing is not innate in human nature and that's why even from a small age, our instinct is keep all that we get for ourselves; leaving the act of sharing to be taught to us by our parents. But even with all the good advice parents give to us when we are infants on sharing what we get, we never learn. Instead of refusing to share our toys for example and having an insatiable lust for more, we continue to have a lust for wealth, fame, and power; refusing to use it for the benefit of others if it doesn't serve our needs first, that is if we don't do so outright.

Why do we work so hard towards outdoing and outperforming each other? Competition is healthy if it is turned inward, to encourage yourself to do better at what you do. But not if it is at the expense of someone else. Christ has called us by His example to be generous and gracious to others. If we are to follow His example, we must not allow cries for help and despair to fall on deaf ears. Jesus Himself said that whatever benevolence we do for even the least of those around us, we do unto Him. This should be enough of a motivation to help and serve others with what we have; always checking our motives to see if our acts of kindness are bringing glory to God and drawing others to Him, or if they are serving our own selfish wants.

May 8

MASTERING OUR CIRCUMSTANCES

"Do not be anxious about anything, but in everything, by prayer and petition, with thanksgiving, present your request to God. And the peace of God, which transcends all understanding, will guard your hearts and your minds in Christ Jesus." -Philippians 4:6-7 (NIV)

Isn't it strange how sometimes Christians love to say that they have surrendered their lives to God, but when push comes to shove, trials reveal that there is so much they still need to let go of? Whenever things don't go our way or something throws a wrench in our life plans, our first response is to whine, gripe, and complain. Then we somehow try to see if, on our own understanding, we can take our circumstances by the horns and master them. However, the bull usually throws us off and we are left not only back to where we started, but with our pride broken as well.

We like to take control of our lives because we think we know what's best for us. After all, it's our life so why should anyone else think that they know better than us and dictate to us how we should live our lives? But the truth is that we cannot control our lives half the time. Even when everything seems to be going according to the plans we have set for our lives, life has a way of sometimes completely derailing everything we've achieved and hoped for. We look to ourselves for solutions, but in our finite understanding we often fail to find any that would restore us completely. We then look to friends and other human sources in hopes that they would have an answer. Sometimes they might give helpful advice because they have the advantage of being a spectator as you live your life. But even they are fallible and prone to error, which results in them giving bad, if not well-meaning, counsel and only prolonging your misery.

Who then do we go to for help? God as revealed through Jesus Christ is the source of all perfect wisdom and comfort. If we surrender to Him, who is perfect and promises to work all things together for good, He will take our hopeless and bleak circumstances and turn them around according to His timing and will. It is hard to surrender to God because of our selfish and rebellious nature. But I have found that when one surrenders his circumstances and requests to God, he will not only be filled with peace, but God will take him on a fantastic journey. It will pull him from misery and despair, to joy and fulfillment in a way that will far exceed his wildest dreams.

May 9

SUFFERING FOR THE FAITH

"For it has been granted to you that for the sake of Christ you should not only believe in him but also suffer for his sake," -Philippians 1:29 (ESV)

The Christian message is an offensive one. It demands people to forsake their autonomy and their desires to a God they cannot see or touch. For this reason Christians are mocked for their perceived irrationality, and persecuted for their non-conformist stance against culture when it goes against the principles of Christ. As Christians, we are to be aware and to be prepared to face opposition for the beliefs and the Savior we have chosen to follow. At times, standing up for the cause of Christ will be hard and uncomfortable to do. However, in the face of opposition, Christ will be our comfort and strength; even when those closest to us have ceased to be so on account of our belief in Him.

At the same time, it is easy to develop a victim mentality. Often I have heard stories from other Christians claiming to have been unjustly slandered for their faith in Christ. Yet when I look at their lives and how they act towards those who do not share the same faith, I can understand why they were. It is important that whenever we go out we should remind ourselves who we represent and acknowledge that we represent Him through our actions, words, and thoughts whether we want to or not. Being inconsiderate, obnoxiously judgmental, and an all-around jerk, and then claiming to be persecuted for your faith when the angry criticism piles on, is not a good witness for Christ. People should be offended by the message of Christ because of its claims, not because of the actions and words of its followers. We must always be willing to examine ourselves and our attitudes, and we should be quick to acknowledge our faults when confronted with them and actively seek to change them. In doing so, we become more effective witnesses for Christ and people around us will take notice. They will respect your beliefs because they truly see a love which can only come from God evident in your life, and that will give you an avenue to share the message of Christ with them.

May 10

ARE WE REDEEMERS?

"For the Son of Man came to seek and to save the lost." -Luke 19:10 (ESV)

Humans love to think that they are all-powerful. That somehow they alone can wrestle with the evil and circumstances that impede their path to glory and happiness, and can do the same for others. Such heroism is not necessarily a bad thing. It often serves as an impetus to address the injustices of the world instead of sinking into a defeatism that renders a person immobile. However, the problem with such an attitude lies in the fact that humans are not all-powerful. If it were so, the world would not be in the state it is in.

Yet it is so easy to think that the fate of everything in this world rests on us and our actions. Even Christians are not exempt from this. How often do Christians catch themselves attempting to take responsibility for the salvation of another person? As if to say that it was by their efforts that the person in question came to a living faith in Christ. Such self-congratulatory attitudes take the glory away from God and place it on human beings. If Christians were solely responsible for the salvation of man, then what is the need for the Holy Spirit who is supposed to work in the world for the redemption of man and strengthen the faithful until the Day of Judgment? Furthermore, even though Christians have Christ working in them, their stubbornness often hinders the work of God in their lives. Therefore, how can an imperfect human redeem another imperfect human? It is important to remember that redemption is the realm of God and not of men. Our responsibility on Earth is to tell the message of Christ. Whether or not they choose to accept the message is between them and God. We should neither force a person to come to Christ nor should we be discouraged when they don't. Jesus Himself said that believers should move on when they encounter apathy from others towards His message. God will continue to work in the hearts and lives of those who have heard His message as a result of our obedience to His call for us. But He will also work in the lives of people where believers are not present. God wants us to be active participants in His mission. However, we must be ever so mindful of our place in His redemptive plan. We are His agents, but we are not redeemers.

May 11

RIGHT THOUGHTS AND RIGHT ACTIONS

"You have heard that it was said to the people long ago, 'Do not murder, and anyone who murders will be subject to judgment.' But I tell you that anyone who is angry with his brother will be subject to judgment." -Matthew 5:21-22a

We all have had people we don't like. Someone who is so insufferable that we cannot bear being in his presence. So obnoxious that it's painful to hear him talk. The only thing that is restraining us from simply strangling him is the fact that murder would be a crime, not to mention the mess it would create. But if this is the only thing restraining us, what if we were in a secluded alley and could get away with murder if we could. I would say that if we could murder someone we completely despise without having to suffer consequences, we would do it in a heartbeat. In light of this how can we call ourselves better than people who openly commit murder? Sure we might look upon a murderer with disgust but how many of us could easily go down that path if the wrong buttons are pushed?

The Laws of the Pharisees focused on outward appearance, but never dealt with the condition of the heart. By implication then it was alright to hate as long as it did not develop into murder. But cannot hate develop into the act of murder? How many acts of genocide in the course of history have begun with thoughts of hatred and malice towards a certain group? Human action is determined by thoughts. Jesus knew this full well and declared that even those who hate in their thoughts are as guilty as committing the physical act of murder. But in light of these standards who can stand? We are truly depraved when we compare our thoughts to the standards of Christ. That is why we need Him; to constantly check our thoughts so that our actions would reflect His work in our lives. Charity done with a grimace loses its purity compared to when it is done with a truly loving and caring heart. Christ by His example compels us to love one another with all of our hearts. We may be able to purge ill-thoughts towards another person if we truly feel we can love them, but only the love of God in our lives can make us love the unlovable. We were unlovable to Him in our sin and yet He loved us enough to pay the penalty for our sins. May we display this love to others around us knowing this fact.

May 12

GREATER STRENGTH

"Moses said to the Lord, "O Lord, I have never been eloquent, neither in the past nor since you have spoken to your servant. I am slow of speech and tongue." The Lord said to him, "Who gave man his mouth? Who makes him deaf or mute? Who gives him sight or makes him blind? Is it not I, the Lord? Now go; I will help you speak and will teach you what to say." –Exodus 4:10-12 (NIV)

How often do we make excuses when we have been given a task? We will use anything to squirm our way out of additional responsibility if it goes beyond our comfort level. "I can't do this because of so and so…" We use things such as our conditions, our lack of time, and our inabilities, to justify our aversion. Sometimes these excuses may be legitimate. At other times they may be only excuses. But both seem to place the capacity to pursue an undertaking or vision solely on human strength and efforts and ignore the fact that there is someone far more powerful and willing to help.

We rarely take the God factor into the equation when presented with a task or a dream. Even if deep down we would really like to see it happen, we dismiss it as being outside of the realm of our abilities and thus it remains only a nice sentiment, never a reality. But who has created our inner most being? Who knows us inside and out? Clearly not us because half the time we can't even understand ourselves. God has created us and He knows exactly what He is doing. Furthermore, His plans for us are good and He promises this for us. It's true we cannot do anything on our own efforts or abilities. But if we were to trust in God, it will surprise us that despite our failings He is able to accomplish His good and perfect purposes in a way that will take our breath away when we look back. We should never doubt the power of God to work in our lives for in our weaknesses He makes us strong.

May 13

RESORTED PAINTINGS

"You created my inmost being; you knit me together in my mother's womb. I praise you because I am fearfully and wonderfully made; your works are wonderful, I know that full well." -Psalm 139:13-14 (NIV)

There is something beautiful about the human race. For all our faults and the constant mistakes we make, nothing can compare to the beauty of humanity. We have been created with such physical and mental complexity in mind that it is truly magnificent. What is even more amazing is that humans, regardless of anthropological or cultural differences share in these complexities. All humans share in the love of being creative and innovative, need rest for their bodies when tired, feel joy and laugh, feel hurt and weep, and desire to love and be loved.

The reason why humans are so beautiful is that every single person has been created in the image of God. Although the fall of man into sin has tainted the image of God, it still exists and still shines through occasionally in the form of human love, compassion, and justice. We can easily be compared to paintings in this regard. A valuable painting is valuable by what it is and not necessarily by its present condition. An art lover specialized in restoration techniques would not simply deem a prized painting worthless if it has in some way become flawed. He would do his best to restore it to its original beauty and would not give up knowing that underneath its flaws is a marvelous painting waiting to be restored so that its entire and complete beauty may shine through. Likewise, God is in the business of restoration. We as flawed paintings cannot restore ourselves. Blemishes in a painting don't just go away by themselves. But only a specialist can restore paintings to the original glory. Thus we must always show respect to our fellow human beings knowing that we all bear the image of God and are waiting to be restored by our Redeemer.

May 14

TAKING SHORTCUTS

"Enter through the narrow gate. For wide is the gate and broad is the road that leads to destruction, and many enter through it." -Matthew 7:13 (NIV)

Shortcuts are dangerous. We have all had times when taking the shortcut seemed like a good idea at the time, only to have to pay the consequences later. Whilst navigating through the chaotic railway terminal in Tokyo and close to missing my train, I had thought I had found a shortcut. Logically, it seemed to work out for my benefit as I reconstructed the map of the terminal in my head. As it turned out however, my shortcut took me to a completely different platform! The subsequent backtracking to my original route cost me half an hour of travel time when I could have easily taken the long route and still make the train, even if I did so by the skin of my teeth.

Humans love to look for shortcuts. Anything that reduces effort and makes things convenient and easy for us is the route that most of us would like to pursue. In some respects this is not necessarily a bad thing. The love that humans have for shortcuts leads them to become innovators and inventors. Many of the technological advances we have today stand testament to the love we have for finding the easiest and quickest method to get done what we need to get done.

However, this cannot be applied to the Christian life. Many of those outside the faith, and even those within Christian circles, feel that the key to fulfillment and happiness in life is the path of pleasure. Is the pursuit of pleasure wrong in itself? No, but it becomes wrong once it has replaced the pursuit of Christ. Yet many who do not want to subjugate themselves to the rigors of the Christian life but still call themselves Christians end up paying only lip service to Christ and following the path of comfort at the expense of living as His true followers. By the time they realize that they have taken a wrong turn, it is already too late. Those who have been able to realize their mistake before it destroys them find that they had wasted precious time pursuing the fleeting pleasures of this world over the eternal pleasures of pursuing Christ and interacting with the world through His eyes. The Christian life was never meant to be easy. In fact it should cause more discomfort than ease because it challenges us to critically look at the world and its assumptions we have grown to become accustomed to. However, the rewards of following Christ far outweigh the suffering and challenges of the narrow path in light of a truly fulfilled and happy life both in the present and into eternity.

May 15

DIVINE VICTORY

"Then the Lord said to Joshua, 'See, I have delivered Jericho into your hands, along with its king and its fighting men.'" -Joshua 6:2 (NIV)

It is often hard for believers to comprehend that all their trials and problems with regards to sin in their lives are ultimately answerable to God's victorious promises. As long as we remain obedient to God and towards His purposes, we will be able to overcome our circumstances by His enabling. Yet somehow we tend to forget this. Either we try to deal with sin on our own strength; the resulting failed attempts to purge ourselves prompting us say to ourselves it is hopeless and continue to live in our sinful habits, or we take advantage of God's grace. Both are wrong from the point of their attitudes on God's proper role in the life of the believer. The former denies the active role God plays in redeeming His creation and the power of His redemptive work. The latter simply and ungratefully treats God as an insurance policy and not their Redeemer to whom they are now indebted to serve and respect.

Human attempts to deal with their own sinfulness are halfhearted at best. Like a diet plan, some believe that they are entitled to sin once in a while because they have worked so hard to be holy, just as how a person on a diet feels entitled to an amount of junk food because they have worked so hard to slim down. But that's not how it should work. Suppose if Joshua did not obey God's instructions and let a few of the people and livestock of Jericho survive. They would have no doubt grown and reorganized themselves in order to challenge Israel yet again. Likewise we cannot compromise on sin. Even a little leeway here and there can set a person back. When we sin they are not entitlements, but they are moments of shame which we surrender to God so that He may forgive and purify us. It is not of our own devising or planning that we gain victory over sin, but only through constant obedience and surrender to Christ's redemptive work can we be saved. Divine victory is within our grasp as followers of Christ. We must take it now if we do not want to drown in defeat.

May 16

WHO DO WE THINK WE ARE?

"Humility and the fear of the Lord bring wealth and honor and life." -Proverbs 22:4 (NIV)

Pride is built into every one of us. As a result of the privileges we obtain or the abilities we already possess, we often think of ourselves as being superior to everyone around us. Even adopting "self-enlightened" or "holier-than-thou" attitudes is a form of pride in that it invariably places oneself as superior over those whom they have deemed as inferior. We love to boast because it satisfies our selfish and sinful nature that wants to be at the center of everyone's attention and thoughts; a role that should be only designated to God Himself. People often lord their wealth and status over those that do not share the luxuries to the point of oppression. Thus they often see themselves as monarchs of the world; having the power of life and death over those they can control and manipulate. However, the prideful always fall for the very reason that the fuel of their attitudes is transient. Money, fame, and power are always fluid and can be lost as quickly and easily as it was gained.

Christians are not exempt from pride and sadly they succumb to it far too often. They often feel that their own piety and righteousness makes them, in their eyes at least, perfect compared to the rest of the world. But are we really? If we are honest with ourselves, even Christians in a living relationship with Christ often stumble and fall far too many times to even count. Thankfully our salvation is not based on the performance of the believer, for if that were true who could stand? Furthermore, what would be the need for God sending down His Son to die for all the sins of humanity if humanity already had the ability to save himself? The truth is humanity cannot save himself and any good that the believer does is done because of the redemptive work of God in his life, not of his own inherent, yet non-existent, righteousness. Paul wrote that he should boast only of the work of Christ in his life. May that also be the boast of our lives as well.

May 17

IDOLS AND IDOL WORSHIP

"Those who cling to worthless idols forfeit the grace that could be theirs." -Jonah 2:8 (NIV)

We always end up worshipping the wrong things. When one thinks of idol worship, the first thought that comes to mind is that it is something only common to Eastern or African cultures where they bow down before man-made statues or images. But the truth is idol worship is a very universal human activity. All men have been created with a desire to worship something. However, because of fallen human nature, they grope at anything to satisfy their desire to worship. How many people in so called "non-idolatrous" societies worship money, success, and relationships? Even

Christians fall into this trap. Putting the local pastor on a pedestal or placing the busyness of Christian ministry over a relationship with God is also considered idolatry and is sadly far too common. Anything that takes you away from God is considered idolatry, no matter how good or pure the thing is in of itself.

Why do humans invest all their faith and time in things which are transient? Perhaps it is because human beings, in their finite understanding, can only grasp and comprehend what's in front of them. There is a false sense of certainty in tangibility, even if the tangible is destined to perish at some point. Thus, people often end up feeling unsatisfied after their idol is crushed and turn to another tangible idol to regain their satisfaction, never learning that everything in this world is fleeting. Thus it makes more logical sense to place one's faith and energy into something that will remain constant and eternal. The pursuit of Christ will be the most satisfying pursuit one will ever undertake, that is if one is truly open and willing to submit Himself before Christ.

May 18

LOVING OTHERS AND LOVING GOD

"Each of us should please his neighbor for his good, to build him up." -Romans 15:2 (NIV)

How easy is it for us to find fault with others and bring them down? It's a habit that begins in the schoolyard and even into adulthood, we catch ourselves doing it constantly, albeit a little more subtly and secretively. Due to our fallen nature, tearing down and oppressing our neighbors with our harmful words and actions comes more naturally; hence the very real fact that considerate and compassionate behavior is not innate and needs to be taught. Somehow, in a backwards and twisted way, tearing down others elevates our own self-esteem and self-worth. A nagging feeling of inadequacy drives us to rag on the inadequacies of others in order to present ourselves as being better or superior.

Such behavior in the Christian should be non-existent. Through the acceptance of Christ's redemptive sacrifice on the cross and our liberation from the shackles of sin, we are made whole and complete in Him who is the source of everything that is right and pure. A Christian should never feel worthless or inadequate because He is highly valued in the eyes of God. The same God who has created the beautiful universe and continues to maintain it, also loves and cares for His followers in the same manner as a loving parent cares for their children. Therefore, we should never tear down others in an attempt to elevate our own position. Instead we should love them and encourage them in the same way Christ loves and encourages us. In addition, whenever we fail to build others up and instead focus on their failings and shortcomings in an attempt to put them down, we implicitly say that God has created worthless beings. God has not. All men have been created in the image of God and when we think, act, or speak with malice and hatred towards someone, we are essentially spitting on that image and grieving God Himself. Christ said that whoever serves even the least among men renders His service unto God, and Paul wrote that whoever acts with kindness and charity towards his fellow man unknowingly entertains angels. As Christians, if we truly want to serve and follow God, we need to start serving, loving, and encouraging those around us, regardless of who they are; instead of trying to destroy them. In doing so we reflect the God we serve. He is a loving, compassionate, and just God who truly cares for the well-being of all peoples and who wants to see them free from the corruption of sin so that they may live in the happiness and peace which can only be found through Christ.

May 19

WHERE IS YOUR TRUST?

"Whoever trusts in his riches will fall, but the righteous will flourish like a green leaf." -Proverbs 11:28 (ESV)

Money can't buy happiness. It's a cliché that we are taught from the time we become aware of the presence of wealth and of its ability to be gained for one's personal use. Yet it would seem that we ignore the warning and live as if the amassing of wealth was the sole purpose of life. Our materialistic culture has taught us that the more we earn and the more we buy, the happier we will be. Commercials, explicitly or implicitly, always say that their product will guarantee the buyer satisfaction and happiness. But how many times has that proven to be false? Yet in our stupidity we always search for a new product, a new material pursuit, only to be disappointed when the object of our desire outlives its use. Subsequently we foolishly place our hopes for happiness and fulfillment in a seemingly new and better material pursuit; imploring us to earn more money to pursue our new material fancy. Often if we step back and look at ourselves, it would seem that living a material lifestyle is like living as if one were a dog chasing its tail; never to be satisfied. One would think that humanity would learn. But sadly, the majority of us never learn from our mistakes.

At the end of the day, when all of us are dead and buried in the ground, our wealth and possessions will mean nothing. We will not be able to take with us anything we have gained under heaven. When we stand before the judgment seat of Christ, there is only one thing that will be of relevance to Him; have we served Him by accepting His lordship over our lives and in doing so have we pursued righteousness and purity in our lives and in the world. Before one thinks that pursuing righteousness and purity for Christ only pays in the afterlife, there are also blessings that will follow in the earthly realm should one pursue such a life. Consider how men with integrity and a sense of honor and justice are much better spoken of compared to the man who is wealthy and has all the material comforts of life, yet has forsaken his morals and honesty. Consider the health of the relationships of those who may not place a strong priority on accumulating wealth with those who always have money and status on their mind. God had asked King Solomon before his ascension, to make it known before Him any gift that he requested. Instead of choosing wealth or power, Solomon chose wisdom. For his decision, God was pleased and not only gave the new king wisdom, but wealth and power as well. Anyone who puts their trust in their own wealth will be sorely disappointed. But God will bless those who pursue righteousness and truth according to His standards. Such people will be far more satisfied and will find the secret of true contentment and happiness knowing that their hope rests not in fleeting thing; but in the eternal assurances of God.

May 20

WHERE DOES MY HELP COME FROM?

"What then shall we say to these things? If God is for us, who can be against us?" -Romans 8:31 (ESV)

As a result of the fallen state of the world, human opposition is bound to block the most noble and just of causes. It can strike at any time and can come from anywhere while wearing many masks. Often when such opposition comes our way, we tend to lose our momentum and shrink back; thinking we've bitten off more than we can chew and consequently, we descend into hopelessness.

It is easy for opposition to get to us and it is easy for it to keep us under the oppressive spirit of defeat and discouragement. But in the wake of opposition God always provides a moment to critically evaluate ourselves and our intentions. Perhaps we have pursued the cause of justice by relying on our own human wisdom and not allowing God to do His work by directing our paths. God will always stand by a just cause because He is by nature just. However, we get easily discouraged and lose valuable time in regaining ground and continuing the fight when we do not have a strong rock on which to stand upon. If his idea of justice and truth is in line with the teachings of Jesus, the Christian has an invaluable ally in Christ; if only he calls upon His name. Only Christ can give the strength and wisdom to pursue truth and justice when it seems that the forces of evil and corruption in the world have overwhelmed such noble, God-given principles. The unscrupulous and corrupt seem to be victorious only for a time. But with God defending those who stand for righteousness and integrity, nothing can overcome them and it is they who shall have the final victory.

May 21

DIVISION AND UNITY

"May the God who gives endurance and encouragement give you a spirit of unity among yourselves as you follow Christ Jesus, so that with one heart and mouth you may glorify the God and Father of our Lord Jesus Christ." -Romans 15:5-6 (NIV)

Why do we love forming divisions? This desire is found in every community; even in the Christian Church. The origins of this question however, seem to lie in the human tendency to form cliques and elite groups to enhance their own self-worth. Since we are human and prone to conditional love, we only like to deal with people who are our like ourselves. Such an insular brotherhood ends up polarizing people; which becomes the source of all conflict.

Division is something that God did not want in His creation. Are there differences in the world He has created? Yes there are. But these differences are meant to complement each other in order so that creation in general and humanity in particular would be unified serving the one true God. When people put their group on a pedestal, claiming it to be the one that truly follows Christ, they are not serving and worshiping Christ. They are serving and worshiping their group. There have been noble attempts to do away with these divisions by human hands, but often they themselves end up becoming elite clubs. The Church is comprised of different parts. But only with Christ bestowing upon His followers the spirit of unity can we become blind to divisions based on earthly criteria. Man's designs for unity and conformity will only divide, but only Christ can unite people together so that they may serve Him with one heart and one mouth.

May 22

THE WISDOM OF HEAVEN

"The wisdom that comes from heaven is first of all pure; then peace-loving, considerate, submissive, full of mercy and good fruit, impartial and sincere. Peacemakers who sow in peace raise a harvest of righteousness." -James 3:17-18 (NIV)

Often, what is advertised as wisdom in the human realm is not actually wisdom. The purpose of wisdom is to set a person on the path to fulfillment and happiness. It is supposed to keep people from harm and preserve them when calamity strikes. But wisdom found in our realm only seems to set us on the path to destruction. I once remember a classmate of mine explaining what she was being taught at a business training session. Sound business advice, as thought by the session speaker, involved crushing the "little guy", trusting no one, and essentially treating the business world as a battlefield where the strong survive and the weak perish. Such is the world's advice. It has not only been applied to the business world, but to every realm of modern human life. When we are taught only to look out for ourselves so that we would not be taken advantage of and prove ourselves to be weak, we become corrupt and violent oppressors; with no qualms about trampling over those who are struggling, and manipulating and sacrificing meaningful relationships for the sake of advancing our own position.

Is this supposed to be the natural order of things in this world? If it was, both the practitioner and victim of such a philosophy would enjoy living under such a system. But the truth is that those on the receiving end are usually saddened and indignant that they must live only to be crushed by those deemed their "superiors". In addition, even if they don't admit it, those who are at the top and have everything in terms of material wealth and possessions feel incomplete; living in the regret of obtaining everything they have at the expense of wholesome and fulfilling human relationships. Life was not meant to be lived this way. We were created to pursue justice, purity, and peace because the God who has created us is the manifestation of all these things. We were created to live together in mutual and equal harmony and service towards one another because the Father, the Son, and the Holy Spirit - the Holy Trinity - which has brought humanity into existence, works together in community. We were created to love unconditionally because God is a God of love, and He loves unconditionally. Humanity can never understand these ideas in the purest sense because their minds have been clouded by the destructive force of sin. Thus, even if humanity tries to reach for these qualities on our own strength or understanding, the noble ideologies we create often get hijacked by human corruption. Only when this cloud of sin is removed from the human mind as a result of truly accepting and believing in Christ redemptive sacrifice can humanity understand the wisdom which comes from Heaven and put it into practice in the world. Not on our own comprehension, but with Christ working through us.

May 23

BE KIND ANYWAY!

"God is not unjust; he will not forget your work and the love you have shown him as you have helped his people and continue to help them." -Hebrews 6:10 (NIV)

How often do we wonder if our charity towards others seems to go unnoticed? While some may truly show their gratitude towards your efforts to act generously and graciously towards them, others may never show their appreciation. In extreme cases, they may even blatantly show their ungratefulness and make it known to you. When those around us have taken advantage of and walked upon our kindness, often we wonder, why do we even bother? It would seem to be in our best interest to withhold our charity from everyone, lest we should be hurt and trampled upon yet again.

Somehow, we have gotten the false view that charity is dependent on us. For most, whether we admit it or not, charity is self-serving. We want to hear people thanking us or showing their gratitude because it elevates our ego and sense of purpose. Since we have this need to fulfill we tend to be elated when someone compliments us on the charity we perform. However, when people stab us in the back and walk all over our charity, suddenly we don't feel like serving others anymore because they have deprived us of inflating our egos and have crushed our sense of purpose.

True charity is not dependent on the actions of others. Neither is it dependant on one's own feelings. It is only dependant on adopting a Christ-like nature which can only be achieved once a person has allowed Christ to work in his life by accepting and believing in His redemptive sacrifice. Humanity spat on, mocked, and crucified Christ; never realizing that Christ came to die for every human being in every period of time, be it the past, the present, or the future. Even now we trample upon the image of Christ when we persist in our sin. Yet He never gives up on us. Despite our failings, He continues to actively seek the redemption of the world and the sanctification of believers, so that sin's chains may be finally broken. The Christian should not perform charity to get something out of it; rather he should expect nothing in return, not even the praise or approval of men.

When one seeks to perform charity because it glorifies His Redeemer, it gives them the strength to perform and continue to perform acts of kindness despite whatever the recipient may think. It has been said that no one has been impoverished because he gave too much and God has a way of preserving those who are faithful to Him in loving and serving others without any strings attached.

May 24

THE LIMITS OF HUMAN WISDOM

> *"Oh, the depth and riches of the wisdom and the knowledge of God! How unsearchable his judgments, and his paths beyond tracing out."* - Romans 11:33 (NIV)

Who can comprehend the mind of God? How can we, in our finite understanding, understand His ways and thoughts? Man often tries to think up seemingly clever ways to discredit or disprove God. But such attempts are like trying to judge an ocean based on a tiny sample of water. He only sees a part of God's actions, a part of His thoughts, and based on that he makes his conclusions on God. But man fails to see the whole picture because our perception is limited and quite frankly, sometimes we are simply too lazy to probe further; content with thinking that our word is infallible and not bothering to challenge our own assumptions.

How can we claim ourselves to be infallible in our thoughts and conclusions about God when clearly humanity is flawed in many ways than one? How easy is it for us to follow figures, with their detrimental ideologies, like sheep? Sure we might claim to be rational in our decisions and who or what we place our faith in, but throw in a charismatic figure with a dash of human desperation and people will follow anything; even if the ideology they are rallying behind flies in the face of everything that is pure and just in the world. We are irrational people. We may be capable of rational thought but we rarely use it half the time. Only through Christ, who is the only perfect being and who bestowed upon humanity the gifts of reason and free will, are we able to consistently use our rationality only through Him can we understand God and the world around us in the truest sense.

May 25

NOT JUST FOR SHOW

"Woe to you, teachers of the law and Pharisees, you hypocrites! You are like whitewashed tombs, which look beautiful on the outside but on the inside are full of dead men's bones and everything unclean." - Matthew 23:27 (NIV)

"I like your Christ. I do not like your Christians. You Christians are so unlike your Christ." For Christian ears those should be the most painful words ever uttered by Gandhi, the man who would forever go down in history as the one who challenged the might of the British Empire and liberated India, its most important colony, through the doctrine of non-violence. He would have made a wonderful Christian and he himself was potentially a few short steps away from fully embracing Christ. But what stopped him from doing so was the hypocrisy he saw amongst those who claimed to be guided by Him. Instead of finding the love of Christ in His children, he found hatred. Instead of finding His children worshipping Christ, he found them worshipping wealth, power, and prestige above all else; to the point of discarding the teachings of Christ in order to satisfy their sinful urges. In Gandhi's eyes, how could Christians, claiming to love and worship a God who embodies justice, truth, and love, support and even actively participate in a system that is based on the exploitation and degradation of other human beings who bear the image of God and whom God loves as much as His children?

Hypocrisy is lethal. It not only destroys us and our walk with God, but it can destroy and discourage others as well. The book of James asks the question, "How can pure water and filthy water come from the same spring?" Likewise, we cannot profess to stand for Christ if the source of our actions, our heart, is not aligned with His purposes. Anyone can say the right words, do the right thing, and create an air of piety and righteousness. The Pharisees of Jesus' time certainly did so. However, if his heart has not been conformed to God, he may fool people for a time, but his heart will eventually betray the façade he has put up for the world to see. Even if he ends up fooling the world until the day he dies, he cannot hide from God's all-seeing eyes. When we stand before Him on Judgment Day we will be asked to call to account all our actions. We cannot lie before God because He already knows what is in our hearts and knows who His children are. The only cure for hypocrisy is for one to enter into a living and close relationship with Christ, and always being humble before Him. When we are humble before Him, we lose the desire to put up an act and we know our place in relation to His. We know that we are sinners in need of a Savior. We know that we are not saved by our outward words or actions, but by Christ entering into our hearts in order to purge us from sin and mold us into the people He wants us to be. It has been said that the true Christian lives out his faith even behind closed doors; where there are no spectators save for God Himself. May it be our prayer that we live godly lives when the crowd is absent so that we may be positive witnesses for Christ when the crowd is present.

May 26

TOGETHER WE RIDE!

"Though one may be overpowered, two can defend themselves. A cord of three strands is not quickly broken." -Ecclesiastes 4:12 (NIV)

Ever heard of the expression, "it would be so much better without the people"? Often we apply this expression to life as well. There are times when people can truly aggravate us. The faults of humanity, especially if we've been victim to those faults, are sometimes enough for us to wish that we could live life away from people altogether; content with just looking at them but never interacting with them beyond the point of absolute necessity.

Such hermit lifestyles are never truly satisfying. Eventually we being to develop a longing for human companionship and seek to have meaningful relationships with others. The reason for this is simple, man was never meant to live alone, but was created by God to live in community with one another. God Himself lives and works in community in the form of the Trinity. The Father, the Son, and the Holy Spirit act together as one for all three existed together before time began, had a hand in the creation of the world, and work together for its redemption from sin. It shouldn't come as a surprise then that this quality of operating in community was infused in humanity when God created us. It is also clear from this fact that God places a high value on human relationships. We should never underestimate or take for granted their importance. The truth of the matter is that we need each other in this often harsh and brutal world. We all go through the same struggles, the same hardships, and, even if we are not willing to admit it, we all share the very same faults that we accuse each other of. This is why we must encourage and build each other up; so that we may grow to be better people and better servants of God. As children of God redeemed by Christ, we have an obligation to pursue and value wholesome human relationships; never doing anything to violate something that God has wonderfully given to us. Furthermore, the Christian life is meant to be lived together in community for the Church is one body interdependent on each other and if we are to be effective witness for Christ, we need to be in meaningful relationships with others so that we may show God's love to everyone and tell them about His desire to set every human being free from the oppression of sin so that they may enter into a beautiful relationship with Him. Though life will come with many struggles and battles, know that we never fight alone. All of us fight as a team and with God on the side of His children; we will be able to overcome any obstacle.

May 27

THE GOODNESS OF CREATION

"God saw all that he had made, and it was very good." -Genesis 1:31 (NIV)

Even from a very young age, I could never buy into the whole notion of the universe coming into existence as the result of a random cosmological event. How could its immense vastness, its marvelous complexity, and its breathtaking beauty, be the result of random chance? There has to be a purpose behind it all. Everything, from the simplest table to the most complex computer, has a maker. The parts aren't simply lying there until they somehow randomly come together without any external assistance. There is a hand which deliberately chooses and determines which part goes where so that the finished product may fulfill its intended purpose.

When we see the sorry state the world is in, and how we as humans seem to partake more towards its destruction than its restoration, it is easy to ask the question, "Why has God created the world?" Has He created it in such a way as to be imperfect? Not at all! The imperfections in creation and in humanity are not the result of God's incompetence, but of human disobedience. How could God, who is the source of all that is good, pure, and just, wish to create an imperfect universe? It would go against His nature. Despite the reality of the fallen state of the world, the original beauty of God's creation still shines through. Everything from the birds of the air, to the fish of the sea, reflects God as our peerless and matchless Creator. He has also created a beautiful order in His creation. Everything depends on each other and if any aspect of the creation is completely wiped out, or fails in its God-given processes, an entire ecosystem can be jeopardized. Even in sinful humanity we can see evidence of the beauty God has bestowed upon us as the crowning glory of His handiwork. There is something about the order and aesthetics of the human form, the brilliance and ingenuity of the human mind, and the intensity and depth of the human heart and soul that is sublime beyond words. All of us as humans bear the image of God, and though that image may be tainted by sin, aspects of it can still be seen. God's creation is meant to draw people closer to the Creator and closer to the right worship of Him. This I have experienced personally. In the past, I used to seriously question God and wondered whether He was even out there, listening to me, watching over me, and always loving me. Yet whenever I looked up into a clear blue sky, or walked through a peaceful forest, or gazed into the eyes of a fellow human being, I have always been left with the conclusion that there has to be a God behind all this beauty. Only the foolish and stubborn would see the beauty of creation and say there is no God. Regardless of its flaws and faults, the world and creation in general is beautiful and is meant to be enjoyed. Therefore, while we are called as God's children to be a part of His mission to redeem the world from sin, we should also remember to look at the beauty around us and praise God knowing, to quote the eighteenth century German poet Johann Wolfgang von Goethe, that His "…works, sublime, eternal, are fair as on the primal day."

May 28

REFINING FIRE

"Give thanks in all circumstances, for this is God's will for you in Christ Jesus." -1 Thessalonians 5:18 (NIV)

When everything seems to be going our way, when all seems to be right with the world, it is easy to thank God and praise Him. We all love it when someone buys us a nice present right? Hence our gratitude when God blesses us. However, when trials and suffering come along our path, we want nothing to do with God. We hold Him responsible for our misfortune and see Him as a cruel saboteur deliberately trying to deprive us of any happiness that we can find in this life. Thanking Him in our circumstances is the last thing on our mind! Only after things return to a relative calm do we thank and praise God for bringing us back into a state of peace.

How wrong we are in our attitudes! If our faith is based on the wonderful things we get from God, then our faith is like a decaying house waiting for the catalyst that will tear it down. God is not the source of suffering because all good things come from God. Yet because of the fallen state of the world, which was the direct result of man's disobedience, suffering exists. God does not allow suffering into our lives because He is spiteful or gets some sadistic pleasure out of it. He allows it because suffering refines character. Just as how metal needs to be bent and twisted in order to create a beautiful finished product, so to must man give thanks in his trials knowing that His Heavenly Father loves him, is in control, and has allowed suffering to befall him in order to turn him into a beautiful person that will be a beacon of hope, love, and life in this dark world. If we go through suffering kicking and screaming and refusing to be molded by our Welder's hands, then we have missed out on a valuable time for growth in our faith and we end up hindering the good and perfect redemptive work that God has planned for our lives. Instead of wallowing in self-pity in the midst of our darkest hour and instead of forgetting God, let us give thanks to Him and let us use this opportunity to hold our Father's hand ever so tightly and seek to learn from Him and understand what He is trying to teach us; always keeping in mind that He has promised to preserve us and lead us into a beautiful future if we continue to hold onto Him.

May 29

SOWING AND REAPING

"Those who sow in tears will reap with songs of joy. He who goes out weeping, carrying seed to sow, will return with songs of joy, carrying sheaves with him." -Psalm 126:5-6 (NIV)

Sometimes, pursuing what is right and just is painful. Perhaps we have been confounded by the corruption and injustice in the world when we have tried to further the call of righteousness and truth. Or maybe, despite all our prayers and efforts, we spend much time in tears as we try to bring a friend or relative out of their destructive behaviors with little to no sign of success. While we as Christians are called to be lights in a dark world, we must confess it can be an awfully painful calling. It is no wonder that the Bible says that those who love much also suffer much.

Consider Christ for a moment. While He was conducting His ministry here on Earth, He had much to weep about. He loved His creation, loved His people. So much so that He personally came down to Earth so that He might save the world from its self-inflicted degeneration and tell us that there is hope for redemption if only we believe and place our trust in Him. Yet people refused to believe Him. It is no wonder then that Jesus, despite His loving efforts to reconcile all to Him, wept over Jerusalem when He encountered the stubbornness and hardness of heart in that city towards His message. While He heard the mocking voices of the crowds as He endured the agony of the cross, it would have pained Him to know that the people in the crowds were not aware that He was dying for them and their salvation from their sins; hence His cry "Father forgive them! For they do not know what they doing!" But he who sows in tears, reaps with songs of joy, and imagine the joy of the face of Christ when someone truly desires to be reconciled to Him by accepting His redemptive sacrifice. The tears and the pain would have been worth it! Likewise, when we grieve that the cause of redemption, purity, and truth, is not being fulfilled, we should persevere through the tears and continue to be faithful to God; asking Him for the strength and wisdom to carry on. With the strength and peace that only God can give, we can then look forward to the hope of singing songs of joy when all will be restored.

May 30

TOUNGE-TIED?

"Ah, Sovereign Lord," I said, "I do not know how to speak; I am only a child." But the Lord said to me, "Do not say, 'I am only a child.' You must go to everyone I send you to and say whatever I command you. Do not be afraid of them, for I am with you and will rescue you," declares the Lord. Then the Lord reached out his hand and touched my mouth and said to me, "Now, I have put my words in your mouth." -Jeremiah 1:6-9 (NIV)

Saying and doing the right thing is often hard for us as humans. Even when we want to comfort with our actions or our words, in hopes that it would help the other person, it sometimes manifests itself in the wrong way and the intended recipient of our sentiments leaves more wounded than uplifted. At other times, when we really need to stand up and speak what is true and right, we become tongue-tied and intimidated by people who seem to be more powerful than us and could easily dismiss anything of the truth. It would seem that if we aren't saying negative things, however well-intentioned, we aren't saying anything at all when it really counts!

The prophet Jeremiah, like Moses centuries before him, also had speech troubles. It is interesting that Jeremiah refers to himself as a child when it comes to this area. If anyone has been around children, they would know that a child often says nonsensical things when expressing himself. This is why children have to be taught by their parents and teachers to speak well and eloquently. Likewise, as His children, God instructs us on how to use our tongues. Moses and Jeremiah never spoke the way they did because of their own abilities. It is clear that they had no ability to do so. But because they walked closely with God and wanted to be taught by Him, God took control of their tongues and enabled them to speak boldly before kings and accomplish great things for His glory. When we feel that our words will be inadequate or feel too intimidated by those around us to speak up, we should ask God for the wisdom and strength to say what is right and He will guide our words in such a way as to fulfill His pure, just, and perfect will. Like children who try to imitate the speech of their parents, our goal is to speak like our Heavenly Father. In our own limited capacity we cannot do it. But with Christ's enabling and His constant refining as a result of His redemptive work in our lives, we can speak with boldness and discernment in any situation. At times, the words which Christ speaks through us may not necessarily be popular with the crowd. But Christ can only speak for justice, truth, and redemption in a fallen world, and because He is the preserver and protector of all these things, He will safeguard the speaker of these things as well.

May 31

OUR ETERNAL GOD

"Jesus Christ is the same yesterday and today and forever." - Hebrews 13:8 (ESV)

Human feelings are often unpredictable and the human heart is often whimsical. One day we may choose to act in kindness and generosity because we feel like it. However, because of circumstances along the way, we could refuse to keep acting in such a manner because we are not in the mood to do so; choosing instead to act in coldness and selfishness towards others. We react to the world around us and, because this world and everything in it is never constant and always fleeting, our feelings are subject to change as well. That is why the cliché to "follow your heart", or to "do what your heart tells you", is a lie. Following one's heart, without Christ residing in it, often leads one to making foolish and destructive decisions because such decisions are based on human feelings which often change and act contrary to one another.

Thankfully, God is not human. It would be terrible and brutal world if He was. Consider the promise He made before Noah to never flood the Earth again in the manner He had done in order to purge sin from His creation. Yet, humanity has continued to insult and grieve God because of their persistence in continuing in their depravity. In my own human understanding, I would have broken my promise and have the Earth flooded all over again so that they would pay for their insolence. But thankfully, God is not human. He always upholds His promises, evident in the fact that the world hasn't been visited again by the calamity that struck the Earth in Noah's time. We as humans can also rest in the assurance that God's love is eternal. Despite our failings and our constant grieving of His spirit, He stays by us, loves us, and works for the sanctification of His children and the world's redemption. God's love never tires when humanity seems to mock and spit on Him, He never throws His hands up in the air and says "I give up!" when it becomes hard to love the unlovable, as we might be when faced with similar circumstances. In a fluid and ever-changing world, how wonderful it is indeed to have your trust placed in a God who never changes. Who remains, and continues to remain, loving, gracious, and just in all His dealings towards His creation.

June 1

TRUE OR FALSE?

"What is truth?'" Pilate asked." -John 18:38 (NIV)

It has been humanity's constant question. In a world full of deceptions and intrigues people have often wondered, just what exactly is truth? Interestingly enough, we know what constitutes as truth more than we give ourselves credit for. We know that the world we live in is not perfect and that we were not meant to live under such imperfect conditions; refusing to accept that evil and oppression were truths that were intended from the start to govern the world. Every human society in history has had a hatred for injustice and tyranny, a loathing for corruption and vice, a high regard for honesty and integrity, and a love for freedom and love itself. Instinctively we know what constitutes as right and what is deemed as wrong. That is why most belief systems and philosophies share a similar view on what consists as righteousness and what is considered sin.

However, because our fallen nature has corrupted and blinded us, we don't know who to attribute these truths to; attributing them instead to man-made belief systems and philosophies. The subsequent problem is that any human invention in these fields either warps the truth or preserves the truth but offers no adequate way to grasp it. So how are we able to understand and take hold of the truth? Jesus Himself stated "I am the Way, the Truth, and the Life". He is the personification of the truth that we all know deep inside our souls. Yet He proves that humanity can never fully realize or grasp the complete truth unless we allow Him to remove the wool of sin that has been pulled over our eyes. Only when we have done that and by doing so allow Him to work in our hearts, can we understand the truth; what the world and humanity was intended to be and how to return back to our intended nature and purpose in life. Truth is absolute. Although some answers - according to C.S Lewis - are "much nearer being right than others," absolute truth, just as in mathematics, can only have "...one right answer to the sum."

June 2

OUR FLASHLIGHT

"Your word is a lamp to my feet and a light to my path." -Psalm 119:105 (ESV)

Humanity has always looked for guidance. Life has often proven itself to be too overwhelming, too complex, and too chaotic for one to navigate its treacherous waters without some sort of counsel or road-map. However, the trouble is that we often find ourselves looking for wisdom in all the wrong places. It's like trying to find a flashlight in a dark room. As we grope in the dark desperately trying to find one, we grab hold of an object thinking that we have found what we are looking for. Judging by the way it feels when we wrap it around our fingers, it certainly feels like the flashlight we need. However, as we attempt to thumb for the button that will bring light into the dark room, we find that it is not a flashlight, but a slender bottle or a hairbrush. Likewise, we blindly grab hold of inadequate philosophies, deceptive superstitions, and flawed belief systems, thinking that it will be a perfect guide but only to be disappointed when it does not appear to be the ideal guide that we hoped it would be.

If we seem to be always grabbing the bottle or the hairbrush, who then is our flashlight? The Word of God, who became flesh in the form of Jesus, is the perfect source of light to illuminate our way as we traverse life. When we read the Word of God, we are reading the heart and mind of God Himself. He, who was there before time began, who created the universe, who was present during the fall of man, and who works for the redemption of His creation, knows all and knows how to deal with human nature and the storms of life far better than ourselves or any contrived philosophy could ever attempt do. The beauty of the Word of God is that it is brutally honest about the nature of man and life itself. If one were to truly read the Word of God with an open heart and mind, he would find that its words in this area strike an unpleasant chord, but one that certainly rings true nevertheless. Yet it offers hope in and through Christ that man can be saved from his own destruction and will be guaranteed a flawless guide to help him as he tries to sort through the chaos of life and find his purpose and meaning in his existence. The lantern is there, waiting to provide light, but we must be the ones to grab hold of it if we want to seek its aid in helping us find our way.

June 3

TO HAVE FEET OF A DEER

"The Sovereign Lord is my strength; he makes my feet like the feet of a deer, he enables me to go on the heights." -Habakkuk 3:19 (NIV)

Have you ever seen a deer run? It's a beautiful sight! There is something about the way its legs pump into the air and land back as it dashes through the woods that is truly inspiring. You would think that the thick foliage of the forest would obstruct the deer's path. But on the contrary it seems to traverse them all with remarkable poise and grace. How about a goat? Different animals with different personalities yes, but I have seen goats in India easily climb hills that no human could even dare traverse without risking serious injury.

We can only ask God for strength if we are in a vibrant relationship with Him and have accepted His Lordship over our lives. We must acknowledge that without Him, we are but dust and are incapable of consistently doing anything of value on our own strength. Adam, the first man, was dust. It took a sovereign, all powerful, yet loving God to take the dust and mold it into a man that has the faculties to overcome anything and take on any challenge as long as they surrender those faculties back to its Giver. When we do things on our own strength, we may seem to succeed for a time. But eventually we cave in and reach our breaking point. When we draw upon God for strength and ask Him to take over, He will give us the nimble legs of a deer and the dexterous hooves of a goat; allowing us to triumph over any obstacle with such grace that people will stop and take notice. Often the best witness for Christ is how we react to challenges and how we deal with them. When others see His children and how they approach situations relying on their Savior and Provider, they will want to know what makes us tick and would thus present a wonderful opportunity to share the redemptive message of Christ. May we constantly rely on Christ to provide us with the strength we need so that we may ultimately bring glory and honor to Him.

June 4

WHO IS YOUR MASTER?

"Large crowds were travelling with Jesus, and turning to them he said: 'If anyone comes to me and does not hate his father and mother, his wife and children, his brothers and sisters—yes, even his own life—he cannot be my disciple.'" -Luke 14:25-26 (NIV)

It would seem odd for Jesus to say this. How could the same God who made it clear in the Ten Commandments to "Honor your father and mother", suddenly turn around and throw filial piety out the window? Is Christ telling us to backtalk to our parents, treat our siblings and relatives like garbage, and be living terrors to our spouses and children? Of course not! It would go against His desire for us to be witnesses for Him through our love and service to others. Families and marriage are gifts from God. How could He call for their destruction?

But like most of the gifts God has given us, we end up worshiping the gift and not the giver of that gift. How often do we place our families, our spouses, and our children on a pedestal higher than God Himself? We have placed them in a position in our lives that should be reserved only for God. Yet when we do this, our minds become clouded to the reality that the people whom we most love and cherish belong to the same human race which has proved is fallibility and sinful nature over and over again. True children of God know that only their Heavenly Father is worthy to be worshiped and adored. Thus, when those around us, and even ourselves for that matter, act contrary or in opposition to the cause of Christ and His plan for His people, our ears and mouths must yield to the voice of truth and righteousness. However, this voice can only be heard if we are in a living relationship with Jesus. No one can serve two masters and Jesus knew full well that the majority of the people in crowds who came to Him would eventually choose their earthly pleasures and comforts as their ultimate master. But may we be the faithful few who choose Christ and in doing so choose life eternal.

June 5

TALKING TO GOD

"And pray in the Spirit on all occasions with all kinds of prayers and requests." -Ephesians 6:18a (NIV)

What is prayer? So often we go through its motions that we lose sight of what it really is. Is it something we do at a specific time in a specific place? Is it a bunch of fancy words we string together before God? Sometimes if we allow the rhythms of prayer to dull our minds, coupled with the expectation of an immediate and favorable answer from God, we begin to feel as if our prayers are going to the wall and thus we feel that they are of no use.

Prayer is something that speaks volumes of our relationship with God. Often we see prayer as the coin we insert to get treats from a vending machine. Once we make a request to God through prayer, we fully expect Him to grant whatever we ask immediately and without fail. But that was not how God wanted His relationship to be with humanity. If God was our vending machine, then He would be our slave and not our Lord and Master. Sometimes we see prayer as our "get-out-of-jail-free" card. When we are in a tight bind it is only then do we remember to pray. But once we are out of the fire, we forget to kneel before God until the next time when trials come our way. What then is prayer supposed to be? Since the Spirit of God has restored us and continues to indwell in us and work in our lives, prayer is supposed to be like talking with your best friend. When we are with our closest friends, we want to share everything with them; from our most trivial joys to our deepest sorrows. Likewise, prayer should be viewed as a wonderful privilege to foster and grow our relationship with the Creator of the Universe, who wants to be our closest friend and enter into a relationship with us. What is even more wonderful is that though our closest friends may sometime be far apart, God is always here with us. He wants us to interact with Him and laugh with us in our joys, weep with us in our despair, encourage us when we are hurt and, if we allow Him to, give us sound advice when we try to pick up the pieces of our broken lives. Prayer isn't something that should be just limited to a set of actions done in a designated place at a predetermined time. It should be something that transcends such limitations, which manifests itself not only externally but internally as well, and becomes a part of every moment of our waking existence; from time we rise to the moment we fall into slumber. If we have failed to spend time with our best friend, may we not lose haste to do so now.

June 6

GET UP AND RUN!

"Do you not know that in a race all the runners run, but only one gets the prize? Run in such a way as to get the prize. " -1 Corinthians 9:24 (NIV)

Laziness is a dangerous trap to fall into. We have all experienced it. There are days when we simply don't want to do anything. Even if we know that it would be in our best interest to act now and do what we need to do immediately, we procrastinate anyway. In an effort to justify our sloth, we say to ourselves, "We have time" or "We are ahead of schedule so we can relax a bit." But laziness is a thief which steals our energy and time. In a blink of an eye, our allowance of indolence leaves us in a quandary that we find extremely difficult to reverse.

It can be same with the Christian life as well. When we become lazy in our walk with God, we end up depriving ourselves of victory in our lives. When we whine and complain about our relationship with God being mundane and routine with Him not doing much, why don't we look at ourselves? Christ cannot do His redemptive work when our hearts are not willing to be molded by Him. A living relationship with Christ, like any other healthy relationship, is never one way. We must be as willing to maintain our relationship with Him and spend time in His presence much as He is willing to do so with us. In addition, when we are lazy, we miss out on opportunities to be positive witnesses for Christ. How often do we hesitate when it comes to sharing our faith with others? We think that we have all the time in the world to share Christ with others. But the truth is that because we have told ourselves this, we never get around to actually witnessing to others. Eventually, what ends up happening is that before we find the courage and diligence to share the wonderful message of Jesus, it is already too late for our intended friend to hear it. Paul was accurate in comparing the life for the Christian with a race. A good athlete trains for the event and never gives into sloth, whether it is in his training or during the main event itself. He is focused on the prize and runs to win it. Likewise we must actively pursue excellence in everything we do; remembering full well that we are representatives of Christ and that our actions reflect Him and His character.

June 7

DISCARDING OUR OLD NATURE

> *"Therefore put away all filthiness and rampant wickedness and receive with meekness the implanted word, which is able to save your souls." -James 1:21 (ESV)*

Why do we sin? Part of it is nature; it is in our blood to do so. As a result of Adam and Eve's disobedience, we are born into the world with a nature that is more inclined to sin. But part of it is also choice. When we were created, God gave us the beautiful gift of free will. He did not want pre-programmed robots to love and serve Him, but He wanted man to love Him because we choose to, not because we are forced to do so. Yet as with every beautiful gift God has given us we, through our own folly, have corrupted that which was supposed to be pure. Sin makes us feel powerful. It fuels our pride, our desire for total autonomy, and places us higher than anything and anyone. When we sin, we cloud our minds to the reality that we are answerable to someone higher than ourselves and instead we think of ourselves as all-powerful and infallible kings.

But are we really? How ironic is it that the very thing that gives us a false sense of freedom and sovereignty over our lives, is the very thing that ensnares us in a mire of bondage and oppression. Sin creates an illusion of happiness, contentment, and liberty. It is a tragedy when we in our own limited human understanding fall prey to these illusions only to find later that we have been deceived and the sinful life we previously idolized has chained us in despair and defeat. How then do we break the shackles of sin in our lives? It begins with a confession. There is no such thing as a prideful confession. A confession means to discard our pride and humble ourselves before God; admitting to Him that we have made mistakes that we cannot reverse on our own and can only be resolved through Christ entering and working in our lives. Due to His sacrifice on the cross, Christ died for the sins of all of humanity in every age and resurrected from the dead to show that He has the final victory over sin and death. But like everything He gives us, we must accept it of our own free will. Christ stands at the door and knocks, but it is up to us to open it for Him. May we discard our sinful habits and with humility be willing to be reconciled to Him.

June 8

A TRUE FRIEND

"Better is open rebuke than hidden love. Faithful are the wounds of a friend; profuse are the kisses of an enemy." -Proverbs 27:5-6 (ESV)

How often do we see friends who are on the path to destruction, but never speak a word to them about it? We fear that if we confront them about the way their life is going, they will hate us and we would have lost years worth of friendship. That's why we are sometimes so hesitant to positively intervene in a friend's situation when we know that there is a potential for hurt on both sides. Fearing that we would rock the boat too much, we keep quiet and watch from the sidelines thinking it would be the best course of action.

But is that true friendship? Inaction, as an option when deciding what to do about a friend's situation, is just as bad as actively seeking his downfall. If we are not preventing our friends from clearly destroying themselves, we are helping them in their downward spiral through our silence. It is at times like these when we who model after Christ need to speak truth and life into those who are struggling. Jesus did the same. He did not sit idly enthroned in Heaven as His creation was slowly decaying. He intervened and came into the world to speak the truth about the state of humanity. Jesus never skirted around the issue that the reason why humanity is so warped is because of their sinful nature. Naturally this did not go over well with many who saw themselves as being decent human beings. But Jesus saw the truth and He saw that they were hurting even if they were not willing to admit it. He had to identify and address their problem to them so that He may provide a solution. This came in the form of His sacrifice in order to free us from our sinful state and be reconciled to God; thus giving us new life and renewed hope. Likewise we must quickly identify and address the root cause of our friend's destructive habits and tell them that such habits are wrong. But at the same time we must not heap condemnation just as Jesus did not; instead offering solutions as He will and letting them know that He has never left their side and never will. We must also let them know that Jesus will guide them on the right path if they allow Him. Just as how Christ suffered with us and continues to do so, we too, if we call ourselves His children, must suffer with our friends and not forsake them with our silence. They may not necessarily like our efforts at first. But by continuing to show the love of Christ while speaking His truth, they will grow to see Him and in the process see their lives completely transformed.

June 9

MEEKNESS EQUALS GREATNESS

"Blessed are the meek, for they will inherit the earth." -Matthew 5:5 (NIV)

It is an incredulous statement. How could the meek possibly lay claim to the world? Our conditioning at the hands of our fallen environment has labeled meek people as incompetent and ultimately weak because of their perceived timidity and compliance. In our eyes, power and greatness seems to only come to those who are assertive, who have no qualms about using unethical means and "realpolitik" to eliminate their rivals and obstacles in order to get what they want.

Our flawed human understanding has a misinformed view on what being meek exactly implies. It means being humble as opposed to prideful, respectful as opposed to arrogant, patient as opposed to irritable, and merciful as opposed to unforgiving. Human eyes may see these as qualities for the weak. But on the contrary, they are the true markers for strong leadership and greatness. The meek are assertive. By their stance, they assert themselves against the injustices and tyranny of those who lord their power over those who are under them. They refuse to accept that deception and heartless decision making must be treated as the principles which must form the basis of good governance and leadership. Often it is the case that the meek leaders are the ones which command the most love and respect. A leader who rises to the upper echelons of power through intrigue and bullying may be feared and wield extraordinary power, but they are rarely truly loved and respected. The leader who is adored is leader who serves the people, who empathize with them, and who truly cares for them and wants to see them advance out of despair and misery. This leader does not reach the height of power through underhanded means, but he reaches it with integrity knowing that he serves a far higher calling than personal glory. Christ Himself was and is the perfect example of what it means to be a meek leader. He served the people not to obtain glory for Himself, but knowing that everything He did was to be done unto the glory of His Heavenly father. When we work knowing that in our toil we are to serve Christ and His people, any sort of prideful ambition should dissipate from our minds. In our humility and service before God and before others, God will reward us with greater responsibilities as long as we obey His call to be faithful to Him in our service. He will replace the arrogant with the meek knowing that those who have adopted a meekness that only Christ can give will be stewards that will breathe life into a world strangled by darkness and corruption. The proud will fall, but the meek will always endure.

June 10

BEING AT PEACE

"The fruit of righteousness will be peace; the effect of righteousness will be quietness and confidence forever." -Isaiah 32:17 (NIV)

Why should we pursue integrity? Why should we live uprightly in this world? When it seems that everywhere we look a sinful lifestyle reaps benefits in the here and now, we often wonder why we even bother to do so. But if we believe that a life lived without a so-called "restrictive sense of morality" is free from anxiety and fulfilling, we are sadly mistaken. Consider for a moment the person who tells a lie to get out of a tough situation. He may be alleviated of any sort of immediate punishment, but his anxiety is added to because he has to continue to heap lies in order to maintain the ruse he has built for himself. Likewise with any sinful pattern, though it may seemingly pay today, it hurts tomorrow. It is no wonder that the Psalms speak of the woes of the wicked being many.

A life spent in the pursuit of righteousness and truth has a benefit that far surpasses any other peace. When people unfairly accuse us of wrongdoing, a life that has striven to cultivate integrity will be our strongest advocate. We will be secure knowing that with God as our witness, we are not guilty of the charges that have been so wrongfully lodged against us. Unless if we in our own folly have pursued vice and thus compromised our witness for Christ, no one will be able to accuse a truly virtuous man of partaking in evil without looking like a fool. Those who pursue righteousness are also respected and loved far more than the one who has gone down the path of wickedness. God has promised that He will preserve the righteous. But this righteousness is not one formed by human effort. We as humans, despite our hardest efforts, will only corrupt any attempt at living a righteous life because of our fallen nature. It is a righteousness that can only come through Christ working in our hearts and refining us into becoming children that reflect the qualities of our Father. Choose the path of righteousness and we will live in peace and harmony with God, ourselves, and with each other. Choose sin and we will be crushed by its weight and the anxieties that come with it.

June 11

JUST DO IT!

"Do not merely listen to the word, and so deceive yourselves. Do what it says." -James 1:22 (NIV)

When I went to Calcutta as part of a missions trip in the summer of 2008, I became acutely aware of the disparity I had between what I believed I could do and what I could actually do. Before I went, I could say with confidence that I could help the poor and the oppressed in perfect love and humility. But to my utter surprise, when I tried sharing my one bottle of water with a group of thirsty street children, I became indignant. How dare they attempt to yank the bottle out of my hand when I am graciously pouring water into their mouths? It was at that moment that God revealed to me that I really don't know how to serve and I needed Him to teach me how to do so. God had to break down a lot of pride that I harbored and He had to make me realize that if my position with the street children were reversed, I would have yanked the water bottle and hoarded it for myself just as violently.

Aren't we full of contradictions? Often we live our lives thinking that we would do what Christ says in a heartbeat. Defend the orphan and the widow? Sure! Love our enemies? Why not? Care for the poor? Of course! But when the moment comes to test our claims, we shrivel back. How many of us would say that we love our enemies only to foster malicious thoughts against someone that we know? How many of us say that we would actively serve the poor and needy around us with love only to avert our gaze from the homeless man lying on the street or to dismiss underprivileged inner-city youth as good-for-nothing thugs? If we truly hold to and believe in the teachings of Christ yet not show any outward application of our beliefs, then we have been merely listening to Christ and letting His teachings go in one ear and come out the other. Faith without works is dead and we need to make a conscious effort to attach actions to our faith. But right actions are determined by right thoughts, and who among us can truly control our thoughts in a way that would be pleasing to God? We need to constantly allow Christ to take captive of our thoughts so that our actions would line up with His perfect will to restore righteousness in us and in the world. How can we be of use to a hurting world when we do not act? Therefore it is imperative that we do, knowing that the engine which drives us to act for the furtherance of God's redemptive plan is Christ Himself.

June 12

REBUILDING WALLS

"Like a city whose walls are broken down is a man who lacks self-control." -Proverbs 25:28 (NIV)

We humans cannot control ourselves. Even if we may present an outward façade to the world showing off our supposed respectability and decorum, we know that there are things in our lives that make us lose the little self control we have. It could be anything from an innocuous binge on a favorite snack to more serious matters such as a fiery temper triggered by even the most trivial of offences. In either case, a lack of self-control destroys us and all the good things that we treasure. Whereas excess consumption of food may destroy one's health, uncontrolled rage can destroy cherished relationships and cause much anxiety and stress to ourselves. All the diet plans and anger management classes in the world can't seem to restrain us completely. Although we may keep our destructive desires at bay for a time, it often feels as if our defenses could give way at any moment to the beast that we so desperately want to keep locked up.

Self-control is perhaps one of the most important qualities we could ever ask for. It is like the wall that protects us from driving off a cliff and plunging to our deaths. With self-control, we gain discernment; to speak and act when we need to do so and to refrain when we must. This will save us from unnecessary shame and guilt, and will help us steer clear of pitfalls that can hinder us in our walk with God. But, self control cannot come from our own strength or willpower. If we are honest with ourselves, we can never say that we have kicked our sinful habits on our own because often, just when we think we have beat them, we regress and defeat the purpose of all our efforts. Paul writes in Galatians that self-control is the fruit of the Spirit. It's only when the Holy Spirit is working in our lives and is refining us into becoming better children and servants of God that we are able to manifest true self-control. This is because Christ deals with the root of a lack of self-control; the sinful desires that we harbor and which like acid deteriorate the walls of self-control that protect us. With those desires under the thumb of Christ, we can focus on rebuilding those walls in order to protect us from future attacks of the passions. No wall can be built single-handed. We need the assistance of the strong to help us in such a task. Likewise, we cannot rebuild the walls of self-control on our own strength, but relying on Christ who is able to restore and rebuild.

June 13

PERFECT TIMING

"For still the vision awaits its appointed time; it hastens to the end—it will not lie. If it seems slow, wait for it; it will surely come; it will not delay." -Habakkuk 2:3 (ESV)

Have you ever had to wait for something? Something that you have dreamed of for a very long time? Waiting for anything is hard enough as it is for us as humans. But it is even harder to wait and be patient when we know that our desires will be granted at some unspecified point. We are always anticipating that glorious day when our long harbored visions will be realized. However, in our impatience we tend to mistake opportunities and events that come our way as the hour we have been hoping for; only to be disappointed when we find out that it is not what it seemed. Then we wonder whether our dreams were ever meant to come true. Despair begins to creep in and defeatism clouds our world.

God has promised in His Word that as long as we abide in Him and walk closely with Him, He will grant us the desires of our hearts. If He has placed a vision in our hearts, He will make sure that they do not simply fade away and will actively work towards their realization. It may not be according to our timing, but it will come to pass according to His will. We may wonder why we must surrender our visions and dreams to Him. After all, they are ours. Don't they belong to us? Suppose we do make mistakes in pursuing our desires, don't those mistakes also belong to us and are there for us to learn from? But if our mistakes do not draw us closer to God in surrendering our deepest hopes to Him, we will continue to unnecessarily repeat those mistakes in our pursuit of those desires. It does not have to be like that. We can trust God with the particulars of how our dreams may be fulfilled because He sees the bigger picture and is not hindered by a fallen human understanding of how our plans must come to their fruition. When we trust in God's timing and allow Him to work things out, He will give us the desires of our heart and fulfill it in such a way that it will leave us awe-struck at His goodness and faithfulness. We will be amazed at how everything, even our mistakes, were used by God to see our desires granted in the wonderful way that they had been. The French author, Alexandre Dumas, wrote in his book "The Count of Monte Cristo" that, "Until the day when God shall deign to reveal the future to man, all human wisdom is contained in these two words: wait and hope." Our responsibility with regards to our dreams is to wait and hope in God; acknowledging that He knows what is best for our lives and trusting that His timing will never fail.

June 14

STAYING STILL

"Be still, and know that I am God;" -Psalm 46:10a (NIV)

We live in a fast-paced world. In an era where everything seems to be instant and convenient, we have become accustomed to our requests being granted immediately. However, in exchange we have lost the ability to be still and patient. Our lives have become so hectic that what concerns us is what is in front of us now and nothing else. We say that we do not have the time to think about God or the world around us; that we should spend our energies watching our own back because that is our immediate concern. Maybe when things calm down then we'll start remembering God and the finer things of life. But that moment never comes and we only end up reinforcing unhealthy attitudes of self-reliance that serves to distance ourselves from God and contribute to our own ruin.

But it is in those hectic and busy moments that we need to hold onto God the most. Our frail human bodies cannot handle the pressure that we place ourselves under. God can help us, but because He has given us free will to act, we must make the conscious choice of being still before Him, knowing that He has the world in His hands. Being still before Him means meditating on Him and His Word, away from the distractions of life, communing with Him, and asking Him for the strength and guidance to carry on. We must acknowledge His authority over our lives if we are to free ourselves from the stresses that we create. When we have taken the time to be still before the One who controls the universe, we see our lives and our situations in a different light. Our priorities are arranged in a manner that would truly benefit us and we will have the wisdom and foresight to avoid the pitfalls that we would have otherwise fallen into in our impatience or in our own human understanding. Being still before Him is the key to living a full and satisfying life. May we all make sure to be still before Him and allow Him to direct our paths.

June 15

A PROMISE IS A PROMISE

"And now, O Lord God, you are God, and your words are true, and you have promised this good thing to your servant." -2 Samuel 7:28 (ESV)

In an age where words are thrown around loosely and where things are said but not meant, the weight and value of a promise has been lost. It used to mean that when one made a promise, they would do everything they could to make sure their promise would be fulfilled; regardless of any changes in their situation. But now promises are said more as niceties and formalities. At the first sight of inconvenience or hardship in keeping our promises we forget them and do what we please. We make up excuses saying that the world is full of trials so we don't want to add to our hardship by going through with a promise that seems difficult to keep.

However, promises are a powerful thing. When we promise something to someone, it brings its recipient a sense of hope, assurance, and comfort. When we break them, all of those emotions are immediately sucked out; leaving the other person hurt, used, and disillusioned. But where humans fail in keeping their promises, God is always faithful. He promises to never abandon or forsake us. The Psalms are filled with examples of God promising His children that they will be delivered from the evil that surrounds them and shows men who sing praises to God because He proved his faithfulness towards them. Perhaps one of the most powerful of His promises is found in Jeremiah 29:11, "'For I know the plans I have for you,' declares the Lord, 'plans to prosper you and not to harm you, plans to give you hope and a future.'" In this uncertain world where we are always wondering about what's around the river bend and if there are smooth waters after the storm, this promise in particular serves as an encouragement to all who hear it. God will never create life only to destroy it. He will work for the restoration of that life and guarantee that even through the hardship and chaos one goes through, His wonderful and perfect purposes will be fulfilled if we allow Him to work in our lives. God will never let us down because He is the manifestation of truth and faithfulness. Thus, it is in His nature to be these things. But since God is always faithful in His promises to us, we should also be faithful in our promises to others. As His children who have adopted the nature of Christ and whose actions reflect upon our Father, may we be sincere in what we say to others and always keep our promises to the end.

June 16

GETTING A NEW HEART

"Thus says the Lord of hosts, 'Render true judgments, show kindness and mercy to one another, do not oppress the widow, the fatherless, the sojourner, or the poor, and let none of you devise evil against another in your heart.'" -Zechariah 7:9-10 (ESV)

It begins with the heart. Out of our hearts, our actions flow. When we see oppression, injustice, deceit, and wanton cruelty in the world it is easy to condemn the perpetrator of such acts as diabolical and purely evil in every fiber of his being. But is the problem with the person or with the heart? God does not create imperfect people. It would go against His nature as a perfect Creator. The real problem is with a heart that has been tainted by the reality of living in a fallen world. The oppressor must have his heart cleansed from his sinful nature and have a spiritual liberation just as much as the oppressed needs both a spiritual and physical liberation. We must acknowledge that we all have the same fallen heart and thus we are all prone to become tyrants and deceivers.

What then is the remedy for a fallen heart? It is but one simple word. Jesus. Only He is able to cleanse the heart and purge it of all sin. We simply cannot because sin is a major problem that we are too small to handle. No matter how hard we may try to purge ourselves of wickedness, it will never work because our hearts, without Christ residing in them, will only continue to persist in leaning towards evil and doing everything that is wrong in the eyes of the Lord. Our hearts without Christ want to be independent and free of any sort of outside control. By being so we allow ourselves to engage in all sorts of foul indulgences. These fallen hearts deceive us with a false sense of freedom and thus we become enslaved to sinful habits and patterns of behavior. Only through a breaking down of all the pride in our hearts that tells us that we are gods unto ourselves can we humbly submit to a God who grants us freedom from our fallen nature by obedience to Him. Only then can we render true judgments, show kindness and mercy, avoid becoming oppressors, and abstain from plotting evil in our hearts. May we continually ask God to purge our hearts of evil so that through Him we may be able to do good.

June 17

HAVING A SERVANT'S HEART

"So when you give to the needy, do not announce it with trumpets, as the hypocrites do in the synagogues and on the streets, to be honored by men. I tell you the truth, they have received their reward in full." - Matthew 6:2 (NIV)

Ulterior motives are hard to get around when we serve others out of our own benevolence. Our pride dictates that since we so graciously serve those around us, we are entitled to a bit of praise every now and then. But when we fail to get praise from others for our good works, our pride comes under attack and we become offended. Soon our service to others becomes not about contributing to the physical and spiritual betterment of the other person, but about making sure our egos continue to be inflated by the compliments that we hope to hear from people.

Such service becomes a corrupted effort in helping others. It's true that people are helped by the kind acts that we do, but in the end, God will be looking at our hearts and not our outward actions. If we have served others only for the benefit of ourselves and our egos while only pretending to be truly concerned about the cause of Christ and those we have served, our works are like filthy rags to our Savior. That is why Christ said that it is better to perform our good deeds in secret; away from the watching crowds, with God as our sole spectator, and away from being tempted by our own pride. But even doing our acts of kindness in secret can make us prideful and disparage others when they are in the limelight while serving others. May we not fall into this trap! Our goal in serving our fellow man is to bring glory to God and in bringing glory to God we must genuinely care about the needs of those we serve. Only with a God who is actively working in our hearts and breaking down the layers of pride that have been built around it, can we truly serve as He wants us to.

June 18

WITNESSING FOR CHRIST

"Whenever you are arrested and brought to trial, do not worry beforehand about what to say. Just say whatever is given you at the time, for it is not you speaking, but the Holy Spirit." -Mark 13:11 (NIV)

I used to be enrolled in a Toastmasters class in order to improve my public speaking skills. As part of the activities that we would participate in, we were asked to pick a random topic out of a hat and speak on it for about two to four minutes. Sometimes you would know something about the topic you have picked, but most of the time you wouldn't know anything at all. I remember when I used to get a topic that I had little knowledge about; it was hard to speak on it even for the short amount of time I was given. I was always worried if I was presenting myself clearly and hoping that I was not making myself look ignorant.

Often when we are put on the spot against our will by those who may view our faith in Christ with cynicism and confront us for our belief in Him, we may react in the same way. Our shock at the sudden nature of the circumstances we find ourselves in, coupled with our nervousness and anxiety in making sure we use the right words to present a bold witness for Christ, leaves us stammering and hoping that our "interrogation" will be over soon. After the pressure is off us, we question whether in that moment we were bold witness for Christ at all.

It is true that we must be prepared to answer opposition and tell them of the life-changing power of Christ. We prepare ourselves for this inevitability by spending time in God's Word and meditating on what He has done in our lives. Yet sometimes, in our moments of weakness, we feel as if we have failed to be the witnesses for Christ that we are called to be; resulting in anxiety overwhelming us. Thankfully we don't have to go through this anxiety. If we allow Christ to speak through us, asking Him to guide our words and control our thoughts, automatically He will give us the words to say and how to say them. When we rely on our own strength to be witnesses for Christ, we will stumble because it was not of our own effort that we were saved from sin. Since we were freed solely because of Christ's sacrifice and Him coming to reside in our hearts, He is the only one who can speak of the redemptive work in our lives and spread His message. All that Christ asks is that we have an open heart for Him to use and to speak to others about His plan for all His creation. The result will surprise us when we have allowed God to speak through us and all we will be able to do is to praise Him. Our words are not to bring glory to ourselves or to our own abilities in living the Christian life, but it should reveal to others that there is a transcendent and powerful God who loves humanity so much that He is actively seeking to restore humanity from its degradation.

June 19

WHO IS TO BLAME?

"Let no one say when he is tempted, 'I am being tempted by God,' for God cannot be tempted with evil, and he himself tempts no one. But each person is tempted when he is lured and enticed by his own desire." - James 1:13-14 (ESV)

We humans love to put the blame on others. If by putting the blame on someone else we can avoid taking responsibility for our own actions, we would do it in a heartbeat. After all, taking responsibility for our deeds means accepting that we have failed in some way and that we must face the consequences, something that infringes on both our pride and our comfort levels. It is no wonder that Adam, when God confronted him about his disobedience, automatically blamed Eve for leading him astray. Adam wanted to have the pressure off himself and be spared from any sort of punishment or feelings of guilt and shame.

Aren't we quick to blame God for our failings and shortcomings? We shake our fists angrily to the sky saying, "I'm in the mess I'm in because of God!" But is God really the culprit of our misfortune? When we have destroyed relationships and squandered the wealth that God has given us because of the poor choices we have made, it is not right to turn around and blame God for actively seeking our destruction. God, because He is the source of all that is good and pure, cannot by His nature seek to act with malicious intent towards His creation. He has given us free will to act because He wants people to make the right choice to follow His ways not because we have to, but because we want to. Therefore when we are lead into temptation and fall into sin, we have only ourselves to blame for being the architects of our own destruction because we have deliberately chosen the wrong path when we knew what was right and pure. True children of God know when they have been in the wrong and realize their need to ask for forgiveness and accept the consequences of their wrong actions if that was the root cause of their despair. But the beauty of Christ is that He will give us the strength to deal with those consequences if our hearts are open to Him. It is a process of making sure that we learn from our mistakes so that we may not repeat them again and be refined more and more into the image we bear as His children.

June 20

REJOICE IN EVERYTHING!

"Rejoice in the Lord always. I will say it again: Rejoice!" - *Philippians 4:4 (NIV)*

It is a universal human trait to seek happiness and to find reasons to celebrate. When we have reason to do so, we love to express our delight and jubilation in a variety of colorful and vibrant ways. But how can we even think about rejoicing in times where there seems to be no cause for merriment? When tragedy comes our way, when struggles become too overwhelming to bear, it is as if all our joy has been sucked away; leaving us desolate and mournful. We long for those days when happiness filled our hearts. Yet no matter how hard we try to reclaim the joy that was lost, sorrow continues to choke us as darkness clouds our days.

What does it mean to rejoice in the Lord? It means acknowledging who God is in relation to our present suffering. Trials and tribulations were things that humans were not meant to handle on their own because we were created for a perfect world free from these things. Suffering was not part of God's original plan for His creation, and yet because of sin's entry into the world as a result of man's disobedience, it has tainted every aspect of life. But God is bigger than our sufferings for He is Lord of the Universe and continues to hold the world in His hands; using whatever evil that befalls the world to turn it around for good. It means leaning on God's promise to never leave or forsake us in our darkest hour. He is there with us in our times of despair; comforting us and reminding us of His plan to see us restored if we continue to follow Him. God's plans for us are not to harm us, but to give us hope and a bright future. We can trust Him in this knowing that He never breaks His word. If we try to look for joy and peace in ourselves it will never happen because our own human limitations and senses can only focus on the present. That is why we see our sufferings as never ending. But by standing on God's promises and seeking Him as our only source of solace and comfort, we will realize that our sufferings are only temporary in relation to His eternity. The joy of the Lord is our strength. With a joy that only God could give, we can rejoice in any situation knowing that God is taking care of us.

June 21

BEING LIVING TEMPLES

"Don't you know that you yourselves are God's temple and that God's Spirit lives in you?" -1 Corinthians 3:16 (NIV)

There is something sublime about old cathedrals. Whenever I enter one, I am always reminded of whose presence I am entering into and what my position is in relation to Him. I am going before a holy and righteous God who loves justice and hates sin. The only reason why I stand before Him is not because of any merit I have gained on my own to earn the right to be in His presence, but of my acceptance of the fact that I need Christ to continue to work in my life and free myself from my sinful nature. The idea behind an impressive cathedral was to remind people that they were entering before the presence of a holy God and to make themselves humble before Him. It is true that Christ is our Friend, but it is equally true that He is the Lord and Master of our lives who requires that we obey Him if we truly want to be free from the consequences of wrong choices. But we do not need to go into a cathedral to be reminded of this fact. The church is not a building, but it is in the hearts of those who have allowed Christ to take permanent residency.

Since we bear God's Spirit, we need to actively seek to sanctify our hearts in order to make it a home fitting for the holy and righteous nature of the Spirit that has taken command over the center of our lives. This means making a lot of tough decisions that will place oneself at odds with our old sinful nature. Inappropriate thoughts and words, destructive addictions and habits, all of these are outward manifestations of issues that need to be addressed and dealt with in order to make ourselves worthy of being God's living temple. But we cannot sanctify ourselves on our own. If we could, what would be the necessity of God coming down to Earth? We need to constantly swallow our pride and humble ourselves before God so that He may continue His redemptive mission in our lives. As our Father, He is always there to help His children in their struggles and gently prod them towards the path of life and true happiness. May we continue to ask God to help us clean our hearts and be careful of what we let into them. The source of all actions is our hearts, and we must take great care in making sure our hearts are pure so that Christ and who He is may be reflected when we come into contact with others.

June 22

NEVER ALONE

"I will not leave you as orphans; I will come to you." -John 14:18 (ESV)

Have you ever met an orphan? In the major urban areas of India such as Bombay and Calcutta, there are many. I have met several orphans and have heard their stories. If they weren't left destitute after the death of their parents, they flee their homes because they are unwanted and abused by their families. They turn to life on the streets in hopes that they would secure a stable and comfortable future. But when you are a pre-teen child from India's underdeveloped countryside coming to the cities to seek opportunity, there is only so much you can do. With a yearly salary picking up garbage for collectors that pales in comparison to what a person in the developed world makes in a week, every day for them is a fight for survival. Food is expensive and hard to come by for orphaned street children. Often the children are brutalized by the police. What is especially tragic is that they have to deal with their every-day struggles alone; with no mother or father to care for them, support them, protect them, and love them.

Loneliness is painful and it affects everyone. Even if we are surrounded by people and with all the privileges this world can offer, we can still feel as if life is an uphill struggle and we have to deal with the struggles that come along our path on our own. But Christ guarantees that He will never leave or forsake those who come to Him wanting to be adopted into His family. Christ is the Good Shepherd and a good shepherd takes care of his sheep as if they were his own children. This means always watching over them, protecting them, and actively seeking to bring guidance and comfort to a sheep that is lost and scared. When we have a Heavenly Father who cares for us in this manner as His children, we are filled with a sense of hope and promise. Christ gives us the comforting reality that we never go through life on our own, but that He is always keeping us in His hands. If we call upon Him, He will always be there to help us and console us through our trials; promising that if we continue to walk with Him, we will have a glorious future awaiting us. In Christ we find our solace and our sense of worth. In Him we find our confidence and strength. He is our ever present Father and Friend. With Him we are never alone and we will be able to find joy and peace in any situation.

June 23

STAYING STRONG

"Consider him who endured from sinners such hostility against himself, so that you may not grow weary or fainthearted." -Hebrews 12:3 (ESV)

The Christian life is not for the faint of heart. Although our Christ-guided lifestyle may earn the respect and admiration of some, it will be a subject of scorn for others. Christians throughout history have been persecuted by people who live lifestyles that are antithetical to the righteousness, integrity, and purity that Christ calls His children to follow with His help. It offends some who believe that Christianity stands against their culture and everything they hold dear. When such people come and try to crush our faith, we may be able to successfully resist their attempts. But we must confess that it is disheartening to see so much opposition to something that we know will save them and the rest of the world from destroying itself.

As children of Christ, we often feel entitled to be loved by everyone. The truth of the matter is that as long as humans continue to bow down to sin and its false promises of freedom, we will be hated for the stance we have taken to choose Christ and His righteousness. We need to accept that we will not be loved by all and that we cannot force anyone to love and accept us. If we do, we risk the prospect of propelling others further away from Christ.

However, before we sink into despair over the fact that we will not be loved by everyone, we must remember that our Savior was hated and mocked as well. Despite His efforts to bring people out of their depravity and reconcile man with God, He was spat on, flogged, and suffered the humiliating death of being nailed to a cross. Yet how did He deal with opposition? By dusting the sandals of His feet and praying for them. This should be our response too. Our faith is not determined by what others think of us, but it is determined by who Christ is and what He has done for us and the world. We shouldn't let opposition get us down knowing that though Christ Himself faced the same, it did not stop Him in redemptive mission. Our Savior, who knew what it was like to be rejected, will be our comfort and strength through those times when we feel alone and hated. We are loved by the Creator of the universe as His own children. In Him, who is the final authority on everything in this world, we find our sense of worth and identity. He will give us the confidence and boldness to continue to witness for Him through all opposition while remembering that we do not save people from themselves. Christ is the one that saves and our detractors need to come to Him of their own free will and in accordance with God's timing and purpose for their lives.

June 24

SOLDIERS OF SALT

"You are the salt of the earth. But if the salt loses its saltiness, how can it be made salty again? It is no longer good for anything, except to be thrown out and trampled by men." -Matthew 5:13 (NIV)

I am a huge military buff. When I was in high school, I briefly entertained the thought of joining the Canadian Armed Forces. To this end, I decided to enroll myself in Royal Canadian Air Cadets; a youth program administered by the Canadian military. Although members are not obliged to join the military, I had gotten a taste of what life would be like if I did. Everything, from drill movements to weapons training, had to be done precisely and in accordance with regulations. The continual repetition of these procedures may seem tedious, but they are there to build discipline. It is a proven fact that any army which fails to keep itself disciplined, organized, and ready for combat, will falter at the first sight of the enemy.

As children of God we have been called to battle. This battle is not against flesh and blood however, but against the forces of evil which continue to poison the world. This struggle is not for the faint of heart. Know that if we ever deviate from the path of Christ even for a moment, wickedness will slowly infiltrate our hearts and sin will walk all over us. If we truly want to succeed in this battle, we have to make it a practice to spend time with God and meditate on His Word. When we do this with an open heart, God will strengthen us for the challenges we face. He will help us maintain our "saltiness" so that we will be able to act as a force by which God can preserve and redeem the world from evil. Salt fights against bacteria which causes meat to rot. May we ask God to preserve our saltiness so that the world will not fall into decay.

June 25

KEEPING IT COOL

"It is to a man's honor to avoid strife, but every fool is quick to quarrel." -Proverbs 20:3 (NIV)

Most of us have either been involved in or picked a quarrel with another person at some point in our lives. Often times, our quarrels are not even about serious things. Even the most trivial of matters are enough to start an argument that could easily spin out of control. Imagine how our relationships would be if we didn't bicker over minuscule things. It would certainly be more peaceful that's for sure. Yet our pride demands that we should always prove ourselves to be right, regardless of the situation. We do not want to admit when we are wrong because that makes us look deficient and weak. In our stubbornness, we sow the seeds of discord when we squabble. This can cause serious emotional and physical damage not only to ourselves, but to the people around us.

Ironically, our pursuit to vindicate ourselves in our quarrels ends up making ourselves look like utter fools. When others see our arrogance in our disagreements with people over insignificant matters, they shake their heads in dismay. Irritability and short-temperedness stem from pride, and pride should have no place in the hearts of those who claim to follow Christ. When He invades our lives, we stay close to Him and we gain the wisdom to know what battles to fight. Our anger should be saved for the things that anger Him; things such as the presence of injustice and sin in the world. There are times when the stance we take as followers of Him will invite strife, and in these moments we must remember to be firm but not hot-headed. Subsequently, we ourselves must not actively look to pick fights. Strife should come to us because of the nature of Christ's message to the world, not because we have provoked conflict through our own behavior. May we continually submit ourselves to Him and may His serenity and peace manifest itself in us so that we may be able to present Christ as the perfect refuge of those trying to escape turmoil.

June 26

ASSURED PROTECTION

"Now Daniel so distinguished himself among the administrators and the satraps by his exceptional qualities that the king planned to set him over the whole kingdom. At this, the administrators and the satraps tried to find grounds for charges against Daniel in his conduct of government affairs, but they were unable to do so. They could find no corruption in him, because he was trustworthy and neither corrupt nor negligent. Finally these men said, 'We will never find any basis for charges against this man Daniel unless it has something to do with the law of his God.'" -Daniel 6:3-5 (NIV)

Jealousy and rancor are some of man's greatest faults. Sometimes, instead of genuinely feeling pleased for someone else's success and wanting to offer our congratulations, we are often overcome with envy. Our pride feels that it should be us up there in the spotlight winning the admiration by everyone around us. This desire to fuel our egos drives us to resort to underhanded and destructive means to see our needs for fame and prestige met. We have also been on the receiving end of such schemes. Just the effort that they make to ruin all our accomplishments and hopes hurts doesn't it? What have we done to offend our assailants? Like a python that coils around its prey, we feel as if we are being suffocated by all the attempts to tear us down.

The best and surest defense against such opposition is to walk evermore closely with God. He has promised in His word to preserve those that follow after Him. Only by actively seeking to conform to Christ's likeness and being in complete dependence on Him in this pursuit, will we see His righteousness and purity shining through us. When people see Christ reflected in us, they may not necessarily like what they see and will try their hardest to find something in us that they can exploit for their own benefit. But if our hearts and our subsequent actions are radiating the likeness of Christ, our adversaries' attempts to derail us will be thwarted because they cannot fight against a God who is the embodiment of truth and virtue working in our lives. Like Daniel's detractors, they will be left to conclude that it will be impossible to find fault in us without looking corrupt and deceitful. When we feel attacked from all sides, take courage, for God protects those who acknowledge Him and His Son. We will be able to walk confidently knowing that though our critics may bear their fangs and hiss, they will never be able to bite if we walk alongside our Lord.

June 27

FOLLOWING CHRIST

"After this, Jesus went out and saw a tax collector by the name of Levi sitting at his tax booth. 'Follow me,' Jesus said to him, and Levi got up, left everything and followed him." -Luke 5:27-28 (NIV)

For a man of his time, Levi had found himself in a relatively good position. As a tax collector for the Roman Empire, he found himself far better off than his fellow countrymen in impoverished Judea. Not only was he employed by arguably the most powerful empire of the day, but he had the power to deceitfully demand "additional taxes" from the people as long as he had given the amount that was due to Rome. Naturally, the Jews would have viewed Levi as a crook and a traitor exploiting his own people. But this wouldn't have bothered him too much. After all, he had money.

So why did he suddenly abandon everything when Jesus told Levi to follow Him? There is something about Christ that pierces the depth of our hearts. When we see who He is through His example and the reading of His Word, we become aware of our own fallibility. All the false promises and comforts of sin are cast aside until all that we see of ourselves is our own depravity. We can either continue to live our lives in denial of this reality or we can accept that this is something which needs a remedy far greater than man himself. When we have opened our hearts to the redemptive work of Christ, we will want to whole-heartedly follow Him because He has made us see the folly of our prior lifestyles and saved us from destroying ourselves. Of course, the remnants of our old sinful nature will try to bring us back into wickedness. But if we constantly surrender every area of our lives to Christ and actively seek to conform ourselves to Him, He promises victory over those desires which threaten to harm us. What are we holding back that prevents us from following Christ to the fullest? May we continue to submit everything we have to Him knowing that He will take us on a beautiful journey that, although not without sorrow, will be filled with an unshakable sense of joy, hope and fulfillment.

June 28

NOTHING IS IMPOSSIBLE

"Jesus looked at them and said, 'With man this is impossible, but with God all things are possible.'" -Matthew 19:26 (NIV)

When I was a child, my grandmother used to tell me stories of the famous French general Napoleon. For me it sparked not only a lifelong interest in the history of modern Europe, but also a broader interest in the histories of the world. His personal life and the crimes that he committed in his conquest of Europe aside, Napoleon's ambition never ceases to impress me. My grandmother always used to repeat one of his most well-known quotations to me; "'Can't' is in the dictionary of fools." This quote of his has always inspired me to take courage when I encounter struggles and always see them as something that can be overcome.

Often when we face trials and obstacles that come along our path, it seems that despite all our efforts to rise above them, our circumstances continue to knock us down. We descend into hopelessness; thinking that these struggles will never leave us and any attempt to challenge them will prove to be futile. But how can we say that when we worship and have placed our hope in a God who is all powerful and all knowing? It would seem foolish to deem our situations as impossible to overcome given what we know of Him and His power. Yet despite this, God understands that we are but dust and that our finite minds can only grasp our present realities. In His love He promises to encourage us and strengthen us in our trials if we allow Him to do so. When we lean on Christ, we will see our circumstances in a different light. We will see them as times that can not only be triumphed over when we have relied on God's strength and wisdom, but also times of growth where our hearts will be further molded to conform to Him and who He has called us to be as His children. May we acknowledge God's supremacy over our situations and allow Him to carry us to victory!

June 29

ALWAYS ON OUR MIND

"Fix these words of mine in your hearts and minds; tie them as symbols on your hands and bind them on your foreheads." -Deuteronomy 11:18 (NIV)

What does it mean to tie the word of God on our hands and on our foreheads? In some traditional Jewish circles, this command is taken quite literally. Called *tefillin*, tiny leather boxes containing portions of Scripture are strapped to the head and arms of those who want a physical reminder to keep the Word of God always at the forefront of their minds. But as we have seen with many of God's commandments to His people, physically tying His Word to our bodies is not necessarily what He is getting at. He is a God concerned more about the hearts of His children than by displays of piety. Outward manifestations of obedience cannot change the heart. True transformation must come from the inside out.

When we have accepted Christ's redemptive sacrifice on the cross and allowed Him to conduct His transformative work in our hearts, automatically we will have a thirst to know the things of God. We want to know what the Word of God says and because we often forget, we make it a habit to dwell upon God's Word frequently through actively reading and meditating on it; asking God to help us grasp what He wants us to hear. Thus, God's Word is always on our minds and we will be prepared to respond in every-day situations according to His teachings and expectations for His children. Our hands, through God's guidance and His enabling in our lives, will fulfill what He has laid out in His Word through the actions that we perform in service to others. Tying the words of God to our heads and hands means to dwell continuously on the Word of God and live out our faith in accordance with what Christ has prescribed. May we do so drawing upon our Savior for strength and wisdom.

June 30

INSEPERABLE LOVE

"Who shall separate us from the love of Christ? Shall trouble or hardship or persecution or famine or nakedness or danger or sword? ... I am convinced that neither death nor life, neither angels nor demons, neither the present nor the future, nor any powers, neither height nor depth, nor anything else in all creation, will be able to separate us from the love of God that is in Christ Jesus our Lord." -Romans 8:35, 38-39 (NIV)

Love is a beautiful thing. It comforts us in our darkest hour, invigorates us to do our best, and gives us a sense that life, despite its challenges and sorrows, is a wonderful adventure. When we know that we are loved by someone for who we are, it can completely transform our outlook on life. The problem is that because of our fallen world, love has been corrupted. As humans we are accustomed to conditional love; a love which is based on a certain criterion that we have to meet. Should we fail to meet the standard in order to be worthy of conditional love, then we are discarded and shunned. If humans can only experience such love, we are also only capable of providing such love. Human pride may claim that we can love without any strings attached, but the truth is that we all have a breaking point to our love. Even the slightest hint of resentment in our hearts will make us refrain from showing our affection towards the one who has offended us.

Who then is capable of unconditional love? To answer this question we must go to the source of all love. It says in the Bible that God is love. His love is perfect in that He is the only one capable of loving us as we are. In our wicked and sinful state, though sin separated us from God, He still loved us. So much so that He laid down His life for us so that we may be free from our depraved nature and be reconciled to Him. When we have accepted this love, absolutely nothing will be able to tear us away from God. Our sins cannot separate us from Christ's love anymore because the blood of Christ has cleansed us of our transgressions. It is hard for us humans, who have been conditioned to experience a love that has limits, to understand the kind of limitless love that only Christ can give. But Christ's love is true and we can always find solace in this fact when we feel that we are unlovable because of something we have done or because of who we inherently are. As children of God, we love others because Christ first loved us. Only by having a heart that has been transformed by Him can we truly practice unconditional love.

July 1

UNSHEATHING THE SWORD ON OUR SHADOW

"For the word of God is living and active. Sharper than any double-edged sword, it penetrates even to dividing soul and spirit, joints and marrow; it judges the thoughts and attitudes of the heart." -Hebrews 4:12 (NIV)

Who are we? It's a hard question to answer. Some wear their true colors, for good or bad, on their sleeves; letting themselves and others know who they really are. Others, out of pride or fear, don a mask to obscure what lies underneath. We present a façade to the outside world in hopes that they would never know what our true selves are like. But often, because we have put on our masks far too frequently, we convince ourselves that the mask that we have created is a true representation of ourselves. We live in denial of the fact that the dark shadow, which we have tried so hard to hide, continues to lurk within our hearts. When it finally reveals itself, we either continue to deny its existence, or we realize that something needs to be done.

We often talk about the Word of God as being the "Sword of the Spirit". But it is interesting to observe that we tend to focus on its external application. The Word of God will help us in our challenges, in times when opposition is pitted against us. It's true that it is these things. But have we ever thought about turning the Sword on ourselves? Whenever I open the Word of God, it always reveals to me who I really am. All the ruses and façades that I have built with my pride have been cut down; leaving only my dark shadow to stand before the Blade of God. His Word tells me that because of this dark shadow I am a sinner; wretched, and arrogant.

Yet I, like every other human being on this planet, has been created in the image of God and therefore we all have an intrinsic worth. It is because of this fact that God, in His love, wants to offer me hope, freedom, and redemption on the condition that I allow Him to slay this shadow. Since God gave us free will, He wants us to choose between the life that He will offer and the death that will occur because we have allowed sin to live. He gives us free will because He wants children who will love Him because they want to, not because they have been forced to. Only by the destruction of this shadow at the hands of Christ can God perform His redemptive work in us. May we allow the Word of God to pierce our hearts and minds so that we may see ourselves for who we really are. May we also choose to allow Christ to draw His Sword upon our wickedness so that his redemptive work may manifest itself in our lives.

July 2

TOWARDS A HARMONIOUS SOCIETY

"Live in harmony with one another. Do not be proud, but be willing to associate with people of low position. Do not be conceited." -Romans 12:16 (NIV)

It is a natural human tendency to look down upon people. In an effort to legitimize and boost our own position, we look for things in other people that we can scoff at. How many times do the privileged belittle those that are not? How many times do people from one region or ethnicity ridicule another? Human society has been wracked by divisions; and even within these divisions there are further divisions. Our pride continually seeks ways to uplift our egos. But when we look for our sense of worth in what we have, we automatically assume that those who do not have what we have are of lesser worth. In turn, those who feel beneath others, hope to restore their shattered egos by looking for people whom they can deem as beneath themselves. It is a vicious cycle of physical and psychological oppression that continues to taint human interaction even to this day.

When God created the world, the concept of equality under Him was not merely a lofty idea written on a piece of paper. It was a constant and beautiful reality. Adam and Eve enjoyed a relationship with God and with each other that was characterized by love, care, and harmony. But this perfect world was corrupted when sin entered the world through man's folly. As a result, man became tyrants towards each other. Christ came to restore man to what he was intended to be; before the entry of wickedness and pride. When Christ enters our lives, we will see everything and everyone in a whole new light. If we allow Him to, He will continue to break our pride so that we may live as true children who seek to emulate their Father. Our God is a God of justice, fairness, love, and compassion. He shows no impartiality towards His creation because He sees all as equal in their intrinsic worth, in their sin, and in their need for redemption. May we seek to emulate these qualities with His help and not allow our pride to hinder the ministry that is due to others.

July 3

LOOKING FOR TEACHERS

"Although the Lord gives you the bread of adversity and the water of affliction, your teachers will be hidden no more; with your own eyes you will see them." -Isaiah 30:20 (NIV)

We love to own our suffering don't we? How often have we said that no one can understand what we are going through? Sometimes it is true. There will be some who will not understand the pain we are enduring or the issues we are wrestling with simply because they have not experienced it yet. At the same time however, we must not make the universal claim that no one can console or advise us in our time of need. When we dwell upon our sufferings and refuse any external solace, it is easy to fall into the destructive trap of self-pity.

Often, we label God as the source of suffering. But how can God be the source of something so vile when He is the source of all that is good and pure? Clean water and filthy water cannot flow from the same spring. Rather, God uses suffering, which entered the world because of man's disobedience, to bring restoration to our lives. It may sound cruel but think of this for a moment. When we feel physical pain, it tells our body that something is not right and that it needs to be dealt with soon. Pain and suffering are blessings that tell us we need to seek help if we don't want to destroy ourselves.

Whom do we go to for comfort and counsel? While He was on Earth, Christ experienced firsthand all the pain that man has to endure in this mortal realm. God even endured the pain of having His Son murdered by the very people who once thronged to hear Him speak about life and salvation. Thus, He is the perfect Counselor because He has gone through all that we will ever go through in this life. Yet God can use others who have gone through the struggles we have faced to encourage us and give us excellent advice. This is why it is so important not to shun those who sincerely want to help us. Their willingness to assist us in sharing their experiences and in giving sound counsel could be God using them to minister to us and refine us into becoming the children that God wants us to be. The rigors of the Christian life are not meant to be overcome on our own. It is prideful to think that we can do so. May we discard our pride and humble ourselves to the guidance of God and the advice of those He will bring along our path.

July 4

BEYOND OUR LIMITATIONS

"Now to Him who is able to do immeasurably more than all we ask or imagine, according to His power that is at work within us," - Ephesians 3:20 (NIV)

Who is God? It is clear that He is someone much different from us. If we could graphically describe His existence, it would be like a circle. Who can tell where a circle begins and where it ends? Likewise, God's existence is eternal; there was never a point where He began to exist, and there will never be a point where He will cease to exist. In contrast, our existence can be described like a line. A line has a clear start point and a clear end point. It is the same with our mortal lives. For us, our existence begins when we are conceived in our mother's womb, and ends on the day when we die.

God is also omnipotent and omnipresent. No feat is too great for Him to perform and He sees everything simultaneously in real time. For us humans however, situations always remind us of our limitations. Even though we wish otherwise, we are neither invincible nor can we be everywhere at once. He is the only one who can create something out of nothing. We on the other hand always have to use pre-existing materials and ideas to create. God is all-knowing, yet ignorance is something we as humans always need to overcome. Not only is God different from us, but He is superior to us in every way. Thus He deserves our respect and worship.

Often, we tend to put God in a box. We catch ourselves thinking that our situations are too difficult even for God to solve. Our own limited human understanding tells us that if no human can solve our problems, not even ourselves, then no one can solve them at all. How wrong we are! We fail to take account of the fact that God is not bound by our limitations and nothing is impossible for Him. What's even more reassuring is that fact that He is not distant from us. He is not a passive observer, but actively seeks to help us out of His love for us as His creation. However, if we truly want His help in our lives, we have to allow Him to enter into our hearts and do His work. God will always be standing at the door of our hearts and knocking, but we must be the ones willing to open that door for Him. When we come before Him, acknowledging His supremacy over our lives and our situations, He will be able to do more than we ask or can even imagine according to His will and purposes. May we surrender our present situations to God knowing that while we may be powerless in our human frailty, He is more than able to help us in our time of need.

July 5

BEING PREPARED

"And now, dear children, continue in him, so that when he appears we may be confident and unashamed before him at his coming." -1 John 2:28 (NIV)

Being caught red-handed doing something you are not supposed to do is always embarrassing. When I was in high school, I used to draw in class a lot. Although for the most part I paid attention to the lesson and took detailed notes, class discussions tended to drag on and become unnecessarily dull. It was during these moments where I would sketch in the margins of my notebook. One day in my English class, I was caught by my teacher. She had asked a question directed to me, but I wasn't listening because I was concentrated solely on finishing my masterpiece of a tree. It wasn't until she stood beside my desk looking over my notebook that I realized that I had been found out! Thankfully, she knew that I was a good student and didn't penalize me. However, it was certainly an awkward moment and I made sure to be more attentive next time.

No one knows when Christ will return. His arrival will be unexpected and without warning; like a thief in the night. We can make all the predictions we want, but we can never claim with absolute authority when exactly Christ will come and under what circumstances. The hour of His arrival is only for God to know. What is of prime importance to us is that we be in a constant state of readiness. Our lives should be reflecting Christ every moment of our existence, in public and when no one is present. What answer will we be able to give to Christ when He returns and catches us in a compromising situation where our sin has been exposed? Like Adam and Eve before us, when they were confronted with their sin, we will try to place blame everywhere else except on ourselves. To save ourselves from such a position, we should live every moment as if Christ could come within the next second. It is a challenge that cannot be overcome by human effort. Our old sinful nature will continue to resist and fight. Yet if we stay in constant fellowship with Christ and rely on Him for strength and wisdom to live a life after Him, we will be ready to meet with our Lord when He comes to set the world aright.

July 6

BEING THE VOICE OF TRUTH

"Shortly after the prophet Hananiah had broken the yoke off the neck of the prophet Jeremiah, the word of the Lord came to Jeremiah: 'Go and tell Hananiah, 'This is what the Lord says: You have broken a wooden yoke, but in its place you will get a yoke of iron.' This is what the Lord Almighty, the God of Israel, says: 'I will put an iron yoke on the necks of all these nations to make them serve Nebuchadnezzar king of Babylon, and they will serve him. I will even give him control over the wild animals.' Then the prophet Jeremiah said to Hananiah the prophet, 'Listen, Hananiah! The Lord has not sent you, yet you have persuaded this nation to trust in lies.'" -Jeremiah 28:12-15 (NIV)

Have you ever been placed in a situation where you had to be the bearer of bad news? It can be a difficult task to take on. Fear of offending or hurting the recipients of our message can lead us into thinking that glossing over the truth and providing false hope is the best option in such a situation. Sometimes, we might even think that doing so will place us in good standing with our hearers; thus leading to an advantageous and beneficial relationship. But nothing can silence the truth. What profit will we gain if we are confronted with the fact that we postponed revealing the inevitable for our own selfish wants?

God is Truth. He cannot be deceitful or dishonest in His dealings with man because it would go against His nature of being the embodiment of truth. In some way or another, He will make sure that truth always triumphs. This is why He expects us to be champions of truth, even in situations where it would seem hard to stand up for its cause. We might be belittled and ridiculed when we proclaim the truth, and this may discourage us. But we must remember that when we speak the truth and bear honest testimony, our strongest advocate is God Himself. It was Him who gave Jeremiah the strength to continue speaking the truth and confront Hananiah's claims of being a true prophet. It was God who gave John the Baptist the strength to call people to repentance in advance of the coming of Christ; even when others called him a lunatic who spent way too much time in the desert. May we take comfort in the fact that truth always prevails and that God will safeguard those who desire to see truth upheld no matter the cost.

July 7

LIVING WITH AN ETERNAL PERSPECTIVE

"Now we know that if the earthly tent we live in is destroyed, we have a building from God, an eternal house in heaven, not built by human hands." -2 Corinthians 5:1 (NIV)

We live in a world where nothing is permanent. All that we value and treasure, could be swept away at a moment's notice. Houses easily fall prey to dilapidation and destruction. Wealth can be lost as dramatically as it can be gained. Time and separation can gently break apart friendships. Even our physical existence is only temporary and death comes to us all regardless of who we are. When we have invested so much of time and energy into these things, it is natural that we feel disappointed and mourn when the time comes for them to pass. But it is important to remember that to cling onto these things reveals who is really the master of our hearts. "Where our treasure lies, there our heart will be also".

God has promised in His Word that He is preparing a wonderful place in Heaven for those who have entered into a relationship with Him. It will be a place free from strife, calamity, pain, and every evil thing. In light of this eternal hope, why do we get so worked up over the things of this fleeting life? But does this mean that we should be indifferent and apathetic to the affairs of the world? On the contrary, we serve a God of excellence and a God who wants to see the world redeemed from sin and its offspring, suffering and misery. Likewise, as His representatives through whom Christ works, our actions should reflect these qualities. Yet when the affairs of the world take control of our lives, it is then we lose sight of God and His divine plan. It is only when we look to Christ and His eternity can we be of any substantial value to the world around us. May we walk closely with Christ knowing that our security rests in Him and that He will give us the strength and wisdom to live in this world with eternity in mind.

July 8

A LOVE THAT KNOWS NO BOUNDS

"Whoever does not love does not know God, because God is love." -
1 John 4:8 (NIV)

What is love? Often, the first thoughts that comes to mind when we hear the word is the romantic love between a man and a woman, or the love between parents and children; brothers and sisters. But if we try to define love by these relationships, we will only obtain a limited understanding of what love really is. Although these types of love are part of the definition, to define love solely by these lenses fails to capture the scope and universality of the kind of love which Christ preached. Love is based on genuine respect and concern for the other. It always seeks to serve, and expects nothing in return. Transcending all boundaries of race, age, gender, and socio-economic status, it is a love that encompasses all and excludes none. This love, because it sees the image of God in every human being, wants to manifest itself in tangible gestures out of a desire to revere God and obey His imperative to love our fellow man.

But are humans capable of such love? Our innate pride and self-centeredness prevents us from loving as Christ did. That is why we are so quick to love others who are similar to us and shun those who are not. It is also why we are so prone to hatred when we have been slighted instead of quickly extending the hand of forgiveness. The voice of our injured pride deems that those who offend us are not deserving of our love. Yet for the child of God saved by grace, we must remember that we too are not deserving of God's love on our own merits. Despite our wretchedness, Christ in His never-failing love reached down to us and offered man through His redemptive sacrifice on the cross freedom from sin and a restored relationship with God. It is in His nature to love because God is the manifestation of love. When we have entered into a relationship with Christ, we strive to conform to His likeness. May we ask Him to help us love impartially and unconditionally, so that the paralyzing specter of hatred will dissipate as the love of Christ invades our lives.

July 9

TURNING WOUNDS INTO VICTORIES

"You intended to harm me, but God intended it for good to accomplish what is now being done, the saving of many lives." -Genesis 50:20 (NIV)

The story of Joseph is perhaps one of the most uplifting and inspiring stories in the entire Bible. Every scheme of man seemed set on making Joseph's life miserable. His jealous brothers sought to get rid of him by selling him into slavery and hoped that he would meet his fate in some far off land. Not only did they get some money by selling off their brother, but they concocted an elaborate ruse to successfully convince their father that their brother had been killed by wild animals. Hurt by this betrayal and torn from his mother and father, Joseph struggled while working as a servant of Potiphar, captain of the Pharaoh's guard. Pleased with his work and diligence, Potiphar placed Joseph in charge of his entire household. Things were certainly beginning to look up. But again human intrigues would shatter Joseph's world when Potiphar's wife deceitfully framed him. Left to rot in an Egyptian prison, Joseph's future looked bleak. At this point of the story, in the face of such injustice, of such cruelty, we often ask the question-why?

I've experienced how it feels to have your peaceful and content life turned upside down. It hurts deeply. We ask ourselves, "What good could possibly come out of this?" But in our limited human perception, we do not see the big picture. God feels our hurt and our pain. He Himself was betrayed and was unjustly crucified as a result. Yet He knew that this moment of darkness would pass, and that He would turn it into something wonderfully magnificent.

While Joseph was in jail, God arranged a way out for him by giving him the opportunity to showcase to his fellow inmates his God given ability to interpret dreams. One of them happened to be Pharaoh's cupbearer. When the cupbearer was restored to his former position, in accordance to Joseph's interpretation, he remembered Joseph when Pharaoh was plagued by dreams himself. Brought before the ruler of the wealthiest empire in the world at the time, Joseph interpreted Pharaoh's dream. His interpretation impressed Pharaoh so much that he was made prime minister; answerable only to the Pharaoh himself. In this position he was not only able to save his family in Canaan from famine, but the lives of many others as well. Likewise, through Christ's death and his glorious resurrection, there is redemption for all so that man would be saved from destruction. In both examples the sovereignty of God's perfect will over man's wicked plans is proven. He is able to take the hurts that have been inflicted on us by man and turn them into triumphs that will restore our spirits and bring glory to Him. If we hold tightly to Christ, we will be guaranteed victory. May we take comfort in His promise that the plans of the unscrupulous will be foiled as He will use them to bring about His good and perfect plan for our lives.

July 10

OUR MEASURING STICK

"I urge you, brothers, to watch out for those who cause divisions and put obstacles in your way that are contrary to the teaching you have learned. Keep away from them. For such people are not serving our Lord Christ, but their own appetites. By smooth talk and flattery they deceive the minds of naive people." -Romans 16:17-18 (NIV)

One of the reasons why Hitler's rise to power was so successful was because of his charisma and his skills as a persuasive orator. During the 1930's, people thronged to hear him speak at Nazi party rallies throughout Germany. Looking back, it seems odd that so many would place their trust in him. Didn't they feel disturbed by his blatant racism? By his willingness to use violence and oppression for the continuation of the German nation-state? Yet for a defeated nation, stripped of its former glory and strength, he seemed to offer hope; hope that Germany could redeem itself and its prestige. Hitler convinced people, through his powerful speeches and commanding personality, that such cruel measures were necessary, even logical, if Germany was to ever regain its prominence on the world stage.

We have proven ourselves to have weak and impressionable minds. Just because someone exudes an air of authority and possesses a magnetic character, we feel compelled to believe that everything they say is true. After all, it takes less effort to simply sit and assume that what a person says is sound and true if he is speaking from a position of authority. But who has the final word? Is it man or is it God? It is of paramount importance that we make the conscious effort to filter everything we hear through God's Word. He is the ultimate source of truth. By reading God's Word and asking Him for the guidance and wisdom to understand it, we will be able to distinguish between what is true and what is false. Attempting to read between the lines and figure out the truth may seem like something beyond our capabilities and time. But does not a child go first to his father in hopes that the father would clear up any doubts that may have arisen in the child's mind? Likewise, we should first go to our Heavenly Father if we want to discern what is true and right. May God give us the discipline to spend time in His Word so that we may not be led astray by the false teachings of the world.

July 11

REACHING OUT IN LOVE AND SERVICE

"If one member suffers, all suffer together; if one member is honored, all rejoice together." -1 Corinthians 12:26 (ESV)

Stepping into the poorer side of Calcutta was like stepping into another world. A world that I had seen every day on my many visits to India, but never really knew at all. It's a brutal world where every manner of vice and suffering imaginable thrives. Yet for every horror story that comes out of this world, there are stories of selfless service and valor. While I was in this world, I came across accounts of street children being generous with what little resources they had in order to help another in his time of desperate need. I even heard of one story where a group of street children prevented two corrupt police officers from assaulting a girl by throwing stones at them. In the midst of the madness that is their reality, these street children look out for each other and protect each other from harm.

Christ foreknew that the weight and bondage of sin would be something that we could not bear. Motivated by His divine love, He initiated His redemptive plan for the world; the climax of which was His willful sacrifice of Himself on the cross for humanity's transgressions. As children of God wanting to follow the example of Christ, we cannot afford to be silent and inactive in the face of human suffering. When our hearts are aligned with the heart of God, what breaks His heart will break ours too. Instead of slandering others or always trying to prove ourselves superior to them, which was part of our old wicked nature, we should instead seek to serve others and be generous with what we have. The key to achieving a perfect world is that man should be in constant communion and fellowship with Christ, allowing Him to help us live in harmony and peace with others. This was how it was before the entrance of sin. Thus, only through His enabling will we be able to serve and love as He did, impartially and with the needs of the other in mind.

July 12

LOOKING FOR WATER

"Blessed are those who hunger and thirst for righteousness, for they will be filled." -Matthew 5:6 (NIV)

All of us are looking to be satisfied. Our quest for fulfillment stems from something that always nags at our hearts, the need to feel complete. We are incomplete people, but incomplete people who were never meant to remain in such a state. For this reason, we try everything possible to fill the gap in our lives. We look to sin and living however we choose as the solution to our problem. But the deception of sin is that it enters us promising thrills and satisfaction, only to leave us with pain, misery, and emptiness. We invest all our energies in our work and in our seemingly "satisfying" relationships with others, hoping to find fulfillment in these things. Yet while these things may be good, they cannot fill the void in our hearts. At some point, these too will pass and will leave us feeling unfilled and lacking.

It says in the Word of God that those who drink of the water that Christ offers will never thirst again. What does this mean? The water that He offers us is His righteousness being poured upon us and working in our lives. We may try to procure our own water by living a righteous life on our own merits. But it will always be tainted by impurities that corrupt and foil every attempt at living a life worthy to the standards of God. He freely gives this water to all who believe and choose to accept Him as Lord. Only by the water He offers can we be purged of our sinful nature and be satisfied completely. Through His righteousness guiding our hearts and actions, Christ will set us on the path to true fulfillment and joy. Christ, by His sacrifice, has offered this water to everyone regardless of who we are or even if we want it or not. However, if we really want to escape the curse of living an unfulfilled life, it is up to us to accept this water. Are you thirsty? Then drink up! Those who actively pursue the righteousness of Christ through His aid will never be in want.

July 13

BELIEVING BY FAITH

"Then Jesus told him, 'Because you have seen me, you have believed; blessed are those who have not seen and yet have believed.'" -John 20:29 (NIV)

How many times have we applied the old maxim, "seeing is believing", when it comes to God and the way He works in the world? We are always expecting to see tangible evidence of Him positively intervening in our affairs. We tell ourselves that if only He would do this for us or that for us, we would be truly drawn to follow Him and become His children. But such a miracle-based faith in God is never lasting. The crowds who gathered to hear Jesus while He was on Earth, bore witness to the miracles He performed. They were amazed and astounded. Yet shortly after, the same people who claimed to believe in Christ had no qualms about putting Him to death. It is no wonder that Jesus says through parable in Luke 16:31, "If they do not listen to Moses and the Prophets, they will not be convinced even if someone rises from the dead."

If we base our faith solely on seeking out miracles and dwelling only on the good things God gives us, then our faith is like a sandcastle on a beach. Once the waves come crashing down on our lives, we angrily shake our fists towards Heaven. But who are we to demand that God should wait upon us? God is not a vending machine, nor a slave bound to do our every bidding. He is the Lord of the Universe! However, because He loves us and sees us with intrinsic worth, He will always seek to intervene for our benefit. But He will do so according to His perfect will and timing; not ours. By continuing to base our faith on the tangible, we not only begin to worship miracles and experience over God Himself, but we deprive ourselves of seeing the big picture God has for our lives. He will always act in our best interests because He is love. God sees what is in the deep recesses of our hearts. If we truly want to understand God and follow after Him, we must come before Him with an open heart and a sincere faith. In doing so, He will teach us to believe without sight by training us to rest in who He is; a loving and just God who will never abandon nor forsake us.

July 14

KNOWING OUR BOUNDARIES

"They said to each other, 'Come, let's make bricks and bake them thoroughly.' They used brick instead of stone, and tar for mortar. Then they said, 'Come, let us build ourselves a city, with a tower that reaches to the heavens, so that we may make a name for ourselves and not be scattered over the face of the whole earth.'" -Genesis 11:3-4 (NIV)

There is a well-known Greek myth that I always used to enjoy reading when I was a child. Daedalus was a brilliant inventor. So brilliant that King Minos of Crete imprisoned him and his son, Icarus, so that he may capitalize on Daedalus' abilities. Wanting to escape his island prison, Daedalus made two pairs of wings out of wax and feathers. Before taking flight, Daedalus warned his son not to fly too close to the sun. However, once they started flying, Icarus became elated over the fact that he was soaring among the clouds. In his youthful pride he flew too close to the sun, only to fall to his death after the wax melted under the sun's heat.

Both Icarus and the people of Babel had one thing in common; pride was their downfall. God has given us beautiful minds. With it we can create beautiful works of art and literature, reason with such skill and aptitude, and invent with such ingenuity and intelligence. Yet because of our pride, we seek to use these abilities to bring glory to ourselves, not to God who has bestowed these abilities on us. As a result, we define progress by our own rules and standards, and live our lives as if we are answerable to no one but ourselves. In doing so, we bestow upon our heads the title of God, for we have trespassed into what was meant to be His realm. But this title is undeserving for us as humans. How can we imperfect human beings, with our own limited understanding, have the audacity to challenge God's authority and His perfect standards? Just as how He dealt with the people who were building the tower of Babel, likewise God will have to humble us the hard way when we have been out of line. But it is important to remember that He does not break us out of spite, but out of love. As with any loving parent who will discipline their child when he has been disobedient and arrogant, so too will God discipline us. He does so for our own good, so that we may not destroy ourselves in our folly. Only by asking God to take control of our lives will we know those divine boundaries ordained by Him, and the wisdom to know that it is within those boundaries we are truly free.

July 15

BETWEEN TWO PATHS

"You adulterous people, don't you know that friendship with the world is hatred toward God? Anyone who chooses to be a friend of the world becomes an enemy of God." -James 4:4 (NIV)

We like to keep everything black and white. For this reason, we like to categorize our lives. It gives us a sense of comfort to draw a line between what is secular in our lives and what is spiritual. This sense of comfort derives from our need to be in control of our affairs. When we begin to categorize, we have control over what is considered what. This power that we have given ourselves, gives us a false sense of comfort in the fact that our lives are in order as long as we keep everything separate from each other. But the reality is that living a double life is a constant juggling act. Invariably, there will come a point in our lives where we will have to choose which path to take. If we are not walking closely with God and are only paying lip service to Him, the secular realm will seep in and take control of our lives once that decisive moment comes around. Before we know it, we will have forsaken Christ and sold ourselves into the false sense of security and fulfillment that the world brings through its empty promises.

No one can serve two masters. It is made plain in God's Word. One is destined to overtake the other. The question that we need to answer right now is who do we choose to serve? If we choose to follow the world, its values will invade our lives. What are these values? Materialism, accumulating as many material possessions as possible will lead to happiness. The pursuit of fame and personal advancement is better than investing in meaningful relationships. Doing what feels right will lead to complete satisfaction. But how many have bought everything that money can buy, only to feel hollow inside. How many have followed the maxim of "business is business" and have either trampled over or ignored their relationships only to feel immense regret later on. How many have decided to follow their hearts only to find out that a heart not directed by God, will continue to deceive and disappoint? God stands in direct opposition to these things. He knows that the things of this world will pass. Thus, He implores that we find our sense of worth and joy in His eternal, never ceasing love for us as His invaluable creation. He recognizes the value of both work and relationships and He wants to help us find that perfect balance. He wants to conform our hearts to His perfect will; promising us that we will never be disappointed and that we will find true happiness in Him. We can trust God because He is perfect, whereas we are clearly not. May we choose Him so that He may invade every area of our lives and put us on the path towards life, joy, and security.

July 16

A DIVINE ORDER

"Thus the heavens and the earth were completed in all their vast array." -Genesis 2:1 (NIV)

When we read the Creation account in the first chapter of the book of Genesis, it is both interesting and assuring to mediate on how God created the world. Each step is meant to be a preparation for the next. Plants need soil to root themselves in, and water and light to aid in their growth. This is why God beforehand created light, the sky, and dry land on the first, second, and third days. Where would the birds fly and where would they rest? Before God created the birds on the fifth day, He created the sky on the second day and the trees on the fourth day. Those trees would not only be sources of shelter, but sources of food as well. On the fifth day God created fish for additional sustenance, which in turn would not survive if God had not created water on the second day. Neither would the livestock or wild animals of the sixth day survive if there was not the land and gathered waters of the third day, the vegetation of the fourth, and fish of the fifth. To top it all off, God created man, and brought him into a world where everything he will ever need will be provided for.

Often, it seems that we can never make sense of our lives. Everything, at least from our perspective, seems to be one random event after another. It can be distressing, especially after we've tried to connect the dots on our own understanding and failed to draw meaning from it all. Yet it is at these moments, when we are perplexed over our destination in life, that we should take comfort in God's perfect will for us as His children.

Nothing is random in God's eyes. He has ordained every event in our lives towards a specific plan; a plan that He assures will never be meant to harm us, but to give us a bright future and hope. More often than not, I find that those seemingly random events and decisions in my life, were actually guided by God to prepare me for something grand and glorious. However, we tend to see this big picture only in retrospect. I have often thought in my moments of confusion that it would be nice if God could reveal to me the entirety of His plan for my life. But then I realize that life would not only be dull and predictable, it would be a life where faith could not grow. It is in the unknown, in times when we seem to be groping in the dark, where we learn to place our faith in God and hold onto Him. May we take assurance in the fact that God has a specific and beautiful plan for our lives. A plan which only requires that we surrender our cares, our confusion, our concerns to Him and place our trust in His perfect wisdom.

July 17

SPEAK UP!

"But when I was silent and still, not even saying anything good, my anguish increased." -Psalm 39: 2 (NIV)

Saying things at the most improper of times is often a flaw that we all have to deal with. We all know of the grief it causes to us and to others when we speak without thinking. In an effort to curb our tongues, we decide to keep our mouths closed. That way, no hurtful words will come from our mouth. But by doing this we fall towards the other extreme; speaking up when we need to. I've had moments in my life when I failed to say something when I really should have. Even though every fiber of my being wanted to speak up, fear paralyzed me and shut my lips. The subsequent regret, to imagine what could have been if we had just opened our mouths, is something that can be a constant thorn in our sides if it is not surrendered to God and we ask Him to help us learn from it.

Admittedly, saying the right thing at the right time is something that can be really hard to practice. If our fear of speaking up does not stem from not wishing to rock the boat, it stems from the fear that our well intentioned sentiments will not come out right. But we should not fear if we allow Christ to speak through us. It is clear that God highly values speech. With words He spoke the world into existence and there is a reason why He created us with mouths and voices. God knows that words are powerful; both to harm and to heal. If we remain silent when we are required to speak life, truth, and justice into the hearts of people, then we have done a great disservice to our fellow man. As God's children who have been called to be a part of His redemptive work in the world, we are required to use words alongside action in our witness. Thankfully, the same God who merely had to speak in order to form the complexity of the world is willing to help in enabling us and giving us the discernment to speak when we need to. May we allow Him to take control of our lips so that we may not have to succumb to the regret of not speaking up.

July 18

BRINGING ABOUT PEACE

"Blessed are the peacemakers, for they will be called sons of God." - Matthew 5:9 (NIV)

September 1938 was a tense time in Europe. Under Hitler, Nazi Germany had invaded the Sudetenland; an ethnically German region belonging to Czechoslovakia. As the prospect of war loomed across the continent, the British Prime Minister at the time, Neville Chamberlain, met with Hitler in Munich. In keeping with the general rule of appeasement which characterized European foreign policy in the years between 1918 and 1939, Chamberlain returned to Britain with a compromise in hand. Under the terms of the Munich Agreement, Germany was allowed to annex the Sudetenland on the condition that Hitler and the Nazi state would promise to cease their expansionist designs.

Chamberlain proclaimed to the cheering British crowds that the agreement had brought "peace for our time".

However, only a few months later, Hitler completely disregarded the Munich Agreement and invaded the rest of Czechoslovakia in March 1939. At this point Chamberlain, along with the rest of the democracies of Europe, realized the failure of appeasement to check German expansionism and resolved to deal with Hitler by force should the trend continue. When Hitler invaded Poland on September 1st, 1939, Britain and France declared war two days later; triggering a war that, although would be bloodiest in the history of mankind, would also see the destruction and widespread condemnation of fascism and ultra-nationalism.

Often we get confused over what it really means to be a peacemaker. In our minds, a peacemaker is someone who makes sure the peace is achieved through the maintenance of the status quo. As long as we don't get on anyone's bad sides, we have done our duty in maintaining peace; even if means ignoring serious issues that lie at the root of the conflicts we have to deal with. But this is not what it means to be a peacemaker. The role of a true peacemaker is to form a lasting peace by tackling the crux of issues; not simply dealing with mere symptoms. Just as how Christ came to redeem the world by addressing the problem of sin, we as His children must also be willing to address the source of the conflicts we have been called to intervene in.

Doing so always comes at a price. In order that the problem of sin may be finally solved and humanity freed from its chains, Christ had to die and rise again. The penalty for sin was death. Only by His willing sacrifice on the cross for all of our transgressions, could that penalty be met. Likewise, to be a true peacemaker we will have to give of our time and energy; continuously opening ourselves emotionally and spiritually in order to speak truth and wisdom even when we are rejected and rebuffed by the very people we want to help. It might not always be the most comfortable and pleasant thing to do, but it is a worthy price to pay for God's truth and peace to flourish. People will know if we are His children by the way we solve conflicts. Only by staying close to Christ and relying on Him for wisdom, strength, and discernment, can we be the peacemakers He has called us to be.

July 19

WHAT DO YOU THINK?

"What about you?'" Jesus asked. 'Who do you say that I am?' Simon Peter answered, 'You are the Christ, the Son of the living God.'"
-Matthew 16:15-16 (NIV)

Who is Christ to us? We cannot question His influence in the world because even two thousand years after His time, people are still talking about Him and debating over who He really was. Some adopt the position that He was a teacher; that His main mission was to instruct people on how to live a virtuous life but nothing more. Others say that He was a prophet; come to call people to repentance before God in an age of decadence.

But it is clear from this verse and Christ's own subsequent confirmation that He is the Messiah and the Son of the Living God. For this reason, many deem Him to have been a lunatic. But how can that be given His eloquence of speech, and the fact that His followers came from many different backgrounds; ranging from the poor to the very peak of Judeo-Roman society. In addition, His disciples, the ones who spent every moment of their lives with Christ during His three year ministry, were killed on account of their faith; with the exception of John who died in exile. If Jesus was a lunatic, why would they willingly give up their lives for Him? Christ was certainly sane and He was certainly more than what people claim Him to be.

Why are we so hesitant to acknowledge Christ as the Son of God; Savior of mankind? Are we afraid that He will get personal? In a time where window-shopping for religion and philosophies is commonplace and the need to be politically correct is paramount, the absolute claims of Christ seem to challenge such attitudes. We are content to keep Him at a distance as a teacher or a prophet. We may admire Him and even want to live out what He taught. But because we want to appear "open-minded", or because we want to retain our so-called "freedom" and live life the way we want to on our own efforts and understanding, we are reluctant to accept Christ as Savior.

However, if Christ is simply a mere teacher to us, then we have missed the point of His whole coming down to Earth. The standards that Christ has set for leading a truly righteous life are beyond the capabilities of man because of our inherent sin. It is because of this that Christ came; so that He may make our hearts His home, destroy the root of our problems, and aid us through His righteousness working within us and not our own. When we say of Christ that "He is a teacher", we will set ourselves up for discouragement and disillusion. But if we say of Him, "He is the Christ, the Son of the Living God" and believe it sincerely like Peter did, we will find true freedom, fulfillment, and an investment secure in the promise of eternal life.

July 20

KNOCKING ON DOORS

"Here I am! I stand at the door and knock. If anyone hears my voice and opens the door, I will come in and eat with him, and he with me." -Revelation 3:20 (NIV)

Can we knock on the gates of Heaven? We like to think we can. Whether we are open about it or not, we feel that with all our good works under our belts and all our theological knowledge in our heads, we are deserving of a place in Heaven. But the truth is that we cannot ensure a place in Heaven with these things. We may have fed every starving mouth in the world in our selfless service and know every theological concept in existence. However, if we have not personally acknowledged that we are sinners in need of salvation and have not allowed God to take care of the wickedness that resides in our hearts, we will never be able to enter Heaven.

No one can enter Heaven by their own merits. According to God's standards on what constitutes as sin, none of us will be able to say with confidence that we have lived a pure and sinless life. God cannot tolerate impurity, however little, because by His nature He is holy. If we find even a small pinch of dirt in a glass of water, do we regard it as being pure or impure? Likewise, despite all our works and knowledge, God cannot allow us into His Heaven if we are still bound by sin.

From the moment that Adam and Eve sinned, God knew that man would not be able to reconcile themselves to Him. He promised Eve that her offspring would crush the head of the serpent, Satan. This referred to the coming of Jesus who through His death and resurrection, has paid the penalty of sin for all of humanity and broken the hold Satan had over the world. Though we cannot reach Heaven because of our own limitations, in His grace, God has come down to humanity so that He may redeem His creation through Christ. He now stands at the door of our hearts and knocks. He will not barge in because He respects the free will He has given us. Once our doors are opened, we have an assured passage to Heaven because we have allowed Him to come into our hearts. The question for us is, why do we deny ourselves divine help when we know we need it to attain salvation?

July 21

TOTAL SURRENDER

"He said, "Take your son, your only son Isaac, whom you love, and go to the land of Moriah, and offer him there as a burnt offering on one of the mountains of which I shall tell you."" -Genesis 22:2 (NIV)

It was an interesting request. God asking Abraham to sacrifice his child? It seems so strange that there has to be something more. What is even more interesting is how God asked Abraham. God specifically instructed him to "take your son, your only son Isaac, whom you love," Born to them while Sarah was old and barren, Isaac was truly a miracle from God. He was the son that Abraham always dreamed of and the proud father did not withhold any love from his son. There must have been countless questions running through Abraham's mind when God instructed him to go to Moriah and sacrifice Isaac. But he did so fully trusting God, that all will work together for good according to His perfect plan. Pleased with his faith, God prepared a ram caught in a thicket for Abraham; drawing his attention to it so that Isaac would not be harmed and the ram would be used for the sacrifice in his place.

What does it mean to surrender to God? We would like to think of it as a partial surrender. There are areas in our lives where we can confidently say that we would be able to willingly hand them over to God. But what about those areas that we don't want to give up to Him? Our life-long plans, our deepest desires, our friendships, our loved ones. All these things may be good in and of themselves. They may have even been bestowed upon us by God Himself. But if we try to manage these on our own strength or understanding, thinking that only we are capable of doing so, we will only end up depriving ourselves of the wonderful things that God can do with what He has given and placed within our hearts. Surrender to God is total, not partial. When we trust in God and allow Him to direct our paths, He will take all that we value and treasure and manage it in such a way as to leave us in awe of His flawless wisdom and perfect will. It can be hard to surrender every aspect of our lives to Him. On our own efforts we will fail in this endeavor. But in His grace, God has given us His Holy Spirit to all who believe in and call upon the name of Christ. Through the indwelling of the Spirit, He will help us surrender where we need to, so that we may live life to its fullest, dwelling in the faithfulness of God.

July 22

SOMEBODY CALL POISON CONTROL!

"Do not let any unwholesome talk come out of your mouths, but only what is helpful for building others up according to their needs, that it may benefit those who listen." -Ephesians 4:29 (NIV)

Words are powerful things. If we consider how words of healing, or a lack thereof, can determine the course of relations from the largest of entities, such as between two nations, to the smallest of entities, such as between two people, the potency of speech cannot be questioned. God Himself created the world through the usage of words, declaring His desires for how the world should turn out. It is truly a privilege that God has bestowed upon man the power of speech. No other created thing on Earth shares our capacity for language and communication. Such a gift has been entrusted to us by God and thus we must use it with wisdom and responsibility.

Yet how many times do we do the opposite! In this fallen world, sin has corrupted the way we use the God given gift of the spoken word. How prone are we to be party to slander, gossip, foul and vulgar talk, and insincerity in our speech? Such things are like poison that flows out of our mouths; slowing creeping in and damaging those around us whether we are aware of it or not. But unwholesome speech does not just affect others! We may think that we can use such words when no one is around. However, even such indulgences will poison us as well; corrupting our thoughts and actions. Even though we may present a clean façade to the rest of the world and try to make sure that we keep a close reign on our tongues, the poison, in part or in full, that has been building within will gush out at some point. If we allow it to consume our private lives, it will come out in situations where it will surprise both ourselves as well as others. Taming our tongues is no easy feat, for out of our hearts the mouth speaks. Only through the indwelling of Christ in our lives will our hearts be cleansed of evil and overflow with His undiluted purity. As a result, Christ will give us the restraint and wisdom to choose our words carefully; making sure that we use His gift to benefit others and build them up, instead of tearing others down and contributing to the persistence of evil in the world.

July 23

USING POWER RESPONSIBLY

"The kings of the earth did not believe, nor did any of the world's people, that enemies and foes could enter the gates of Jerusalem. But it happened because of the sins of her prophets and the iniquities of her priests, who shed within her the blood of the righteous." -Lamentations 4:12-13 (NIV)

History has proven countless times that oppressive governments and empires never last long. Even if they seem to be unassailable, they will crumble as long as they continue to exploit the innocent and shed their blood in order to maintain power. In the last century, we have seen the rapid rise and destruction of ultra-nationalistic and fascist states, the disintegration of the old colonial empires, and the fall of the vast majority of totalitarian communist regimes. Although these evils continue to persist in the present age, the promise that truth and justice will ultimately triumph continues to encourage those who live under and fight oppression and tyranny.

These words in Lamentations however, should serve as strong reminders for us as leaders. All of us are leaders to some degree and have been entrusted by God with authority over someone or a group of people. It could be at work, in our circle of friends, or within our own families. But too often our tendency is to abuse the power we have been given. When we know we are in a position of authority, we are inclined to use it for our own gain. Consequently, we become manipulative, cold, and heavy-handed towards those whom we have been charged with.

Lording our power over others and always trying to prove with our authority that we are the boss, satisfies our egos and our pride. But this is not what God intends when He gives us authority. Although there will be times when we need to be firm, God wants us to be servant-leaders; to use our authority for the benefit of others so that Christ may be glorified in our service. When we use our power to feed our pride and to elevate ourselves instead of God and others, we will do things that will go against God's requirement for us to pursue His righteousness and integrity in our leadership. Like King Saul who had his God given authority taken away when he abused it, God will take away the powers He has bestowed upon us when we use it to harm and exploit others. He will hand it over to those who will pursue virtue and truth, as He did with King David, for God will always stand by a righteous cause.

As children of God, we are His representatives on Earth and all our actions should point to His perfect character. How then are we to use the authority we have been given responsibly? When the Spirit of God is within us and we dwell upon the perfect leadership advice that can only be found in His Word, we will be able to use our authority for His glory. By doing so, we will be able to not only contribute to well being of others, but to ourselves as well; living together in peace and harmony.

July 24

LOOK FOR HEAVENLY GUIDANCE

"Glancing this way and that and seeing no one, he killed the Egyptian and hid him in the sand." -Exodus 2:12 (NIV)

Life is full of situations that force us to make important decisions. When such situations come along our path, it takes us aback and we feel compelled to make a decision as soon as possible before it's too late. In our haste we formulate plans based on our own understanding and, because we want to make sure that we are doing the right thing, we seek advice. However, the problem with seeking advice when we have already drawn our conclusions based on our understanding is that we end up looking for accomplices. We tend to only consider and take to heart the counsel that falls in line with our plans. Thus, it leads us to make rash and destructive choices.

Such was the case with Moses. When he saw the Egyptian slave driver beating the Hebrew slave, his emotions ran high. He knew that he couldn't simply stand back and watch; he had to do something. But in his emotional fervor he ended up taking the life of the slave driver. This brought Moses much misery and grief, for it placed him at odds with Pharaoh. Once he heard of Moses' crime, he sought to kill him. Fleeing from the royal household and from Egypt would have been painful for Moses. After all, it was his adopted home. It is interesting that the Bible mentions that he glanced this way and that before he committed the foul deed. He looked everywhere around him, but failed to look towards Heaven.

Why is it so hard for us to first consult with God about our plans? As Wisdom personified, isn't He the best person to approach when we are faced with a decision? Too often He is an afterthought in our decision making process. As a result, we will sometimes seek counsel from His Word only to try to make it fit with our plans. It should not be the case. The Word of God should not conform to our desires. Rather, our desires should conform to the Word. We could spare ourselves from so much pain if from the start we abandon our desires and with humble hearts consult God's Word; sincerely listening to Him and asking Him to guide our actions and words according to His perfect will. God assures us that when we first consult with Him, He will make our paths straight and will help us make the right decision. We will not have to suffer as Moses did, for regret and scandal will be far from us when we allow Him to guide our lives.

July 25

LET THE RAIN FALL DOWN!

"Let us acknowledge the Lord; let us press on to acknowledge him. As surely as the sun rises, he will appear; he will come to us like the winter rains, like the spring rains that water the earth." -Hosea 6:3 (NIV)

While I was working at a summer camp in western Ontario, we once had three consecutive days of unbearable heat. The moment we stepped out of our cabins, it would feel like we stepped into a desert! Compounding this was the fact that the campground, although quite beautiful, was also quite large. It required a lot of walking to get from one point to the other. One can imagine how exhausting it must have been to do camp activities under such circumstances. I could see on the sweaty and fatigued faces of child and counselor alike that we all hoped for rain. When it came the next day however, all of us greeted God's provision with jubilation and ecstasy. Regular activities were brought to a halt as everyone allowed the cooling rains to soak every bone in their bodies. We even brought out small cups to collect raindrops and throw them on each other! Although naturally I caught a cold after our adventure in the rain, it was completely worth it!

We all go through times where our situations seem too difficult to bear. Hoping to find deliverance, we look in many places, only to find that they can bring only temporary relief. Such faulty remedies do not adequately deal with our situations and leave us in our despair. At other times, in order to escape the heat of our circumstances, we look for shelter. Thinking that we have found where we need to be, we don't realize that the shelter we have chosen is ready to come crashing down on us at any moment. When that time comes, we are left destitute and broken. But God promises in His word that He will bring relief and provision to those who call upon His name and acknowledge Him. Like the refreshing rains, He will bring peace and restoration for the parched soul. The once previously barren gardens of our lives will flourish and teem with life. However, God gives us choices. We can choose to acknowledge Him or to reject Him. If we reject Him, we will have to go through this life on our own; trusting our limited wisdom and wandering through the desert of our circumstances chasing one unfulfilling mirage after another. But if we choose Christ and are in complete dependence on Him, He will be faithful in His promises to provide for those who call upon Him and we will rest in the assurance that He is always faithful.

July 26

POINTING TO CHRIST

"For since the creation of the world God's invisible qualities — his eternal power and divine nature — have been clearly seen, being understood from what has been made, so that men are without excuse." - Romans 1:20 (NIV)

I was never one inclined to the study of mathematics. However, after learning about fractals, I never looked at trees the same way again. In essence, fractals are progressively miniature replications, though not exactly the same, attached to a shape that serves as the original model. We can see this sequence in trees where a tree trunk splits into two large branches, which then each split into two smaller branches, and so on. The fascinating thing is that it is universal in all trees. It is beautiful to observe! Even snowflakes and plants, such as ferns, follow this pattern. This fact continues to remind me that God does nothing without reason, and governs the world through principles and laws that are derived from His perfect wisdom and character.

Some use creation to disprove God. Others go towards the other extreme and worship creation as God. But if anything, creation's intended purpose was to point heavenward towards God. From the created world around us, we can obtain so many truths about God's character, and how He expects us to live as His children. Jesus knew this full well. He implored those who heard His words to be as industrious as an ant, and as carefree as a sparrow who finds rest in God's provision. However, we cannot ignore the fact that creation, although it has retained some of its primordial splendor, is largely fallen. We can see clearly that death, physically and by sin, has tainted the created order. This was not meant to be. When God sent His Son to die on the cross for the sins of humanity, it was to inaugurate a restorative mission that would not only redeem man, but all of creation as well. In the new world which will come after Christ's second coming, the lion will sleep with the lamb, and the infant will be able to put his hand into the snake's den without being harmed. Creation bears testimony to the power and wisdom of God, and can open our eyes to His truths and His plan of salvation for the world. But it is only by acknowledging the Creator, Jesus, as our personal Lord and Savior will we be able to partake of the restored world that is to come.

July 27

WHAT WILL WE REAP?

"A man reaps what he sows." -Galatians 6:7b (NIV)

Some have taken the Biblical idea of reaping what we sow as equivalent to the Hindu concept of *karma*. However, there is one fundamental difference. *Karma* is tied to the idea of reincarnation; that when we die we are reborn into another life on Earth. Under the idea of *karma*, the actions of our previous lives determine the consequences in our present lives. Not only is this unfair, because essentially we have to bear the consequences of wrong actions that were committed in a previous life that we cannot even recollect, but it also becomes hard to attach responsibility. There is no way to determine whether or not the consequences we face in the present, good or bad, are a result of actions committed by ourselves in the present, or by a former self in our past lives. The system of *karma* can also give license to someone to indulge in sin in the present, with the nominal acceptance that they will pay it off in their next lives. Thus, it can be easy to dodge responsibility for our present actions.

But the Bible is very clear. According to Hebrews 9:27 man is destined to die once and stand before God's judgment seat. The consequences that we face in the present are not attributed to actions, pure and wicked, committed in a supposed previous life, but those committed in the here and now. Responsibility for our actions is squarely placed on what we have done in the single, present life that God has given us and we will pay for those actions in this life as well. It is paramount therefore that we be careful in our actions. If we sow the seeds of sin, folly, and wickedness in our lives, do not be surprised when the damaging consequences of our actions come knocking at our door. God allows us to endure the ramifications of sin now so that we would reconcile ourselves to Him. In doing so, we realize our need to pursue righteousness only by walking closely with Him and relying on His constant help and grace. Conversely, God rewards those who sow virtue and purity. We can take great comfort in the fact that He will bless the faithful who have been obedient to His Word and continue to persevere in living in love and integrity. When we walk closely with Christ, our eyes will be opened to what we are sowing and, with His wisdom and guidance, we will be able to reap a harvest of righteousness even in times where turmoil surrounds our lives.

July 28

STANDING FIRM

"Therefore, my dear brothers, stand firm. Let nothing move you. Always give yourselves fully to the work of the Lord, because you know that your labor in the Lord is not in vain." -1 Corinthians 15:58 (NIV)

Sometimes, the road which God has called us to walk can become hard to endure. Despite our faithfulness and diligence, obstacle after obstacle, and discouragement after discouragement, seem to be our only rewards. In the face of such adversity, it is easy to lose hope. We begin to question why we are even on this path and look for ways to escape. But as the prophet Jonah would find out centuries before us, running away from our problems is not the solution. God, with gentleness and firmness, will always bring us back to the point where we will have to confront the mission which He has laid out for us.

When God has placed us in situations, it is not without reason. Although we may not see it immediately because of the limits of our human perception, God is fulfilling His perfect will for our lives and for others. He never calls us to a task only to watch us fall. It would go against His nature, and His promise to never abandon us. Our role is to simply carry on the work He has called us to do and trust Him in His divine plan. When we encounter hard times and the pressure is against us, it is in these moments where our faith in Him who is able to overcome will be strengthened; that is if we continuously hold on to Christ. Resting in His promises to always catch us when we fall and that any good work done in His name will not return void, will encourage us when hardship seems to be our lot. By standing on the promises of

God we will be able to labor diligently and joyfully knowing that victory belongs to Him. In this assurance, we will be able to enjoy watching His plan unfold before us and stand in awe of His infinite wisdom.

July 29

LOVING OUR BROTHERS

"If anyone says, 'I love God,' yet hates his brother, he is a liar. For anyone who does not love his brother, whom he has seen, cannot love God, whom he has not seen." -1 John 4:20 (NIV)

In my teenage years, I never understood Christians. I understood and loved Christ, or at least I thought I did, but not His followers. Seeing the decadence, hypocrisy, and coldness of some who called themselves Christians, I slowly developed a distrust and aversion for anyone who claimed to be a follower of Christ. I thought I was living the Christian life and honoring God by obeying His teachings and witnessing to my non-Christian friends. But God had to show me that if I was accusing Christians of being hypocrites, I was guilty of that sin as well. I claimed to be a child of God while refusing to obey His call to love unconditionally; a love that was to extend to everyone regardless of who they were and what they have done, for I myself am in need of God's grace! He had to teach me how to love as He did and bring me to the realization that unconditional love does not pick favorites.

God is love. John 3:16 doesn't say, "For God so loved this people…" or, "For God so loved that group…". It says that, "For God so loved the world that He gave His only begotten son so that those who believe in Him will not perish, but have everlasting life." His redeeming sacrifice was meant for all because He sees everyone, past, present, and future, as having intrinsic worth and deserving of His love and grace. He will never close the doors of salvation on anyone. Therefore, there can be no room for hatred in the hearts of His children. Not only will hatred suffocate us and deprive us from enjoying the life God has given us to the fullest, it will also harm our witness for Christ. When we accept Christ as Lord and Savior we enter into a process where, through His help, we conform ourselves to His likeness. This means to surrender all our inhibitions and simply love those around us regardless of their identity and their past actions. In doing so, we will see all people as Christ sees them; as being equal in bearing the image of God, and equal in their need of His grace. Anyone can hate, and anyone can show love to those who will reciprocate that love. But it takes Christ to help us love those who seem to us as being unlovable. If we truly love God, we must ask Him to help us love unconditionally as He has done for us. This in turn will show the world that His wellspring of love will never run dry.

July 30

BEING GENEROUS AND JUST

"Good will come to him who is generous and lends freely, who conducts his affairs with justice." -Psalm 112:5 (NIV)

Our culture has taught us to be tight-fisted. When we have been fed with subtle messages which tell us to essentially hoard as much as we can and trust no one, we tend to become rather insular in our giving. Consequently, generosity is looked down upon as a sign of weakness and naivety because it requires us to open ourselves and all that we have; thus making us susceptible to manipulation and exploitation. Since we don't want that to happen, we harden ourselves and become guarded in an effort to protect what we have and our self-esteem. Why should we open ourselves only to get trampled on? But, when we have built our sense of ease on material things, the distrust and possessiveness we have fostered will only cripple us.

God has implored us to be good stewards of what He has graciously given to us. In response, our stewardship should lead us to generously give to others all that is truly His. He loves a cheerful giver; one who gives out of love and concern of the other while not expecting anything in return. It is how Christ loves us. He was generous with Himself by sacrificing His own life in order to pay for our sins so that we may be free from its shackles and have eternal life. Therefore, there can be no room for avarice in the heart of the child of God. When we begin to see that nothing truly belongs to us and that everything really belongs to God, we will know the weight of our so-called treasures in relation to God's eternity. All our wealth and possessions will count as nothing to us and when we surrender them to God, we will be able to be a blessing to others and find that we too will be blessed. We will also be reminded of the importance of not taking advantage of other people's charity. Just as we cannot take advantage of the grace of God by deliberately persisting in our sin, we cannot abuse those who graciously extend the hand of kindness. When the Spirit of God has consumed our lives, we will be able to be obedient to His calling on our lives to be generous with what we have and to likewise act with integrity when under the benevolence of someone else. By doing this, we will show to those around us that the God we serve is one of compassion and justice.

July 31

WHERE IS YOUR SECURITY?

"Keep your lives free from the love of money and be content with what you have, because God has said, "Never will I leave you; never will I forsake you." -Hebrews 13:5 (NIV)

Materialism is a lie. It promises us security and the perfect lifestyle through the accumulation of wealth and possessions. But rarely does it deliver on its promises. If anything, it makes us more insecure over the fact that we don't own enough. When we are governed by materialism we are always chasing the proverbial carrot; ignoring everything else and never being completely satisfied. Materialism teaches greed, and greed is never content with what it has. It will do anything to accumulate more, even if it is at the expense of ourselves and those around us. We trade everything, including the things that materialism is supposed to promise, for a false sense of security that will unravel itself the day when all our wealth and possessions are gone.

There is nothing inherently wrong in trying to better yourself. However, if our whole lives revolve around the pursuit of money and material wealth, we will be trapped in a cycle that will never bring us true happiness. Where our treasures are, our hearts will be there as well. Yet why is the draw of materialism so appealing? In a world that is often chaotic and confusing, we yearn for a sense of security and comfort. Seeking to meet these needs through material things is tempting because they are tangible. We can see them, feel them, and therefore keep track of them. But we were not meant to find our security and worth in things that will pass away. We were meant to find it in the eternity of God our Creator. However, when we deliberately chose sin we separated ourselves from Him. Yet in His perfect love and compassion for us, He sought to redeem us through His death and resurrection so that sin's grip over our lives may be broken and our relationship with Him would be secured. When we willingly choose to be a part of His family, our satisfaction and security will be complete knowing that our rest is found in our eternal Heavenly Father who will never abandon or forsake us.

August 1

NOTHING TO HIDE

"There is nothing concealed that will not be disclosed, or hidden that will not be made known. What you have said in the dark will be heard in the daylight, and what you have whispered in the ear in the inner rooms will be proclaimed from the roofs." -Luke 12:2-3 (NIV)

We detest the feeling of being exposed. It is never a comfortable or desirable experience. We dread the moment when the reputation that we have worked so hard to build unravels, because of our deliberate desire to indulge ourselves in sin. This is why we like to do and say everything in secret; so that we can pursue our errant desires without our reputation being comprised or our pride coming under attack. It is even better when we have an accomplice. To know that there is someone else who secretly engages in the same vices as ourselves gives us a sense of comfort and even a justification for our actions. As long as we are not caught and are not seemingly harming anyone, we persist in our sinful habits convincing ourselves that it is okay.

Nothing is hidden from God. He sees all and knows all. He not only hears every word that comes out of our mouths and sees every act that is done in secret, but He knows the state of our hearts as well; something that no human being, not even ourselves, can accurately perceive. To think that we can get away with anything is a lie. God, because He is a God of truth and righteousness, will make sure that what has been said and done behind closed doors will be revealed publicly in the streets. The consequences of what we have tolerated and said in private will catch up with us; often unexpectedly because we have fostered our habits to the point where we are not even conscious of it. God allows the consequences of our actions to teach us that what we have done is wrong and that we need to conform ourselves to His standards. But He knows that we cannot meet His standards on our own power or wisdom. That is why He has given us Christ. Through Him dwelling within our hearts, we will become acutely aware of wrong habits and attitudes in our lives; actively seeking to change them with the help of Christ in our lives. If we want to truly live without regrets, we must embrace Christ and allow Him to take control of our lives so that we may have nothing to hide before Him and before others.

August 2

HOW TO BE EXALTED

"But God chose the foolish things of the world to shame the wise; God chose the weak things of the world to shame the strong. He chose the lowly things of this world and the despised things – and the things that are not – to nullify the things that are, so that no one may boast before him." -1 Corinthians 1:27-29 (NIV)

To Roman eyes, Judea was a backwater. It certainly didn't have the prestige of Rome itself, nor could it boast the wealth and productivity of other provinces in the Empire, such as neighboring Egypt. Its people, although respected for the antiquity of their Jewish faith, were viewed by the Roman authorities as a stubborn people, who were always rebelling against the Greco-Roman culture and religion. No one would have expected any major historical figure to arise from such a region. Yet Judea would be the birthplace of Christ, the Name that is above every other name, the King of kings, and the sole greatest figure in human history who has and will never be surpassed by anyone else.

Throughout Scripture, God uses the most unlikely of people and the most obscure of places to exalt them and fulfill His perfect will. Why does He do this? We often like to think that to be of use in this world, we have to be wealthy and wise according its standards. Subsequently, we look for people who meet these standards and try to emulate their lives. However, we will find that our efforts to be successful by following the world's standards only end up reinforcing pride in our hearts. We feel that we are entitled to be blessed by God on the basis of our accomplishments achieved by our own toil and understanding. But God does not look at the material riches of man. He looks at our hearts. If our hearts are not obedient to Him, then we have no right to demand that He bless us. Moreover, He will use people who we thought were beneath us to humble us and draw our hearts closer to Himself. God stands behind those who stand up for truth and honor Him with their lives and their obedience. People who do so transcend all socio-economic divisions. When we humble ourselves before God, pride will dissipate as we allow Him to teach us the true meaning of success, and what we must do to be exalted in His eyes and in the eyes of those around us.

August 3

WE ARE CHRISTIANOI!

"Since we are surrounded by such a great cloud of witnesses, let us throw off everything that hinders and the sin that so easily entangles, and let us run with perseverance the race marked out for us." -Hebrews 12:1 (NIV)

What is a Christian? The actual term originated in ancient Rome as the Christian faith was spreading throughout the Empire. Its first recorded use is found in Acts 11:26, when Paul and Barnabas were in the city of Antioch in modern day Syria. The pagans in the city began to label them in Greek as Christianoi, meaning "people of Christ". Some have translated this word more liberally to mean "little Christs", which is stronger in illustrating the fact that we are called to be imitators of our Savior. However, both meanings indicate that Christ is the one who is at the center of our being, and the one we seek to emulate. The fact that the term Christian was first coined by those who were not His followers shows that they are very much aware of who we represent.

Whether we like it or not, the truth is that the world is watching those who declare themselves to be children of Christ. The moment we let others know of our faith in Christ, they will be looking to see if our words match our actions and beliefs. This is why it is critical to keep a close guard on our thoughts, words, and actions; constantly bringing them before Christ and allowing Him to be our filter. Although we are living in the world, we are called to be not of it. This means to not conform ourselves to the values of this world. Consequently, this requires us to seriously consider what we are allowing to permeate our minds. We may think that whatever we watch, read, or listen to will not affect us. But if we do not allow these things to come under the scrutiny of Christ, that which is evil in reality, though we may not see it, will ultimately destroy us and our witness for Him. If we truly want to be strong witnesses for Christ and run with perseverance the race He has called us to run, we must allow Him to sift through our hearts. When we ask Him for the wisdom to discern what is right and wrong and allow Him to purge any evils in our hearts, we will be able to bring glory to Him and hold the torch of Christ high for all to see.

August 4

WE ARE NEVER FORGOTTEN

"Are not five sparrows sold for two pennies? Yet not one of them is forgotten by God." -Luke 12:6 (NIV)

When modern cities first began to appear, one social problem that emerged was that people began to experience feelings of isolation and loneliness. It would seem to be a paradox. How can one feel alone when surrounded by a sea of people? But the sheer size of these urban areas made many, who were used to the intimacy and familiarity common amongst those who lived in rural areas, feel like a mere drop in the ocean. Conditions at work only seemed to solidify such attitudes. Life in the rapidly expanding factories of the city was squalid, harsh, demanding, and mundane; with workers feeling more like cogs in the industrial machine rather than individual human beings. In the face of such conditions, quite a number turned to crime in hopes of finding a sense of brotherhood and belonging; using the anonymity of being in a large city to their advantage. Others, separated from family and friends and living in such desperate conditions, succumbed to depression and suicide. Although much has been done to rectify such attitudes and problems in the past two centuries, they have not disappeared entirely.

We yearn for human companionship. God, because He works in community with the Son and the Holy Spirit, has created within us this same need for relationship with others. However, even when we are surrounded by people, our search continues to prove fruitless. We want someone who will stand by us regardless of the situation and who will genuinely care for our struggles and seek to see us through them. When we fail to find such people, it is easy to feel that we are forgotten. But what a friend we have in Jesus! If He cares for the sparrow's every need, how much more will He care for us as human beings who all bear His image? He seeks to have a relationship with us; loving us so much that He Himself died for our sins so that the gap of sin that separated us from Him would be bridged. He came down to Earth to experience what we as individual humans experience and thus can empathize with our struggles. When we have Christ as our friend living within us, we will never feel alone or neglected knowing that He will rejoice with us in our delight and mourn with us in our grief. Moreover, He wants to actively be a part of our lives towards our benefit; so that if we willingly take His counsel we may live in true fulfillment and spared from regret. Human relationships will come and go, but God is eternal. What a privilege and blessing it is to have a friend who will stand by us both now and into eternity!

August 5

THE NECESSITY OF THE LAW

"For the Lord is our judge, the Lord is our lawgiver, the Lord is our king; it is He who will save us." -Isaiah 33:22 (NIV)

Our view of authority has been skewed. We have seen people abuse the power that has been given to them. Instead of being upholders of the law and acting in the best interests of the people, they use their influence to exploit the helpless. They misuse the power of the law by decreeing commandments that put the powerless under their oppressive thumb. They circumvent or pervert just statutes and honorable principles in order to fulfill their own unscrupulous agenda. In the face of such wanton corruption it is only natural to develop apathy towards law and order, and distrust towards those who represent it. We then decide to become authorities unto ourselves; living however we wish according to our own wisdom and understanding. However, one of two things will happen. Either we will become the architects of our own destruction, or we will become the very oppressors that we hate.

What does freedom mean? Does it mean living by no standard other than the ones which we set up for ourselves? If we were granted the freedom to act as we see fit, this world would be rife with anarchy; where bloodshed and vice would be rampant. Human nature is selfish and wicked. It is inclined towards evil and would only consider doing what is right if there was something to gain. That is why God, in His perfection and wisdom, has set boundaries for us to live within. He has set these limits not to tyrannize us, but so that we may live in a manner that would be of true benefit to us and spare us from ruin. God cannot set laws in place to harm us because it would go against His divine nature; which is being the epitome of love and justice. But to match God's law is not for man to attain on his own strength or effort. Only by accepting God's willing sacrifice of His Son, Jesus Christ, as satisfying the penalty for our individual sins and by giving us a new nature through His resurrection from the dead, can we obey the laws He has placed before us. With Christ working through us, we will be able to grasp the true nature of His statutes and obey His commandments with all our hearts. A life without limits will make us slaves to depravity. But a life living within the borders that Christ has defined will liberate us from the shackles of decadence and grant us true freedom.

August 6

DON'T BE HASTY!

"Careful planning puts you ahead in the long run; hurry and scurry puts you further behind." -Proverbs 21:5 (The Message)

We are such a hurried race. In this fast-paced world of ours, we have been trained to believe that we need to be able to make snap decisions. Motivated by this culture's emphasis on values such as instant gratification, we often make choices based on the immediate benefits that we would gain. In addition, we want to make these decisions as quickly as possible before someone else seizes the opportunity. Certain actions need and often should be taken immediately; actions such as notifying the proper authorities in the event of an emergency. But then it seems that even for those decisive choices which could shape our futures, we haste; not spending enough time to really think about what we are getting ourselves into.

We need to be patient in our thought processes and allow God to show us where He is leading us to go. God wants to help us choose the right path, and He wants us to consult with Him through prayer and reading His Word. We know that we can rely on His counsel because He sees the bigger picture of our lives and He knows us better than we know ourselves. But if we simply pray to God for direction and soon after come to a resolution based on our own limited wisdom, then we really haven't been still and allowed Him to speak. When we make rash choices, we set ourselves up for misery and failure. Thus, we cannot turn around and blame God for leading us into sorrow. In reality, the blame should be on us for being impatient and not spending enough time counting the cost with God as our guide. When we take the time to think through important decisions and ask God for guidance and clarification, we will find that the choice we have made according to His faultless wisdom was far better than what we initially thought of doing. As we wait upon God and allow Him to build up patience and wisdom in our lives, we will be able to rest in the arms of Christ knowing that He will help us make choices that will be in accordance with His pleasing, perfect will, and free of regret.

August 7

WATCHING OUT FOR TRAPS

"Be self-controlled and alert. Your enemy the devil prowls around like a roaring lion looking for someone to devour." -1 Peter 5:8 (NIV)

There is a reason as to why lions are both admired and feared. Although regal in appearance and powerful in strength, they are also very cunning. With stealth they quietly stalk their prey, taking advantage of anything that would conceal their presence. The prey itself might not even be aware of the lion's presence and will carry on its activities oblivious to its coming fate. Once the prey has reached within range of the lion however, the lion springs into action; devouring its hapless prey using its powerful claws and strong jaws. Those who are alert, who see the warning signs before the lion can catch them, or those who move together in groups, are more likely to escape a lion's grasp.

Satan is always looking for opportunities to draw people away from Christ. He is constantly setting traps for us; waiting for us to take his bait. Often times, his bait will look innocuous, and in our human naivety we will gravitate towards it; not realizing that there is a concealed hook that will spell our end. At other times, we will be completely oblivious to the nature of our actions, and we will deliberately persist in sinful lifestyles. In our own human perception we think that we are not harming anyone by the choices we make when in reality the clock is ticking towards the moment when Satan will pounce upon our lives.

That is why it is important to be vigilant, to be aware of the nature and consequences of our actions, thoughts, words, and attitudes. But how can we do so? How will we obtain the wisdom to see through the traps of Satan and becomes aware of our folly? Although human wisdom can sometimes be helpful in this regard, it is not the final word. Human wisdom, because it comes from an imperfect source, must be filtered through the Word of God. Only by staying close to Christ, allowing His wisdom to invade our lives through His perfect Word, will we be able to have the foresight needed to not fall prey to the devil's snares.

August 8

AGAIN AND AGAIN

"The unfolding of your words gives light; it gives understanding to the simple." -Psalm 119:130 (NIV)

I had a professor who would always implore us to constantly read the Bible. Even if we've read through all of it once, his advice to us was to read through all of it again, and again, and again. The point he was trying to make was to not be lethargic in our reading of God's Word. Rather, we should be actively seeking for God to reveal to us new truths in the Scriptures so that our understanding may be widened and that we may apply them to our lives. He made it very clear that if we are lax in our reading of God's Word, then our relationship with Him will suffer as well. We cannot separate the two for they are intricately woven together.

Often times, we feel that because we have so much Bible knowledge in our heads, we feel that we don't need to spend that much time reading the Word of God. How arrogant we are to think that we know all that there is to know! In our self-righteousness we imply with our attitudes that we don't need to read God's Word because we live perfect lives as Christians. But we seem to be blind to the fact that we are a forgetful race; who constantly needs reminding to stay on the path of God with the help of Christ in our hearts. When we spend consistent time in His Word, He will give us the wisdom and discernment to live in this chaotic world. Things that we may have overlooked will suddenly become clear to us, and God will use His Word to speak to us in our situations. If we truly need Christ and want Him to work in our lives, we must be willing to read His Word and listen to what He has to say. Those who choose deliberately to refuse to heed to His words revealed in the Scriptures, will find themselves set on a path to ruin. But those who choose to heed to the words of Christ will find life abundant.

August 9

HARDENING OUR HEARTS

"As has just been said: 'Today, if you hear his voice, do not harden your hearts as you did in the rebellion.'" -Hebrews 3:15 (NIV)

There are many reasons as to why we can end up hardening our hearts towards the voice of God. It could be that we refuse to give our lives over to the perfect direction of Christ. In our flawed human understanding and in our sheer selfishness, we want to remain in control of our destinies. We want to voraciously cling onto all that we treasure in this world and we refuse to give up those vices that we take pleasure in. It was Pharaoh's hunger for power, to remain in control over his Israelites slaves, that his heart was constantly hardened towards God's command to let the Israelites go. His deliberate disobedience to the will of God cost him the lives of many of his subjects and resulted in the widespread devastation that would visit his kingdom.

Our lack of faith could also result in a hardening of our hearts. Throughout their time in the desert, the Israelites always doubted the wisdom of God and the direction He was leading them towards. Despite being witnesses to God's miraculous provision and perfect guidance, they always displayed an arrogant disbelief that hardened their hearts towards God when hard times came. When such moments occurred, they thought that they knew better than God by saying that it would be better to return to the so-called pleasures of Egypt than to die in the wilderness; completely ignoring the fact that they were under the oppressive yoke of their Egyptian overlords. This constant hardening of their hearts would bar them from entering the Promised Land for forty years because they failed to believe that God would overcome any difficulties that they would face.

When we harden our hearts to the voice of God, we are really depriving and destroying ourselves. God promises in His Word that the plans He has for our lives are meant for good; for our benefit so that we may be given hope and a future. But when we willingly try to drown out the voice of God, we will set ourselves on the path to desolation. It will come to a point where we will be so deaf to His voice that we will not pay even the slightest heed to what He has to say. God, because we have ignored His warnings, will then have to physically allow the consequences of our unbelief and disobedience into our lives so that we may realize what we are doing to ourselves and to those around us. In most cases such a wakeup call will not be pleasant. However, God's grace knows no bounds. Even when we feel that we have passed the point of no return, Christ will be waiting with outstretched arms to save us from destruction and set us on the path to freedom and true fulfillment by coming to dwell within our hearts. We can save ourselves so much pain and grief if we simply listen to His voice; allowing His wisdom and truth to melt our hardened hearts as we trust Him and His perfect will.

August 10

ESCAPE TO CHRIST!

"No longer do they drink wine with a song; the beer is bitter to its drinkers." -Isaiah 24:9 (NIV)

I had often heard stories of people drowning themselves in drink to numb their pain. But I would see it with my own eyes for the first time when I was in India. As part of our outreach in Calcutta, I was paired with a local pastor to minister to the poor gathered around the city's hectic Howrah train station. We would sing, in Hindi and Bengali, songs of Jesus and the sure hope He offers. Afterwards the pastor would give a short lesson from the Bible. One day as we were singing, a woman came and sat amongst us. She was silent for a while, then burst into tears. The pastor asked her what was wrong. With tears flowing she explained to us that her infant son had recently died. In an effort to cope with the pain, she turned to alcohol. But drink as she might, she couldn't escape her grief.

As I prayed for the woman, I couldn't help but think how often people turn to the wrong things for comfort when hard times come. Alcohol is one such thing. When we turn to alcohol as the solution to our problems, we may find some form of temporary solace. But in exchange, we are left not only with our problems unresolved, but also with an addiction that can eventually destroy ourselves and others physically, mentally, and emotionally.

Indulging in any sort of escapism, be it through alcohol or anything else, does more harm than good. Suffering is not something that can be avoided because it is an inescapable fact of life in this world. Rather, suffering is to be met head on with Christ Himself paving the way through it with us. As frail human beings, we cannot do so through our own wisdom or understanding. If we attempt to tackle our struggles by ourselves, we will crumble under the weight of our miseries. However, God has promised that through Christ we are victorious over every evil in this world. When we have allowed Him to dwell within us and when we have grounded ourselves firmly in His Word, we will be able to weather the storms of life knowing that Christ preserves those who honor Him. We will begin to see that our trials are meant to build up our character and our faith if we allow Christ to guide us through our circumstances. When our situations become too burdensome to bear we must avoid the traps of pursuing any form of escapism; instead falling upon Christ and casting all our burdens upon Him.

August 11

COMING UNDER THE MAGNIFYING GLASS

"See if there is any offensive way in me, and lead me in the way everlasting." -Psalm 139:24 (NIV)

We don't like to be honest with our faults. As much as possible, we would like to deny their very existence in our lives. It's no wonder that we get irritated by people who confront us regarding our faults when our behavior has brought our imperfections to the forefront. We dismiss their concerns, saying that they don't understand us and we come up with reasons to justify our actions. However, even if we know in our hearts that they are right, we don't want to admit it because we fear that to do so will be interpreted as a sign of weakness and vulnerability. Thus, we choose to remain in our wrong patterns of behavior; making every effort to deny that they exist in hopes that our pride and our reputation will remain intact.

If a light bulb blows a fuse in our home, do we not rectify the problem by installing a new one? Who would say that nothing is wrong when their source of light is suddenly snuffed out? When we grope and stumble in the dark, will we still say that everything is alright? Likewise, it seems rather foolish to deny or ignore the sinful attitudes in our lives when it is brought to our attention. If we tolerate evil in our lives by our deliberate inaction, it will grow to the point where it will consume and destroy us. Often times, God uses people in our lives to make sure that we are aware of our blemishes. Even when we pay no heed to the warnings He gives us, He will continue to expose that which is impure in our hearts until we come before Him in humility and the realization that we need Him to correct the vices that we harbor. When we truly ask Him to search our hearts and see if there is any wickedness in us, He, just as a skilled potter, will make a masterpiece out of us that will reflect His glory and love. We must be willing to acknowledge that we are sinful creatures in need Christ's redemptive work in our lives. Living in denial of our sin will only serve to be a contributing factor towards our own demise. But when we allow Christ to deal with our sin according to His perfect wisdom and unhindered by our stubbornness, we will be set on the path to life everlasting free from the mire that our transgressions will trap us in.

August 12

WHOM DO WE TRUST?

"The gullible believe anything they're told; the prudent sift and weigh every word." -Proverbs 14:15 (The Message)

Wouldn't the world be such a wonderful place if people were simply honest in their speech and conduct? All the intentions of men would be laid bare and we would be able to test with confidence the purity of a person's words and actions towards us. Sadly however, this is not the case. Since humanity is fallen, people conceal their wicked motives with their charisma, using soothing talk and benevolent deeds to deceive others and bring their hidden agendas to fruition. They might try to convince us that they stand for truth, and assure us that we will not fall into harm if we follow them. But when we realize that their claims are false and they are exposed for who they really are, we feel hurt and betrayed; resolving to never trust again.

We should never abandon trust. Along with love it forms the bedrock of human relationships. If we refuse to trust, we will never enter into relationships with others. We will be trapped in our own cynicism; depriving ourselves of that which could be wonderful and fulfilling. However, we should also not go towards the other extreme by giving ourselves to naivety. We are often referred to as sheep following our Good Shepherd, who is Christ. But how often do we act like sheep before men by believing everything they say without testing their words and motives against the Word of God? Christ will never betray us or abandon us. We can place our trust and faith in Him because He is the manifestation of all that is true and good. In contrast, because of the fallen state of man, we cannot expect the same guarantees. When we are walking closely with Christ, spending time with Him through prayer and the reading His Word, He will give us His wisdom and discernment. With these we will be able to see whether or not a person is pursuing purity and integrity in their speech and interactions with us. When we place our trust in men, we will open ourselves to exploitation and disillusionment. But when we place our trust in Christ, He will enable us to act in honesty, love, and service while keeping in mind that all are prone to wickedness and need His redemptive work in their lives.

August 13

GET UP!

"Then Jesus said to him, 'Get up! Pick up your mat and walk.'" - John 5:8 (NIV)

There are many things which can hold us back. It could be things such as our past, our perceived limitations, or our own cynicism. When we cling onto these things, we use them to justify our inaction when God calls to do a certain task. But when we wallow in our self-pity, we are essentially depriving ourselves. Our woeful attitudes will become a hindrance to the redemptive work of God in our lives. We, because of our own unwillingness, will fail to see the wonderful plan that God has for us unfold in our lives. It will cause our faith in Christ to stagnate and decline as well, for by continuing to grasp onto our qualms, we have deliberately shut any opportunity for Christ to build up our faith in Him.

Do we doubt the power of God? He stands supreme over the universe. He can calm the roaring oceans and raise the dead from their graves. Through His death and resurrection, the battle over sin and death is won and in Him we have victory over all our circumstances. When He tells us to do something, it isn't so that He can watch us fall. His plans for us are for our good; to guarantee us a hope and a future. All that He requires of us to do is to step out in faith knowing that He is the one who enables us and who will preserve us on the path He has called us to walk. What are the "mats" in our lives? What are those attitudes in our hearts which chain us to the ground and prevent us from living abundantly in the life God has graciously given to us? When we surrender those attitudes to Christ and make the conscious choice to "get up" in faith, He will take us on a journey that will not only surpass our wildest dreams, but will open our eyes to see the world in the light of His eternity and never-failing love. Those who are slaves to their mats cripple and limit themselves. But those who heed the voice of Christ will be able to taste the joy and freedom of living in His glory and loving provision. Our mats will become a testimony for others to see that, though once bound, we now walk because of the power of Christ in us.

August 14

AN EVERLASTING PEACE

"I am not saying this because I am in need, for I have learned to be content whatever the circumstances. I know what it is to be in need, and I know what it is to have plenty. I have learned the secret of being content in any and every situation, whether well fed or hungry, whether living in plenty or in want." -Philippians 4:11-12 (NIV)

We would all like to possess eternal happiness. It's the driving force behind humanity's utopian aspirations, where a world would be brought into existence where sorrow is absent and joy abounds. Many ideologies have sought utopia only to be dashed by the reality that as long as sin and wickedness persists in the world, a utopia is impossible to achieve by human hands. Thus, our contentment comes to depend on our circumstances. One day we may be elated because something wonderful has happened to us. The next day, we could be mournful because suffering has knocked on our door. It can be painful sometimes to endure this cycle of emotions and we long to find that sense of peace and contentment which will remain with us regardless of our present conditions.

Where then can we find that eternal sense of contentment? It cannot be found in anything of this world. Though we may find temporary solace in the things that this world may offer, it will not deliver on its promises of providing lasting contentment. Sometimes, such remedies will cause more misery than healing. True peace can only be found in Christ. Through His crucifixion and resurrection, He conquered the two sources of suffering in the world; sin and death. Christ, through His blood, has broken the grip sin has held over humanity so that those who believe in His sacrifice may allow Him to dwell in their hearts and begin His redemptive work to clear the remnants of our wickedness. But the sting of death has also been rendered helpless for through His resurrection, Christ has conquered the grave and promises that all who believe in Him will spend eternity with Him in Heaven; the only true utopia. Our whole perspective on life will change when we view our circumstances in the light of the hope we have through Christ. Will we still feel suffering? Yes. But for those who find rest in Christ, suffering will never be able to oppress us as we allow the peace that only He can give to invade our lives. It begins now!

August 15

GETTING SIDETRACKED

"Whoever works his land will have plenty of bread, but he who follows worthless pursuits lacks sense." -Proverbs 12:11 (ESV)

We can become quite distracted at times. Situations and opportunities may arise that, at first glance, would seem inviting and pleasing to pursue. Thinking that such avenues may not open up again, we rush headlong into them; abandoning the path that we know we should be on. Our willingness to run after these distractions, although we do not see them as being those initially, can be attributed to a variety of reasons. It could be that the previous path that we were on became too challenging, or we suddenly lost interest in it. However, the moment we realize that what we thought was a worthwhile pursuit was really a distraction in disguise, we become regretful over the fact that we have strayed and wasted so much time and energy investing in something that was not meant for us to do.

Difficulty is an inescapable fact of life; even for those who claim to be God's children. If we think we can escape difficulty by avoiding it and allowing ourselves to get sidetracked by distractions, we are mistaken. Luke 9:62 says that, "No one who puts his hand to the plow and looks back is fit for the kingdom of God." God has set us on the course we are on for a reason and He promises to preserve those who trust in Him and continue to be faithful in the task that He has called them to accomplish. When we on our own effort and understanding try to navigate around the difficulties in this life, we will only end up running in circles pursuing distraction after distraction. Instead, we must seek God's direction and allow Him to give us the strength to face those hurdles and to stay on the path He has called us to walk. By holding onto His hand as we walk through trials, our faith in Him will be strengthened as He, in His omniscient wisdom, fulfils His wonderful and perfect will for our lives. When we are faithful in working on the field which God has graciously given to us, we, through His enabling, will be able to reap a lasting harvest that will outshine any sense of satisfaction that mere distractions may promise.

August 16

TRUE LOVE

"But God shows his love for us in that while we were still sinners, Christ died for us." -Romans 5:8 (ESV)

In our minds, we always have ideal images of the various social roles that exist in human experience. We all have our own notions over what constitutes such roles as the perfect parents, the perfect friend, the perfect spouse, or the perfect children. However, problems arise when we bring these ideals and try to impose them on others. Our love for them then comes to depend on how well they match our expectations for the part that they play in our lives. When they fail to do so, our love for them begins to dissipate; with intolerance becoming the extreme and ultimate result. We will keep trying to find people who will fit our ideals. But our search will be in vain; leaving us with only disappointment and regret.

Romans 3:23 says, "For all have sinned and fall short of the glory of God." If God, who is holy and knows all which transpires in the hearts of men, says that there is no one on Earth who can claim perfection, what makes us think that we will be able to find perfection in humanity? When we allow our ideals to color our view of people, we will be blinded to the reality that every member of the human race is flawed. Does this mean we should give ourselves to hate? Not at all! Christ did not reject us because of our sin. Rather, He loved us to the point of giving up His own life so that the penalty for all our sins may be satisfied and that through His resurrection we can have a restored relationship with Him. Having that unconditional love that Christ will build in our lives if we allow Him to, does not mean being ignorant to a person's faults. It means loving them and standing by them in spite of those faults; knowing that all are created in the image of God and that Christ loves them just as much as He loves us despite our iniquities. When the love of Christ invades our lives, we will not oppress others by imposing our self-serving expectations onto them. Our love for them will be true and lasting as we, through Christ's eyes and enabling, begin to love others for who they are and through His direction, seek to make that love tangible through acts of unconditional and consistent service towards them.

August 17

A WARNING AGAINST AVARICE

"As soon as Jezebel heard that Naboth had been stoned to death, she said to Ahab, 'Get up and take possession of the vineyard of Naboth the Jezreelite that he refused to sell you. He is no longer alive, but dead.' When Ahab heard that Naboth was dead, he got up and went down to take possession of Naboth's vineyard." -1 Kings 21:15-16 (NIV)

King Ahab wanted Naboth's vineyard. Seeing it as a fitting place for a vegetable garden near his palace, Ahab placed an offer before Naboth; give up the vineyard in exchange for a better one, or the total worth of vineyard itself. However, for many generations the vineyard belonged to Naboth's family. Refusing to surrender what was passed down to him by his father; Naboth would not give up the vineyard for any price that Ahab would offer. However, instead of accepting the fact that Naboth would not offer up his vineyard, Ahab grew sullen. Noticing that Ahab pined after Naboth's vineyard, his wife Jezebel assured him that the object of his desire would be in his hands. Through an elaborate and deceptive plot, Jezebel had Naboth executed on false charges of blasphemy against God and the king. With Naboth out of the way, Ahab was able to take possession of the vineyard, which he gladly did.

This story has been echoed throughout history, and continues to be a reality for many in the world today. Where human greed and wickedness persists, it will compel people to take what doesn't belong to them and fulfill their own unscrupulous agenda at the expense of the powerless. However, for all the intrigues and brutality that man may commit out of their avarice, God will not stand silent in the face of oppression. He says in Proverbs 14:31 that, "He who oppresses the poor shows contempt for their Maker…" Although the corrupt may prevail in deceiving those around them, God sees the truth and will take up the cause of the oppressed. Soon after Ahab had taken Naboth's field, God promised that disaster would visit his household and that Jezebel would be eaten by the dogs. When Ahab was killed in battle, not only did dogs come to lick his blood, the calamities which God promised would visit his family after his death were fulfilled.

It has been proven that any empire or state which runs on injustice and exploitation will ultimately crumble. Those who take the brunt of tyranny can take refuge in Christ. He sees each tear that falls, and promises that through Him deliverance from wickedness, both internally in our hearts and externally at the hands of others, is assured. At the same time, Naboth's story gives a solemn warning to those who claim to be God's children. Resorting to intrigue and deception to get our way should be far away from us. We should be content knowing that God will provide for our every need and that greed can only be cured if we allow Christ's redeeming work in our lives. When we succumb to greed, it makes us stoop into sin. But when we allow Christ to prevent greed from rearing its ugly head, we ourselves will cease from acting out of covetousness. By allowing Him to teach us how to be a servant-leader, abundant living according to His perfect standards will be our reward; using our influence for His glory and the benefit of others.

August 18

BEAUTY FROM THE INSIDE

"Your beauty should not come from outward adornment, such as braided hair and the wearing of gold jewelry and fine clothes. Instead, it should be that of your inner self, the unfading beauty of a gentle and quiet spirit, which is of great worth in God's sight." -1 Peter 3:3-4 (NIV)

It is no secret that the fashion and cosmetics industry is worth billions of dollars. But not only is it lucrative, it permeates our lives. After all, it's what we wear! Whenever we turn on the television or walk down the street, we are bombarded by advertisements featuring young, attractive models subtly promising that we can look just like them if we buy the product they are marketing. We all want to look appealing. When people compliment us on our appearance or attire, we feel accepted and loved. However, such affection will not last long if it is based on outward impressions. We could be impeccably dressed and spruce ourselves to look like models. But if the condition of our hearts remains depraved, the physical façade of beauty that we have built up for all to see will melt like wax before fire.

Proverbs 11:22 says, "Like a gold ring in a pig's snout is a beautiful woman who shows no discretion." Scripture is clear that the maintenance of our hearts is far more important than safeguarding our physical beauty. It is out of our hearts that we speak and act. Even if we try to conceal our sins from others, we are not fooling God. He sees everything done in secret and in the deep recesses of our hearts. Thankfully He is not here to condemn us, but to save us through His redemptive sacrifice on the cross. When we allow Him to convict us of the wrong attitudes and desires that we harbor and acknowledge His power over sin, He will restore and cleanse us of all our wickedness. We will understand that we are beautiful in the eyes of God because we were wonderfully created by Him in His image. Through the indwelling of His Spirit in our lives, we will be given an irresistible beauty that will shine forth from within; enhancing the natural beauty He has bestowed upon us in ways which the products of the world will never be able to accomplish.

August 19

LIFTING OUR MINDS ABOVE

"Set your minds on things above, not on earthly things." -Colossians 3:2 (NIV)

I am a huge fan of the Bengali poet, Rabindranath Tagore, who wrote during the late 19th and early 20th centuries. The period in which he wrote was arguably the most turbulent and violent in the history of the world. Amid the drums of war, the bloodshed of oppression, the cries of revolution, and the rise of ultra-nationalism, Tagore wrote these words to God, "Give me the strength to raise my mind high above daily trifles." Although his view of God was far removed from what children of Christ know to be the unquestionable truth, he recognized that humanity needs divine assistance in order to be lifted out of the mire of squabble.

How often do we allow miniscule things to take control of our attitudes? We quarrel with others over things that are of no real consequence, and get anxious over things we really need not worry about. When we succumb to these inclinations we become paralyzed by bitterness and bound by fear. Although we see clearly the consequences of our attitudes, we find it hard to rise above such attitudes on our own strength. We become like birds that dream of flight, but are trapped by a cage that they cannot break free from out of their own volition.

Philippians 4:8 says that as Christ's children, we must dwell on "…whatever is true, whatever is noble, whatever is right, whatever is pure, whatever is lovely, whatever is admirable." But can we do so through our own efforts? Try as we might, our mind slowly drifts downward into thoughts that will only serve to feed irritability and discord. However, when we let Christ to take control of our thoughts, He will fill us with His peace and His serenity. By allowing Him to tilt our heads upward so that we may dwell upon His love and eternity, we will be aghast at the destructive power and sheer folly of permitting small trifles to cloud our minds. What good will come of anger? What good will come of worry? Only through His constant intervention in our thought lives will we find His love and tranquility permeate our hearts and our relationships with others. The Holy Spirit will warn us when we are about to fall into the quicksand of quarrelling and fretting over the insignificant. We must listen to that voice, and allow Christ to mold our attitudes so that we may live and interact together in the way He intended His children to live; in the completeness that comes with resting in Him.

August 20

INTENTIONS IN PRAYER

"When you ask, you do not receive, because you ask with wrong motives, that you may spend what you get on your pleasures." -James 4:3 (NIV)

Man makes many requests before God. Even those, who would otherwise not come before Him in prayer, are not above calling upon Him for help in their hour of need. How many students, before they enter the exam hall, beg God to help them pass? How many people, wanting riches, ask God to rain wealth upon them from above? But how many of these people, when their requests are not granted, become angry and bitter with God? We misinterpret God's love to mean that He is bound to grant every desire of our hearts. But this is not the case and like spoilt children, we whine and complain when God doesn't give us what we believe to be rightfully what we require.

God knows the hidden intent of every prayer that comes before Him. He knows whether we are coming before Him with sincerity and humility, or with selfishness and malice. If our hearts are not aligned with Christ, and His perfect standards and desires for our lives, then we cannot expect Him to answer prayers that are tainted by our own corrupt nature. Just imagine if He granted every prayer that came out of the mouths of those who were not reconciled to Him and had no genuine desire to be. The world would plunge into chaos! Like any good parent, God will withhold from a child that which will only end up bringing harm to himself and to others around him.

God is no genie that grants our every wish. He is our Heavenly Father; sovereign over all, and who acts in accordance to what is best for us and for all His creation according to His perfect wisdom. When we allow Christ to dwell in our hearts by accepting that He died for our sins and that through His resurrection we have eternal life, we will become aware of our intentions when we pray. The Holy Spirit, which comes to reside in us, will convict us when our thoughts behind our prayers are not in line with what God expects of us and our relationship with Him. Can we bring our seemingly small requests to God? Of course! He loves us, and is interested in every detail of our lives whether good or bad. Yet Psalm 37:4 says, "Delight yourself in the Lord and He will give you the desires of your heart." When we do this, our desires will automatically align with God's wonderful will for our lives and He will grant them according to His flawless timing.

August 21

FORGIVING OUR DEBTORS

"At the end of every seven years you must cancel debts. This is how it is to be done: Every creditor shall cancel the loan he has made to his fellow Israelite. He shall not require payment from his fellow Israelite or brother, because the Lord's time for cancelling debts has been proclaimed...Remember that you were slaves in Egypt and the Lord your God redeemed you. That is why I give you this command today." - Deuteronomy 15:1,-2, 15 (NIV)

Human beings thirst for power. We love to lord it over others even more. Just imagine how much power high ranking leaders in the political and business realms have over those under them. With a single word or decision, they can either send a person to the heights of euphoria, or make a person's life a living hell. Many throughout history have protested against the use of absolute power for unscrupulous ends. Even to this day, the oppressed seek to seize power with the promise that things will be run differently when they are in control. But despite the lofty promises of freedom from tyranny and a better society for all, the oppressed become just as cruel and unmerciful as their former masters. A classic example is the Russian Revolution of 1917. Although it had the perfectly justifiable aim of overthrowing the brutality of the autocratic Czarist monarchy, it would become notorious not only in establishing a regime just as tyrannical, but the said regime would become a precedent for many other countries around the world to follow. The desire to avenge past crimes consumes the oppressed to the point where they cannot even tell between the innocent and the guilty.

What can break this cycle of oppression? God knew that it could be only one thing - forgiveness. He tried to instill within the Israelites the importance and value of forgiveness by commanding that if any was a creditor, there would come a time where he would have to forgive his debtor. But in our selfish pride, we don't want to give up power. Why should we show mercy? When we in a position of advantage over someone, especially over those who we dislike, why should we think that they are deserving of clemency and forgiveness?

The answer is simple; because we ourselves are undeserving of it. Christ came and forgave us of our sins not because of anything we have done on our part, but because of His unconditional love for us. He knew that it would be impossible for us to clear the debt of sin on our lives through the good deeds we perform on our own. Our righteousness are like filthy rags to Him. What is the value of a righteous act when our hearts are impure? Only through Christ's indwelling in our hearts, as a result of our personal acceptance of His death and resurrection in order to break the hold of sin over humanity, are we free from the oppressive weight of our wicked nature and cleared of our debts. That is why we must be quick to forgive, remembering that Christ has forgiven us of much when we were at the mercy of the consequences of our fallen nature. But we are unable to forgive on our own strength. It is only when we allow the Holy Spirit to mold our attitudes and take control of our actions will we be able to forgive regardless of what we feel the other person owes us.

August 22

TRULY LIVING

"He who has the Son has life; he who does not have the Son of God does not have life." -1 John 5:12 (NIV)

What does it mean to have life? When we describe someone as being lively, we mean that the person is exuberant and joyful; someone who finds happiness in everything life has to offer. We could find our sense of contentment in a variety of things. It could be in our jobs, in our reputation, in our relationships with family and friends. But if these things are our only sources of delight, they delude us into thinking we have life. Since we have laid the foundation of our happiness on things that will not last, it will be inevitable that when these things pass away, our joy will pass away as well. When we lose the job we loved so much, when our reputation is shattered, when we lose relationships to the natural passing of time or to man's wicked designs, we slip into misery and begin to see our true selves.

Without Christ, we are dead in our sinful nature. We could have all the pleasures of the world, yet be dead on the inside. Once all the fleeting things of our existence which gave us satisfaction are taken away, we are left with the realization that sin and its detrimental consequences will always be with us unless we set out to destroy its hold over our lives. But if we think that we can break the power of wickedness and reclaim our joy through our own wisdom and understanding, we are sadly mistaken. Depravity will continue to taint every attempt we make to realize our pursuit of bliss and completeness. Christ offered Himself up on the cross so that we may have life through Him. When we accept with our hearts that through His sacrifice the chains of sin are broken over our lives, and that through His resurrection death has been conquered, we are assured of the eternal life that Christ brings when we allow Him to invade our hearts and carry out His redemptive work. Our joy will be complete, our security will be unshakable, and our anxieties will be put at rest when we rest in His eternal, unconditional love and faithfulness. Through His wisdom, He will teach us what it means to truly have life; showing us how to enjoy the earthly existence He has given to us in the manner which He intended, yet always looking heavenward towards the promise of a beautiful and perfect existence in the presence of our Father.

August 23

JUDGE NOT!

"Do not judge, and you will not be judged. Do not condemn, and you will not be condemned. Forgive, and you will be forgiven. Give, and it will be given to you. A good measure, pressed down, shaken together and running over, will be poured into your lap. For with the measure you use, it will be measured to you." -Luke 6:37-38 (NIV)

I remember once watching a sitcom in which one of the main characters witnessed her neighbor fighting with a traffic cop. While commenting on how disgraceful her neighbor's behavior was, her daughter recognizes the traffic cop and asks her mother whether she had fought with the same one. The mother quickly dismisses that prior incident by stating it was different. Immediately there is a humorous flashback to the aforementioned incident where the mother is not only fighting with the traffic cop, but in the exact same manner as her neighbor. Clearly the mother was not pleased by the fact that her standard on proper public behavior was being used against her. Instead of willingly admitting that she was guilty of the same transgression as her neighbor, she denied that she was.

How quick are we to point out each other's flaws and pass judgment? By doing so, we fuel our pride and ego. It gives us an air of superiority when we criticize others for their moral shortcomings. However, we fail to realize that often times we are guilty of the same dishonorable things that we accuse others of committing. Suddenly we find ourselves feeling justified in condemning others, but cry foul when our hypocrisy is brought into the open.

God is a God of truth and of justice. He will make sure that the contradictions in our lifestyles and attitudes will be brought to our attention. Our ideas on what constitutes as sin cannot stand against the standards of God. According to His holy standards, all men are guilty of sin for even our wicked thoughts and attitudes are deemed as sin before Him. What right do we have, as imperfect human begins, to heap condemnation when we ourselves are just as depraved? God knew that man could not meet His standards. For this reason, He sent Christ to die for the sins of humanity; so that all who call upon His name and believe in His atoning sacrifice will be able to count themselves among the redeemed.

When Christ invades our hearts, He gives us a new nature and an awareness of who we are in relation to Him. Part of this nature and awareness is the desire to be imitators of Christ. Thus, we too must be quick to forgive for Christ has forgiven us of all our misdeeds. We also begin to realize that judgment does not belong to us. It belongs to the One who can claim perfection. Although we must take a strong stand against moral decay, we must not become conceited in our self-righteousness. Our responsibility as children of Christ is to allow the Holy Spirit to teach us humility and enable us to love and forgive. When we do so, others will be drawn to the God we serve and to His standards; which we are able to meet not by any effort of our own, but because of His power in us.

August 24

ANSWERING THE OPPOSITION

"Then I said to them, "You see the trouble we are in: Jerusalem lies in ruins, and its gates have been burned with fire. Come, let us rebuild the wall of Jerusalem, and we will no longer be in disgrace." I also told them about the gracious hand of my God upon me and what the king had said to me. They replied, "Let us start rebuilding." So they began this good work. But when Sanballat the Horonite, Tobiah the Ammonite official and Geshem the Arab heard about it, they mocked and ridiculed us. "What is this you are doing?" they asked. "Are you rebelling against the king?""" -Nehemiah 2:17-19 (NIV)

In all of our hearts, God has placed desires to be used for His glory. When we become aware of these desires and surrender them willingly to Him, He reveals to us the path that we are to follow so that His pleasing and perfect will for our lives may be fulfilled. As long as we continue on the path He has laid out for us and walk in His wisdom, we will be assured that we are doing what is right in His eyes. But God does not promise a smooth journey. By choosing to follow Him and His will, we will often earn the opposition of others on account of the stance we have taken. For their own ulterior motives or for their lack of an eternal perspective, they will try to dissuade us from continuing on the road God has explicitly called us to follow. They will even misuse the Scriptures in an effort to deter us.

Under these conditions it can be easy to get discouraged. Doubts cloud our minds and it becomes increasingly tempting to give in to the pressure of their voices. But we must resist through prayer; asking God to give us the strength to carry on in the task He has called us to accomplish and the wisdom to handle the antagonism lobbed against us. When we try to handle hostility towards us in our own wisdom and understanding, we will more likely than not end up sabotaging our witness for Christ. However, when we pray and ask God to control our thoughts, words, and actions, we will be given the discernment to either answer our critics in love but without compromise, or to not deliver an answer at all. When our security and our definition of ourselves are found in what others think of us, we will be forever bound to their desires and whims. But when our sense of assurance is found in the love of Christ and what He has done for us through His redemptive sacrifice on the cross, even the most violent of opposition will not shake us. We will be able to carry on knowing that God will not call us to a task that was not meant to be finished, and is faithful to those who truly serve Him and seek His will.

August 25

A QUESTION OF CITIZENSHIP

"You are no longer foreigners and aliens, but fellow citizens with God's people and members of God's household." -Ephesians 2:19 (NIV)

Most countries do not allow their citizens to adopt another nationality. However, certain countries have provisions for people who were born within their borders, but have taken on the citizenship of another country. Such arrangements allow people to freely live, work, and travel to and in the land of their birth. However, there are certain restrictions. They are not allowed to vote or hold public office because of their decision to retain the citizenship of their adopted homeland. Thus, even if someone wanted to participate and serve in the government of their native country, they have no business doing so. They have voluntarily pledged their full allegiance to another nation; making the commitment to uphold its interests and obey its laws.

When we choose to follow Christ and allow Him to live within our hearts, we obtain a heavenly citizenship. Our earthly citizenship, which we gained at birth, is not relinquished, but becomes subordinate to our new identity in Christ. He has allowed us to partake in all the wonderful things He has created for our benefit and enjoyment. However, because we are Christ's citizens, we are called to enjoy the pleasures of this world according to His laws and standards. As a result of the corruption of sin, we formed our own standards dictating how we are to live life on this Earth. But these were guided by our own limited wisdom and fuelled by our wicked desires.

Realizing the futility of following after principles of our own devising, we are now drawn to the holiness and perfection that we can obtain through Christ. By personally accepting His atoning sacrifice and victorious resurrection, we make a commitment to allow Him to help us uphold His standard in our lives. This means standing against all unrighteousness and impurity; using our entire lives to be ambassadors for Christ and what He stands for. To follow the world and its values as citizens of Christ is "spiritual treason". But thankfully, Christ is merciful and is always willing to pardon our transgressions. In light of this, we must never forget who we belong to; where our true allegiance really lies. It is only by allowing Christ's Spirit to take reign over our hearts and minds that we will become true citizens of God's Kingdom; and as citizens of God's Kingdom we make the commitment to be, with His enabling, lights to the world around us.

August 26

SELFLESS GIVING

"Then the righteous will answer him, 'Lord, when did we see you hungry and feed you, or thirsty and give you something to drink? When did we see you a stranger and invite you in, or needing clothes and clothe you? When did we see you sick or in prison and go to visit you?' The King will reply, 'I tell you the truth, whatever you did for one of the least of these brothers of mine, you did for me." -Matthew 25:37-40 (NIV)

When I was a child, there was a short story written by the Russian author Leo Tolstoy that left a strong impression on me. It began with a cobbler practicing his trade in a small village. Falling asleep one cold winter's night, he had a dream. In his dream, Christ appeared to the cobbler declaring His intention to visit him tomorrow. When tomorrow came, the cobbler was glued to his window; waiting adamantly for his Savior.

At different times of the day he saw through his window a poor soldier, and a destitute woman with an infant child; both under the mercy of the frigid winter and their desperate circumstances. Without hesitation, he opened the door of his home; providing them with food, warmth, clothing, and companionship. As night began to fall however, he became discouraged; thinking that Christ had decided not to visit him. But when the cobbler fell asleep, Christ revealed to him that He had indeed visited his house and directed him to Matthew 25:40, "...I tell you the truth, whatever you did for one of the least of these brothers of mine, you did for me."

In this self-centered world of ours, we often ignore Christ's call for His children to be hospitable towards others and generous with all that He has graciously given to us. We make excuses saying that we are too busy or that we do not have the time. Sometimes we allow cynicism and distrust to callous our hearts towards others; saying that they do not deserve our charity based on past experiences. However, in most cases, the real reason for our aversion is that we are bound by our avarice. We have been so conditioned to look only after our own needs and our own pleasures that we have become blind to the plight of those around us. So tainted are we by the vices of greed and suspicion that even when we do give, we seek out what we can gain from our charitable acts.

But Christ willingly gave up Himself; dying for all of humanity's sins while expecting nothing in return. He does not demand that we accept His sacrifice. His gift of salvation is open to all who would choose out of their free will to allow Him to carry out His redemptive mission in their hearts. Those who have allowed Christ to invade their lives will realize that they have no claim to anything in this world; for naked they entered it and naked they will depart. They will give not out of self-interest or duty, for they will not be concerned about what others will do with their generosity. But they give because of a natural outpouring of Christ's love; desiring to please the One who redeemed them from sin and condemnation.

August 27

SURRENDERING OUR BURDENS

"Humble yourselves, therefore, under God's mighty hand, that he may lift you up in due time. Cast all your anxiety on him because he cares for you." -1 Peter 5:6-7 (NIV)

Why do we feel the need to prove our strength? Although we don't deny that we have our struggles and dilemmas, we feel that to save our pride we have to present ourselves as being fully capable of dealing with the storms that come our way. However, we soon realize the limits of our individual human wisdom and capability. Yet despite this, our pride dictates that we must make every effort to cover up our weaknesses; portraying ourselves as stoic and unassailable in the face of adversity. In this way we succumb to the folly of refusing the help of an all-powerful God and the people He brings alongside our path whilst we continue to bear, with bent backs and trembling knees, the burden of our troubles.

We are not helping ourselves when we attempt to wrestle with our difficulties and anxieties on our own finite power. If anything, we are only delaying the inevitable fate of crumbling under the weight of what we have tried to master. Christ promises to give rest to all who come to Him. In His omnipotence He stands above our worries and in His love He offers to take all of our burdens; dealing with them according to His infinite wisdom and perfect will. But when we are given the offer, why do we hold back? Why do we in name surrender our troubles to God while at the same time try to dictate to Him what He needs to do? If we seek the wisdom and power of God while still wanting to master our struggles on our own strength and wisdom, we have not truly surrendered our circumstances to Him. Our pride and our desire to retain our autonomy prevent us from allowing God to fulfill His redemptive and wonderful plan for our lives. It is only by the total surrender of every area in our lives to His will that we will emerge victorious over our situations. When we allow Christ to reside in our hearts, we will know that the best way for us to handle our anxieties is to give them all up to Him, trusting in His will and resting in the assurance that He works everything together for good.

August 28

OUR VICTORIOUS LORD

"Therefore, in the present case I advise you: Leave these men alone! Let them go! For if their purpose or activity is of human origin, it will fail. But if it is from God, you will not be able to stop these men; you will only find yourselves fighting against God." -Acts 5:38-39 (NIV)

Persecution comes in many forms. For Christians living in certain parts of the world, it is violent and lethal. For those Christians living in places where the right to worship freely is generally respected and upheld, their persecution is more subtle and psychological. In both cases it can cause great discouragement and we doubt whether if Christ's message really does possess the final victory.

However, if we look at history we will find that even through the most brutal of persecutions, Christ and His Church have always emerged triumphant. The Soviets, at the height of their power, boasted that they would parade the last Christian in the U.S.S.R on state television before executing him. Yet in the end, it was Communist state which crumbled while the Church continued to grow. A more contemporary example can be seen in China. Despite vicious crackdowns on Christians during Mao's Cultural Revolution in the 1960's and 1970's, and government persecution which continues even to this day, the Church in China is experiencing exponential growth. Many are not only accepting Christ into their lives, but are remaining steadfast in their devotion to Him even under threats of imprisonment or torture.

If something is ordained by God to be fulfilled, it will happen. God is sovereign over the world. Who can stand before His omnipotence and all-knowing wisdom? The greatest examples of wisdom and power amongst men are but examples of foolishness and weakness before Him. Nothing and no one will be able to resist His good and perfect will. As His children, we can take comfort in the fact that since He has initiated His redemptive mission for humanity, He will bring it to its fruition. God will bring about the day when, as Paul describes in Philippians 2:10-11, "…at the name of Jesus every knee shall bow, in heaven and on earth and under the earth, and every tongue confess that Jesus Christ is Lord, to the glory of God the Father." Paul himself realized the futility of fighting God's will for he was once Christianity's most ardent adversary. What will be our decision? Will we in our stubbornness fight a battle that we cannot win? Or will we embrace Christ and partake in the victory we have in Him?

August 29

THE BEAUTY OF CHRIST

"One thing I ask of the Lord, this is what I seek: that I may dwell in the house of the Lord all the days of my life, to gaze upon the beauty of the Lord and to seek him in his temple." -Psalm 27:4 (NIV)

Have you ever met someone who instantly made a good impression on you? There was something about their demeanor, their speech, or their outlook on life, which attracted you towards them. Although there is always the fear that they could be putting up an act, those fears are quickly quieted when we realize that they are truly genuine and sincere in their conduct. Such magnetism compels us to say of them, "I can trust this person", or "I want to model my life after this person's example". We enjoy their company and want to spend time with them not only because they have won our admiration, but because they have also won our love and loyalty.

There is something irresistible about Christ. Why else would His disciples instantly abandon everything they knew to follow Him? When they gazed upon Christ, they knew that He was no ordinary man; that He was someone much more than all the exalted men of the world put together. However, if we really want to see for ourselves His beauty, we must put aside what others say about Him and allow Him to speak about Himself through His Word. Who would pass final judgment on a person based solely on what someone else has said about them? Today, we would label that as being prejudiced because we have not actively sought out the whole truth. When we come to His Word with an open-heart and mind, we will be in awe of what we discover. We will be humbled by His holiness and perfection in wisdom, reassured by His faithfulness and providence, assured by His stance on justice and integrity, and comforted by His never-failing love and redemptive mission for humanity.

What will our response be? Will we ignore the beauty of Christ, or will we accept Him? He gives the freedom to choose the path that we want to take. If we live our lives knowing the truth about Christ as revealed through His Word, but not making that personal commitment to Him, we deprive ourselves. It won't be long before we realize that His claims about the destructive power of sin and the futility of living morally on our own wisdom are indeed true. When we allow Christ to invade our lives, we will find true peace, security, and joy. We will desire to gaze upon His beauty and seek Him in His temple because of what He has done for us through His redemptive sacrifice on the cross and His promise of life everlasting to all who believe in Him.

August 30

THE SHIELD OF THE LAW

"Great peace have they who love your law, and nothing can make them stumble." -Psalm 119:165 (NIV)

The monsoon season in India is notorious for its torrential rains. During this time, it is not uncommon for the streets to be submerged underwater. The first monsoon I experienced was when I was in Calcutta. I was certainly not prepared! Without an umbrella and wading through filthy shin-deep water, I was especially concerned about the possibility of tripping over something that I could not see. The murky water I had to traverse did not aid me in this regard. I was greatly relieved when we found warmth and shelter in the form of a restaurant. A few weeks later I was in an auto rickshaw when the rains began to pour again. Had I stuck my arm or leg out, that part of my body would have become completely drenched. But as long as my body was inside the vehicle, I knew that I would be safe and dry.

When we live in sin we expose ourselves to its consequences. Although sin entices us with promises of pleasure and fulfillment, we find that we have been deceived when pain, regret, and a loss of security seem to be our only rewards. We try to pick up the pieces of our shattered lives in an attempt to restore what was lost. Yet because of our sinful nature, such attempts result in us stumbling and groping in the dark. However, where humanity falls, God never fails. He is in the business of restoring what has been destroyed by sin and wickedness. His offer of salvation is open to all who choose to accept in their hearts His death as satisfying the penalty of our sins, and His resurrection as the assured promise of having eternal life in Him. Through His indwelling in our lives, we will be able to understand the true purpose and intent of His law, and put it into practice in our lives through His enabling.

When we live our lives according to His law, we will be assured that sin and its consequences will be far away from us. Our hearts will be filled with His peace knowing that obedience to His law will be our shield and our strongest advocate when fingers are being unjustly pointed towards us. May we never think that His laws are meant to oppress us and restrict our freedom. Rather we must always remember that His laws are a manifestation of His love for us. He has set them in place to protect us from harm so that we may live in the completeness and bliss which comes from resting in Him.

August 31

THE GOODNESS OF GOD

"I am still confident of this: I will see the goodness of the Lord in the land of the living." -Psalm 27:13 (NIV)

Sometimes when we are overwhelmed with images declaring the declining state of the world, it is easy to wonder whether God is really fulfilling His redemptive plan for creation. But if we reflect on human history from the moment of His resurrection to the present day, we can clearly see His goodness at work. It was missionaries who established throughout the world, hospitals to care for the sick and dying, and schools that taught young minds to stand up for truth and justice. It was people like William Wilberforce who, answering God's call to defend the poor and the oppressed, spearheaded what would become the wholesale condemnation of all forms of slavery on the basis that all humans are created equal, and created in the image of God. The legal systems of the world that uphold the cause of justice find their source in the Ten Commandments. Even to this day, there are people whom God is using to further His purpose of bringing healing and restoration to this fallen world.

We should never doubt the goodness of God. Since our human perception is so limited, we cannot see the work of God in its entirety. He loves His creation immensely and He works tirelessly to redeem what has been lost to sin. If we allow God to open our eyes, we will see that He has not given up on the world. Even when we don't see tangible evidence of His work, His faithfulness to humanity is always steadfast; working every event that occurs in human affairs towards His glorious and perfect will. But what is our response? Are we but mere spectators? God has called us as His children to be willing to play the role He has allocated for us in His redemptive mission. Can we do so on our own strength? We cannot, for it is not our place to redeem people. That honor belongs to Christ. Our role is to be a light bearing Christ; willing instruments that will display to the world who He is and what He can do for them. When we walk closely with Christ, dwell upon His word, and ask Him for the strength and wisdom to put His words into practice, the light in our hearts bearing His goodness will not grow dim.

September 1

OUR PRIDEFUL SELVES

"As long as Uzziah sought the Lord, God gave him success. ... But after Uzziah became powerful, his pride led to his downfall." -2 Chronicles 26:5b,16a (NIV)

Worshiping God's blessings instead of God Himself can be dangerous. In our misguided adoration toward the success that God has blessed us with, we slowly turn away from the fact that it was Him who gave us victory over our situations and circumstances. We begin to deceive ourselves into thinking that we've gotten to where we are now because of our own talents and our own wisdom. Swollen with pride, we allow it to taint our judgment and destroy our relationships. In our deluded state, we make decisions that no wise man would make, and refuse to listen to sound counsel when it is given to us. We feel that because our skills and capabilities are far superior to others, we will not drink of the cup of failure and suffering.

As long as we place our confidence in our own limited capacity, we will always be let down by ourselves. God, because He allows us to exercise the free will He has given us, will allow the consequences of trusting in our own wisdom to visit us. He does so not to maliciously harm us, but so that we may humble ourselves before Him and see the folly of allowing pride to take control of our minds. Who are we before God? We are but dust! Genesis 3:19 says, "...for dust you are and to dust you will return." Yet in His love, He offers to transform us into beautiful works of art according to His perfect wisdom if we allow Him to invade our hearts. When we dwell in the presence of God, we will realize our place in relation to His eternity, power, and wisdom. In humility, we will want to ask Him to guide our paths and enable us to use the gifts and abilities He has given us to their full potential. We simply do not have the cleverness to skillfully master the abilities God has given us. But thankfully in our weakness He makes us strong. When we see the work of His wisdom and aptitude exhibited in our lives, we will be awestruck and praise God for enabling us to do what He has called us to do.

September 2

GUIDED BY HIS WISDOM

"Be very careful, then, how you live - not as unwise but as wise, making the most of every opportunity, because the days are evil. Therefore do not be foolish, but understand what the Lord's will is." - Ephesians 5:15-17 (NIV)

We all have moments in our lives where we have regretted a past decision or action. What we wouldn't give for the ability to go back in time with the wisdom we have now! We would have expressed ourselves differently, stayed away from those situations that ensnared us, and thought through our choices more carefully. But as much as we would like to, the reality is that we cannot undo the past. Sometimes we refuse to accept even this simple fact. How much time and energy do we waste brooding over what could have been? Instead of allowing God to help us learn from our past mistakes, we cling onto them; thereby sowing the seeds of bitterness and hopelessness in our hearts.

God's wisdom is perfect. In His omnipotence He sees what we as humans cannot. He knows what transpires in the minds of men. He knows the consequences of every action we will undertake. Moreover, His judgment is not clouded by the corruption of sin. Our judgment is tainted by wickedness. It is for this reason that we often act out of sinful impulses and selfish gain. But God, because He is holy and just, can only act out of righteousness and purity. In His love, He offered up Himself to us on the cross so that, through His cleansing of our sinful nature and through Him indwelling in our hearts, He will be able to guide our lives according to His flawless wisdom. As long as we stay within His good and perfect will, we are assured of the promise that our evil desires will not ensnare us and that the poison of regret will not consume us. How do we discern the will of God? It is only through prayer and the reading of His Word. By spending time in His presence, He will give us the strength to abandon all that is holding us back, and the wisdom to make the most of every second of the life He has given to us by allowing Him to guide our steps. With Him as our compass, let us look forward with hope and embrace the glorious future He has planned for us!

September 3

BEING A VIGILANT SOLDIER

"So Gideon took the men down to the water. There the Lord told him, "Separate those who lap the water with their tongues like a dog from those who kneel down to drink." Three hundred men lapped with their hands to their mouths. All the rest got down on their knees to drink. The Lord said to Gideon, "With the three hundred men that lapped I will save you and give the Midianites into your hands. Let all the other men go, each to his own place." -Judges 7: 5-7 (NIV)

God was helping Gideon recruit an elite group of fighting men to defeat the Midianites in battle. He knew that Gideon would need the cream of the crop; the best of the best. They needed to be strong, but also vigilant and loyal. The latter two qualities were what God wanted to see when He tested Gideon's army at the spring. When a soldier, wanting to satisfy his thirst, dunks his face into the water, he has made himself vulnerable. An enemy combatant could exploit the fact that the parched soldier has failed to cover all his possible blind spots; easily killing him with the art of stealth. However, if a soldier gathers the water in his hands and, bringing it to his mouth, laps from it, his senses are not submerged in the water. His ears are alert and his eyes are on a swivel; constantly aware of his surroundings and always remembering that he is on a battlefield. It was also a test of loyalty. The soldiers who drank voraciously from the spring revealed something about where their allegiance truly lay. If they fell into the hands of the enemy, would they be loyal to God's cause, or to the material pleasures of this world? No commander wants soldiers who would easily switch allegiances for food or drink.

As children of Christ we are in a constant battle. But this battle is not against flesh and blood. It is against the evil powers of this world that attempt to sabotage the Christian's walk with His Savior. That is why it is imperative to keep our eyes focused on Christ. When we do so, through being in constant communication with our Lord in prayer and the reading of His Word, we will be vigilant against the traps of our adversary. God will give us the strength and wisdom to resist temptation when it strikes, and to lightly cling onto the pleasures of this world. Even the most noble of desires can lead us astray from Christ if we allow it to consume our minds and distract us from being what He has called us to be as people who walk blameless and humble before Him. On our own efforts in pursuing righteousness, we will never be able to emerge victorious over sin for our wicked nature will continue to snatch victory from our grasp. It is only when we personally accept Christ into our hearts and allow Him to begin His redemptive work in our lives will we be able triumph over sin. When we permit Him to train us in godliness and in reliance on His abilities to overcome depravity, we will stand firm in the face of temptation and fulfill His call upon our lives to be the salt and light of the world.

September 4

WALKING WITH CHRIST

"So then, just as you received Christ Jesus as Lord, continue to live in him, rooted and built up in him, strengthened in the faith as you were taught, and overflowing with thankfulness." -Colossians 2:6-7 (NIV)

Sometimes, we tend to approach Christ's gift of salvation and the Christian life with the expectation that the storms of life will not visit us. As long as we have Christ in our hearts, we feel that life will be full of green pastures and meadows until the day we met our Lord in Heaven. Such an attitude leads us to become complacent in our walk with Christ. However, when the realities of living in a fallen world visit us, our faith wavers. In our frustration and anger we begin to cry out to God asking why He has failed to deliver on His promises to guarantee us a life free from suffering; something that He never promised to us in the first place.

Christ does not promise us the peace that the world gives, but the peace that only He can give in His perfect wisdom and faithful provision. The peace that the world gives has at its core the elimination of suffering. However, such a belief ignores the fact that as long as this world remains mired in sin, suffering and hardship will persist in rearing its head. The peace that God gives works through suffering. Despite the turmoil around us, we will find our source of comfort in Christ as He works everything together for good if we trust and hold onto to Him. He allows trials to come along our path to strengthen our faith in Him. When we fail to walk closely with Him and see our circumstances through His eyes, the weight of our struggles will overwhelm us and suffocate our faith. But when we stay rooted in Him through prayer and the reading of His word, allowing Him to speak into our situations, we will find a true and lasting peace knowing that God's perfect will for our lives is being fulfilled. In the light of this truth we will be able to rejoice both in our joys and in our sorrows; knowing that we are safe in the Word of God and that it is Christ who enables and sustains us in the midst of suffering.

September 5

LOVING IMPARTIALLY

"If you really keep the royal law found in Scripture, "Love your neighbor as yourself," you are doing right. But if you show favoritism, you sin and are convicted by the law as lawbreakers." -James 2:8-9 (NIV)

Who is my neighbor? For the Jewish expert in the Law, who asked this question in the tenth chapter of Luke, it was not only just fellow Jews, but those Jews who followed the Law of Moses to the letter. However, the Jewish teacher's idea of who qualified as his neighbor was far too narrow according to God's standards. Jesus, through His Parable of the Good Samaritan, revealed to the Pharisee that his neighbor was not just the people who looked and talked like him, but also those he had absolutely no intention of interacting with. Jews viewed Samaritans as heretics who defiled the Jewish faith by mixing it with Greek religion and philosophy. Naturally, the Samaritans resented this and both parties would do as much as possible to avoid contact with each other. Jesus, by illustrating the picture of a Samaritan helping a Jew in his time of need, was clear in His message; and it wouldn't have sounded pleasing at all to the ears of the time.

Are there people in our lives whom we refrain from showing the love of God? We could be perfectly warm and charming people around those whom we deem worthy of our concern, but cold and antagonistic towards those who for whatever reason are contemptible in our eyes. However, Christ's love knows no boundaries. He loves each and every individual on this Earth for we all bear the image of God, despite the fact that we are all equal before Him in our sin.

His love does not pick favorites for He never said that His redemptive sacrifice was reserved for a select few. It was meant for all, regardless of who they were, who would come before Him with hearts full of humility; yearning to see sin's hold on them broken and their relationship with God restored. If we are selective in our love towards others, then we have failed to understand God Himself and what it means to follow Him. Our righteousness and piety is meaningless if the love of Christ is not paramount in our lives. When we allow the Holy Spirit to invade our hearts and impart to us the love of Christ, we will be able to see everyone around us as being equal under His unconditional love and equally deserving of His grace.

September 6

THE LAST COMMANDMENT

"All authority in heaven and on earth has been given to me. Therefore go and make disciples of all nations, baptizing them in the name of the Father and of the Son and of the Holy Spirit, and teaching them to obey everything I have commanded you. And surely I am with you always, to the very end of the age." -Matthew 28:18-20 (NIV)

There is something powerful about a person's last words. If they come from someone whom you truly love and yet may never see again for a long time, our ears and hearts want to remember their parting request or encouragement. How much more would we want to remember the last instructions of God Himself after dwelling in our world as man? After three years of being constantly in His presence and bearing witness to His death and resurrection, the disciples must have been waiting with anticipation to hear the final words Jesus would speak before ascending into Heaven. His last command to His disciples was to go to the four corners of world telling everyone of the hope available to them through His redemptive sacrifice and guiding them along on their Christian journey. We know through historical records that all the disciples took Christ's final instruction very seriously; proclaiming His truth and training others to walk in His ways even if it cost them their lives.

In an era where religious pluralism and political correctness seem to stifle any meaningful presentation of Christ's message, we often become apprehensive about sharing our faith in Christ. Fearing that we will be ignored, ridiculed, or not have the ability to present what Christ has done for humanity, we excuse ourselves by saying it is beyond our capability. However, in our weaknesses Christ makes us strong. If we allow His Spirit to indwell within our hearts and allow Him to take control of our speech and actions, we will be able to boldly proclaim the message of Christ. It was because of the Holy Spirit's enabling that Peter, in the second chapter of Acts, was able to preach Christ's truth eloquently amidst the voices of ridicule and scorn. It is because of Christ's Spirit imparting upon His followers the strength and confidence to carry out the task He has called them to accomplish, that even today they go out and make disciples of His Word even at the risk of much grief and suffering. We are not the ones who bring about salvation in the lives of individuals, for how can the imperfect build perfection? Rather Christ is the one who draws people to Himself. Our role is to simply be willing to be the conduit through which God speaks and acts for the furtherance of His redemptive mission for the world; taking refuge in His promise to be always by our side until the day He comes to consolidate His eternal and wonderful Kingdom on Earth.

September 7

CARING FOR THE DOUBTING

"Be merciful to those who doubt." -Jude 1:22 (NIV)

Why are we so afraid of doubt? Our pride deems doubt to be a weakness and something that should be silenced for it will not bring glory to ourselves. We want to present ourselves as impervious to doubt; that our Christian life is in perfect order and never disturbed by the uncertainty that doubt brings. What is worse is that we often look down upon those who are going through a period of questioning in their lives. In our delusion, we expect that they should know all of the answers just like us; ignoring the fact that there may be doubts of our own still lingering in our minds. However, doubt itself is not necessarily something detrimental. On the contrary, it can lead to a strengthening of one's faith. It is when doubts are left suppressed and unaddressed that they fester and grow; eventually evolving into something that can seriously sabotage the believer's walk with God.

It is a natural human reaction to doubt. Admittedly, it is hard at times for our limited human perception to grasp the total gravity of who God is and His limitless power. If we are truly honest with ourselves, we can point to moments in our Christian walk where doubts plagued our mind. Yet our response shouldn't be to frown upon a man who has questions about their faith in Christ. As fellow children of God, we are to come alongside that person; strengthening his faith by directing him to the Word of God. We, out of our own wisdom and understanding, cannot resolve doubts in a person's mind.

Only the Word of God is able to speak truth into a person's situation. However, this must never be done out of condescension or derision, but out of the love and patience that only Christ can give. He never gets frustrated with us when we come before Him with our doubts. He is always willing to reveal His truth and dispel our uncertainties; even if it means explaining it to us and reminding us over and over again about His promises when we fall into doubt. What reason do we have then, as imitators of Christ, to act in a contrary manner towards our brothers and sisters in Him? Our role in helping a person overcome doubt is to simply be willing to allow Christ's Spirit to speak through us. When we do this, we will find that He will illumine our minds as well; thereby strengthening our faith as well as those around us so that together we may find rest in who He is and allow Him to help us conform ourselves to His likeness.

September 8

DON'T GLOAT!

"You should not look down on your brother in the day of his misfortune, nor rejoice over the people of Judah in the day of their destruction, nor boast so much in the day of their trouble." -Obadiah 1:12 (NIV)

Human tendency is to gloat, especially if we feel someone has gotten what they deserve. When we see someone suffering the consequences of their behavior, or when truth vindicates us in a dispute, our first reaction is to smirk and adopt an "I-told-you-so" attitude. However, where is the love and mercy of Christ, that we are called to display, in such a response? Our pride thirsts for moments to prove our superiority, to boost our confidence in our own so called righteousness and purity. But the very fact that we gloat over another's misfortune is ample evidence to prove that we are just as wicked and cruel. By slandering those who have fallen, we breed hate, contempt, and malice in our hearts; things that should be absent from someone who claims to be a child of God.

All of humanity has sinned and fallen short of the glory of God. It is for this reason that none can enter Heaven solely because of their righteous deeds. Our wicked and sinful nature corrupts any good work that we perform out of our own effort. Yet Christ did not come down to Earth to condemn the world in its sinful state, but that through Him we may be saved from destruction. The only basis upon which we can claim righteousness is that we are made pure and holy through Christ's redemptive sacrifice and His indwelling in our hearts. Christ did not look upon our failings with scorn, but with mercy and love. He has forgiven our sins by His blood and promises eternal life through Him even though we were deserving of death because of our iniquities. Therefore we must not look down upon others for their shortcomings and for the injustices they have done. Instead of performing a victory dance celebrating our righteousness over the wickedness of others, we should look upon our fellow man with the mercy, grace, and love that Christ shows us. When we allow Christ to take control over our attitudes, words, and actions we will be able to see ourselves and others in light of the grace of God and actively seek to let others know of the hope of redemption that can be found in Him.

September 9

UNDER THE WINGS OF GOD

"The earth is filled with your love, O Lord; teach me your decrees."
-Psalm 119:64 (NIV)

I love elephants. Majestic as they are, they are also immensely powerful. As the largest land animal on Earth, none can stand before an elephant's strength. Not even a lion would dare challenge an elephant in its prime; preferring to go after the weaker or newborn members of the herd, and even then being careful not to alert the rest of the group. It is for this reason that a baby elephant sticks close to the herd and in particular under the towering legs of its mother. As long as it stays within the loving protection of its mother, the young calf will be safe from the predator's grasp. Should the child fall into villainous hands however, it can be assured of the fact that its mother will do everything in her power to save her child from harm.

There are many examples from nature which reveal God's love. Jesus Himself described His love for the city of Jerusalem as comparable to how a hen desires to gather its chicks under its wing. His love for us is not self-serving in nature. It is selfless; always concerned about us and our well-being physically, psychologically, and most importantly spiritually. The very fact that we exist, that He provides us with breath and the faculties to sustain ourselves, is an expression of how much God loves us. When sin entered the world, He did not want any to perish under its destructive hold. Thus He offered up Himself on the cross so that by His death we are saved from the grasp of sin and by His resurrection we can enjoy everlasting life.

By voluntarily accepting what Christ has done for us and asking Him to enter into our hearts, He will begin His redemptive work in our lives through enabling us to live according to His holy standards. When we allow Him to help us live in righteousness and integrity according to His decrees, we will be protected from our own folly and falling into the hands of the devil. But should we stumble, we can rest in the assurance that Christ in His grace will lift us up again if we allow Him to. As long as we are under the shelter of our Savior, taking refuge in who He is and seeking to obey His statutes, sin will never wrap its claws around us. Instead, we will enjoy the peace and joy which comes from dwelling under His protection, grace, and love.

September 10

DOING WHAT IS RIGHT IN HIS EYES

"To do what is right and just is more acceptable to the Lord than sacrifice." -Proverbs 21:3 (NIV)

It is actually quite easy to abide by all the outward signs of the Christian walk. Anybody can spend their Sunday mornings sitting in church. Anybody can sing Christian hymns and worship songs. Anybody can open their Bibles and read its words. But if we claim to be children of Christ solely on the basis of our obedience to ritual, we delude ourselves. All of our acts of piety are useless if we have not allowed Christ to occupy the primary position in our lives and His Word to permeate every aspect of our being. Our lives must reflect the reality of Christ living within us. If our lives fail to reflect who Christ is in every moment of our existence through our thoughts, words, and actions, then we must ask ourselves who it is that we really serve.

God is pleased when we live according to His perfect standards of righteousness and integrity. But how can we, as imperfect human beings, live up to the holy standard He has placed before us? If we are truly honest, no one, not even ourselves, would be able to stand before God and claim any sort of righteousness. It is this fact that makes us fall into spiritual lethargy; being content with obedience to ritual because we think it impossible to obey His standards. But we fail to see that living the Christian life is not dependant on our attempts at righteousness. God, in His loving provision, has given us His Son so that all who believe in His redemptive sacrifice and allow Him to reign in their hearts may be freed from the bonds of their sinful nature and be made righteous through Him. We are redeemed from our sin not because of any effort of our own, but solely because of what Christ has done for us through His death and resurrection. Only through His enabling will we be able to live a life of holiness that honor God by doing what is right and just in His eyes.

September 11

MY REDEEMER LIVES!

"I know that my Redeemer lives, and that in the end He will stand upon the earth." -Job 19: 25 (NIV)

Job's assertion is powerful when taken in the context of what he had recently gone through. Every horrible thing that could possibly happen to a man happened to Job, and in relentless succession. His abundant wealth was stripped away. His beloved children were dead. Disease afflicted his body and darkness was his closest friend. To twist the knife further into him, the men who came to supposedly comfort Job in his hour of need did exactly the opposite! They accused him of bringing this destruction upon himself through his deliberate decision to sin against God; even though Job knew very well in his heart that he had done nothing wrong. Job had every reason to do as his wife said; to curse God and die. But despite the severity of the suffering he was undergoing, he refused to abandon God. As long as His Redeemer lives, he had faith that God, in His love and justice, would ultimately stand triumphant.

When suffering seems to suffocate us and anguish torments our soul we often tend to ask where God is in the midst of it all. Does He see our suffering? Does He care? The wonderful truth is that He does! He knows our pain and sees each tear that falls. Suffering was never meant to be a part of His perfect Creation for how can God, who is by nature good, create evil? Though we were the ones who brought sin, and therefore misery, into the world, it grieves Him to see us, His beloved creations made in His image, suffer under its yoke. He is our Redeemer. It is His desire to see us delivered from sin and suffering; working tirelessly towards the salvation of every single person on this Earth. We as His children can take assurance in the fact that as long as God remains eternal, He will work everything together for His good and perfect will. But the question remains, will we allow ourselves to abandon our imperfect will and surrender ourselves to His? When we allow Christ to reign in our hearts through our personal acceptance of His redemptive work on the cross and His glorious resurrection, we will be able to face the trials of this life knowing that God will always be faithful to His wonderful plan for us; that life is worth living just because He lives!

September 12

INNOCENCE VERSUS PURITY

"Blessed are the pure in heart, for they shall see God." -Matthew 5:8 (ESV)

What does it mean to be pure in heart? Often we confuse it with being innocent. The key difference between being innocent and being pure is that innocence carries connotations of ignorance. When we describe a person as being innocent, we imply that they are unable to commit an evil deed simply because they are not aware of the existence of the act or the possibility of carrying it out. Innocence is therefore a weak shield in the face of the reality of sin in the world. Once we become aware of sin, our sinful nature will fight to ensure that we are bound by it. To live in purity on the other hand is a conscious decision to choose and pursue righteousness and integrity despite our awareness of sin. But admittedly, it is hard to be pure in heart when sin seems to consistently pull us back.

We simply do not have the capability to make ourselves pure through our own efforts. Despite our best attempts, our impure hearts, tainted by the corruption of sin, will always serve as a detrimental force in our lives. But Christ, in His mercy and love, offers to us the hope of being made pure through His redemptive work in our hearts. By personally accepting Christ's sacrifice on the cross and allowing Him to take reign over our thoughts, words, and actions, we will be able to live in purity through His enabling. As long as we stay close to Him through prayer, the reading of His Word, and constantly asking Him to direct our steps, we will find that sin, though it surrounds us, will not ensnare us. Our understanding of who God is and what He has done for us will not be clouded by the wickedness in our hearts. We will be able to see Him in His totality; praising Him for His love, faithfulness, and mercy in our lives.

September 13

HEY LISTEN!

"He who has an ear, let him hear what the Spirit says to the churches. To him who overcomes, I will give the right to eat from the tree of life, which is in the paradise of God." -Revelation 2:7 (NIV)

Throughout the second and third chapters of the book of Revelation, God is addressing seven churches situated in what is now modern-day Turkey; then the Roman province of Asia. Each exhortation ends with the phrase, "He who has an ear, let him hear what the Spirit says to the churches." Those are powerful words! It reminded its hearers that an omnipotent, sovereign God is speaking directly to them, and attaches an urgency to follow His commandments. But how many times do we as the church, the body of Christ, allow His words to fall on ears that are not willing to do what He says? Jesus had something to say about instances when we do not pay heed to His Word. There's even a whole song, based on His parable in Matthew 7:24-27, dedicated to it! When we fail to listen to His Spirit and fail to build the foundation of our lives upon His Word to us, the rain will fall, the floods will come up, and we will be overtaken by the storms of life; drowning in the waters of misery.

In a time where everything seems to be more about our own selfish needs and wants, we either ignore God's Word completely, or misuse and twist it in such a way as to rationalize our own ideas and desires. If we think we are walking in obedience to God's will by doing the latter then we are sadly mistaken. We as His children are simply called to do what He says; not follow our own impulses justified by our own interpretations of what we think He says. We cannot pray to God expressing our desire to seek His will and asking Him to direct our path only to turn around and do what we feel is right. Prayer is a two-way street; a conversation between us and our Savior. When we pray without taking time to listen to Him, prayer becomes more of a nominal act we do to make us feel justified in the decisions we have made on our own faulty wisdom and understanding. But if we want to truly obey His commandments, we must allow His Spirit to give us open minds and hearts that will be receptive to His Word. We must ask Him to purge us of any attitudes, opinions, or emotions that will prevent us from understanding His Word and putting it into practice uncolored by what we think. When we obey the will of Christ by allowing Him to enable us to follow His Word, we will be rewarded with His perfect peace and joy; taking assurance in the fact that He will reward us in Heaven for our faithfulness on Earth.

September 14

COMMITTING OUR SPIRITS

"Into your hands I commit my spirit; redeem me, O Lord, the God of truth." -Psalm 31:5 (NIV)

Living a life of righteousness and purity is not easy. Despite our most ardent of efforts to pursue holiness, it always seems to be an uphill struggle. Our sinful nature continues to ensnare us; preventing us from walking in integrity and holiness. We soon realize that it is futile to live a life of virtue on our own strength. But this is the key moment. It is one thing to realize this fact, but another matter to decide what needs to be done in light of this fact. Often we descend into hopelessness, wallowing in our sin saying that there is no point in attempting to live a life that is impossible to live. However, instead of finding relief, such an attitude only leads to our own destruction and misery.

In our over-reliance on our own strength and abilities, we fail to take into consideration the redemptive power of God. Through His loving sacrifice on the cross He has broken the hold of sin on humanity and through His resurrection He promises newness of life in Him. When our spirit is weighed down by the weight of our sin and our circumstances, we can take hope in the fact that when we commit our spirit to Him, He will restore us. We might say that we have gone too far down the path of depravity to take comfort in any hope of redemption. Yet the truth is that Christ's grace is without boundaries. There will never be a point where He will refuse to carry out His redemptive work if we ask with total sincerity and abandoning our trust in our own capacity. All we have to do is simply call upon Him; surrendering our spirit into His hands and allowing Him to renew our hearts and minds. When we permit Him to conform our spirits to His perfect will for our lives, we will be able to dwell in the joy and freedom that comes from walking closely with Him and allowing Him to direct our thoughts, words, and actions.

September 15

CHOOSING OUR BATTLES

"A fool shows his annoyance at once, but a prudent man overlooks an insult." -Proverbs 12:16 (NIV)

We can be quite irritable at times. Instead of taking everything in stride, our annoyance can flare over even the slightest of offences. It could be over a person's minor idiosyncrasies or something that they unintentionally said. In our anger we refuse to acknowledge that the issue we have chosen to quarrel over is really of no important significance, though we delude ourselves into thinking that it is, and ignore their pleas for forgiveness and grace. Suddenly we get into arguments which spiral out of control and we end up saying things that we don't really mean. After the damage is done, we lament over the destruction we have caused; realizing the sheer folly of contending over such a trivial issue and wishing that we had been more patient and understanding.

Our God is a God of great forbearance and love. How many times do we grieve His Spirit by choosing sin over life in Him? By nature He is holy, and cannot tolerate sin. Yet despite this He sought to break the shackles of sin in our lives through His redemptive sacrifice, and continually seeks to redeem us from our wicked nature. He does so because all of us bear His image and because of this we are loved by Him as having intrinsic worth. His grace knows no bounds and He is always willing to forgive us for our iniquities. As imitators of Christ, why then should we be quick to anger and slow to show forgiveness and grace? First we must be willing to ask Christ to search our hearts so that He may identify and purge us of any attitudes that does not conform to His perfect standard of righteousness. Once we have been tested for such attitudes we must take up, through the indwelling of Christ, Paul's challenge to us in Ephesians 4:2 to be "...patient, bearing with one another in love." Does this mean we should simply ignore one's faults? No, but we must allow Christ to give us the wisdom to determine what is really worth fighting for, and tact to address them not in a spirit of rage or confrontation, but with much gentleness and grace. When we allow Christ to speak through us and control our actions, He will enable us to pick our battles wisely and fight them in such a way as to bring others into a closer relationship with Him.

September 16

LEADING BY CHRIST'S EXAMPLE

"Teach the older men to be temperate, worthy of respect, self-controlled, and sound in faith, in love, and in endurance." -Titus 2:2 (NIV)

All of us have seniority. As long as we are older than someone else, we are placed in a position of leadership and authority over that person regardless of our awareness or enthusiasm. With any such position comes the responsibility to use the powers we have been given with wisdom, grace, humility, and love. Yet how often do we use our seniority to silence any criticism of our behavior? We demand respect and the total obedience of our subordinates even while we are clearly abusing our authority and living in blatant hypocrisy. Although we will get obedience, it will be devoid of respect and love. It will only be a matter of time when the resentment of those under us will develop into open conflict, slowly destroying relationships that we cherished.

As children of Christ we are called to follow His example of what leadership truly is. He certainly has seniority, for He is older than time itself! Yet, in His perfect goodness and wisdom Christ demonstrated that a true leader does not demand obedience, but lives in such a way so that obedience would be a natural response from those who want to follow Him. In His righteousness He demonstrated the need for leaders to live in integrity and stand up for the truth. In His love He emphasized the need for leaders to be understanding and serve the physical and spiritual needs of others in total humility. The very fact that Christ Himself was willing to come down to Earth in the form of man, in all our frailties and weaknesses, and experience the sufferings and trials we undergo in order to lead us towards redemption, shows that we cannot claim to be leaders by holding onto our pride. It is for these reasons that people continue to be drawn to Christ and seek to obey His will for their lives. We cannot reach Christ's standards for leadership on our own effort, for it is in our nature to protect our pride and be self-centered. Only through Christ's indwelling in our hearts will we be able to lead in love and humility; thereby drawing people to Christ because of what He has done in our lives.

September 17

WALKING IN INTEGRITY

"You love evil rather than good, falsehood rather than speaking the truth..." -Psalm 52:3 (NIV)

We lie for a variety of reasons. However, in many cases we lie to cover up things we shouldn't have done, or things that we should have done but didn't do. The option of lying becomes attractive when we fear the consequences of our actions and thus because we don't' want to bear the full brunt of those consequences, lying seems to be the perfect defense. But although lying attracts us with the possibility of securing a lasting peace, in actual fact it often secures only a short tem reprieve from the inevitable. Once we lie, we have set into motion a ticking time bomb that is waiting to explode and destroy all in its wake once the truth is revealed. But even if the truth is not revealed, we are left with an unbearable guilt that makes us feel filthy and depraved.

A lie sets the precedence of tolerating evil practices in our lives. If we make it a habitual practice of lying when confronted with our sin, we will slowly become calloused towards not only the act of lying, but also towards the sin we are trying to hide. Guilt, like pain, tells us that something is wrong with us morally and spiritually. If we become hardened towards that intuition, we set ourselves on the path to destruction. God is a God of truth and He does not want to see falsehood reside in the hearts and minds of His children. We are called to be a people set apart in holiness and living in integrity. But we cannot lead this life on our own efforts for when the pressures are against us, we tend to give ourselves to sin. Only through our acceptance of Christ's redemptive sacrifice on the cross and His indwelling in our hearts will we be free from the shackles of sin and live a life that will bring glory to Him. When we allow Him to direct our actions and attitudes, He will give us the strength to be able to stand up for the truth, even if we have to bear the consequences of the decisions we made in our own human fallibility. He will give us wisdom and enable us to lead a life that will not require us to lie, for we will be walking blameless before Him and before our fellow man.

September 18

TO OBEY IS BETTER THAN SACRIFICE

"But I did obey the Lord," Saul said. "I went on the mission the Lord assigned me. I completely destroyed the Amalekites and brought back Agag their king. The soldiers took sheep and cattle from the plunder, the best of what was devoted to God, in order to sacrifice them to the Lord your God at Gilgal." -1 Samuel 15:20-21 (NIV)

God, speaking through the prophet Samuel, gave King Saul specific instructions about how to deal with the Amalekites. Saul was to destroy every trace of the Amalekities, not sparing even their livestock from the sword. However, Saul failed to follow God's instructions to the letter. Not only did Saul bring back the Amalekite King, Agag, alive, but he also took the best of the destroyed kingdom's livestock. When God confronted Saul about his disobedience, the king not only placed the blame on his soldiers, but he tried to justify his actions by stating his intention to sacrifice the animals to God. This was not what God wanted and because of his disobedience, Samuel warned Saul that his days as king were numbered and that God will appoint a new king to take his place.

We have a hard time coming to grips with the fact that God demands our total obedience in every area of our lives. When we voluntarily allow Christ to enter into our hearts and guide our paths, we cannot simply ignore His call when He asks us to do something that makes us uncomfortable or requires us to give up something that we desperately want to hold on to. God can only act in our best interests for He is by nature good and loving. Just as how King Agag would have worked to undermine the Kingdom of Israel if he remained alive, so too will our toleration of sin work to destroy us.

God knows our innermost thoughts and motives. Thus, He will never buy into our declarations that we hold onto the things He requires us to surrender to Him so that we may bring glory to Him. If we really analyze ourselves, our intentions will run contrary to our claims. Are there any areas of our lives which we are not willing to bring under God's refining fire? If we completely surrender ourselves to His perfect wisdom and obey His commandments to us, it is only then that we will be able to enjoy the eternal joy and peace which surpasses all understanding that comes from obeying His good and perfect will.

September 19

WAITING UPON THE LORD

"Rejoice in the Lord your God, for he has given you the autumn rains in righteousness. He sends you abundant showers, both autumn and spring rains, as before." -Joel 2:23 (NIV)

Waiting can be hard, even painful at times. When we see showers of blessings pour upon the lives of others, we often become impatient, and even a little bit envious. We cry out to God asking Him when our time will come; when will we be able to see His blessings pour upon our lives? The desires that we yearn to see fulfilled may be pure, good, and may have been placed in our hearts by God Himself. But in our impatience we make decisions in an attempt to, in our limited minds, hasten the work of God. However, we soon realize that the method we have chosen in our faulty wisdom hurts us and others more than it does good; leaving us with not only more anxiety, but with regret as well.

God has a wonderful plan for each and every one of us. Best of all, it is specifically customized for each individual person. He knows us better than we know ourselves and therefore He knows, even if we are not aware of them, all the intricacies of our personalities and the deepest desires of our hearts. God is love, and He wants to fulfill His perfect will for our lives so that we may find true joy and peace in Him. If we have allowed ourselves to let Christ carry out His redemptive mission work in our hearts and have permitted Him to direct our paths, we should not take His silence as a sign of inactivity and thus give ourselves to impatience and envy. God is constantly at work fulfilling His wonderful plan for our lives and, just as the rains have their divinely appointed season in which they arrive to water the land, He has ordained everything to happen according to His perfect will.

As long as we stay within His will by walking closely with Him through prayer, reading His Word, and putting it into practice, He will grant us the desires of our hearts. Not only will He do so in a manner that will bring us total satisfaction, but His methods will also reflect His righteousness. Trying to take control of our own destiny using our faulty wisdom and motivated by our sinful impulses will only lead down the path of destruction. But if we wait upon God and His faithful provision we will never be in want; taking refuge and joy in the fact that God, in His perfect wisdom and love, has a wonderful plan in store for us.

September 20

TRUST IN THE ONE TRUE KING!

"But the people refused to listen to Samuel. 'No!' they said. 'We want a king over us. Then we will be like all the other nations, with a king to lead us and to go out before us and fight our battles.'" -1 Samuel 8:19-20 (NIV)

People are not always who they seem to be. The Israelites thought that if they had a king, he would look after them, protect them, and bring Israel glory and honor. They ignored Samuel's warnings that having a human king over Israel would only exploit and oppress them all. Blinded by their own faulty foresight and their desire for a monarchy, they pressed on for a king. But once they got what they wished, the Israelites realized their folly. Although there were good examples of kingship in the forms of David and Solomon, most of Israel's kings, such Saul and Ahab, were wicked and deceitful. Such men did not meet the Israelite's expectation of an ideal king and they had to learn the hard way that power corrupts; even the most righteous and honorable of men as the latter part of David and Solomon's lives show.

If we place our total and complete trust in humanity we will be continuously disappointed. We are all tainted by sin and therefore, even if we present ourselves as being noble and benevolent, we are prone to bend to our wicked and ignoble desires. None of us can match the perfect standards of behavior that we have set for each other. However, the very fact that we have such high ideals about how a person should conduct himself indicates that we were destined to be in relationship with someone perfect in whom we could place our confidence and trust. God, because He is love and because He is holy and just, will never let us down. He is always faithful; never acting out of deceit because He is the embodiment of Truth. He will always care for us and protect us, for His plans are not to harm us, but to give us hope and a future. Through His redemptive sacrifice on the cross, God promises that all who accept Him as Lord and allow Him to carry out His redemptive work in their hearts will find true peace, joy, and security in Him. When we allow the Holy Spirit to open our eyes, we will see the frailty and weakness of humanity. However, we will not be averse to interacting with our fellow man, but love them all the more as we allow Christ's love to flow through us; displaying the hope, joy, and confidence that could be theirs if they choose Him as the foundation of their lives.

September 21

SOME DEBTS SHOULD REMAIN

"Let no debt remain outstanding, except the continuing debt to love one another..." -Romans 13:8 (NIV)

It is never good to leave a debt outstanding. To do so is to present ourselves as inconsiderate and ungrateful; willing to take advantage of a person's benevolence if it serves our temporary needs and wants. That is why we are taught from a young age itself that when someone extends the hand of generosity, we are to return it in kind. But how many times do we exercise kindness in the same manner as if we were giving or paying a loan? If the sole reason for acting out of goodwill is to be free of our indebtedness or to ensure that we can secure the assistance of others when we need it, then in reality our benevolence is self serving.

Such a mercenary attitude is devoid of the selfless love that we are called to display as children of Christ. His redemptive sacrifice on the cross is for all of mankind; regardless of whether they individually want it or not. As long as we live in the temporal world, His offer of grace will always be open to us. He allows us to exercise our free will by giving us the choice to personally accept His sacrifice as paying the penalty for our sins and allowing Him to work within our hearts. Therefore, He does not withhold His gift of salvation based on what we can do for Him because the salvation which He offers is based on what He has done and continues to do in our lives. In the same manner we, just as how Christ selflessly in His love works towards our sanctification, must also continuously act in a spirit of love towards others; not expecting anything in return. We must never feel as if we have done all that is required of us in the area of service, for the love of Christ is never-ending and ever-flowing. Only through His enabling in our lives will we be able to act in the selfless, unconditional love He has called us to abide by; continuing in our service and not allowing our debt of love towards one another to be paid.

September 22

LIGHTING OUR PATH

"You were once darkness, but now you are light in the Lord." - Ephesians 5:8 (NIV)

When I was in elementary school we went to an outdoor education camp for a week. One of the activities that we were to participate in was a night walk. Armed with only a small flashlight we were to navigate through the forested darkness from our starting point back to our dormitories. As a child who only knew the comforts of the city, I was scared and I feared that I would get lost. But then I saw my classmate further ahead of me turn on his flashlight. In response I turned on my own and suddenly the darkness that surrounded me was dispelled, illuminating my path in the process. As long as my flashlight was on and didn't lose sight of the light ahead of me, I knew that I would be safe. In turn, the light that emanated from my flashlight would also serve as a guide for the person behind me, giving him security in the fact that as long as he saw the light, he was on the right path.

Without Christ we are all blind. Sin clouds our vision to the point where we cannot even see where our steps are taking us. If we try to navigate through the darkness of our sin and find that path that we are supposed to walk, alone and without a Light to direct us, we can only go further into the darkness and therefore further into insecurity and sinful patterns of behavior. However, God does not want to see us, His precious creations, stumble about in the darkness of our wickedness. He wants to draw us to Himself so that we may set ourselves on the right path and find true peace and security in Him. When we personally accept His redemptive sacrifice on the cross and invite Him into our hearts to carry out His good and perfect work in our lives, He will be the Light which guides our feet away from sin and towards our loving Heavenly Father. As His children, we are also called to be aware of those around us who are lost and wanting to find the Truth. Therefore it is imperative that we live as those who are walking in the Light. We must never permit anything to dim the Light that is at work within us; constantly allowing Christ to work His righteousness through us so that others may see Him and know that as long as they follow the Light, they too will be saved from stumbling in the dark.

September 23

LETTING GO OF OUR HATE

"And when you stand praying, if you hold anything against anyone, forgive him, so that your Father in heaven may forgive you your sins." - Mark 11:25 (NIV)

How often have we come before God in prayer while holding grudges in our hearts? Our grudges, if we hold onto them, become like a poison which seeps into us and contaminates every area of our lives by its destructive touch. Clinging onto bitterness invariably breeds hate, and hate consumes our thoughts, taints our words, and even corrupts our prayers. How often do we catch ourselves wishing God to inflict His divine wrath and punishment upon the cause of our resentment? But although we deceive ourselves into thinking that such requests stem out of our need for justice, it really stems out of malice and our twisted, wanton desire for revenge.

God does not pander to our sinful desires and therefore He will not grant our requests if they are asked with wrong intentions. He is holy and pure, and He has called us to live by a higher standard that is in direct contrast to our wicked human impulses. The Christian life is characterized by mercy and forgiveness. These qualities cannot be found in human nature, for our nature, corrupted by sin, demands that when we are slighted we give ourselves to hate. The problem is that hate not only destroys others, but also ourselves; dragging us into a pit devoid of peace or joy.

In His mercy and love, God offered His Son, Jesus Christ, to die for us on the cross so that through our personal acceptance of His sacrifice and resurrection we are forgiven of our sins and are given a new nature in Him. We must realize that just as Christ forgave us of our sins even though we did not deserve it, we must also be willing and ready to forgive others regardless of what they have done to offend us. Hatred and spite are the marks of the old nature that we were previously bound to. But as imitators of Christ we must ask Him to help us abide by the new nature which He has given us. When we allow His Spirit to enable us to be genuinely merciful and forgiving towards others, our grudges will disappear and His righteousness will reveal itself not only in our prayer lives, but in every fiber of our being.

September 24

LIVING IN RIGHTEOUSNESS

"Woe to those who call evil good and good evil, who put darkness for light and light for darkness, who put bitter for sweet and sweet for bitter." -Isaiah 5:20 (NIV)

We live in an age where moral confusion has become a disease that has seeped into our culture like a poison. Abandoning absolute and universal moral values, we have adopted the position that morality is subjective and solely dependent on what the individual feels. Some might take this as a sign of progress; that such an attitude heralds an age of peace and happiness. But such a peace comes at a dire price. In the name of toleration and a wish to make everybody content, we have rationalized inherently evil practices as being acceptable, turned a blind eye to injustice, and have restrained ourselves from condemning both wickedness itself and the practice of allowing it to persist. If human society continues to degrade itself in this manner, we will silence the voice of truth, righteousness, and justice; instead becoming mindless slaves of our own depravity.

Humanity is meant to live under a set of guidelines. Without them, we have nothing to hold back our carnal nature. God, in His Word, set in place His righteous and pure standards for proper human conduct. These standards are not there to oppress us, but to protect us from the ravages of falling prey to our sinful nature. Yet if we try to obey God's Laws, we will fail because His standards are too lofty for humans to attain through any action of our own. This is why in His love and grace, He sent His Son to Earth to die for us on the cross; so that by His blood and His glorious resurrection sin's hold over us is broken and we can enjoy a restored relationship with God. When we allow Christ to work within our hearts, we will know exactly what is right and wrong for His righteousness will be worked out through us. Only through Christ's indwelling in our hearts and our constant obedience to His voice will we be able to live according to God's standards. Through Him we will be able to stand confidently for truth, righteousness, and justice; never forgetting that all are deserving of God's love and grace and that all can achieve salvation from their depravity if they allow Christ to work in their lives.

September 25

AN UNBREAKABLE PROMISE

> *"This is what the Lord says: 'If you can break my covenant with the day and my covenant with the night, so that day and night no longer come at their appointed time, then my covenant with David my servant—and my covenant with the Levites who are priests ministering before me—can be broken and David will no longer have a descendant to reign on his throne.'"* -Jeremiah 33: 20-21 (NIV)

There is something wonderfully assuring about seeing the sun rise and set. Regardless of the chaos on Earth or the corrupt ambitions of man, nothing can alter the cycle of night and day. It is far beyond human capability to do so. God is the only one who is able to cause dawn and dusk to appear faithfully to signify the beginning and end of each new day. Just as how nothing can interfere with God's divine ordination of the sun and moon to appear at their appointed hour, no human design can interfere with a promise that He has made. To this day God's covenant with David and the Levites has not been broken. It remains intact through Christ who is, and will be eternally, the Davidic King and Levitical High Priest for the entire world.

As sure as the rising and setting of the sun, we can take assurance in the fact that God never breaks His promises with us. In a world where promises have lost their meaning and can be easily broken, our conditioning asks if this is truly possible. But God is not tainted by human failings. He is the embodiment of truth, love and justice. Therefore, when He says that He will do something, He will do it. If we have allowed Him to enter into our hearts by accepting His redemptive sacrifice on the cross for our sins and His resurrection, we can find rest in the fact that His hand is upon us and that we will see His wonderful plan for our lives come to fruition. The redemptive work of Christ in the world cannot be stopped. No matter how bleak the world around us may be, no matter how desperate our circumstances may seem, we can find comfort in the fact that God is the world's Redeemer and Restorer. He will mend the brokenness of our world and lives, if we allow Him to, according to His good and perfect will. Our trust is not misplaced when we place our hope in God and His promises.

September 26

INTO ETERNITY

"Naked a man comes from his mother's womb, and as he comes, so he departs. He takes nothing from his labor that he can carry in his hand." -Ecclesiastes 5:15 (NIV)

In most ancient cultures, when a king or ruler died, all of his possessions would be buried with him in a tomb. The rationale behind this practice was that the sovereign would need them in the afterlife. All manner of things, from food and jewelry to horses and slaves, would be buried so that they would be of use to the dead king in the hereafter. But as archaeologists would find out, the material things of this world cannot be taken with us when we die. Everything that the kings thought would be with them in the afterlife remain sealed in their tombs and if their possessions did not fall prey to natural decay, they are displayed in museums all around the world; even then in environments where there is no guarantee that they will survive forever.

We often seem to be oblivious of this basic fact of life; naked we enter this world and naked we will return. We spend so much time accumulating wealth; hording material possessions in an effort to boost our prestige. But for what? When we succumb to the inevitability of death, our wealth will be divided amongst others; our houses and possessions sold to strangers. Even a reputable name will eventually be forgotten underneath the sands of time. This then begs the question, is there anything which can claim eternity? There is, but it is something not of this world.

God is eternal, and before we disobeyed Him and allowed sin to enter this world, humanity was destined to live forever. Once wickedness corrupted us and the world however, the life-giving relationship we shared with God was ruptured. But because God is love and wanted none to perish, He offered His Son to humanity so that through His redemptive sacrifice on the cross and His resurrection, we may have our relationship with God restored and partake of the eternal life He offers. The redemptive work which Christ initiated on the cross is eternal and once we choose life in Him, it will never be snatched away. When we choose to invest in the treasure that will not give to rust and decay, we will find the unshakable security and peace which comes from knowing Christ in a personal way. Our priorities will be re-aligned as we find our source of fulfillment not in what we can obtain for ourselves, but what God does through us as He brings to fruition the wonderful and eternal plan He has for the entire world.

September 27

RISING ON WINGS LIKE EAGLES

"...but those who hope in the Lord will renew their strength. They will soar on wings like eagles; they will run and not grow weary, they will walk and not be faint." -Isaiah 40:31 (NIV)

I loved wearing my school uniform. Every morning I would make sure that it would look neat and crisp before I went to classes. What I loved most about it however was that emblazoned on my tie and vest was an eagle with an outstretched wing. Written underneath were the words "Isaiah 40:31". Whenever I was going through anxious times in school, I would always find hope in the promise that was written on my uniform. As long as I placed my hope and faith in the Lord, He would never fail to renew my strength. He will raise my spirit above the concerns and cares of this world on the sure assurance that He will be the one to carry me through the dark times I face.

Why do we give into excessive worry and fear? When the clouds of misery and grief darken our skies, it is a natural response. We feel as if the burdens of our circumstances are meant to be borne solely on our own shoulders. In our limited human perception, we see no other alternative. But humanity was not meant to bear such a burden. We were meant to live in the peace and joy that comes from knowing and relying on our Heavenly Father. Once sin entered the world through our deliberate choice to disobey, not only did suffering enter as well; but the blissful relationship we shared with God was severed because of our wickedness. Yet God is the restorer of all things. Through His loving sacrifice on the cross and His glorious resurrection from the grave, we are all given the hope of being redeemed from our sin and our relationship with God restored if we allow Him to carry out His restorative work in our hearts. As Christ's children who bear His presence, we must never forget that we do not live this life on our own. We will always have Christ who, if we allow Him to, will strengthen us when we feel weak, revive our spirits when they are crushed, and comfort us in our darkest hour. When we place our hope in Him, His peace will overflow through us; bearing witness to all who see us that there is a God who can and will lift them up if they call upon His name.

September 28

SPEAKING THE WORDS OF GOD

"If anyone speaks, he should do it as one speaking the very words of God…" -1 Peter 4:11 (NIV)

We have often heard the maxim, "Actions speak louder than words". But by no means does it indicate that we should neglect the way we conduct ourselves in our speech. If anything the words which we say, and the way we say them, reveal something about our character, our values, and our entire outlook on life. Anybody can act in a kind and charitable fashion. However, when we are in environments where we are not hindered by mere social convention or when the wrong buttons have been pushed to arouse our ire, it will be our words which will betray any façade we have created. Out of the heart, our mouths will speak and our words will reveal to others what we really serve and hold dear.

It is interesting to note that God reveals who He is not merely through His actions, but primarily through His words.

The words He used to speak the world into existence reveals His creativity and loving provision. His commandments and decrees to His people and prophets reveal His nature as being, pure, holy, and just. His constant assurances towards those who are undergoing or entering into a period of trials and suffering, display His great love and faithfulness. The very fact that we have the Bible, literally God's Words to humanity, shows the importance that God places on words and speech. As His children who are called to be His witnesses on Earth, every part of our lives must display His character being manifested in us. The tongue is no exception. Our words should reveal our Lord as being uncompromisingly holy, faithfully just, and irresistibly compassionate. When we allow Christ to take reign over our hearts and mouths, we will be able to speak life into the hearts of those around us; using our tongues as a witness for who He is and what He can do for all who call upon His name.

September 29

KEEPING IN STEP

"Since we live by the Spirit, let us keep in step with the Spirit." - Galatians 5:25 (NIV)

Anyone who has been involved in a dance troupe or has danced in a formal ballroom setting knows the importance of keeping in step. If even one person in the troupe or couple fails to be in perfect co-ordination with their partners, the entire performance of the group will look unsynchronized even if the others were carrying out their part flawlessly. What will amaze the audience is not just the aesthetic beauty and complexity of the movements the dancers perform, but also whether the dancers are working together in harmony with each other. That is why they undergo constant training; making sure that everyone is in step so that their performance will be without blemish.

The Christian life is meant to be lived while being constantly in step with the Holy Spirit residing in our hearts. When we personally accept Christ's redeeming sacrifice for us on the cross and allow Him to guide our paths, we acknowledge His leadership over every area of our lives. He is leading us towards making choices that will perfect His righteousness in our lives so that we may live life in its true beauty and bliss. When He prompts us to do something that will contribute to the realization of His will in our lives, our role is to simply obey and trust that everything is in His hands. If we refuse to obey His leading and go off on our own direction and faulty wisdom, it will be just as if a dancer decided to spontaneously deviate from the pre-arranged choreography of the group. He may think he is doing everything right when really he is making a fool of himself. Likewise, people will look at our lives with puzzlement and scorn when they see us claiming to be Christ's children, but living contrary to everything He stands for through our thoughts, words, and actions. When we surrender our lives to Christ, abandon all our wrong attitudes and values, and permit Him to guide our steps, He will lead us in a dance that will allow His righteousness to shine forth; leading others to be astounded and drawn to the redemptive work of God in our lives.

September 30

HIS GRACE IS ENOUGH

"But he said to me, 'My grace is sufficient for you, for my power is made perfect in weakness.' Therefore I will boast all the more gladly about my weaknesses, so that Christ's power may rest on me." -2 Corinthians 12:9 (NIV)

We all have areas in our lives where we fall prey to temptation and ensnare ourselves in sin. Although our pride would like to tell us that we are of a perfect breed cut above the rest, if we are truly honest with ourselves, we can all point to areas in our lives which reveal our human weakness and fallibility. In light of this fact, it is easy to become discouraged and chained by despair. We tell ourselves that we are not good enough; that we have not attained that state of perfection, which everyone else around us seems to have achieved, in order to serve God. Such an attitude not only hinders us in our Christian walk, but it also sows the seeds of bitterness and insecurity in our hearts.

Throughout the Bible, God uses sinful people to fulfill His perfect will. Moses was a murderer and yet it was he whom God choose to lead the Israelite out of Egypt. Jonah was disobedient towards God and disliked the people of Nineveh; deeming them to be not worthy of God's mercy. Yet God was able to use him to bring that city into a right relationship with their Creator. Paul, the man responsible for writing much of the New Testament, struggled with what he referred to as his "thorn in the flesh." What Paul actually meant when he said this is uncertain, but it is sometimes interpreted as an area of his life that often harassed him with temptations. God, because He is loving and all-powerful, is able to work through us despite our sinful inclinations. Yet

He can only work through us if we have accepted His redemptive sacrifice on the cross for our sin and allowed Him to dwell in our hearts. We are not saved because of how holy we are, but solely because of God's grace which He has lovingly bestowed upon us.

Though sin's hold on our lives has been broken through the shedding of Christ's blood, there will be times when, because of our human weakness, we will fall into sin. Yet as long as Christ lives and works within our hearts, there is always forgiveness if we come before Him with a repentant spirit. Satan would like us to believe that we are of no use to God because of our wickedness. But God says that He will pick us up when we fall. In His love and compassion He will never give up on us. If we allow Him, He will empower and strengthen us to do His work despite our weaknesses so that we may not boast of any efforts of our own; but boast in the redemptive power of Christ and what He can do for all who come to Him.

October 1

MAN IS BUT A VAPOR

"Fear of man will prove to be a snare, but whoever trusts in the Lord is kept safe." -Proverbs 29:25 (NIV)

People can be intimidating, especially if they command an aura of authority and strength. Since we can never truly predict the reactions of people, we often shy away from saying or doing anything that would, in our minds, provoke or offend them. As a result, we become paralyzed by fear. Every thought and prompting from God suddenly becomes subject to what others would think or say. When this happens, our fear of people's reactions takes precedence over God's call to display His love and stand up for His truth. But this shouldn't be! Who is man that we should cower in fear before them? We all share the same sinful and mortal nature; prone to error and destined to one day face death. None can claim superiority over another for we are all equal before God. Yet all too often we tend to forget this fact and remain enslaved to the opinions of others.

When we place our trust in God, we are assured of the fact that He never forsakes those who call upon His name. As beings created in the image of God, He sees us as having intrinsic worth and are therefore intensely loved by Him. When we allow Him to enter into our hearts through accepting his atoning sacrifice for our sins on the cross and partaking in the new life he offers through His resurrection, we will be able to dwell in the assurance that He never abandons His children. He will always remain faithful and steadfast in His love and provision. In light of this assurance, the opinions of others become irrelevant and meaningless. With Christ's guiding our minds and hearts, we will be able to see that their opposition to His truth stems from their own faulty wisdom and their corrupt attitudes. Why then do we listen to the voice of men? Why do we bend our knee to the imperfect when we should heed the voice of the One who is the embodiment of perfection? Through Christ's power in us, we will be able to stand boldly before men and proclaim His truth and love; knowing that our sense of security and confidence comes from One who is greater than man and who will always defend those who obey His voice.

October 2

STANDING FOR CHRIST

"Blessed are you when people insult you, persecute you and falsely say all kinds of evil against you because of me. Rejoice and be glad, because great is your reward in heaven, for in the same way they persecuted the prophets who were before you." -Matthew 5:11-12 (NIV)

Sometimes being the bearer of God's truth can be a formidable and daunting task. Not everyone will want to hear it, for God's truth has the tendency to pierce deep into the inner recesses of the soul and reveal areas in our lives where His cleansing power needs to wash us of sin and wrong attitudes. This fact makes people uncomfortable. Out of a desire to hold onto their wickedness or to tolerate its presence in an effort to not disturb the peace, others will do all that they can to snuff out the truth and drown its voice. In such a climate it is easy to give into discouragement and question whether we did what was right in taking a stand for God's righteousness and truth.

God never promised that upholding His cause would be an easy task. If the examples of the prophets and of Christ Himself are an indicator, standing up for what is right and pure in a sinful world can often be dangerous, painful, and lonely. But God, in His goodness and love, promises that those who call upon His name and are obedient to His call to proclaim His truth never fight alone. If He has given us His torch of righteousness to bear and go forth into the darkness, He will see to it that it is never snuffed out. Through the suffering and opposition we may endure, He will be the one to help us raise His torch when we are weak and give us the boldness to speak when our mouths fall silent. As long as we allow Christ to guide our steps towards the fulfillment of His perfect will for the world, we can be assured in the fact that our simple obedience to Him will not return void; that God will work out His redemptive mission even in the face of vehement opposition. As children of Christ who know that their security and strength comes from God, we must always be ready and willing to stand up for His truth and for what is pure and just. It may not be the most comfortable of tasks and it may result in conflict. But God sometimes needs to shatter the false sense of peace and façade of righteousness we have created if true restoration and peace is to flourish.

October 3

CHOOSE WISDOM!

"Now, O Lord my God, you have made your servant king in place of my father David. But I am only a little child and do not know how to carry out my duties. Your servant is here among the people you have chosen, a great people, too numerous to count or number. So give your servant a discerning heart to govern your people and to distinguish between right and wrong. For who is able to govern this great people of yours?" -1 Kings 3:7-9 (NIV)

There is something admirable about Solomon's choice. When God offered to give him either riches and power, or wisdom and discernment, Solomon chose the latter. There is no hint of pride or of a desire for selfish gain in Solomon's request. He wanted wisdom not so that he could boost his own reputation or authority, but to serve God's people in the manner that He would have intended; in righteousness and justice. Solomon wanted to be a good steward of whatever God would give him, yet he knew that he couldn't be that good steward through his own fallible understanding. He needed God's wisdom and guidance to help him make choices that will benefit the people while bringing glory to God. For his humility and willingness to be guided by heavenly counsel, God promised Solomon wealth and power; not through any ability of his own, but because they would be by-products of Solomon's continued obedience to Him.

How many of us would choose the opposite? Choosing wealth and prestige over the wisdom to manage it? We would like to think that we are wise enough to manage our own affairs; that our wisdom is not prone to error. But the truth is that we often make selfish and destructive decisions that help neither ourselves nor others. If we were given absolute power and wealth to use according to our own discretion, we would mostly likely squander our wealth, abuse our power, and bend to our prideful and avaricious nature. God assures us that if we willingly choose to surrender our hearts to Him and allow His Spirit to reside in us and guide our steps, we will be able to become good stewards of what He has given us. Our eyes will be opened to what He values and we can be assured of the fact that when we live through the Spirit's enabling according to the Laws of God, we will find success and peace in the truest sense. God's plans for us are good and perfect. He will never lead us towards our destruction because not only is it counter-productive to His redemptive mission for the world, but it goes against His very nature as being loving and just. Riches and power are fleeting. But having the power of God residing within us and His wisdom guiding us will help us to live life to the fullest and to be responsible with whatever we have.

October 4

LETTING GO WITH GRACE

"...a time to search and a time to give up, a time to keep and a time to throw away," -Ecclesiastes 3:6 (NIV)

Autumn has always had a special place for me as a season. Not only is it wonderful to see hues of red, orange, and yellow painted on the leaves, but watching the same leaves fall gracefully from the trees has always illustrated an essential truth for me. God has appointed a time for each and every leaf to detach itself from the tree; thereby making it bare. But suppose if a tree refused to give up its beautiful shades of color? Afraid of being stripped of its glory, what if the tree defiantly retained its leaves of red, orange, and yellow throughout the snows of winter? If that happened however, how will the new leaves grow? How will the blossoms of spring flourish? The two simply cannot co-exist together.

Often we do not want to let go of certain things in our lives. They could be perfectly wonderful things in and of themselves. Material possessions, successful careers, fulfilling relationships, all of these can be extremely hard to let go. But when the hour has come for them to pass, we are hesitant to accept that fact. We become angry and bitter with God for allowing such suffering to visit us. In our limited human foresight we fail to see that God has a wonderful plan for our lives. Just as the autumn leaves need to part in order to make room for the beauty of spring, God promises that if we surrender everything to Him and let go of the things that are holding us back, He will bring about beautiful changes in our lives that will bear witness to His love and faithfulness. All He expects of us is to simply wait on Him and allow Him to fulfill His good and perfect will for our lives. The only thing that will stand between us and true restoration and healing is our unhealthy attachment to the past and to wrong attitudes that we harbor. With grace and with Christ's indwelling in our lives, let us leave behind all that which needs to be let go and embrace the future He is preparing for us, knowing that Christ is the one who will sustain and preserve us through all uncertainty.

October 5

GRASP HIS HAND!

"Now a man crippled from birth was being carried to the temple gate called Beautiful, where he was put every day to beg from those going into the temple courts. When he saw Peter and John about to enter, he asked them for money. Peter looked straight at him, as did John. Then Peter said, 'Look at us!' So the man gave them his attention, expecting to get something from them. Then Peter said, 'Silver or gold I do not have, but what I have I give you. In the name of Jesus Christ of Nazareth, walk.' Taking him by the right hand, he helped him up, and instantly the man's feet and ankles became strong." -Acts 3:2-7 (NIV)

Often times we are just like the beggar. When uncertainty or trials weigh heavily on our lives, we ask God for deliverance. But in our own limited wisdom, we expect God to deliver us according to what we see as the solution to our woes. We feel that if only our desires met, if only our plans are fulfilled, only then will our problems be solved. With this in mind we pray, hoping that God will grant us what we want to see accomplished in our lives. However, we do not realize that our plans will only treat the symptoms of our problems instead of the root. The beggar's dependence on the alms of others may have bought him a meal, but it wouldn't have cured him from his crippled state.

God's ways are far better than our own. In His infinite wisdom He knows exactly what we need even before we ask it of Him and even before we come to the realization that we need what He has to offer. What's more is that His plans will always work for our ultimate good. He will never call us to step out in faith only to watch us fall. If we abandon ourselves and our circumstances to His perfect will for our lives, He will give us more than we could ever ask for. Clinging onto our own plans and desires for relief, will serve to deprive us of the hope which could be ours in Christ. But if we personally accept His redemptive sacrifice on the cross and allow Him to enter into our hearts we can take great assurance in the fact that if we grasp onto Him and permit Him to guide our steps, He will be faithful. We will be constantly affirmed of the fact that He will never turn back on His promise to us to lift us out of our circumstances through His omnipotence. Resting in this assurance, we will find true joy and fulfillment knowing that Christ is the one who will eternally sustain us according to His flawless understanding; not our own.

October 6

THANK GOD FOR THE PEOPLE!

"I thank my God every time I remember you. In all my prayers for all of you, I always pray with joy..." -Philippians 1:3-4 (NIV)

It is so easy to thank God for the people we love. These are the individuals in our lives in whom we take great pleasure in just by being in their company, and who makes our eyes light up at the thought of them. But what about those people in our lives whom we look upon with hatred and anger? Whenever they come up in our minds, we want to do everything but thank God for them and pray for them with joy. If we continue to foster a seething malice toward them in our hearts and minds, it will consume us; crippling us in our walk with Christ and prevent us from showing His love. Our focus will shift away from God and onto the hatred which we continue to nurture; thereby becoming a destructive idol which will only enslave us in bitterness.

Hatred will only breed more hatred. We enter into a vicious cycle that will eventually destroy ourselves if we contribute in any manner to the growth of spiteful attitudes towards those who are the objects of our anger. There is only one way to break this cycle in our lives; by allowing the love of Christ to permeate every area of our being. When we personally accept Christ's redeeming sacrifice for us on the cross and allow Him to conform our minds and attitudes to Himself, we will see others in a whole different light. We will see that all of us are fallen souls; all needing redemption and deserving of God's grace and love. By submitting our attitudes and hate to the love of Christ in us, His love will work through us. Through Him we will be able to thank God for each and every life; that fallen as a soul may be, as long as God sustains life there is hope for that soul under the assurance that God's grace knows no limits. For this reason we can pray with joy knowing that when we pray for our enemies, Christ love will overpower both our hate and their attitudes as He fulfils His wonderful redemptive work for all our lives.

October 7

AN ETERNAL REFUGE

"Trust in the Lord forever, for the Lord, the Lord is the Rock Eternal." -Isaiah 26:4 (NIV)

When I was traveling through the Himalayan foothills, I was awestruck by the beauty that surrounded me. Driving on winding roads through mountain forests, while mist danced around their boughs, was truly a breathtaking experience. It is no wonder that India's erstwhile British rulers often came here to get away from the heat and troubles of the plains, and that Buddhist monasteries dot the landscape. Mountains have the effect of creating an atmosphere of safety and refuge; a place where one could retreat to when the world seems too chaotic and overwhelming to bear. Yet in an age where machines of destruction can soar above the peaks, and modernized armies can penetrate the hills, it would seem that not even mountains can offer the same degree of protection and security that they once promised.

We turn to all manner of things in an effort to gain a sense of peace and sanctuary. But all too often, we place our trust and hope in things that will eventually pass away. Everything under the sun is transient; be it nations, material possessions, people, or even ourselves. If our security is based on the fleeting things of this world, then our sense of security and worth will be fleeting as well. This is why insecurity and fear grips our hearts and minds. But we were not meant to live with these feelings. We were meant to place our hope in something that is eternal and transcends this world. Man was destined to live under the loving and faithful provision of our Heavenly Father. Yet because we choose sin, our relationship with Him was severed. But in His love and compassion He sent His Son, Jesus Christ, to die on the cross so that through Him, the wall of sin that separated us from God may be broken. When we personally accept Christ's sacrifice for us and allow Him to dwell within us, we will find that when we rely on Him, He will be our impregnable fortress. Where the world fails us, we can be assured of the fact that Christ never will; that when we take refuge in Him alone we will find a lasting peace and hope which will carry us through whatever our temporary circumstances may be.

October 8

FINDING THE WAY

"All a man's ways seem right to him, but the Lord weighs the heart." -Proverbs 21:2 (NIV)

The human heart is corrupt. As long as sin continues to permeate our being, our wisdom and reason will be sabotaged by our wickedness. This is why sin continues to make a mockery of any philosophy or ideology formulated and implemented through human wisdom alone. Although in our eyes we might seem to be doing what is right and true, our depravity blinds us from seeing the true scope of our actions. God takes our sinful nature into account and because He cannot tolerate sin on account of His holiness, any sort of self-proclaimed righteousness of our own is like filthy rags before Him. No amount of good or good intentions can justify what evils we commit, what principles we bend, in order to achieve our goals; even if the goal we aspire to fulfill is noble in and of itself.

However, God does not wish to leave us with a sinful heart. He sees the consequences of sin in our lives and grieves over the fact that it will consume and destroy our lives no matter how hard we try to overcome our wickedness on our own strength. In His love and grace He has provided us His Son so that through a personal belief in His death and resurrection our sinful nature is washed away and we can partake of a new life in Christ. When we allow Him to perfect His wisdom in us, we will be able to act in a manner that will fulfill His wonderful will in our lives. As long as we remain within His will and allow Him to enable us in His righteousness so that we may obey His perfect commandments, we will not be ensnared in the mire of sin in our pursuit of what is good and pure. Human wisdom and good intentions alone will never be able to bring us happiness or heal a hurting world. It may ironically serve to do the opposite. But if we allow our hearts and minds to be molded by Christ, we can trust in the hope that His wisdom will never fail us, and is there so that we can live abundantly in Him; at the same time being lights that will shine forth His truth and righteousness into a world engulfed by darkness.

October 9

DON'T COMPLAIN!

"Do everything without complaining or arguing, so that you may become blameless and pure, children of God without fault in a crooked and depraved generation, in which you shine like stars in the universe" - Philippians 2:14-15 (NIV)

Sometimes, we whine and complain when in reality there is no reason to do so. Our circumstances could be absolutely wonderful and even envied by others. Yet blinded by our selfishness and greed, we voraciously demand for more. Instead of being gracious and grateful for the opportunities given to us, we take advantage of the goodwill shown to us by finding unscrupulous ways to satisfy our avarice. Under illusory injustices or blackmail we convince others to support us in falsely vilifying and extracting "compensation" from our hapless victims. However, there is a fine line between fighting injustice and committing extortion. Although we might convince everyone around us that our cause is true and pure, God is the one who tests the heart. If our complaints stem from our selfish wants and not out of a desire to uphold His truth and righteousness, God will make sure that our ulterior motives are brought to light.

As children of Christ we are called to serve while bearing with one another in love. When we allow Christ to invade our hearts and conform ourselves to His likeness, we will want to serve others in a way that would edify them and bear witness to the goodness of Christ residing in us. Making unjust complaints and using deception to get what we want runs contrary to who we are representing on Earth. Wherever we are placed, God has appointed people in our lives so that we may display His mercy, grace, and love in our service and interactions with them. Unless the people we serve truly overstep God's Laws, we are not to raise our voice in resolute opposition towards their benevolence. When we allow Christ to purge us of our sinful nature, we will be able to see through His eyes the truth of our circumstances and the world around us. Where God's righteousness and truth are upheld, we are to continue in its preservation and not seek to destroy it. Where injustice truly rears its head, we are to condemn it. However, we should not condemn injustice by committing more injustice. Rather we are to fight against it in a manner that is in keeping with God's expectations for us to live a life that is above reproach. In this way, through God's power and guidance, we will walk in a manner that is set apart from the crooked and depraved of this generation; bearing Christ's Light to the world.

October 10

TAKING UP THE CAUSE

"Defend the cause of the weak and fatherless; maintain the rights of the poor and oppressed. Rescue the weak and needy; deliver them from the hand of the wicked." -Psalm 82:3-4 (NIV)

Our world is full of people who are under the yoke of oppression and poverty. To be blind to this fact only accentuates the ignorance that we have allowed to cloud our minds as a result of living a life where our major concern is solely looking out for our wants and needs. Sometimes, we deliberately want to shut out images of suffering in this world. We do not want our lives to be disturbed or inconvenienced by what injustices are permeating the world we reside in. In some cases, we may even profit by tolerating evil and exploitation in our midst. But if we are not resolute in our denouncement of injustice and tyranny, even if we remain silent before its presence, we are contributing to its existence. Brutality thrives and innocent blood flows where apathy and appeasement are the order of the day.

As children of Christ we are called to display His light within us by serving one another in love and being vehement in our opposition towards wickedness and injustice. When we allow Christ to reside in us and allow Him to carry out His redemptive work in every area of our lives, He cleanses our hearts and minds of all impurities. But His restorative mission is not just for our individual selves. It is meant for every single person in this world. If God does not tolerate wickedness in our lives, what makes us think He would be lenient towards wickedness in the world at large? Our actions reflect Christ in us. When Christ molds our attitudes and directs our steps, others will see that God is not one to stand idly by when the world is convulsing in pain. He is a God who actively seeks to uphold His truth and justice, bring deliverance to the oppressed, and restore the world from its fallen state. Passivity and indifference when confronted with the realities of living in a world tainted by sin is not an attitude from God. Through His enabling and our obedience to His call to stand for His righteousness and truth, Christ will fulfill His mission to redeem the world from both its physical corruption and spiritual depravity.

October 11

CONFORMING OURSELVES TO CHRIST

"May the words of my mouth and the meditation of my heart be pleasing in your sight, O Lord, my Rock and my Redeemer." -Psalm 19:14 (NIV)

Hypocrisy begins when we have not brought every area of our lives under the scrutiny of Christ residing in us. We are sadly mistaken if we think we can be successful in living a life where our faith in Christ does not inform our inward thoughts and outward actions. Slowly our minds and hearts will begin to dwell on things that are not becoming of a child of Christ. Slowly, our words will no longer bear witness to Christ and His righteousness. Our desires to cling to our own attitudes, our own values, will eventually cripple our witness for Christ. We will find ourselves drawing further away from Him and from the safety and security that comes from living within His good and perfect will.

In an age where to conform to something has been labeled as negative and totalitarian, we have made ourselves as the supreme authority. Only our judgments and our interpretations are valid and right. But the problem with placing authority on ourselves is that we are fallen creatures. In our wickedness and faulty wisdom we superimpose our errant beliefs on issues and even use them to interpret the Word of God in an effort to justify our wayward convictions. What we will find is that by idolizing ourselves and our own sinful values we uphold the cause of depravity instead of righteousness. When we allow Christ to enter into our lives and break our wicked nature, He will begin the process of restoration in our hearts by conforming us to Himself in His perfect righteousness. The only thing that will slow this process is our own stubbornness and our hesitance to surrender every area of our lives to Him. We can trust His perfect will for He guarantees that He never works anything for evil, but always for the good of His children. By conforming ourselves to Christ and allowing Him to make our words and thoughts synchronize with His perfection, we can rest in the fact that in all our actions we bear witness to Christ working within us His wonderful redemptive plan for us and for the world.

October 12

CALLING FOR HELP

"O Lord my God, I called to you for help and you healed me." - Psalm 30:2 (NIV)

In our stubbornness and pride we often deny that we need healing and restoration in our lives. We do not want to portray ourselves as weak or deficient in anyway. Conversely, in our timidity and insecurities, we feel that it is not our place to ask for assistance when we desperately need it. We have the very wrong impression of thinking that we are unworthy to do so. Both extremes however, result in us constructing a façade of contentment and joy in an attempt to convince others and ourselves that everything is well with our soul when it is really not. If we persist in this manner, our physical and spiritual aliments will not only betray the façade we have attempted to maintain, but we will rot from the inside as a result of not crying out for help.

When we enter into a relationship with Christ it is not one of distance. God wants to be involved in every area of our lives, no matter how insignificant they may seem. He wants to rejoice with us in our joy, and grieve with us in our sorrows. In His great love for us He wants to help us. It pains Him to see His precious children suffer and He wants to use His omnipotence and wisdom to help us for our benefit. What a privilege we have when we have allowed Him to reside within our hearts! Through Christ in us, we have a personal relationship with Almighty God. The very same God, who created the highest peaks in all their glory and the oceans in all their majesty, cares for each and every person on this Earth. We do not have because we do not ask. It would be simply wrong to complain about how horrible our situations are when we have not even asked our Heavenly Father to come to our aid. When we call upon His Name asking for deliverance and healing, He will be faithful to our cries and will intervene in our circumstances according to His good and perfect will for our lives. Is there anything that is weighing us down? Make it known to God and rest in the assurance that He will bring healing and restoration to our lives through His infinite power.

October 13

WHAT ARE WE REAPING?

"What benefit did you reap at that time from the things you are now ashamed of? Those things result in death!" -Romans 6:21 (NIV)

Sin accomplishes nothing in our lives. Its purpose is to crush and destroy anyone who falls within its grasp. Although it deceives us with benefits, with fulfillment and pleasure, it strips us of our dignity and our joy. Instead we reap shame and regret, which leaves us in a state of misery. Yet why do we find ourselves returning to sinful patterns? Why do we, as Proverbs 26:11 says, return to our wickedness just as how a dog returns to its vomit? Even though we know of the consequences of indulging in sin, we conveniently forget about them in the heat of the moment. Thus the cycle of falling into sin and feeling guilt repeats itself; resulting in us succumbing to a feeling of hopelessness as we become slaves of our own folly.

God never wanted His cherished creations to live under the hopelessness of sin. In His great love for humanity He gave us His Son so that through His redemptive sacrifice and His resurrection, we have the hope of being free from our sinful nature. Once we allow Christ to reside within our hearts and allow Him to mold us in His righteousness, we will find that in being slaves to righteousness we are free from the suffocating clutch of wickedness. This is why the child of Christ feels a great sense of remorse when instead of following the voice of Christ he bends to the remnants of his own depravity. He has essentially exchanged the truth of God for a lie; that even though he knows full well the destructive power of sin, he still falls for its lies claiming bliss and contentment. But thankfully God is ever forgiving and patient with us. Once He has begun His good work in our lives, He will see it to its completion. That is His promise. As long as we abide in Christ and fix our eyes upon Him, we will be able to stay away from the pitfalls of sin; instead walking in the freedom of living in His righteousness and truth.

October 14

BEING OUR BROTHER'S KEEPER

"Then the Lord said to Cain, 'Where is your brother Abel?' 'I don't know,' he replied. 'Am I my brother's keeper?'" -Genesis 4:9 (NIV)

We live in a culture where we are reluctant to take responsibility for our actions. We have misunderstood freedom as the ability to do whatever we wish unhindered by any form of restriction. However, this view of freedom is a lie. We are not free to do as we see fit. There is a clear definition of right and wrong and the moment we cross that line, there are devastating consequences that follow. Just as how Abel's blood cried out of the ground when Cain denied before God the fact that he murdered his brother, so too will the consequences of our action or inaction haunt us when we fail to uphold God's righteousness and integrity. Nothing is hidden from God and there will come a day when we will have to give an account of our deeds on Earth.

We are not solely responsible for ourselves and to make sure that our individual lives are in order. As children of Christ, we are all called to be responsible for each other. In showing the love of Christ being made manifest in us and allowing His righteousness to shine forth through our lives, we must never act in a manner that would run contrary to who we stand for. Out of hatred or malice, we must never inflict suffering on another. Out of apathy or indifference, we must never turn a blind eye to injustice and tyranny. When we see someone struggling in life and in their walk with Christ, instead of shunning them we are to come alongside them and minister to them while allowing Christ Himself to guide our words and actions. Being our brother's keeper can be a hard task. It requires us to put aside ingrained attitudes, place ourselves in uncomfortable situations, and restrain our depraved impulses. But when we personally accept Christ's redemptive sacrifice on the cross; allowing Christ to reside in our hearts and break sin's hold over our lives, our attitudes will change. We will want to reach out to others in love and look out for their best interest. Not because we do so out of our own human inclination, but because the Holy Spirit within us wants to fulfill His perfect redemptive mission for the world through our lives; enabling us to live in a manner that honors God and those around us.

October 15

WHO'S INFLUENCING WHO?

"Do not make friends with a hot-tempered man, do not associate with one easily angered, or you may learn his ways and get yourself ensnared." -Proverbs 22:24-25 (NIV)

The company we keep often tells something of who we are. As much as we would like to think that a person's individual behavior and attitudes has no effect on our own, the truth is that it often does. The more that we spend time with a particular person, the more likely it is for us to adopt the behavioral patterns, values, and temperaments of that person. For better or for worse, this subconscious mimicry can slowly alter our personalities and our attitudes. Slowly we become more irritable. Slowly we begin to tolerate things which should never be excused. It is folly to maintain a stance of indifference when confronted with the destructive conduct and errant beliefs of a friend. If we do not make a stand against evil, wickedness will slowly creep into our hearts and minds.

Our role as children of Christ is to be agents of influence; to display His love and righteousness being worked in and through us. If we find ourselves allowing sinful attitudes and beliefs to permeate our lives, we must truly question whether we are allowing God to carry out His redemptive work in our lives. The conduct of the child of Christ is not informed by the people around them, but by his Heavenly Father whom he ardently seeks to emulate with the assistance of the Holy Spirit residing in him. Only by spending time in His presence through prayer and the reading of His Word will we be able to emerge as the stronger influence; actively showing Christ to those around us without getting caught in the wickedness of others. As long as we continue to align ourselves with Christ and permit Him to mold us according to His perfect wisdom and righteousness, no other harmful influence will be able to control our lives. But the moment we step outside the will of God, man in their sinfulness will hold sway over us. Which will we choose? Will we choose to live as slaves under the wickedness of man and contribute to our own destruction, or to be free under the leadership of Christ and through Him act as lights in a world engulfed by darkness?

October 16

THE SPIRITUAL BATTLEFIELD

"For our struggle is not against flesh and blood, but against...the spiritual forces of evil in the heavenly realms." -Ephesians 6:12 (NIV)

The Christian life is a battlefield. In an age where human wickedness and depravity are steadily permeating every aspect of our culture, the child of Christ cannot afford to be complacent. Although the assured final victory over sin and death is accomplished through Christ when we accept His redeeming sacrifice for us and allow Him to dwell within our hearts, there are still battles to be fought until the ultimate realization of that victory. The remnants of our wicked nature will relentlessly attempt to divert us from following the will of Christ for our lives. Through its deceptive lures promising bliss and fulfillment, sin will ensnare us in destructive patterns that will leave us with misery and emptiness. Such feelings will invariably result in us entertaining the delusion that we are beyond God's grace and sin will exploit this by using it to keep us under a paralyzing enslavement. To live in denial of this fact reveals our sheer ignorance of Christ's redemptive mission for the world and our place within that mission.

We must never forget however, that we do not fight the battle against sin on our own. If we think of ourselves as one-man armies diving headlong to confront sin in our lives, we will be overcome by our own depravity instead of us overcoming it. But where we in our human weaknesses fail, Christ is more than sufficient for us. If we allow Him to enable us, we can be assured of the fact that through His omnipotence and righteousness, we will be able to emerge victorious over those areas in our lives where sin continues to assail and bombard us with temptation. No soldier fights alone. They all fight together to achieve victory under the leadership of their superior and the teamwork of their comrades-in-arms. Likewise, while willingly and continuously subordinating ourselves to the perfect wisdom and power of Christ within us, we should always seek out others who are fighting the same battle under His direction. When we do so, they will not only be a source of accountability and encouragement, but we will be able to be the same to them. Though wickedness vies over our soul, we can take courage in the fact that as long as we remain united with and under Christ, the forces of evil shall never prevail.

October 17

HIS WORD IN OUR HEART

"I have hidden your word in my heart that I might not sin against you." -Psalm 119:11 (NIV)

Living with sin in our lives is never something desirable. Initially when we are lured by its false promises of bliss, it seems logical and pleasurable to pursue a lifestyle that eschews righteousness and truth. However, when we realize that by allowing sin to reside in our hearts we have essentially sold ourselves into a self-destructive slavery, we eagerly search for ways to break out of our sinful habits and attitudes. We seek guidance and counsel in friends, teachers, self-help books, and man-made philosophies. But we fail to realize that these sources are tainted by the fallible wisdom of man; that our reliance on these sources alone will never free us from our wickedness. They may even serve to do the opposite by digging ourselves deeper into sin and vice.

How quickly do we forget that the Bible, the Sword of the Spirit, is the sharpest blade to use when combating sin in our lives? God knows the destructive power of sin and in His loving provision and perfect wisdom, He has made known to us through His Word the way in which we must live so as to not fall under the yoke of wickedness. When we consult the Word of God and allow His Laws and wisdom to seep into our minds, we will find that they will be our best defense when temptation comes knocking at our door. Studying the Scriptures alone is not enough however. We could memorize verses yet still find ourselves under sin's oppression. It is only when we allow the Word, who became flesh in Christ, to reside in hearts that we can live in a manner which pleases God. When we personally accept Christ's redeeming sacrifice for us, so that through Him we may be free from the hold of sin, we will be able to live in the assurance that as long as we allow His righteousness to work through us and spend time in His Word, sin and its devastating consequences will be far away from us.

October 18

THE HEART OF THE LAW

"Then Jesus asked them, 'Which is lawful on the Sabbath: to do good or to do evil, to save life or to kill?' But they remained silent." - Mark 3:4 (NIV)

The Pharisees were looking for a reason to accuse Jesus of disobeying the Laws of God. When Jesus saw a man with a shriveled hand in the synagogue, the Pharisees took notice of this as well. They thought that this was their chance to finally trap Him, for it was the Sabbath and to do any work on the Sabbath was a direct violation of the Law. But Jesus knew of the Pharisees intentions full well. Before He healed the man with the shriveled hand, He asked those present which was more important; a legalistic obedience to the Law, or the restorative work of God Himself. His audience's silence spoke volumes. The people deliberately chose to cling onto their own misconstrued interpretation of the Law instead of accepting the true heart of the Law as Christ Himself revealed.

Legalism is a dangerous idol. Our worship of it, like any other idol, can hamper the redemptive work of Christ in our lives. Legalism is particularly destructive because not only does it cripple us, it turns our faith into something ineffectual and venomous. Instead of bringing the restoration and healing which only Christ can offer, our blind devotion to tradition and needless regulation only serves to turn us into insular and unnecessarily judgmental people. This in turn affects our witness for Him and those around us obtain a colored view of who Christ is and what it truly means to be His children. In Matthew 22:40, Jesus says that the entire Law and the sayings of the Prophets can be summed up in two simple commandments; "Love the Lord your God with all your heart and with all your soul and with all your mind" and 'Love your neighbor as yourself'. When we accept Christ's redemptive sacrifice for us on the cross and allow Him to work in our hearts, He will fill us with His love. Only when we have His love overflowing from within us, will we be able to obey the Law in its truest sense and realize its purpose; to draw others to the holiness of God. Through Him we can partake of the wonderful hope of being free from sin and of being made pure through Christ's restorative work.

October 19

LET HIM DO THE LIFTING!

"Carry each other's burdens and in this way you will fulfill the law of Christ." -Galatians 6:2 (NIV)

Carrying each other's burdens seems like a formidable and even undesirable task. Our natural response would be to ask why we should carry another person's burdens when we have our own struggles to deal with. However, such an attitude leads to indifference. Though we certainly do not wish to add to their suffering, we do not want to go through the unpleasantness and discomfort which we see as being tied to the notion of carrying another person's burdens. That task, we feel, should be left to someone nobler than ourselves. But although we may justify our indifference as being sensible and even compassionate in our hopes that someone else will come alongside them, our indifference is a passive selfishness. The truth is that if all of us remained in this passive selfishness of solely looking after our own interests, no one will reach out in love to one another and we will all collapse under the weight of our struggles.

If our excuse for not helping others is because we have our own troubles to deal with, we fail to take into consideration that Christ is sufficient for us. We delude ourselves into thinking that we can handle trials on our own. Our faith in our own strength is misplaced for if we are truly honest with ourselves, we are frail and fragile people. Yet God, in His abundant love, did not wish to see us in such a state. He knows that to be under the weight of sin and suffering is an unbearable load for us to bear. Through Christ, we have the hope that when we personally accept His redemptive sacrifice and allow Him to work in our hearts, we can take refuge in His faithfulness. When we surrender our troubles to Him, He will be the one to break the yoke of sin in our lives and carry our burdens Himself through those times when we undergo suffering. Just as how He has shown our love to us in this manner, we are to display His love to others. Through His enabling we will be able to pour out His love into the lives of others; bringing healing and restoration to those who desperately need it. Only when His love is made manifest in us will we be able to walk in obedience to Him and fulfill the role He has called us to carry out as His children and active participants in His redemptive mission for the world.

October 20

WHAT IS WORTHWHILE?

"Turn my eyes away from worthless things; preserve my life according to your word." -Psalm 119:37 (NIV)

We often attribute worth to things which actually have no real importance. It fact, they could even prove to be damaging to us if we cling onto them. An insatiable lust for acquiring wealth and prestige, a compulsive obsession over body image and popularity, a wanton desire to hold onto sinful habits and attitudes; all of these can be our ultimate undoing. We place worth on these pursuits because we are deceived into thinking that our worth will be validated by them. But truth is that although they may promise these things, they always leave us feeling empty and worthless. When we have given everything of ourselves, our trust, and our devotion, to these idols, they will swindle and rob us of our joy, peace, and security like thieves who have no regard for their prey.

However, where there is hopelessness Christ promises that He will lift up those who call upon His name. In His love and omnipotence, He promises to bring full restoration in our lives if we simply believe in His redemptive sacrifice and glorious resurrection, and allow Him to reside and work within our hearts. When we allow Him to fill us with His Spirit and dwell upon His Word and love, we will be able to see the folly of elevating anything else to the position of God in our lives. Our worth is not found in the material things of this world, which will eventually give way to decay, but in the knowledge of who Christ is, and what He has done and continues to do for us in our lives. In His eyes we have intrinsic worth because we are created in the image of God and, though we were wicked and depraved; He came down to deliver us from sin so that we may not destroy ourselves. Immersed in His eternal love and faithfulness, we will find full satisfaction in Him; a satisfaction which nothing of the worthless things of this world can match.

October 21

BEING LIKE CHILDREN

"People were bringing little children to Jesus to have him touch them, but the disciples rebuked them. When Jesus saw this, he was indignant. He said to them, 'Let the little children come to me, and do not hinder them, for the kingdom of God belongs to such as these. I tell you the truth, anyone who will not receive the kingdom of God like a little child will never enter it.' And he took the children in his arms, put his hands on them and blessed them." -Mark 10:13-16 (NIV)

Why are we called children of Christ? In popular imagination, children are seen as being innocent; uncorrupted by the wickedness of the world. However, this view of children can lead us to misinterpret this verse; leading us to think that in order to be accepted by Christ and enter His fold, we have to approach Him as sinless people. But anyone who has spent time with children knows that they are far from the ideal of perfection that we have associated with them in our minds. Even before they can talk, the selfishness and greed which is characteristic of our fallen human nature can be seen through their behavior; though they themselves may not be aware of it.

Why the comparison then? What is Jesus trying to say? He is drawing attention not to a presupposed view of a child's innocence, but to their faith. A child is dependent on his parents for almost everything. It needs to be fed, taught, and looked after; all of which the child depends on the faithful and loving provision of his parents. The child does not worry about what he will eat or where he will sleep. He simply trusts that his parents will take care of all his needs. Likewise, Christ does not require that we make ourselves righteous if we have any hope of becoming His child. That is His job to do if we allow Him to work His righteousness in our hearts. He simply requires that we come before Him with that childlike faith, that faith which trusts in the perfect goodness of our Heavenly Father to deliver us from wickedness, and provide for us according to His flawless will. Is cynicism holding us back from tasting and seeing that the Lord is good? Know that we deprive and cripple ourselves when we allow jaded attitudes to reign paramount in our lives. Only by abandoning such attitudes and by faith entering into a relationship with Christ will we be able to experience the inexpressible joy and security which comes from being His children and co-heirs of His Kingdom.

October 22

TAKE CARE OF HIS SHEEP!

"...Jesus said, 'Simon son of John, do you truly love me?' He answered, 'Yes, Lord, you know that I love you.' Jesus said, 'Take care of my sheep.'" -John 21:16 (NIV)

What does it mean to love God? We have many different ideas of what this means. We may think that simply going to church is proof of our love for God. Some of us may take it a step further, that being actively involved in the inner workings of the church is an indicator of a man's devotion to Christ. Further still, we may think that those who preach, or talk about God and Christ through theological debate, are the ones who truly love the Lord. These things are good in and of themselves, but they alone do not reveal a love for God. The truth is that anyone could do these things. We could participate in church services, be active in planning church functions, and argue theological concepts for hours upon end. But if we have failed to heed the voice of Christ and take care of His sheep, the love of God is absent from us.

Who are His sheep? They are the people around us who are lost and confused. They are the people around us who are hurting and need healing and restoration. They are the people around us who have been led astray by sin and are living in destructive lifestyles with only oblivion awaiting them. Christ has called us to love His sheep, to nurture and take care of them by addressing both their physical and spiritual needs. But can we do this on our own? We delude ourselves if we think we can. Our love simply does not have either the patience or the capacity to show the kind of compassion that Christ requires of His children. It is only when we allow Christ's Spirit to reside in our hearts that we are able to love others unconditionally. When we personally accept His loving sacrifice for us on the cross, so that we may live as forgiven men free from our sinful nature, and surrender every area of our lives to Him, He will work out His immeasurable and ever-patient love through us. We cannot be good shepherds through our own actions. But only through His indwelling in our lives are we able to obey His commandment to take care of His sheep. When we do so, God will honor us; not because of any ability of our own, but solely because of our obedience to Him in allowing His love to shine through us.

October 23

WHOM HAVE WE ENSHRINED?

"What, after all, is Apollos? And what is Paul? Only servants, through whom you came to believe - as the Lord has assigned to each his task." -1 Corinthians 3:5 (NIV)

A dispute had arisen within the Corinthian church. On one side of the quarrel were those who claimed loyalty to the teachings of Paul; on the other, those who adhered to the teachings of a man named Apollos. As the church quarreled over which man could claim legitimacy, Paul stepped into the fray. His answer brought the whole issue into perspective. Who was he? Who was Apollos? They were but mere men, yet served a God far greater than any human being on Earth. It was through Christ that Paul and Apollos were able to teach and preach His Word; not through any ability of their own. Therefore, only Christ is to be glorified for He is the Center of the Word and the Enabler of our faith.

It is human tendency to make idols out of anything. Our admiration of people can be taken to the extreme of putting them on a pedestal. Instead of allowing Christ to consume our minds, we pay our homage to His servants; those He has appointed to minister to us. Suddenly we find ourselves yielding to the authority of those we have enshrined in our minds instead of the greater authority of Christ. We may have constructed an image of perfection in our minds regarding the person of our worship. But the problem with placing our hopes in man is that we are prone to error. Once the reality of this fact is made known to us, we will realize how fragile a faith in man can be. When we place our hope and faith in Christ, allowing Him to work in our hearts and minds, we can take assurance in that fact that He is the Truth. Only He is mighty to save and only through Him we will be able to gain understanding of His Word. Christ is sovereign and He is able to take fallen men and use them to fulfill His perfect will for the world. But may we remember that an idolatry of man will only serve to lead us astray from the true Author and Perfector of our faith; the one who is deserving of all glory and praise.

October 24

A PRESENT AND FUTURE HOPE

"He will wipe every tear from their eyes. There will be no more death or mourning or crying or pain, for the old order of things has passed away." -Revelation 21:4 (NIV)

Often times it seems that the world is devoid of hope. When injustice thrives, when decadence flourishes, when humanity never seems to learn from the mistakes of the past, it appears that the world will be forever locked in a destructive cycle of wickedness. Sadly this is the truth. As long as humanity, in its fallen and depraved state, continues to bend to its sinful nature, we will continue to see corruption prosper and history repeat itself in all its gruesome violence. No humanly constructed ideology or philosophy, no matter how well intended, will ever be able to overcome this one essential reality. If man continues to ignore the fact that they are inherently corrupt and continues to persist in this state, their wickedness will overtake them.

But despite this there is hope! Not through any hope that the things of this world can offer, but by what Christ has done and is actively doing to redeem His creation from sin. Depravity was not part of God's plan for His world and we were not designed to live under its yoke. Through His death and resurrection He offers to all who personally accept Him into their hearts the hope of breaking the cycle of wickedness in our lives. In Him there is newness of life, and if we allow Him to restore us, we can be assured of the fact that He will mold us according to His perfect righteousness. But His redemptive mission is not just for the individual, but for the entire world itself. His will is to bring restoration and healing to every area of His creation. Once He has begun a good work, He will see to its completion. In His omnipotence and wisdom nothing will be able to prevent the realization of His vision and we can take comfort in the hope that there will come a day when He will restore the world to its full glory in all its perfection and purity. With Christ there is victory and when we allow Him to work in our hearts and minds, our lives will bear witness to everyone around us of hope that as the Holy Spirit continues His perfect work, all will be made right.

October 25

SEEKING TRUE KNOWLEDGE

"That the God of our Lord Jesus Christ, the Father of glory, may give you a spirit of wisdom and of revelation in the knowledge of him, having the eyes of your hearts enlightened, that you may know what is the hope to which he has called you, what are the riches of his glorious inheritance..." -Ephesians 1:17-18 (ESV)

We all desire knowledge. We all seek to understand the world around us and our place in it. It has motivated the meditations of philosophers and the investigations of scientists for centuries. However, because our reason is flawed by the wickedness of our human nature, we can only perceive an incomplete view of the truth. Though we may grasp certain aspects of the truth, our desire to retain our autonomy and live independently of God distorts what has been perceived by our human minds. This is why the answers provided by manmade philosophies insufficiently answer the purpose of human existence. Despite their attempts to come to a sound analysis of humanity, they fail to acknowledge the fact that we are fallen people; flawed because of our innate rebellious nature.

Our pride leads us to worship our own fallible reason and wisdom. Even when we see that our understanding is in error, we stubbornly refuse to acknowledge that fact. We insist that our reason is perfect and thereby we cling onto the deception that the knowledge we have of ourselves and of the world is without fault. But if we seek to possess true knowledge, we must come humbly before our Creator. God is the master of the universe. He was the One who brought it into existence. Naturally, just as how an architect knows his work intimately, He is the One who knows the inner workings of the universe and all that resides in it. Moreover, He wishes to impart His knowledge to us. For this reason He sent His Son, Jesus Christ, to die for our sins. Through His death and resurrection, the barrier of sin which separated us from God is broken and we have a restored relationship with our Creator. When we allow His Spirit to indwell within us and work in our lives, He will open our eyes to His perfect wisdom and Truth. Only by submitting ourselves to His Spirit within us and living in obedience to Him will we understand ourselves and our destiny. Though we were born in sin, Christ came to redeem us from the yoke of our depravity; setting us on the path to everlasting life with Him in Heaven and being a part of His restorative work for the entire world.

October 26

IS IT OUR OWN?

"You may say to yourself, 'My power and the strength of my hands have produced this wealth for me.' But remember the Lord your God, for it is he who gives you the ability to produce wealth." -Deuteronomy 8:17-18a (NIV)

When we are blessed with success and wealth, it is easy for our heads to swell with pride. We buy into the myth that we, by the strength of our hands and the capacity of our minds, have bestowed upon ourselves victory after victory. But who was the One who gave us legs to walk? Who was the One who gave us hands to work? Who was the One who gave us a mind so beautifully complex that not even the most powerful supercomputer can match it in ability? We delude ourselves when we think that we have achieved success independent of God. The truth is that we are dependent on

Him for every bodily function we perform, right down to every breath we take, for He is the One who created us.

Until we realize that we are nothing without God, we will continue to deceive ourselves; arrogantly thinking that we are responsible for the success in our lives. But soon we will find that, though we may have seen our own abilities and strength as infallible, our trust has been misplaced. Suddenly we will come to the realization that we are capable of making foolish and destructive decisions, and that our strength is subject to decay and limited in what it can do. But in our weakness, God is strong. When we approach Him with humility of heart, asking Him to deliver us from the corruption of sin and dwell with us, He will carry out His restorative work within us. By asking Him to impart to us His wisdom and allowing Him to guide our steps, He will direct us in the proper use of all that He has graciously given us. Under God's guidance, we can trust in His perfect will; that He never seeks to lead us into destruction, but to a life that will reflect His glory and faithful provision in our lives. When we submit all that He has given us to Him and walk while holding tightly to His hand, we will be blessed knowing that He will lead us towards a beautiful future.

October 27

IS THAT ALLOWED?

"Everything is permissible" - *but not everything is beneficial. 'Everything is permissible'-but not everything is constructive."* -1 Corinthians 10:23 (NIV)

We live in a society where everything and anything goes; where taboo after taboo is slowly being broken and cast aside. The prevailing attitude seems to be that everything is permissible. In a sense this is true. As long as we are mobile, and capable of using our minds and our five senses, what is there really stopping us from indulging in sin? But just because we have the ability to commit sin does not mean that it is beneficial in any way. Though we may be fully capable of sin, we will have to bear its destructive consequences. Wickedness has the effect of not only degrading others, but the individual himself. Our minds and hearts slowly become warped and callous, becoming more like the animal who obeys their carnal desires than men who are the crowning glory of God's creation. Anything, even that which in and of itself is good, can become corrupted by our wickedness if we elevate it to the status of God and allow it to take our eyes away from Christ Himself.

While we lived under our sinful nature, we were slaves to our own depravity. We knew of nothing else to serve and therefore, we were bound to live under the yoke of sin. But when we accept Christ as our Savior; allowing Him to free us from the shackles of sin and to carry out His redemptive work in our lives, we have a choice to either listen to His voice, or to the voice of the remnants of sin that reside in our hearts. When we fall into the hands of wickedness while we claim Christ as Lord, it is of our own deliberate choice to pay no heed to His voice and to indulge in that which is impure. But thankfully, Christ is always forgiving and abounding in grace. When we listen to His voice and allow Him to pull us out of the mire of sin, He will restore us and make His righteousness manifest in us. However, we can avoid the consequences of sin by simply obeying Christ from the start, submitting ourselves to His perfect will and allowing Him to carry out His restorative work in our lives unhindered by our own stubbornness. When we choose to hold onto the hand of Christ, we are safe knowing that He will lead us not on the path of destruction, but to life everlasting through Him; a life that is free from the ravages of sin.

October 28

NEVER GIVE UP!

"Let us not become weary in doing good, for at the proper time we will reap a harvest if we do not give up." -Galatians 6:9 (NIV)

Sometimes, when it appears that evil seems to be emerging triumphant everywhere we turn, it is easy to throw our hands in the air and give up. As wickedness threatens to suffocate our stand for what is right and true, we ask ourselves whether there is any point to fighting what seems to be a losing battle. But can you imagine how the world would look like if everyone simply walked away from upholding righteousness when opposition came their way? It would be a brutal and cruel world, where we would be slaves under an unchecked wickedness. If we truly desire to see change happen in the world around us, be it in our homes or in the public sphere, we must be willing to fight for it. Depravity and injustice thrive under the silence of those who know what is right.

As children of Christ we are called to proclaim His righteousness revealed through His perfect standards. But if we think we can do this on our own, the reality is that we cannot. His righteousness needs to be made manifest in our lives first. Only when we have allowed Christ to reign in our hearts and see the world through His eyes will we be able to make a consistent stand for His truth and justice. For this stand, Christ guarantees that we will face opposition and trials from those who wish to silence the proclamation of Himself and His righteousness. But though we may feel that we are under the mercy of the forces of evil, we can dwell in the assurance that when we are on the side of Christ, we are already victorious through Him. It is Christ who will give us the strength and courage to slay the monster of wickedness wherever it lurks. It is Christ who will help us hold up His torch of Truth when our arms waver. Though we may not see the fruit of our stand immediately, we can rest in the fact that God, in His perfect timing, will emerge triumphant. All He asks of us is to be lights for Him in our actions, in our words, and even in our thoughts; holding onto His hand all the while. When we do this, we will rejoice when God in His faithfulness brings about the deliverance and restoration that we hoped and prayed for at His appointed time. Romans 8:31 says that if God is for us, no one will be able to stand against us. Under this promise we can hold our light for Him with confidence and resolve knowing that He is the one who will sustain us in the midst of darkness.

October 29

AN EVERLASTING FAITHFULNESS

"Know therefore that the Lord your God is God; he is the faithful God, keeping his covenant of love to a thousand generations of those who love him and keep his commands." -Deuteronomy 7:9 (NIV)

God never breaks a promise. In His perfect goodness He always remains true to His word. Throughout the Bible we see evidence of His faithful provision, even when we ourselves act in a spirit of ungratefulness. Despite their grumblings and complaints God fulfilled His promise to Moses by delivering the Israelites out of Egypt and bringing them to the Promised Land; faithfully providing them with manna along the way. Even though humanity persists in indulging in sin, God continues and will continue to remain faithful to His promise to Noah to never again destroy the Earth and all that is in it by flood.

But perhaps the greatest mark of God's faithfulness is His provision of Christ; the fulfillment of His promise to Eve that her descendant will be the One to crush the power of Satan over God's Creation. Through Him there is deliverance from our sinful nature and even though we may reject Him, His arms are still wide open; always willing to embrace those who wish to be free from the shackles of wickedness. Never doubt the goodness and faithfulness of God. In a world of broken promises, it is easy to apply our experiences to how God will act towards us. But God is not bound by human depravity. When He says He will do something, He will see to its fulfillment. It is not in His will to seek the destruction of man. On the contrary, it is to restore us from the ravages of sin and to dwell in His wonderful faithfulness. He is the embodiment of what is pure and good and we can trust that His plans, as expressed in Jeremiah 29:11, are to prosper us and never to harm us. When we grab the hand of Christ, allowing Him to carry out His redemptive work in our hearts, we will see for ourselves that the Lord is good and He lovingly provides for those who seek to reside within His will.

October 30

IT'S NOT A BUFFET!

"On hearing it, many of his disciples said, 'This is a hard teaching. Who can accept it?'" -Mark 6:60 (NIV)

We seem to conveniently ignore those teachings of Christ which make us uncomfortable. When He informs us of something we need to grasp, why do we not take hold of it? When He implores us to let go of certain things, why do we hold on? In our refusal to surrender all that we have to Christ, we make excuses. We say that it is impossible for us to go that extra mile for our Lord; even going to the extent of misconstruing the Word of God to justify our attitudes. If our faith is based on grabbing hold of those teachings of Christ which humors our ears and shunning those which bring us discomfort, then we have no right to claim that we are seeking after Christ. If anything we are seeking to please ourselves; to bring comfort to ourselves at the expense of living in and for Christ.

When we enter into a relationship with Christ, we do not accept a portion of Him, we accept all of Him. His restorative work in our lives is total and in order to make His righteousness perfect in us, we must surrender ourselves to His will and yield to His teachings. Christ does not expect us to grasp and live up to His teachings on our own strength and effort. He knows full well of our limitations and our propensity to error. It is only when we allow Him to mold our hearts and attitudes, asking Him to illumine our minds and make ourselves malleable in His hands, will we be receptive to His Truth, seeking to understand it and apply it to our lives. The Christian life is not a smorgasbord where we have the opportunity to pick and choose what teachings we should hold on to. As children of Christ, we live in total obedience to our Father, dwelling in the faithful and tangible assurance that God promises good things for His children and that it is not in His will to seek harm. If we truly desire to have His redemptive and restorative mission in our lives, we must actively seek to conform ourselves to Him; allowing Him to enable us to conform ourselves to His likeness so that we live under the joy and security of being in total synchronization with Him.

October 31

WHO IS SPEAKING?

"A man finds joy in giving an apt reply - and how good is a timely word!" -Proverbs 15:23 (NIV)

Words are powerful. They can either build up a person's life or shatter it completely. In most cases the turning point in the life of a person, either for better or for worse, was usually something that was said to them which either uplifted them or brought them great discouragement. In those critical moments, an encouraging or wise word from someone else can do wonders for their soul. But if we think that just saying something damaging or untimely to a person undergoing a crisis is detrimental, our silence is equally so! How many people could be spared from the misery of being bound to crippling insecurities and destructive lifestyles if someone simply came alongside them and ministered to them through their presence and by telling them of the hope found in Christ?

As children of Christ, we witness not solely through our actions, but through our words as well. Christ gave us mouths for that purpose; to praise and glorify Him and to bear testimony to His love and righteousness in us. Sometimes we remain silent out of fear. We ask ourselves whether if we could really intervene in a given situation through our words and provide comfort, healing, and encouragement. But we do not out of our own wisdom and ability. When we have allowed Christ to reside within our hearts and permitted Him to make Himself manifest in our lives, He will be the one who will give us the words to speak. In our weaknesses and our inabilities, He is the one who enables and empowers us. When we allow Him to speak through us when He has called us to minister in specific situations, we will have the wonderful privilege of bearing witness to His redemptive work in our lives as He places those timely words in our mouth. We should never allow our insecurities in our own abilities to hinder Christ's redemptive mission. It is only when we surrender our mouths to Him that He will fill us with His wisdom and love so that He may bring healing and restoration to a broken world.

November 1

PURGING WICKEDNESS

"For you are not a God who is pleased with wickedness; with you, evil people are not welcome. The arrogant cannot stand in your presence. You hate all who do wrong;" -Psalm 5:4-5 (NIV)

In His perfect holiness God cannot tolerate sin. It breaks His heart when He sees man, created in His image, under the mercy of tyranny and injustice. Therefore, it is no wonder that in Isaiah 1:17, God calls His children to, "…learn to do right! Seek justice, encourage the oppressed. Defend the cause of the fatherless, plead the case of the widow." We can take assurance in the fact that God will always stand behind a just and righteous cause for it is in His nature to do so. He is the God of Truth, and though men may deceive and malign, He will expose their lies and will make sure that His Truth alone triumphs over all.

But how quick are we to overlook the wickedness that we allow to reside in our hearts? It is easy to condemn others for their failings and we may even take a twisted pleasure in declaring that the wicked will pay the penalty for their depravity. However, doing so elevates our pride in our own self-righteousness at the expense of ignoring our own glaring faults. Unless we come to the realization that all men, including ourselves, have fallen short of God's holy standards and that man can only be made righteous through the indwelling of Christ, we are in no position to speak against the decadence of those around us. We must remember that God hated wickedness so much that He sought to redeem the world from its grasp. Through the sacrifice and resurrection of His Son, Jesus Christ, all who come to Him are free from the oppression of their sinful nature. As children of Christ, wickedness will only persist if we have failed to allow Christ to carry out His restorative work in our lives. When we go astray, God will make it known to us through His Holy Spirit residing within us. Only if we listen to His voice and allow Him to purge us of all unrighteousness will we be able to stand up for His truth and righteousness in the world around us. Through Him we will come to the understanding that sin needs to be crushed not only outside ourselves but within as well through God's redemptive power.

November 2

ONLY THROUGH HIM

"Jesus answered, 'I am the way and the truth and the life. No one comes to the Father except through me.'" -John 14:6 (NIV)

We do not like to hear absolutes. Our ears have been conditioned to cringe the moment someone speaks of there being only one, singular truth. As globalization brings the world closer together, we have become more aware of the diversity of the world in which we live, along with the many conflicts and tensions that exist between cultures and beliefs. In an attempt to accommodate everyone, we have succumbed to the view that truth is subjective; that another person's truth is just as valid as someone else's truth. However, is such a view sound? Can we really grant validity to two conflicting truths? This is the problem with relativism. Though it claims to bring harmony, in actual fact it destroys it. In the name of toleration, it not only allows that which is harmful and detrimental to humanity to persist in its destructive work, but numbs humanity to the point where we do not know right from wrong and we fail to take a strong stand for what is truly reprehensible.

Jesus said He is the Way, the Truth, and the Life. Often we ignore these absolute claims and label Him as one of the many ways man can follow. But clearly this is not what Christ intended Himself to be or for people to understand Him as. He is the only Way that man can be saved from sin. No matter how hard we try, we cannot save ourselves from our wickedness. Only when we acknowledge that He alone has the power to save and personally accept His sacrifice on the cross as having paid for the penalty for our sins will our relationship with God be restored. Through Him we are placed on the path to Heaven; knowing that it is Christ alone who takes us there when we choose to submit to His redemptive work in our lives once we have allowed Him into our hearts. He is the only Truth for He is the embodiment of truth as revealed through His creation, the prophecies contained in His Word, and Christ Himself; whose perfection and validity was affirmed not only by His disciples, but even His most ardent persecutors. In Him there is Life, for He is the Giver of Life. Through His resurrection we have newness of life and are active participants in His restorative mission for the entire world. Only through Him will His perfect righteousness and love be made manifest in us and overflow from us to bring healing to this broken world. When we accept the absolute claims of Christ, we can rest in the fact that our trust is not misplaced, and that through Him there is an assured hope and restoration for all as He reconciles man to Himself.

November 3

CUT IT OFF!

"If your right eye causes you to sin, gouge it out and throw it away. It is better for you to lose one part of your body than for your whole body to be thrown into hell. And if your right hand causes you to sin, cut it off and throw it away. It is better for you to lose one part of your body than for your whole body to go into hell." -Matthew 5:28-29 (NIV)

Why is amputation still considered to be a valid medical procedure? From ancient times right to the present day, it is still regarded as the most effective way of dealing with an infection that is spreading throughout the body. Naturally however, amputation is not desirable. It is an excruciatingly painful process which could completely change a person's lifestyle; severely limiting their mobility and ability to perform even the most mundane of tasks. Although, modern medicine has made strides in circumventing the need for amputation, it is generally held that if the infection seems to be spreading unabated regardless of the amount of treatment given, amputation, though agonizing, is necessary to prevent death and to save the life of the patient.

Every human being born into this world has been infected by sin. No matter our attempts to treat it by our human hands, its diseased presence continues to fester and grow; spreading into every area of our lives. The only way by which we may be healed of this disease is that Christ will have to enter into our hearts and cleanse us of our sinful nature; cutting off any area of our lives that is propagating wickedness in our lives. Though this is the only way through which we may be healed of sin, we are hesitant to receive this treatment. Christ's radical measures require us to part with areas of our lives which we, in our sinfulness, have nurtured and cherished. But if we refuse to allow Christ to cut off from our lives those areas where the poison of wickedness is apparent, we are destroying ourselves and contributing to our own inward decay. Holding onto sin in our hearts will place us on the path towards death. But we are guaranteed life through Christ if we permit Him to carry out His surgical work in our lives and eliminate sin at its source.

November 4

A SELFLESS MERCY

"Blessed are the merciful, for they will be shown mercy." -Matthew 5:7 (NIV)

We are very hypocritical when it comes to the idea of showing mercy. On the one hand, we think of it as something that only the weak and particularly gullible show to those who are in an unfavorable position under them. We ask ourselves what right they have to demand clemency from us. What have they done to deserve merciful treatment? We refrain from showing mercy because for the most part it is certainly not advantageous to us. Yet when we are shown unconditional mercy, how often do we seek to capitalize on it? We see it as a chance to restore ourselves and our reputations while conveniently forgetting to be merciful to those who are in a similar position as we were when we were shown mercy.

If we have adopted such a self-serving view of mercy, we cannot expect mercy to be shown to us. In this life, where our positions are always in a transitory state, we cannot demand that pity and forgiveness be given to us in our times of weakness, when we have failed to display the same qualities towards others in our times of strength. We as sinners, as willful transgressors of God's holy standards, are not deserving of divine mercy. But despite this, God sent Christ for all of humanity so that through Him we may be freed from our wickedness and rest in the promise of everlasting life. In His perfection and eternity He lacks nothing, and therefore He gains nothing from showing mercy to us. However, it is because of His great love for us that He seeks to pardon us for our sin and reconcile us to Himself for our benefit; so that we may not destroy ourselves as a result of our bondage to sin. As children of Christ we are required to show the selfless mercy which was shown to us by Christ Himself. But until we choose Him as Lord and allow Him to carry out His restorative work in our lives, we will not be able to ascertain how that looks like. Only when we have accepted Christ into our hearts and allowed His Spirit to enable us in living up to the righteousness we have through Him will we be able to show that unconditional mercy to others; drawing them into the knowledge of who Christ is and what He can do for them.

November 5

HOW TO LIVE IN PEACE

"When a man's ways are pleasing to the Lord, he makes even his enemies live at peace with him." -Proverbs 16:7 (NIV)

It can be exasperating dealing with particularly difficult people. In our eyes, it seems that they are bent on not giving us a moment's peace; deliberately trying to cause conflict in order to sabotage the already tense relationship we share with them and arouse our ire. The worst thing we could do however is to allow our rage to take reign over our thoughts and actions. Not only will we serve to be contributors to disunity and strife, but it will blemish our witness for Christ. We must always be aware of the fact that in our actions and reactions, we bear witness to Christ living within us. True peace will not flourish if we have permitted sin to taint our anger and indignation.

How then are we to live in peace with those around us? Dwelling in harmony with those whom we consider our enemies seems like an impossibility that will never be realized. But when we listen to Christ's Spirit living within us, allowing Him to help us live in a manner that is fitting of one who is His child, He will guide our thoughts and actions in such a way as to display His love and righteousness through us. If we try to create peace by attempting to live according to Christ's example and His teachings through our own efforts and strength, we will fail. His standard on how His children should act in love and forgiveness is too lofty for us to attain because our flawed human nature dictates that if our enemy takes out our eye, we should take out not only his eye but his leg too! Only when we allow Christ to enter into our hearts and break sin's hold over our lives will we be able to live as children of Christ through His enabling. People may be relentless in their antagonism towards us. But when we choose to remain in Christ, allowing Him to purge us of any malicious attitudes we may have and guide our thoughts, words, and actions, our adversaries will not be able to remain justified in their anger. When they see Christ's love and grace overflowing from our lives, they will slowly see that no weapon of theirs can overcome the goodness that is Christ our Lord. They will be drawn to the restorative work that He is doing in our lives, and can do for them as well if they choose to seek after Him.

November 6

SEEKING TO BE GUIDED

"But seek first his kingdom and his righteousness, and all these things will be given to you as well." -Matthew 6:33 (NIV)

There are times in our lives when uncertainty seems to plague our soul. Like a foreboding cloud it hangs over us as we fret about our future plans, our careers, and our relationships. We seek for guidance in every possible source only to find that their answers are unsatisfactory, sometimes placing even more doubts and fears into our already troubled minds. How we wish we had a map that would tell us exactly where to go and what to do at each leg of this journey we call life. But despite the realities and worries that characterize life here on Earth, we have someone who is willing to lead us through those times where we feel lost, confused and afraid.

When we seek the face of Christ and to dwell in His presence, He will be our perfect Guide. His plans for us are never to harm us, but to give us hope and a radiant future; with Him providing for our every need according to His perfect will and flawless timing. This is what He promises to us. However, He gives us the choice of claiming this promise for ourselves. When we try to sail the seas of life using the fallibility of human understanding and wisdom as our compass, we set ourselves on the path of misery and hopelessness. But when we seek the Kingdom of God, by allowing Christ within our hearts to be the sole proof of our citizenship in His Kingdom, and seek to allow Him to make His righteousness manifest in us, He will lead us on the path that He has intended for us to follow. Sometimes this path may seem treacherous and even undesirable. However, as long as we walk with Him and keep in step with His Spirit residing within us, He will slowly reveal, piece by piece His perfect will, His faithful provision and His unfailing love.

November 7

WITH OPEN ARMS

"The Lord said to me, 'Go, show your love to your wife again, though she is loved by another and is an adulteress. Love her as the Lord loves the Israelites, though they turn to other gods and love the sacred raisin cakes.'" -Hosea 3:1 (NIV)

God wanted to use Hosea and his wife as a living and graphic example of His love for humanity. Despite the blatant infidelity of his wife, Hosea was to love her with unwavering faithfulness and mercy. If we were in Hosea's position however, how many of us would actually obey God's call to love in such a radical manner? Often times we can barely love and forgive those who slight us even over the most trivial of matters, let alone the breaking of a holy sacrament given by God Himself. Betrayal hurts, especially if it comes from the people whom we love and thought we could trust. But our hurt can easily turn into hatred; to the point where it consumes our minds and becomes a poison that corrupts every area of our lives.

Yet if we truly look at the state of our hearts and see the depravity that exists, we will find ourselves as being a mirror image of Hosea's wife. When we give ourselves up to our sinful desires, we break the heart of God and prove our unfaithfulness to Him. As His children, our decision to indulge in sin cannot be justified outside of the fact that deep in our hearts we actually enjoy doing so. God has every right to be angry with us when we sell ourselves to wickedness because He cannot tolerate sin on account of the fact that He is holy. But in His wonderful love He does not seek to destroy us because of our disobedience towards Him. On the contrary He seeks to save us from it. Through Christ He offers the hope of forgiveness and being reconciled to Him. His arms will always be wide open to receive all who are truly repentant before Him no matter how many times we stumble and fall. When we make ourselves as slaves before sin, we degrade ourselves. But when we enter into a relationship with Christ; where we are immersed in His love and seek to live under His faultless direction and enabling, He will give us life eternal. By living in obedience to Him and His perfect will, we will be able to be the conduits by which He will fulfill His restorative mission to the world as we allow His love and forgiveness to be made manifest in our lives.

November 8

A LOVING DISCIPLINE

"Those whom I love I rebuke and discipline. So be earnest, and repent." -Revelation 3:19 (NIV)

In this permissive age we live in, we seem to have lost the value and importance of discipline. To ears of many in this present time, discipline has authoritarian and negative connotations; an imposition of the will and values of others upon the individual. But can you imagine what society would be like without rules? If we were without sin and faultless in every way, we would not need regulation and we would live quite happily without it. But the truth is that we are imperfect and fallen people, and this is where an anarchist vision of a utopia fails. By subscribing to a misunderstood view of human nature as being inherently good, it assumes that everyone will naturally act in a manner that benefits others and well as themselves without the need for a set of laws. However, unless we have just boundaries to live under and those boundaries are enforced, our propensity towards sin will result in us residing under a state of chaos that will serve to destroy ourselves and those around us.

God has set in place universal principles for humanity to live by. When we truly read His Word and seek to understand His statutes, we can see the holy perfection of God. His Laws are not meant to oppress us. On the contrary, they are there so that we may not fall slave to our depravity, and live in harmony with God and with each other. Far from disciplining us out of hatred or malice when we go astray, He disciplines us because He loves us. He weeps over us when we live in disobedience towards Him because He sees the damage that sin can do to ourselves as well as to fellow men. Therefore in His never-failing love for humanity, He disciplines us so that we may live under His life-giving Lordship free from the degradation of our wickedness.

No discipline is pleasant to endure. It will require us to endure the consequences of our wrong choices, and give up to Him areas of our lives that we don't want to surrender. But if we allow Christ's Spirit to enter into our hearts and allow Him to refine our hearts in His holy fire, the temporary pain we may undergo pales in comparison to the joy and peace which comes from living under His Law. We are able to live in accordance with God's Laws only if we have allowed Christ to make His righteousness manifested in our thoughts, words, and actions. When we disobey the voice of God, we can take assurance in the fact that His discipline, painful though it may be, will draw us closer to living a life of purity and holiness in Him; where we are not bound by the destructive grip of sin and live in blissful harmony with God and each other.

November 9

MADE HOLY THROUGH HIM

"If you, O Lord, kept a record of sins, O Lord, who could stand? But with you there is forgiveness;" -Psalm 130:3-4a (NIV)

If I was brought before God, in all His majesty and holiness, I would not be able to stand before Him on any account of my own. Despite the sincerity and dedication in my attempts to lead the moral life, I could never reach the perfection of God through my own efforts. Even the slightest hint of sin in my life is enough to count me amongst the wicked and depraved. We delude ourselves if we think that because we are essentially good people, we can claim a righteousness that will enable us to stand before God and guarantee us a place in Heaven. The truth is that because God is holy, He cannot tolerate the presence of wickedness in our lives, and if we honestly measured ourselves against God's standards of perfection, every one of us can claim to have failed in meeting those standards. Holiness, according to God's definition, cannot be achieved by human hands.

However, God wants to reconcile His creation to Himself. Though sin has separated us from God, He seeks to destroy the tyranny of wickedness over His creation and redeem humanity, whom He deeply loves because we are created in His image. Through Christ's death and resurrection He offers forgiveness and restoration to all who come to Him in humility and weary of the weight of sin on their shoulders. When we allow Christ to dwell within our hearts and allow Him to carry out His redemptive work in our hearts, we are made holy and righteous through Him. Only by submitting to His Spirit residing within us will His righteousness and love be made manifest in our lives and be poured out into the world around us. Never feel that you are not good enough and have gone past the line of no return in your wickedness. We are reconciled to God not because of what we have done based on our own human understanding or virtue, but solely because of what Christ has done through us in bestowing upon us His holiness and righteousness. His grace knows no boundaries, and His arms of forgiveness will always remain open to those who come before Him in humble repentance. In this assurance of forgiveness and restoration, we can take hope in the fact that we are saved from the ravages of sin through the power of Christ alone, and that He is preparing a place for us in Heaven so that we may dwell with Him in His perfect goodness and love for all eternity.

November 10

ACKNOWLEDGING OUR FAULTS

"The man said, 'The woman you put here with me-she gave me some fruit from the tree, and I ate it.'" -Genesis 3:12 (NIV)

When Adam and Eve ate the fruit from the tree of the knowledge of good and evil, it soon became apparent to them that they had done something horribly wrong. Realizing their shame, they quickly tried to hide themselves from God; oblivious to the fact God knew the truth the moment they committed their foul act of disobedience. It is enough to make our heads shake in derision as we read Adam's answer to God when He confronts Adam with his sin. Instead of taking responsibility for his actions, Adam first blames Eve for leading him into sin, and indirectly blames God for placing him with such a wayward woman. Not once does he acknowledge that the fault is his own; deliberately ignoring the fact that he was with Eve when she sinned. He could have not only refused to eat of the fruit which was offered to him, but he could have prevented Eve from taking that fatal bite!

Before we condemn Adam and his invalid excuse however, how many of us would act in the same manner? As descendants of Adam are we not prone to the same reaction? When we are caught in our sin, our first response is to look for something to blame; anything to take the pressure off of ourselves. We use other people, our circumstances, even God Himself as our scapegoat to cover up our blunders. Yet we are not fooling anyone. God in His omniscience knows the truth, and deep in our hearts we know full well who is really to blame for our wickedness. Sin is a choice dependant on no one else but ourselves. When we have Christ working within our hearts, the only legitimate reason we can give for our disobedience is that we deliberately chose to ignore God's call in our lives. By choosing to pursue vice, we must bear the consequences of our actions as well; whether we want to or not. But God never leaves us to suffer in our sin. Through Christ there is reconciliation and restoration for all who repent and seek to be made right with Him. This does not mean that the consequences of our sin will go away, rather He will use them to teach and instruct us in His righteousness while giving us the strength to endure the ramifications of our disobedience. However, by simply staying close to Him and obeying His voice, we will find ourselves living within His perfect will; away from situations where the temptation to blame is present.

November 11

A DAILY BLESSING

"This is the day the Lord has made; let us rejoice and be glad in it."
-Psalm 118:24 (NIV)

In every human being there is something called the *medulla oblongata*. It is an amazing little organ! Located just below the brain, it is what prompts us to inhale and exhale. Should anything happen to this organ, it will prove to be fatal and we would have died simply because we were unable to perform the motions of breathing. God, in His loving provision, ensures that this organ is always functioning. Every time we wake up and take in that first breath of a new day, it bears witness to the fact that He is the one who sustains us, who provides for our every need, and who has given us life so that we may enjoy all that it has to offer.

It must break His heart therefore when we unnecessarily gripe and complain about our lives. We are so quick to point out the negative in our day-to-day existence; often times making issue out of things that do not deserve to be made into grievances. Pessimism, although often disguised as being realistic, has the effect of numbing our minds to the blessings that we already have. We begin to take for granted those provisions which God has graciously bestowed upon us and become bitter and angry people. Of course there will be times when we may have a legitimate excuse for our grief. Pressed under the weight of our sufferings we may find it hard to rejoice in our circumstances. But when we have accepted Christ as Lord and allowed Him to work in our lives, we can take assurance in the fact that He is faithful. In His abounding love and perfect will He provides for our every need. He gives us life so that we may bear witness to His wonderful goodness; which is neither too late nor too early. Every day is a gift from God and we can rejoice and be glad in the fact that we are in His loving hands.

November 12

THE PERFECT EXTINGUISHER

"A soft answer turns away wrath, but a harsh word stirs up anger."
-Proverbs 15:1 (ESV)

Mirrors are fascinating things. Whenever we act before it from our first-person perspective, the mirror reflects back an image of ourselves doing the very same thing. It continues to be a source of amusement for children, as well as some adults too! But often times we act like mirrors ourselves. When someone lashes out in anger and malice towards us, how many of us would respond in kind? I would dare say that it is our default response. Sin has numbed our minds to how we are meant to act and react. Thus, our standard for action becomes dependant on the actions of others. The problem with this however is that by responding harshly to an angry word, we only serve to stoke the fire of rage in ourselves and in others; realizing our folly only when the damage has been done.

In our foolishness we often see answering in gentleness in the face of fury as something for the weak and submissive. However, it is anything but. Anyone can use their tongues for destruction for it is embedded in our sinful nature. But it takes someone with wisdom and courage to respond with words of healing and reconciliation amidst the wrathful cries of others. Yet can this gentleness come from ourselves? It cannot for if we honestly look into ourselves, we can see that our innate wickedness prevents us from acting as such despite our most sincere efforts. Only through Christ's Spirit dwelling within our hearts are we able to act in gentleness and restraint. When we allow Him to cleanse us of our sinful nature through our acceptance of His redemptive sacrifice on the cross, He clothes us with His righteousness and gives us His Spirit to help us perfect this righteousness. However, we have a choice. When we fail to listen to the Spirit and instead obey the voices of our old sinful nature, we will allow anger to leave destruction in its wake and deprive us and others of peace. But when we listen to the Spirit and seek to keep in step with Him, He will guide our actions in such a way as to allow His gentleness and love to flow through us; quenching the fires of anger in all who bear witness.

November 13

REMAINING STEADFAST IN LOVE

"Let love and faithfulness never leave you; bind them around your neck, write them on the tablet of your heart." -Proverbs 3:3 (NIV)

They are perhaps the most important qualities anyone could have. In all human relationships, love and faithfulness binds people together. That unconditional, selfless love which places the needs of others over oneself, combined with that faithfulness which promises to remain steadfast no matter the circumstances, serve as bonding agents which foster a sense of belonging and community amongst people. Families and friendships are built upon these qualities and their abundance, or a lack thereof, often determines the overall health and nature of the relationship in question. Humanity was created to live in harmony with one another. Just as how the Father, the Son, and the Holy Spirit dwell with each other in unity, we too are also meant to live in relationship and community with God and with our fellow man.

But can we really say that we have the capability to love unconditionally? Can we really say that we would never falter in our faithfulness to one another? The truth is that we cannot. Since we are corrupted by sin, our love and our faithfulness has become warped and distorted. Suddenly our love is based on if they love us back, and our faithfulness on whether they have been faithful to us. Love and faithfulness therefore become self serving, seeking to only boost one's ego and pride. Yet God calls us to a much higher standard. Despite our deliberate disobedience and our repeated rejections of Him, Christ still loves us and remains faithful to His promises. No matter what we may say or do, His arms will still remain open to all who come to Him in humble and sincere repentance. How many of us would be able to show such a powerful love? If we are truly honest with ourselves, we would shun those who shun us and embrace those who embrace us. But the love of Christ loves and continues to love even when that love is not appreciated or reciprocated. Human love is fleeting and is heavily dependent on whether our needs are being met. Divine love however is eternal because its Source is eternal and therefore it transcends human selfishness and pride. When we allow Christ to work His nature in us, His never failing love and faithfulness will be written on our hearts and overflow from our lives. Through His enabling in our thoughts, words, and actions, we will bear witness to the world that our God is a God who cares so much for humanity that He is willing to redeem us at all costs from the degradation of sin and wickedness.

November 14

DON'T GIVE IN!

"Do not let your heart envy sinners, but always be zealous for the fear of the Lord. There is surely a future hope for you, and your hope will not be cut off." -Proverbs 23:17-18 (NIV)

At times, the success of the wicked completely baffles us. We often see those steeped in sinful lifestyles live seemingly happy lives without experiencing the consequences of their decadence. As we observe this and struggle in upholding Christ's righteousness, we may wonder if the age old idea of good triumphing over evil is a lie. We may be tempted to ask ourselves if there is really any point or merit in living a life of holiness and integrity. Before we take that plunge into a lifestyle of wickedness however, we must consider a very important fact – sin is an excellent deceiver. With promises of hope, bliss, and fulfillment, it misleads us into thinking that we can have a wonderful life by living in whatever way we see fit. But like a disease which initially has no outward manifestation, it will slowly cause us to decay from the inside.

In sin there is no hope. Though all around us we may see the wicked prosper and live in contentment, such luxuries are fleeting. The only certainty of sin is that it leads to death and those who tread along that path will not only face the consequences of their wrong choices here on Earth but also in the hereafter if they choose to remain in their errant ways. However, through Christ we have a secure hope. When we have personally accepted His redemptive sacrifice on the cross for us and allowed Him to dwell within our hearts, He clothes us with His righteousness. This is a righteousness which will guarantee us a place in Heaven not through any effort of our own, but what Christ Himself has done for us.

Yet this righteousness is not meant to be dormant, rather we must allow Christ to perfect this righteousness in us so that others will be drawn to Him. This process will often require us to make lonely stands for His holiness when the world around us rejects what Christ has to offer, and this can be very discouraging at times. But we must always remember and take assurance in the fact that in Christ we have a hope that will never be snatched away from us; a hope which sin can never offer, and promises joy, fulfillment, and life eternal.

November 15

WHO IS ON THE THRONE?

"Put to death, therefore, whatever belongs to your earthly nature: sexual immorality, impurity, lust, evil desires and greed, which is idolatry." -Colossians 3:5 (NIV)

All sin is idolatry. When we indulge ourselves in wickedness, we are essentially bowing down before our sinful nature. In an effort to satisfy our inner corruption, we worship it through committing sinful acts that run contrary to the perfect righteousness of Christ as revealed through His Word. If we have failed to make Christ the center of our lives, by default we have given that position to our own innate wickedness. The problem with this is that our sinful nature is a brutal taskmaster and once we have allowed it to occupy the throne of our lives, our freedom is sacrificed. It will constantly demand that we bring before it sacrifices of vice and sin; sacrifices that will only continue to push the boundaries of our own integrity and dignity. In this way we are enslaved to sin; a slavery that will eventually result in our own destruction as we sacrifice our very lives to its needs.

In Christ there is freedom, and only Christ can free us from this slavery. When we personally accept His redemptive sacrifice for us on the cross and allow Him to reside in our hearts, He will break the chains which bind us to our sinful nature. Before we knew Christ, we knew only sin's iron hand. But once we have Christ, He begins His restorative work of perfecting His righteousness in and through us. The only thing that will hinder His work is our own stubbornness and our willful desire to disobey Christ and voluntarily submit ourselves to sin's yoke. Christ, because He has given us free will, allows us to exercise that free will in our choices. The question is whether we will make the right choice. If we choose to place our sinful nature at the forefront of our lives, we will suffer under the consequences of pandering to our sinful nature's every whim. But when we choose to place Christ on the throne of our hearts, He will deliver us from our wickedness and give us freedom from it by molding and refining us in His righteousness. We cannot save ourselves. How can one steeped in sin save himself from something embedded in his nature? Only through Christ is our old nature broken, and through His enabling and power will we be able to put to death all those wicked practices that ensnare us, thereby living up to the new nature of righteousness which He has given us.

November 16

RUN TO HIS WORD

"My soul is weary with sorrow; strengthen me according to your word." -Psalm119:28 (NIV)

We live in a world of sorrows. Despite the joys of life we must remember that as long as this world is tainted by the corruption of sin, suffering and disappointment will always remain an ever-present reality. When grief strikes our heel and casts a dark cloud over our lives, where do we turn? We want something that will support and strengthen us in our time of weakness. However, because we are fallen creatures, we turn to the material, and often detrimental things of this world to find solace and comfort. How many tried to wash away their anguish with alcohol? How many have tried to run away from their problems by burying themselves in work? How many have sought to find assurance and fulfillment in illicit relationships? All of these things will never be able to console us. In fact they will only serve to make us more miserable by binding us to destructive lifestyles and habits.

In Christ there is an unshakable hope. He is acquainted with the sufferings we must undergo on Earth for He bore witness to our sorrows while He dwelt among us. Yet in His omnipotence He stands above our trials. When we meditate upon His Word, and take refuge in His promises, we can rest in the fact that He will never leave nor forsake us. Christ does not eliminate suffering. Rather he works through it, for often times suffering builds character and faith. In His love Christ promises that He is there with us when we undergo times of darkness and that no matter how bleak our circumstances may be, there is restoration and deliverance in Him. He never leads us into darkness only to watch us fall. On the contrary, in His goodness, He takes us through the fires of hardship to refine us in His righteousness and strengthen us in our faith for our benefit. If we seek relief in the things of this world, we will only end up wallowing in self-pity and woe. But when we take hold of the promises of Christ as revealed through His Word, we are assured of the fact that our sufferings are temporary in light of His eternity, and that he takes us through them only to display His wonderful love, His faithful provision, and His redemptive work in our lives.

November 17

PICK ME! PICK ME!

"Then I heard the voice of the Lord saying, 'Whom shall I send? And who will go for us?' And I said, 'Here am I. Send me!'" -Isaiah 6:8 (NIV)

When I was a child, I loved to volunteer. The moment my teacher asked for helpers, my hand immediately shot up in the air. This was especially true for the task of taking the attendance to the school office. For a strange, inexplicable reason it was the most coveted role that a young elementary school student could get. Perhaps it was because we could see a world that we would otherwise rarely see, that little glimpse of the people who ran our school busily at work. I would try everything to get the teacher's gaze to fall upon me; even to the point of stretching out my arm so far that I needed my other arm to support it! Whenever I was selected, I took my role very seriously, yet found joy as the messenger. I was honored that the teacher chose me and that fact alone was enough to motivate me to perform whatever task I was called to do with much diligence.

When God calls us to a task, how often do we ignore His voice? We have a whole array of excuses to justify our unresponsiveness. In our own human wisdom we may deem it as an undertaking which is impossible, irrational, or undesirable. We fear that God will call us to a task that is arduous with no hope of bearing any fruit or benefits. Yet this is not God's will. He never calls us only to lead us into a bottomless pit. He promises that His plans are for our benefit and in the service of His redemptive mission to the world. If we ignore His call, we are actually depriving ourselves of a wonderful journey with Him. God requires nothing from us except our willingness to say "Here am I. Send me!", and to remain obedient to His perfect will. Sometimes we may feel that God has indeed led us into despair and that all hope is lost. But it is in those times where Christ develops our faith. When we rest in His promises we will be reminded of the fact that God has chosen us for a reason. As our faith deepens in Him, we are awakened to the fact that it is Christ who empowers us. If we remain close to Him, we will see His will accomplished and His faithfulness made manifest in our lives. Christ has already chosen us. Will we choose Him and benefit from responding obediently to His call?

November 18

WHITE AS SNOW

"...Though your sins are like scarlet, they shall be as white as snow;" -Isaiah 1:18 (NIV)

Thinking about the inevitability of winter makes me shiver. I would much rather prefer the heat of summer over its frigid touch. But if there is one thing about winter I look forward to seeing, it is the first snowfall. Every time the season comes around, I stop whatever I am doing to simply gaze out the window and watch as the snowflakes gracefully descend from the sky. Covering the autumn earth with a glistening white blanket, it reminds me of the grace and forgiveness we have through Christ. Though we were dead in our sins, through Christ we are covered by His righteousness. It is His restorative work in our lives which makes us pure as freshly fallen snow.

Sometimes we feel that we are outside of the grace of God. Looking at the depravity of our sin, we say to ourselves that there is no possible cure for us. We find it hard to believe that God can forgive us of our wickedness because we feel that we cannot forgive ourselves. But the truth is that where our forgiveness has limitations, His grace does not. Just as how the falling snow covers all that it touches, the forgiveness and grace we have through Christ is total. His love is greater than our sin and His redemptive sacrifice is not deficient. Christ underwent only one death and one resurrection, so that through Him we are completely cleansed and restored. Will we grab of that which Christ has promised us? When we allow Him to enter in our hearts and take hold of the hope that we have through Him, we are made spotless and pure by His blood shed for us on the cross. In believing that His death and glorious resurrection was meant for us, His Spirit takes up residence within our hearts. Clothed with His righteousness that comes with being made one in Christ, we now embark on an intimate journey with Him that promises life eternal.

November 19

BEING A WITNESS THROUGH CHRIST

"When they saw the courage of Peter and John and realized that they were unschooled, ordinary men, they were astonished and they took note that these men had been with Jesus." -Act 4:13 (NIV)

We often think that we are unsuited to share our faith with others. Pointing to those who are eloquent in speech and educated in the nuances of the Scriptures, we ask ourselves whether we are truly capable of bringing forth an effective witness for Christ. Yet when we look at Peter and John, we see this assumption debunked. Though they could not boast of any considerable education in the Scriptures, they were able to boldly proclaim Christ and His Truth to the amazement of Sanhedrin, the council representing the Jewish religious elite. How was this possible? It was evident even to the religious teachers that Peter and John had spent time with Jesus. They had heard, seen, and experienced His Word in action. He was the core of their witness. The Sanhedrin recognized that the courage and speech displayed by Peter and John did not come from within themselves, but from their relationship with Christ.

Sometimes we may use our inabilities as a convenient excuse to shy away from those opportunities where God is explicitly telling us to proclaim His Name. But the truth is that wherever we are, Christ has called us to be witnesses for Him and we are to be ready to tell others about what it means to be His children. We can only do so when we have entered into that relationship with Christ ourselves; personally accepting His redemptive sacrifice on the cross and allowing Him to dwell within our hearts. When we submit ourselves to Christ's perfect will and permit Him to enable us to live according to the righteousness He has bestowed upon us, He will guide our speech and our study of His Word in order to draw others to Himself. Our witness for Christ is not based on our own actions and knowledge, but solely by what Christ does and is doing through our lives. A living relationship with Christ is the most effective witness for Him, and this is accessible to all who genuinely desire to be in His presence and to be made whole in Him.

November 20

OUR TIMING OR HIS?

"'I am the Lord's servant,' Mary answered. 'May it be to me as you have said'..." -Luke 1:38 (NIV)

Mary found herself to be in quite the situation. Though she was told by God that she would be the bearer of the Messiah, the Savior of Mankind, it opened a whole host of questions. For a young virgin to be found pregnant, especially if she was betrothed, was a grave dishonor. Her parents would be enraged. Her fiancé, Joseph, would be devastated. The entire community would be whispering behind her back and would have treated her as an outcast. In addition, who would have believed her if she said that her pregnancy was divinely ordained? It would have been slightly easier for Mary if this announcement came shortly after she had married Joseph. But why now? Yet Mary's obedience to God's will is an example to us all. Despite all that could potentially befall her, she had faith that God will carry out His perfect plan and will lovingly provide for her through whatever she may face.

Sometimes we may wonder what God has planned for us. When He has called us to a task or into a particular situation, in our own human wisdom we give ourselves to doubt. We question whether He really knows what He is doing and whether His timing is really perfect. Of course we would gladly do His will when we feel the circumstances are advantageous and suitable. But how easily do we cringe when His will conflicts with our visions and schedules. In our wisdom we cannot see the wider picture. Sin has limited our perception to only think of our desires, our wants, and our goals. However, what we yearn to see for ourselves is not always what is best for us. A sinful heart can only deceive us into thinking that our plans are perfect and ideal. However, when we listen to the voice of God and allow Him to carry out His will through us, we will find that His infallible wisdom never fails and He has a plan which is greater and bigger than anything we can imagine. Will we cling onto our own desires, or allow Christ to foster in us a spirit of obedience by which we align our desires with His perfect will?

November 21

STUBBORNLY STAND FIRM!

"But the house of Israel is not willing to listen to you because they are not willing to listen to me, for the whole house of Israel is hardened and obstinate. But I will make you as unyielding and hardened as they are. I will make your forehead like the hardest stone, harder than flint. Do not be afraid of them or terrified by them, though they are a rebellious house." -Ezekiel 3:7-9 (NIV)

God was calling Ezekiel to a task that seemed impossible. The Israelites, God's chosen people, were yet again living outside of His will by indulging in sinful practices and disregarding His divine standard. Right from the start however, God warned Ezekiel that the prophet's task to call Israel to repentance and reconciliation would not be an easy one. Their stubbornness and hardness of heart will prove to be a challenge to Ezekiel and will be the source of much frustration and discouragement. But God, in His wonderful goodness, humorously assures the prophet that He will make Ezekiel just as stubborn and uncompromising in upholding His truth and righteousness. Ezekiel could face the Israelites with his head held high knowing that God was the One who was enabling and empowering Him to carry out what he was instructed to do.

When we come across opposition, it is easy and tempting to fall back and retreat. Antagonism towards our calling can often result in us shrinking into a corner and asking God in our anxiety whether He has pushed us into the lion's den armed with only a twig. But this is far from the truth. When God calls us to fulfill His will, He will equip us with whatever we need to see to the furtherance of His perfect plan and desires. The question is whether or not we will take hold of this supernatural aid which He graciously provides for us. In our own strength and capacity, we will not be able to bring to fruition what He has called us to accomplish. But when we abandon our trust in our own abilities and allow the power of Christ to flow through us, we will be able to not only endure, but flourish despite the circumstances we may face. The voices and inactivity of those around us may try to silence and stifle that which has been placed upon our hearts. But when we are assured of the will of Christ, He will give us the boldness and tenacity to stand firm in the face of adversity.

November 22

AN ETERNAL COMFORT

"Comfort, comfort my people, says your God." -Isaiah 40:1 (NIV)

We live in a broken world filled with broken people. As much as we would like to ignore this fact, it is an ever present reality. No matter how hard we may try to deny its existence, either within others or within ourselves, there will come a point when we will have to confront the misery and emptiness that is characteristic of life here on Earth. We all seek after something that will fill this emptiness in our hearts, heal this brokenness that we hide, and bring peace and joy to our troubled souls. But often times we do not know where to turn. In an attempt to find solace and comfort, we easily throw ourselves onto things that may promise healing only to find that they have swindled us by ultimately contributing to our misery, let alone seeking to bring restoration in our lives.

Outside of Christ there is no hope. If we seek to be comforted by running to the material things of this world, we will only find disappointment. Their temporary and tainted nature will fail to bring the relief we seek. It is only through Christ that we are assured of the hope which will never fail and a source of peace which will never run dry. When we have personally accepted Christ's redemptive sacrifice for us and allowed Him to dwell and work within our hearts, we can take refuge in His perfect, never ending love, and find hope in His faithful provision in our lives. These wonderful blessings found in Christ are not meant to be kept to ourselves however. It is God's will that all would be reconciled to Him and know of the beauty and wonder which comes from walking intimately with Him. In His restorative mission for His creation, our role as His children is to simply be vessels for His love to be poured out into the lives of others. Are there people in our lives who need to be comforted with the love of Christ? When we allow His love to overflow from within us, it will bring life to a lifeless world, hope to a world immersed in despair, and healing to those who need to be restored.

November 23

NEVER FEAR!

"Then Jesus said to his disciples: 'Therefore I tell you, do not worry about your life, what you will eat; or about your body, what you will wear. Life is more than food, and the body more than clothes.'" -Luke 12:22-23 (NIV)

It is a natural concern of ours. To reflect on where we are in our lives, and the direction in which it is headed, is a perfectly human question that we must all wrestle with from time to time. A healthy worry about the future is quite normal, even productive, as it keeps us on our toes and serves as an impetus to work hard towards our goals. But often this worry about the future becomes distorted as we turn it into an unhealthy anxiety. When pressures, real or imaginary, make us feel that time is slipping from our grasp and we are only a step away from collapse, fear grips our minds. We stress, panic, and submit ourselves to the fear that if we do not measure up to our standards of success, all will be lost.

How hard it is for us to reconcile ourselves to the fact that there is more to life than our material needs! How much harder it is for us to realize that our God faithfully provides for all our needs! We have succumbed to this false view that we are the commanders of our destiny. We have come to believe that success is dependent on our own aspirations, accomplishments, and our ability to enhance our lives; the failure to ensure that these things come to their fruition as a sign of worthlessness. But God does not measure success in the material. We could be in possession of all the wealth in the world yet be morally and spiritually bankrupt. As children of Christ, we are called to something greater than our material needs; to be molded in His righteousness and to be bearers of His light to the world around us. Our worth is not found in the abundance or lack of the things which we have accumulated in this world. Rather our worth is found in the love of Christ and what He has done for us on the cross to free us from our sin. When we have personally accepted Christ's redemptive sacrifice for us and have allowed Him to work in our lives we can take assurance in the fact that He never abandons His own and will always provide for us what we need, both materially and spiritually, according to His perfect will that will fully satisfy.

November 24

DON'T BE FORGETFUL!

"Praise the Lord, O my soul, and forget not all his benefits-" - Psalm 103:2 (NIV)

How easy it is to praise God! When everything is going our way and the floodgates of Heaven have showered blessings upon our lives, we find ourselves gushing with thankfulness and adoration for God's love and faithful provision. In our elation we make promises to surrender our lives to God and to be unwavering in our service and faithfulness to Him. But how easily do we forget these very things! When the storms of life turn against us, we fail to remember the goodness of God. Instead, we use our struggles as evidence of God's malevolence; pointing to our trials as indicative of His failure to provide. Yet when circumstances again turn in our favor, we return to that attitude of praise and gratitude. How opportunistic are we in our relationship with God!

When we focus upon the chaos around us we will forget about God. This is exactly what Satan wishes to do. By drawing attention to our miseries, he will attempt to pull us away from that life-giving relationship we have in Christ. But while he may claim that God Himself has brought this suffering upon us, this is far from the truth. It was never in God's will for His creation to be tainted by suffering and sin. Yet because man chose to disobey God, we have caused the world to descend into its fallen state. Trials therefore, are not willed by God, but are the result of living in this corrupted world. However, God stands above our trials and He uses them to strengthen and develop our character. He is unchanging in His nature and He will always be loving, faithful and just. He is not one to simply discard His children; rather He will lead us through tribulations if we allow Him to do so in our lives. When we see our lives through the eyes of Christ, we will be able to remember His faithfulness with joy. We will dwell in the assurance that though we may face despair, He will lift our gaze to rest on Him.

November 25

WINNING THE FAVOR OF CHRIST

"Obey them not only to win their favor when their eye is on you, but like slaves of Christ, doing the will of God from your heart." -Ephesians 6:6 (ESV)

We want to be liked. For a variety of reasons we feel the need to please others whatever the cost. It gives us a sense of worth and usefulness when we are appreciated by others. At times, we may believe that it is necessary to maintain the peace and the status quo. However, in our effort to not jeopardize our position, we compromise our devotion to

Christ. When we find ourselves seeking to align our attitudes and values to those of others, wanting to be loved and accepted by them, we have failed to take into consideration one important fact. Human opinion is subject to change and human existence itself is fleeting. If we have placed our worth and value in these, we will find ourselves having not only turned against the principles of Christ, but have brought into our lives much grief and pain whilst gaining nothing in return.

When we have accepted Christ in our heart; believing in His redemptive sacrifice and allowing Him to work out His righteousness in our lives, our worth and value is found in His eternal and perfect love. If our worth is found in anyone else, then we have exchanged the truth of God and the freedom we have in Him, for a deceptive slavery that seeks to keep us under its thumb. This is not to say we must be always antagonistic towards people. On the contrary, the Scriptures tell us to live in harmony with one another so that Christ may shine forth through us. But if we have become more concerned about pleasing those around us than serving Christ who is above them, then we are bowing down before an idol that will enslave us to our detriment. When we obey others knowing that in our service we serve Christ, we will be able to serve with a whole-hearted joy while remembering that we are not bound to man. We will be able to stand for His truth and justice knowing that our foundation is secure in Him.

November 26

RICHLY LIVING IN CHRIST

"Let the word of Christ dwell in you richly as you teach and admonish one another with all wisdom, and as you sing psalms, hymns and spiritual songs with gratitude in your hearts to God." -Colossians 3:16 (NIV)

It is easy for us to fall into the trap of dead habit. How often do we find ourselves simply going through the motions of the Christian life and ministry? To subscribe to ritual is appealing because it does not require us to think and be challenged. All it asks of us is to simply do what we have always done and this rote obedience to habit gives us a false sense of satisfaction that we have fulfilled our obligations. But such an approach to the Christian life is empty. If we are truly honest with ourselves, we notice that something is missing. Our prayers feel monotonous. Our minds feel numbed to the Scripture. Our worship feels dry, and our work for Christ seems to be disconnected from ourselves.

Paul is imploring the Colossian church to "...let the word of Christ dwell in you *richly*..." We may have the word of Christ in our hearts, but it is another thing to allow it to mold us and shape our minds. The Christian life is not a passive one. It is an active relationship with Christ whereby we allow His Spirit to refine us and draw us closer to Himself. The only thing that is preventing us from living abundantly in Christ is our own attitudes and our desire to cling onto our obedience to ritual. Are we bowing down before the idol of ritualistic duty instead of directing our worship to Christ? When we allow Christ to conform our attitudes to Himself and seek to be made One in Him, our entire lives will take on a whole new character. Our prayers will be vibrant. Our minds will be receptive to the truths it contains. Our worship will edify and strengthen us, and our work for Christ will be effective and transformative both for ourselves and for others. When we seek Christ and allow His Spirit to work within us, we will experience the joys of living in tune with Him.

November 27

WHICH MASK ARE WE WEARING?

"'I tell you, whoever acknowledges me before men, the Son of Man will also acknowledge him before the angels of God. But he who disowns me before men will be disowned before the angels of God.'" -Luke 12:8-9 (NIV)

We often live our lives by carrying a wide array of masks with us. Depending on the situations we are placed, we put on a different mask in an effort to blend in. When we are in our churches, we put on a "church mask" which presents ourselves as model Christians perfect in devotion and piety. However, when we are in our schools or workplaces, we often put on an entirely different mask which presents ourselves as being utterly depraved and willing to adjust our values according to the standards of those around us. Yet if we think that we can live as children of Christ while conveniently donning a mask to conceal our faith when we wish, we are sadly mistaken. Jesus Himself clearly states in Matthew 6:24, "No one can serve two masters…"

When we enter into a relationship with Christ, we are to surrender every area of our lives to Him. Christ's redemptive work in our hearts seeks total restoration and this means that we must allow Christ to work out His righteousness in whatever situation we are placed. Are there areas in our lives where we are failing to acknowledge Him and allowing His restorative work to be made manifest in our daily interactions? Our true loyalties will be made known to us when we feel that sacrificing our relationship with Christ is a small price to pay for conforming to the so-called "real world". Unless we acknowledge Christ in all our ways and are unafraid to bear witness for His truth, we cannot expect the blessings of God to rain down upon us. Only when we desire to align ourselves with Him and remain in His will are we able to partake of the blessings and joys of being covered under His protective umbrella. We are only allowed to wear one mask in this life of ours. Will we choose to wear the mask of Christ and continually bear witness to the hope and restoration that is available through Him?

November 28

THE KEY TO JOY

"Be joyful always; pray continually;" -1 Thessalonians 5:16-17 (NIV)

Where do we find joy? Where do we find peace? It is a universal desire that humanity yearns to posses; that we may find these things in abundance in our lives. Philosophers throughout human history have sought to find the key to obtaining that unshakable joy and calm which we all seek. Some say it is through living the moral life, others through the accumulation of wealth and the pursuit of pleasure. Still others claim that lasting human happiness can be achieved through the creation of a harmonious society where all live in equality and unity. The reality however, is that societies rise and fall, wealth and pleasure are fleeting, and living a truly moral life is seemingly impossible; all because of the fallen state of ourselves and the world around us.

We were created for one purpose alone, to live in relationship with God. In His eternity, man's hope was secure, and in His goodness man's joy was complete. However, because of our sinful nature, we are separated from God and with that separation our eternal joy and peace is lost. Yet it is in God's plan to mend this broken relationship we have with Him. He sees that sin has only wrought misery and insecurity upon our souls and wants to restore our hope and bliss. When we accept Christ's redemptive sacrifice for us and allow Him to dwell within our hearts, we not only have a restored relationship with Him, but our relationship with Him is direct and personal. Being in relationship with Christ is the key to true happiness and peace. As He enables us to live according to His righteousness we are free from the degrading control of sin. When we invest in that relationship through prayer and allowing His Word to permeate our minds, we will find that in Him we are made complete and that nothing can take away the hope we have through Him.

November 29

WATCHING AND WAITING

"But as for me, I watch in hope for the Lord, I wait for God my Savior; my God will hear me." -Micah 7:7 (NIV)

Waiting is hard. How easily do we give ourselves to worry whenever we are placed in a situation where we are unexpectedly obligated to wait? It is at these times that we constantly bombard ourselves with questions. What is going on? Is everything okay? Can we still hope in the possibility that everything will work out according to plan? Perhaps what frustrates us most is that this period of waiting has placed us in a seeming state of helplessness. When it appears that we must resign ourselves to the practice of patience, it makes us feel that we have no control whatsoever over those areas of our lives that we wish to have under our control; thus resulting in much anxiety and stress.

The truth is that in our own human capabilities we cannot control the world around us. As much as we would like to, we must accept the fact that we cannot control our own destiny, and if we could, we would most likely bring ourselves to the doorstep of destruction. But thankfully we have someone who is greater than our limitations and who wants to serve as our guide. When we personally accept the redemptive sacrifice of Christ and allow him to dwell within our hearts, we enter into a restored relationship with Him. This is characterized by a dependence on His perfect will and loving providence. Why then do we worry when we have someone who promises to take care of our very need? Is it because we refuse to give up control over our lives and stubbornly trust in our fallible wisdom? If we try to impatiently and impulsively master our circumstances, our efforts will be rendered futile. But it is only in waiting upon the Lord that we are filled with his peace and joy knowing that it is He who commands our destiny according to His good and perfect desires for our lives.

November 30

WHEN WERE YOU BORN?

"...for we were born only yesterday and know nothing..." -Job 8:9 (NIV)

I wasn't born yesterday! How many times have we caught ourselves saying this phrase? We often use this exclamation when we sense that we are being tricked or deceived by someone else. As much as it signals to the listener that we are not easy to fool, it also assures us that we are not gullible people. But despite our claims to being shrewd, we prove ourselves time and time again that we are quite the opposite. How often do we fall into the traps of misery and woe? How often do we allow sin to deceive us into submitting ourselves under its yoke? Though we are able to see through these deceptions and avoid these traps, we are a forgetful race. When we fail to remember the lessons God has taught us through our lives, our neglect of His teachings will be our undoing.

The Christian life is a discipline. It is a discipline based on remembrance; a concept which is echoed throughout the Bible. God calls His people to remember His commandments and to remember His faithfulness. Like a teacher training his students, God continues to remind us of these things for He knows that wisdom and knowledge easily depart from our minds. The remnants of our sinful nature would like for us to forget His teachings and draw ourselves away from Christ. Our only defense against sin's devices is to abide with Christ and allow His wisdom to illumine our minds. When we make that choice to walk closely with Him and spend time in His Word, He will remind us of the viciousness of sin, and the hope and joy we have by being in

His presence. No one can claim to be wise for our erstwhile wicked nature continues to vie for our loyalty. It is this struggle within our souls which prevents us from achieving full perfection in the wisdom and righteousness of Christ. But when we have allowed Christ to reside in our hearts and opened our ears and minds to walk in His ways, we will be able to live within His perfect will knowing that it is He who gives us wisdom and ability to apply it in our lives.

December 1

BE A LIGHTHOUSE!

"No one lights a lamp and puts it in a place where it will be hidden, or under a bowl. Instead he puts it on its stand, so that those who come in may see the light." -Luke11:33 (NIV)

Before modern technology transformed sea travel, lighthouses served as guides for ships on their journeys. Not only did the presence of a lighthouse indicate a port, it also warned sailors of dangerous formations such as cliffs or rocks which would otherwise be obscured when visibility was poor or when night would fall. Now suppose the lighthouse keeper, for whatever reason, decided to neglect his work. Perhaps he was weary of the lonely and seemingly unrewarding task of being a keeper of the light and decided to extinguish his lamp and go home. Imagine the chaos that would ensue! With nothing to guide them, sailors navigating through the darkness will find themselves lost, confused, and afraid. They may even meet a grisly end as they unknowingly shipwreck themselves amongst the rocks. Lighthouses are meant to save lives and guide others along the right path. It benefits no one therefore if their lights do not shine.

We too may sometimes grow weary of bearing the light of Christ in our lives. The loneliness and ostracism we face because of our stand for Christ may serve to discourage us. In our eagerness to conform ourselves to the world around us, we may deliberately try to hide the light of Christ in our hearts underneath a guise that is deemed acceptable in the sight of fallible men. As children of Christ however, we are called to bear witness to His truth and righteousness being made manifest in our lives. Through His indwelling in our lives, He will draw others into a knowledge of Himself and lead them in the path of everlasting life. We live in a world where humanity is seeking for salvation and guidance. No man-made philosophy can serve as an adequate compass. Only Christ, who has overcome this world, can be the Perfect Guide and He has chosen us to be bearers of the hope we have in Him. Though we may face trials and isolation because of this calling Christ has placed on our lives, He will be the One to strengthen us when our arms grow weary. When we abide in Christ and live in obedience to His will for our lives, His light shining through our lives will steer others away from destruction and point towards Him who is the giver of life.

December 2

AN ETERNAL FOUNDATION

"Heaven and earth will pass away, but my words will not pass away." -Mark 13:31 (ESV)

Persecution has been the Church's lot. From the time of its inception it has faced brutal opposition. Even to this day the Church in many parts of the world still undergoes horrendous suffering and suppression. Yet it is amazing to reflect on the fact that while the Church has endured much hardship, it continues to thrive and grow. No matter how many churches are destroyed, no matter how many Christians are murdered, no matter how many Bibles have been burnt, the Church's persecutors, be they the Romans of the Ancient world or the totalitarian regimes of the modern era, have never been able to extinguish her. Despite the relentless attacks mounted against it, the Church has stood for over two thousand years!

Clearly there is something supernatural sustaining the Church. Its foundation is not in the material things of this world, but it is founded upon Christ who has transcended the world. Sometimes when we undergo unwarranted hostility because of our witness for Christ and are overwhelmed by the opposition against us, we may wonder if there is truly victory through Christ. We may feel that His Word fails to resonate with people today and that His Truth is being drowned by deceptions and injustice. But as history has proven, persecutions may come and go, yet His Word will remain firm. The foundation of the Church is not a building, neither is it found in the numbers who enter its doors. It is founded entirely on Christ. Therefore, the victory of His truth is assured and nothing will be able to hinder the realization of Christ's ultimate goal for the entire world to be reconciled to its Creator. When we have allied ourselves with Christ, personally accepting His redemptive sacrifice for us and allowing Him to work in our hearts, we can rest knowing that while the world may try to silence us, Christ will always emerge triumphant.

December 3

MAKING THINGS RIGHT

"Fools mock at making amends for sin, but goodwill is found among the upright." -Proverbs 14:9 (NIV)

What does it mean to make amends? It is a two-fold action. First there is an acknowledgement that we have done something wrong and that we are at fault. The second step is to seek reconciliation by practically showing the offended party that you are repentant and that you wish to make things right. But how hard it is for us to even take that first step! In a world where humanity seeks to do whatever it wishes heedless of the consequences, we want to hide the fact that every sinful action comes with a responsibility that we must bear. Our pride wants to deny that we have done wrong and we come up with a variety of excuses to justify our behavior. However, underneath the surface we know that we are not innocent and that we need to mend that which is broken.

We are called to live in peace and harmony with one another. But we have created a superficial peace if we have simply ignored issues between each other. Like a ticking time bomb, we will pay the consequences for letting grievances simmer in the hearts of those whom we have offended. Christ has called His children to stand up for His truth and that means admitting that we have sinned before God and against others. He has also called His children to take responsibility for the wrongs we have committed and make things right. Just as how through His death we are reconciled to God, so to we must seek to be reconciled to others when we are guilty of sin. When we seek to be made right with those around us, we bear witness to Christ's righteousness working within our hearts. Our decision to seek amends draws attention to the fact that we serve a God who takes sin seriously and does not wish to see it separate people from Himself and from each other. We might claim that this is a task beyond our capabilities. But only through Christ's indwelling within our lives and our submission to His will can our prideful spirit be broken. Once this spirit has been shattered, Christ will strengthen and enable us to take those steps necessary for true peace and harmony to flow.

December 4

DON'T WALK AWAY!

"He who mocks the poor shows contempt for their Maker; whoever gloats over disaster will not go unpunished." -Proverbs 17:5 (NIV)

The poor and suffering are all around us. Whether they are images on a television screen, people we encounter on our streets, or even within our own circle of friends and relatives, they are there as an ever present reality. What is our reaction to such situations? How often have we borne witness to scenes of poverty and misery by simply saying to ourselves "I'm glad it isn't me". I daresay that this has become our standard response. Not only does it reflect a highly individualistic and indifferent attitude towards those afflicted by suffering, but it is essentially flaunting our perceived success in the faces of those who are in torment. The truth is that in this earthly world nothing is permanent, and all our treasures could vanish in an instant.

Christ has called us by His example to not only show concern for the poor and downtrodden, but to tangibly assist them in their hour of need both physically and spiritually. All men, whether rich or poor, content or distressed, are created in the image of God. As such, to adopt an attitude of indifference or a perceived sense of superiority over others because of our own pleasant circumstances shows a disdain for God Himself. When our hearts are filled with pride, we idolize our achievements and become selfish with the resources God has given us. But when we surrender ourselves to Christ by personally accepting His redemptive sacrifice for our sins and allowing Him to invade our hearts, He will work to shatter our egocentric attitudes and replace them with His love. When we allow His love to overflow through us, our interactions with those around us will change dramatically. We will look for opportunities to display the love which Christ has shown us; seeking to be by His enabling, living examples of who He is and the hope which is available through Him.

December 5

HOW ARE WE LISTENING?

"'Consider carefully what you hear,' he continued. 'With the measure you use, it will be measured to you—and even more.'" -Mark 4:24 (NIV)

Often when God is speaking to us through His Word, we adopt either one of three types of hearing. The first is passive hearing. Though outwardly it may seem that we are attentively listening to the Word of God as it is being brought to us, inwardly our thoughts are scattered everywhere else. Bogged down by the concerns of this world and our daily lives, we miss hearing those important truths that God wants us to apply in our lives for our own benefit. The second is a tendency to lean towards selective hearing; gleaning only what we want to hear and ignoring what appears to be uncomfortable to us. Perhaps we may even go to the extreme of distorting the truths contained in God's Word to justify our own fallen ideas and beliefs instead of allowing Christ Himself to speak to us.

What then is the third type of hearing? When we are intently listening to the voice of God, taking in all of His Truth and seeking to apply it in our lives without any interference from ourselves or others, we are practicing active hearing. Christ has called us to active listeners of His Word and to ensure that it soaks every aspect of our being. When God is speaking to us through Scripture, what we choose to take in or avoid affects our spiritual life. If we have failed to listen to His Truth, our spiritual life will remain stagnant and we will slowly drift away from Him. If we have only partially accepted His Truth or have made it conform to our own desires, we will be discouraged and disillusioned when we feel that God has failed in pandering to our ideals and whims. However, when we are actively immersing ourselves in His Word, allowing Christ to give us open ears and hearts to understand the fullness of His Truth, we will be able bask in the joy and peace of living within His perfect will.

December 6

WE NEED A GATEKEEPER!

"Above all else, guard your heart, for it is the wellspring of life." - Proverbs 4:23 (NIV)

Picture for moment a city. This is no ordinary city however, but the centre of a vast and beautiful kingdom. As the capital, this city is what sustains the life of the kingdom and therefore occupies a very important role. Consequently, what happens in the capital, good or bad, affects the other cities, towns, villages, and territories it governs. Now suppose there is an enemy kingdom who seeks to ultimately destroy this prosperous and content neighbor. Instead of invading the kingdom outright however, they adopt a more subtle approach by discreetly sending spies into the capital. At first their presence is not noticed, though their numbers continue to grow. If remained unchecked however, they could instigate a rebellion that would lead to an overthrow of the government. With the capital in rebel hands, the business of subjugating and enslaving the remainder of once magnificent kingdom would be comparatively easy. Of course, no wise king is ignorant of this fact. For this reason he erects walls around his capital, and hires guards to keep a close watch upon who enters the city.

Our heart is the capital city of our soul. What we allow to enter into our hearts affects the thoughts we think, the words we say, and the actions we carry out. Depending on who and what we choose to permeate our hearts, they can either be the source of life to our entire being, or a poison that will corrupt every aspect of our lives. But are we fully capable of choosing what is right and beneficial for the well-being of our souls? Often times in our ignorance and willful acceptance, we permit wickedness to take root within us. What then is the option available to us if we do not wish to see ourselves engulfed by sin? Our only hope is that we personally accept Christ's redemptive sacrifice for us and allow Him to enter into our heart. When we do this, He will be the gatekeeper of our hearts; rejecting that which is harmful to us and accepting that which will build us up. Christ is perfect in righteousness, and when we allow Him to be that filter in our lives, we can rest in the assurance that He will preserve our hearts so that our entire soul will flourish in Him.

December 7

WHERE ARE OUR EYES FIXED?

"Before long, the world will not see me anymore, but you will see me. Because I live, you also will live." -John 14:19 (NIV)

Where is God? It is a question that we have all asked ourselves at some point in our lives. We wonder if there truly is a loving God watching over us and actively intervening in the world. With our human faculties we cannot perceive God physically and His seeming inactivity in the face of individual trial and collective human suffering leads us to question His existence. But perhaps the reason why we do not see God is that we have focused our attention on ourselves and our circumstances. Often times, we are like a hiker who fails to see the beauty of the valley around him for his mind and thoughts are solely concentrated the arduous path he must travel. Where our eyes are focused affects our view of the world.

Christ has promised that those who seek Him will find Him. When we personally accept His redemptive sacrifice for us and allow Him to work in our hearts, we are not only given new life through Him, but a new perspective about the world around us. By lifting our gaze towards Christ, He will open our eyes to His Truth and see the reality of our surroundings. His Truth distinguishes itself from the counterfeit truths of the world because Christ is perfection and truth personified. Unlike us humans, Christ is not bound by our human limitations. He was present before even time began and presently stands as a victorious King over the fallen world. Through Him we will be able to see that while there are still battles to be fought against the remnants of sin, the war is won. We will bear witness to the hand of Christ actively working towards His unstoppable mission to bring restoration to ourselves and the world around us. If our focus is pointed downward towards the world, we will only find disappointment and despair. But when we turn our eyes upward to see Christ, we will see the world for what it is while taking hope in the fact that He has overcome the world and will use our lives for His good purposes.

December 8

CORRECTING OUR VISION

"Have we not all one Father? Did not one God create us? Why do we profane the covenant of our fathers by breaking faith with one another?" -Malachi 2:10 (NIV)

We are all related to one another. Though we may possess unique qualities which distinguish ourselves from each other, all of us share something in common. Each and every person on this Earth is fearfully and wonderfully made; molded by a Divine and Sovereign Creator in His image. He has given us breath and every life is precious in His sight. Yet how often do we forget this fact! Our failure to see others as having an intrinsic worth by virtue of being created by a loving God is the prime cause of strife in this world. Instead of seeing each other through the eyes of Christ, we allow prejudice and hatred to color our perceptions of people; thereby setting into motion a cycle of pain and sorrow which only serves to degrade humanity.

Sin has not only separated us from God, but it has separated us from each other as well. Ever since Adam and Eve's rebellion and the entrance of sin into the world, we can see the evidence of its corrosive touch in human interaction.

Why do we fight amongst ourselves? Why are insults and betrayal so prevalent in our behavior? Has sin numbed our sensitivity to us seeing the image of God in other people? The only cure for our blurred vision is Christ. God wants people to be reconciled to Himself and to their fellow man. But this can only happen when sin is purged from our lives. We cannot cleanse ourselves of our sin for we are corrupted by its influence. How can one clean himself in his filthy state? That is why God sent down His Son Jesus to die for humanity, so that through Him we may be washed of our wickedness and restored into a beautiful relationship with God. When we allow Christ to place upon us His garments of righteousness and help us see others through His eyes, our interactions with others will be wonderfully transformed. His unconditional love poured out through us will define our exchanges with the people around us as we seek to draw others into a knowledge of Christ Himself. Through the enabling of Christ in our lives we will be able to live together in the manner God intended; in harmony and joy as brothers and sisters under the loving and faithful care of our Heavenly Father.

December 9

HIS LOVING MERCY

"Who is a God like you, who pardons sin and forgives the transgression of the remnant of his inheritance? You do not stay angry forever but delight to show mercy." -Micah 7:18 (NIV)

Mercy and forgiveness are just as embedded in the character of God as His righteousness and justice. In His perfect holiness, God has no tolerance for sin. Therefore, He allows the consequences of man's sinful choices to come to pass. However, He does not do this out of spite, but only so that we may realize the destruction that wickedness causes in our lives. God does not take pleasure in inflicting suffering upon us. On the contrary, it grieves Him whenever He must use the rod of correction. Sin in our lives has separated us from God. This was not part of His perfect will. Man was meant to live in a fulfilling relationship with God, finding lasting peace, hope, and worth in Him and His eternal love. Throughout Scripture, we see God extending the hand of mercy and forgiveness toward humanity, the greatest example of which was the sending of His Son, Jesus Christ, to die for our sins so that we may be reconciled to Him.

What is most beautiful about His gift of salvation to humanity is that we are not deserving of it. Man continues to reject God by his attitudes and lifestyles, thereby rebelling against what He, in His divine wisdom, has ordained for humanity. Yet God does not withhold the gift of Christ because of our rebellion. He seeks to redeem us from the ravages of sin, and knows that we are unable to attain His righteousness on our own strength or wisdom. For this reason, He sent Christ so that, through Him, we are forgiven. The debt of our sin is paid by His blood. When we personally accept Christ's redemptive sacrifice and allow Him to work within our hearts, we enter into a restored relationship with Him and partake in the abundant life we have in Him. As children of Christ, we are called to bear witness to the mercy and love He has shown to us by displaying these attributes to all whom God places along our path. Only by submitting ourselves to the will of Christ and permitting Him to take control of our thoughts, words, and actions will we be able to show the unconditional grace and forgiveness of Christ; drawing others to the hope which is available through Him.

December 10

PRAYING FOR OTHERS

"He is patient with you, not wanting anyone to perish, but everyone to come to repentance." -2 Peter 3:9b (NIV)

Paul's heart broke for his nation. Being a former religious leader of prominence, he knew full well of the delusion such people were under. Though they were zealous for the things of God the religious leaders were far away from Him. Ironically, their legalism ensnared them in sin for they made an idol out of the Law by placing it above obeying God Himself. Their strict interpretations of the Law made them miss the heart of God; turning them into oppressors who took pride in their self-righteousness. When Paul encountered Christ and allowed Him to invade his life, his eyes were open to what true righteousness really is. It is not through any effort of our own that we are made righteous, but we are made perfect only through the redemptive work of Christ in our lives as He conforms our hearts to Himself.

Yet despite having this knowledge, Paul doesn't scorn or look down upon them. We see in Romans 10:1 that he prays for them, earnestly seeking that they too will be saved and brought into the knowledge of their Savior. How often do we adopt an attitude contrary to that of Paul! Too easily we give ourselves to attitudes of condescension and hate towards those who do not understand the message of Christ and who may persecute us because of it. We see them as enemies to be vanquished instead of men and women created in the image of God. Where is the love of Christ in such perceptions of people? His redemptive mission on Earth is to draw the world to Himself, restoring the fallen into a life giving relationship with Him. Our role as emissaries for Him is to pray for this world and allow Christ's love and righteousness to shine through us. When we align our hearts with the good purposes of Christ and pray for those around us, we will see our attitudes change from one of malice to one of selfless love. By looking through the eyes of Christ we will see the people God brings along our path as those similar to ourselves before we encountered Him; as lost souls in need of salvation.

December 11

KNOWING WHEN TO DO BATTLE

"Better a patient man than a warrior, a man who controls his temper than one who takes a city." -Proverbs 16:32 (NIV)

A good general knows how to pick his battles. He knows when to stand his ground and when to retreat so that he and his men can fight another day. With discernment he refuses to allow impatience to taint his judgment. Only until all the intelligence has been collected and all the potential factors are weighed in, does he carefully plan out his attack and determine its execution. More importantly however, he keeps the bigger picture in mind. He does not waste time or resources over a fruitless objective; but is always considering the ultimate goal and his decisions in relation to that goal. A general can be neither overly aggressive nor excessively passive; but must with discernment determine what is really worth fighting for.

In our stubborn impulses we often do things that only serve to tear ourselves and others down. How many of us have wasted time and energy trying to force circumstances to fit our will? How many of us have brought anxiety and grief upon ourselves and those around us through attempts to prove ourselves right even over the most trivial of matters? God understands the value of patience and calls His children to cultivate this virtue in their lives. But patience is not something that can be fostered through our own wisdom or discipline. It is mentioned in Galatians 5:22 as the fourth manifestation of the fruit of the Spirit. When we have allowed the Spirit of Christ to carry out His redemptive work within our hearts and humbly submit ourselves to His perfect plan for us, He will guide us according to His wisdom. In doing so, our actions and reactions to situations will bear witness to the restorative mission of Christ being worked out within our lives. By allowing Him to lift up our eyes towards Heaven, we will be able to discern what battles must truly be fought and what must be surrendered in accordance to His faultless will.

December 12

WATCH WHERE YOU'RE GOING!

"Ponder the path of your feet; then all your ways will be sure." - Proverbs 4:28 (ESV)

When I started my first year of university, I used to travel between home and classes by bicycle. One day as I was returning home, my mind was drifting when I suddenly collided into something. Thankfully I was not hurt. But the irony of the situation was that as I looked up to see what obstructed my path, my eyes met with a giant red stop sign. Had the sign not been there, I would have biked casually away from the security of the sidewalk and onto the main road; thereby placing me in a potentially dangerous situation. Signs are there for our benefit. They prompt us to consider the route we are taking and travel with the safety of both ourselves and others in mind.

How often do we fail to think about the steps we take? Sometimes we are so absorbed with seeing that our desires be met that we do not heed the voice of God. When Christ's Spirit is residing within us He will stir our hearts in order to get our attention and help us discern how to proceed according to His plan for our lives. He will speak through His Word, and through the people He brings along our path, His wisdom and truth. It is not in His will or nature to seek our destruction. On the contrary He is the giver and preserver of life. Christ has already provided for us the means by which we can live within His protective umbrella. The question is will we choose to pay attention to Him? Will we choose to reflect on our actions through His divine wisdom and listen to His Spirit's prompting? If we have made an idol out of our human wisdom and desires, we will be numb towards Christ and oblivious to His voice when He warns us of danger. But when we make that decision to listen to His Spirit and walk in obedience to His will, only then will we find security and confidence in the path we travel.

December 13

A PERFECT COMPASS

"Neither the pillar of cloud by day nor the pillar of fire by night left its place in front of the people." -Exodus 13:22 (NIV)

Getting lost is never a pleasant experience. The mere thought of being stranded in a foreign environment without guidance and the means to meet our basic needs overwhelms our minds with fear. This is why culture shock can be so jarring for many. Unfamiliar sights and language barriers to overcome can leave us with feelings of frustration and helplessness. In a sense, the Israelites also underwent culture shock. Though they were slaves in Egypt, they could at least have boasted about having a roof over their heads and food to eat. But God had brought them into the hostile and barren environment of a desert. In the face of the hardships characteristic of desert life, we may ask along with the Israelites, why?

God never calls us to walk alone. Through Him we are assured that, whether in specific situations or life in general, He will always be there to guide us along. Just as how God provided the Israelites with the cloud and the pillar of fire to guide them through the desert, Christ is the cloud and pillar of our lives. He has given us His Holy Spirit to direct us in the way we should go, and His Word is there before us to help us discern His will. In His perfect will and goodness He does not lead us into death and despair, but into eternal life through Him. What will be our choice? We can choose only one of two options. One path is to reject His guidance and wander in bitterness and grief; all the while complaining about our circumstances. The other is to simply trust in God's good purposes for us and allow Christ to be the compass of our lives. God is not distant from us. He never has been nor will He ever be. The question is, are we distant from Him? Are we, out of pride or fear, deliberately refusing to take His hand and lead us into a bright and glorious future? Outside Christ there is only misery. But only through Him there is life.

December 14

WHAT IS GREATNESS?

"But you, Bethlehem Ephrathah, though you are small among the clans of Judah, out of you will come for me one who will be ruler over Israel, whose origins are from of old, from ancient times." -Micah 5:2 (NIV)

Why Bethlehem? What was so important about this little Judean town? On its own it could not boast of any inherent prestige. It was certainly not the political, economic, and religious centre which Jerusalem was. On the contrary, it was an unassuming town of shepherds and had little, if any, weight in the affairs of the wider Jewish nation. Its greatness however, is not derived from any achievement of its own, but solely from the good purposes God has for its history. It was from Bethlehem that God chose David, that very ordinary shepherd boy, to be the finest earthly king Israel has produced. Now it is remembered as the birthplace of Christ, the King of kings and the Savior of the World. Bethlehem is exalted today because it was God Himself who declared and made it great.

Often in our insecurities we may see ourselves as unimportant and insignificant. When we see those around us who have everything man could wish for in possession and ability, we may feel dwarfed by such people. This leaves us wondering about our purpose in life, and if we can truly match the greatness of others. However, God has a wonderful plan for each and every one of us. His measure of success is not defined by what we can do to be prosperous in this world, but what He can do for us if we take hold of Christ. When we make that choice to grasp His hand and trust in His perfect wisdom, He will take us on a journey that will leave us breathless in the face of His goodness and faithfulness. If we see ourselves as less than great by the standards of the material world, then we have inadvertently placed as the highest good the pursuit of treasure which will not last. But when we see our treasure as being found in the perfect will of Christ, we will stand firm in the knowledge that through Him we have significance and worth.

December 15

TOWARDS A LASTING PEACE

"How good and pleasant it is when brothers live together in unity!" - Psalm 133:1 (NIV)

All of us desire peace. We want to be at that place in our lives when we are at peace with those around us. Yet at times the peace that we hope and yearn for proves to be elusive. In our sinful impulses and human failings, we quarrel over things which have no real consequence, say things that we do not really mean, and act in a regrettable manner towards others. When we see the damaging effects of our petulant behavior we know that this is not meant to be the way in which we must live. That is what motivates our quest for peace; the cherished calm and joy which comes from living with one another in harmony.

However, if we try to cultivate that peace through our own wisdom and efforts it will not last. As long as sin continues to exhibit a hold on our lives, serenity will continue to slip away from our grasp. The source of strife is our sinful nature. It is what compels us to act in ways which ultimately fail to bring us peace. Our only cure is when we allow Christ to reside in our hearts; accepting His redemptive sacrifice for us and permitting Him to break the chains that sin holds in our lives. When we make that choice to submit our attitudes and thoughts to Him, He will fill us with His everlasting peace. By resting in the peace which Christ gives us, only then will we be able to dwell with each other in love and unity. He will give us His Spirit of discernment to choose our words carefully and act according to His righteousness through His enabling. When we choose to step outside His perfect will and fail to allow Him to take reign over our thoughts and actions, we will not find peace either with ourselves or with others. But when we choose to live in accordance with Christ, we will be able to live in harmony with those around us; bearing witness to the assured hope of the human race being restored through Him.

December 16

SPREADING THE HOPE

"I consider that our present sufferings are not worth comparing with the glory that will be revealed in us. The creation waits in eager expectation for the sons of God to be revealed. For the creation was subjected to frustration, not by its own choice, but by the will of the one who subjected it, in hope that the creation itself will be liberated from its bondage to decay and brought into the glorious freedom of the children of God." -Romans 8: 18-21 (NIV)

Sometimes we may wonder why we are placed in this world. When we have allowed Christ to invade our hearts and work out His redemptive purposes in our lives, we may ask for what purpose does He keep us here on this Earth? Everywhere we turn, we are confronted by the fact that the world in which we live is one marked by suffering and torment. Often this fact overwhelms us and we ask God why we must endure the horrors of this world; yearning for the pleasures we are promised in Heaven. But if our acceptance and desire to follow Christ is motivated solely on the basis of gaining a one-way ticket to Paradise, then we have subscribed to a highly individualistic view of the Christian life that is not within the will of God.

There is a specific reason as to why we are placed in this world. God has called His children to be active participants in His restorative mission for humanity. Far from retreating from the world and waiting for the day we enter Heaven, we are to abide ourselves in His love. When we do this, we are enabled and empowered by His Spirit residing within us to draw others to the hope that is available through Christ as His love overflows from our lives. While we can look forward to the blessings of meeting with God in Heaven, we must keep our eyes on the task at hand; to bring others into the knowledge of Christ so that they too may partake of the blessings and joy which come from knowing Him intimately. Though the world may weigh us down Christ has overcome the world, and we can be assured that through all the trials we may face in this life, He will be the one to sustain us because He is Life.

December 17

BEING A WATCHMAN

"At the end of seven days the word of the Lord came to me: 'Son of man, I have made you a watchman for the house of Israel; so hear the word I speak and give them warning from me.'" -Ezekiel 3:16-17 (NIV)

In most cases, the first image that comes to our mind when we think of a prophet is that of a lone messenger proclaiming the words of God. But it would seem that there is another dimension to the idea of being a prophet. God had appointed Ezekiel to be a, "watchman for the house of Israel." What does it mean to carry out this role? Watchmen exist for the purpose of protecting the people. This involves seeing to the maintenance of a standard of behavior that would contribute to the welfare of the people while speaking up against violations of that standard. The function of watchmen therefore is an important one. Without him to hold the people accountable to the standard set in place, there would be chaos and injustice everywhere!

God has called us to be watchmen wherever we are. As His children we are to draw those within our circle of influence towards the righteousness and truth found in Christ. But can we do so by our own strength or will? Can the watchman properly uphold the principles of the law without obtaining an intimate understanding of it? Likewise unless Christ's righteousness is being made manifest within our lives, our stand for His precepts will be weak and brittle. When we have allowed Christ to enter into our hearts and have given Him free reign to carry out His restorative work within us, only then will we understand what true righteousness is and seek to uphold that which Christ has given us. Being a watchman may place us at odds with those who oppose our stand for the instructions of Christ. However, when we lean on the power of Christ within us, He will enable us when our voices falter; boldly proclaiming His truth and seeking to bring others into a restored relationship with Him.

December 18

IT'S HARVEST TIME!

"Do you not say, 'Four months more and then the harvest'? I tell you, open your eyes and look at the fields! They are ripe for harvest.'" - John 4:35 (NIV)

We seem to be experts in the field of procrastination. For almost every activity under the sun we would put it off if it meant enjoying the short term pleasure of undisturbed idleness. Our excuses for our sloth vary. Amid claims of not being ready and that there is plenty of time to do what we must, we wait whilst we resolve to act when we feel that the time is right. But how often does that moment never come? Our laziness prevents us from acting decisively when it is required of us. By the time we realize the urgency of the task we have been called to carry out, it may perhaps be already too late, and we lament over missed opportunities and our own unwillingness to strike while the iron was hot.

In our own spiritual lives we often suffer from the same malady. How often do we make excuses before God; claiming that while we are willing to do what He says, we do not feel that it would be ideal at this time. But who are we to make such excuses? Do we see what He sees? Do we presume to know better than omnipotent God by our attitudes? In His flawless wisdom He knows exactly when we should act in accordance with His perfect will. When we have the Spirit of Christ residing within us, He will prompt us; telling us that the harvest is now. Yet if we refuse to listen to the Spirit's promptings and live according to our excuses, we are essentially cheating ourselves out of the joys and blessings which come when we walk in obedience to Christ. When we allow Christ to open our eyes and step out in obedience to Him, our insecurities and apprehensions will fade away. We will be strengthened by the fact that He will provide us with all we need to reap His harvest in our lives and the world around us.

December 19

SECURING OURSELVES FIRST

"Brothers, if someone is caught in a sin, you...should restore him gently. But watch yourself, or you also may be tempted." -Galatians 6:1 (NIV)

Lifeguards and sailors are trained to follow a specific protocol when confronted with a situation in which a person is drowning. While any well intended person would rush headlong in order to save the hapless victim, this is actually not a good idea. A person who is drowning is often thoroughly frightened and afraid. Flailing madly in order to save himself, the victim ironically becomes a danger to the uninformed rescuer; able to accidentally drown them both in his panicked state. Proper rescue techniques are meant to aid the victim while at the same time ensuring the safety of the rescuer. A potential rescuer must first make sure that he himself is in a secure position before attempting to save the life of another.

When we have acknowledged Christ as Lord, we are called as His children to play a part in His restorative mission for humanity. But if we rely on our own human wisdom and strength in order to pull someone out of sin, we will find ourselves slowly being dragged into wickedness. Good intentions are simply not enough, for the human heart and mind is easily malleable. Unless we are firmly rooted in Christ and are allowing His Spirit to help us act in accordance to His wisdom, we will end up bending to the remnants of our own sinful nature in our efforts to aid another in his struggle against sin. We must first check our hearts and see if our relationship with Christ is in order. By surrendering every area of our lives to His refining power and applying the truths we glean from His Word, we will be able to address sin not by any authority of our own, but solely by Christ's redemptive work being made manifest in us. When we are immersed in our relationship with Christ and our foundation is built on Him, sin will never be able to carry us away; thereby allowing Him to draw others to Himself and His righteousness.

December 20

IT WILL BE MADE PLAIN

"Woe to those who go to great depths to hide their plans from the Lord, who do their work in darkness and think, 'Who sees us? Who will know?'" -Isaiah 29:15 (NIV)

What are we trying to hide from God? Human nature is drawn to sin. That is why our first reaction is to conceal our wickedness instead of being honest about it. Though we may know that our sinful choices are inherently deplorable and destructive, we go to great lengths to indulge secretly in degrading pleasures simply because we do not want to let go. We feel that as long as we can keep up appearances and are careful to ensure that our hidden lives are not make known, we can hold tightly onto our sin without having to face tangible consequences. But while in our human wisdom we may think that we are clever in our efforts to obscure our sin from the eyes of others; to God our attempts are akin to those of a child who has sloppily tried to hide his deviant behavior when his parents have caught him red-handed.

Nothing can be hidden from God. We are truly fools if we believe that somehow His omnipotence is blind to our acts of depravity. He knows us intimately well; being able to perceive our thoughts even before they come to our minds. Therefore, He knows every act committed in secret, whether good or bad. If we have made it a practice of covertly holding onto sin in our lives, the light of His Truth will expel the darkness and expose our wickedness. Sin always has its consequences and although they do not always appear instantaneously, they will slowly manifest themselves, much to our horror, in our lives and attitudes. But while God's Truth will reveal our innate corruption, He does not leave us in this state. He has given us His Son, Jesus Christ, so that we may live as men free from our bondage to sin. Through our personal acceptance of the redemptive sacrifice of Christ and by allowing His Spirit to enter into our hearts, He will cleanse us and make us spotless before God. When we walk in obedience to His Spirit and permit Him to display His righteousness in our lives, we will have nothing to hide before God; enjoying the unshakable peace and wonder which comes from an unhindered relationship with Him.

December 21

TO LOVE INDISCRIMINATELY

"Then Jesus said to his host, 'When you give a luncheon or dinner, do not invite your friends, your brothers or relatives, or your rich neighbors; if you do, they may invite you back and so you will be repaid. But when you give a banquet, invite the poor, the crippled, the lame, the blind, and you will be blessed.'" -Luke 14:12-14a (NIV)

Who do we allow into our circle of friends? If we take a careful look around us, we may find that they share two things in common. The first of these is that they are similar to us. Human tendency is to congregate with others who are alike in appearance, status, tastes, and outlook. Invariably, people find a sense of affirmation and security in their identity by conforming themselves to a certain group. The second common factor is that they are of benefit to us. Somehow being in relationship with them maintains our own status, and we act out of kindness assured that its recipient will be able to return the favor. But what about those who make us feel uncomfortable; who do not fit in nor have anything to offer us? Does our love extend to those people as well?

Human love is actually not love at all. Rather it is a self-gratifying emotion that is dependent on the usefulness of others in boosting our ego and providing us with benefits. If these were taken away, and they could vanish easily, our love would dissipate along with it. True compassion is not birthed out of ulterior motives, but out of the selfless love of Christ. He had nothing to gain Himself by reaching down to draw us out of sin for as the Lord of Creation He lacked nothing. Yet because He did not want to see us perish under the weight of our wickedness, He came into this world as a vulnerable human being, endured the sufferings of this world, and experienced the agony of the cross for our sake. His gift of salvation is open to all, regardless of who we are, and will never be withdrawn or withheld. When we personally accept His death and resurrection and allow His Spirit to enter into our hearts, we will be transformed by His unconditional love if we surrender our pride to His refining work. As our selective, conditional love is replaced by His indiscriminate, unconditional love, through the work of His Spirit, we will truly understand what it means to be a child of Christ who identifies with his Father in Heaven.

December 22

DO WE KNOW HIM?

"The man who says, 'I know him,' but does not do what he commands is a liar, and the truth is not in him." -1 John 2:4 (NIV)

Do we truly know God? Many in this world, including ourselves, claim to have a full understanding of God and who He is. However, human wisdom is not able to comprehend the truth about God. If we rely solely on our fallible minds to understand God we will either gain a partial picture of who He is, or a distorted portrait altogether. God cannot be simply reduced to a subject. He cannot be understood through the reading of a textbook or being debated about in the company of others. Even the Scriptures, if we are reading them with the wrong lenses, will skew our understanding about God; not because the Scriptures themselves are incorrect, but because our interpretation of them is flawed.

How then is it possible to know God? To know Him intimately and acquire a complete knowledge of who He is requires us to do something quite radical and personal. Only when we accept the redemptive sacrifice of Christ and make that personal choice to allow His Spirit to reside within us, will we be able to obtain a true understanding of God. We can only comprehend Him when we are walking in obedience with Him; submitting every area of our lives to Him in order to gain the Truth. When we cast aside our trepidations and step out in faith, He will prove His faithfulness in our lives and provide for our needs according to His flawless timing. By abandoning the idolatry of our faulty wisdom and allowing Christ's Spirit to help us see, we will be able to understand the Scriptures; which bear witness to a God who is infinitely just and abounding in love. God is not a concept that is to be studied, but a living and personal being who is to be experienced in a relationship.

December 23

OCCUPIED BY LITTLE GAMES

"If anyone has material possessions and sees his brother in need but has no pity on him, how can the love of God be in him?" -1 John 3:17 (NIV)

"The Night They Burned Shanghai" is a poem written in 1938 by Robert D. Abrahams. It describes an American couple in Philadelphia set amidst the backdrop of the Battle of Shanghai, one of the bloodiest battles of the Second Sino-Japanese War. As the beautiful Chinese city is under relentless assault at the hands of the Japanese military, the couple, far away from the unfolding carnage, are on their way to play cards at the house of a friend. As they drive, the couple talks about how next year they will consider the affairs of the world; how they will travel and "...fight for ancient liberties..." outside their relatively comfortable circle.

What is tragic about this poem is that the couple also plans to travel to Shanghai at some point. But with a hint of indifference in their voice they say "...they're burning that tonight – And not tonight - we have a date tonight," When the couple reach the house, their host laments about the mess the Far East has become, and while they nod in agreement, they become absorbed in their game of cards without giving Shanghai a second thought.

Too often, when we are blessed with all the pleasures and comforts man can ask for, we forget that we live in a world full of suffering. Though we may pay a token acknowledgement to those who are in the pit of despair, we rarely lift a finger to do anything about it. Our unwillingness to make a difference in this world may stem from the fact that we do not want to sacrifice the life of ease we have created, and disturb the routine we have grown accustomed to. But if we claim ourselves to be infused with the love of Christ, such indifference cannot co-exist within our souls at the same time. Christ is God Incarnate; the Lord of Heaven and Earth. Yet despite His position He dwelt among us in human form, with all the limitations that entails, so that He may save humanity from sin through His death on the cross. His love disregards the self; seeking only to bring restoration and healing to the lives of others. Do we have His love overflowing from our hearts? If we remain calloused to the world around us, not only have we failed to be obedient to the Spirit of Christ residing within us, but we will encounter a slow process of inward degradation. In the final two verses, the poem ends with a solemn warning:

"Tonight Shanghai is burning,
And we are dying too.

What bomb more surely mortal
Than death inside of you?
   For some men die by shrapnel,
And some go down in flames,
But most men perish inch by inch,
In play at little games."

December 24

DEBUNKING THE PROPAGANDA

"In God I trust; I will not be afraid. What can man do to me?" - Psalm 56:11 (NIV)

   Throughout human history those who have exercised absolute power have always made extensive use of propaganda. From the time of the Pharaohs to the totalitarian dictators of the present day, its purpose has remained the same. By portraying the limitless power and infallibility of a leader or party, the object of propaganda is to instill awe and fear in the hearts of the people. In doing so, they lessen the chances of disgruntled citizens questioning and rising up against the will of those in control. But while statues and broadcasts may try to appear convincing in the depiction of their subject's godlike status, the fact is that they are not. In reality, the figures which propaganda tries to elevate are very much human; suffering from the same limitations and flaws as any other person.

   We too have fed ourselves false propaganda. How often have we cowered before men? In our minds we have exaggerated their power and abilities over us. Yet when we have constructed this image in our minds, we become paralyzed with fear. Afraid of what may happen to us if we take a stand for something they are not in favor of, we become immobilized; unable to boldly proclaim the righteousness and justice of Christ. But how can this be when we serve an omnipotent God? Why do we fear men when Christ, who is God Incarnate and who gave man breath, promises to be our stronghold and fortress when we walk in obedience to Him? Through Him we have conquered those diseases that plague man, sin and death, and assured of the hope of dwelling with Him in Heaven. Who therefore is man that we should allow them to intimidate us? When we have allowed Christ's Spirit to reside within us and look through His eyes, we will be able to see people as they really are; not as invincible supermen, but souls in desperate need of salvation just as much as ourselves. He will give us the courage to speak fearlessly His truth no matter the audience and no matter the cost.

December 25

THIS IS CHRISTMAS!

"But the angel said to them, 'Do not be afraid. I bring you good news of great joy that will be for all the people. Today in the town of David a Savior has been born to you; he is Christ the Lord.'" -Luke 2:10-11 (NIV)

One of my favorite Christmas songs is "Mary Did You Know?", written by Mark Lowry. In this song, the tender moment of Mary holding the newborn Jesus is placed into perspective in light of who He is and is destined to be. His mission to redeem humanity from sin is illustrated in the final line of the first verse; "This child that you've delivered, will soon deliver you.", and concludes with a powerful line describing His divine nature; "This sleeping child you're holding, is the Great I Am." The entire song essentially summarizes why every year Christians all over the world take great joy and celebration on this day. It marks the entrance of hope into a world of darkness; the hope that through Christ will come man's deliverance from sin and despair.

What is the true meaning of Christmas? Over two thousand years later, it has become saturated by an excessive consumerism; exploited by those who are obsessed with gaining wealth and prestige. Yet while we know that this rampant materialism has failed to attach meaning to Christmas, we try to find its meaning elsewhere. One place is in the warmth and joy spent with family and friends. But though this is important and good, it is not the reason why Christmas is celebrated. We may even pay a nominal acceptance of the fact that it is about Christ and erect our Nativity scenes depicting baby Jesus. However, unless we have gone beyond the image of the infant Christ, have understood the true purpose of His coming down to Earth, and have personally allowed His Spirit to carry out His restorative work in our lives, the celebrations of Christmas hold no meaning. To truly celebrate Christmas is to dwell in the joy of knowing that on this day our Savior, Jesus Christ was born. In His infinite love He had one sole purpose; to save humanity through His death and to give us life through His resurrection. Outside of Christ there can be no other meaning to Christmas. No other substitute will be able to match the glory of Christ's entry into the world, and the implications it has for all mankind.

December 26

A DAY OF GIVING

"If one of your countrymen becomes poor and is unable to support himself among you, help him as you would an alien or a temporary resident, so he can continue to live among you." -Leviticus 25:35 (NIV)

In certain countries within the British Commonwealth, the tradition of Boxing Day remains strong. Falling on the day after Christmas, it is presently known as a day where people throng department stores in order to take advantage of great sales that only come once a year However, this was far from its intended purpose. Instead of acquiring more possessions, the day was focused on addressing the needs of the poor. Families would make gift boxes and pack food, toys, and clothes in order that they may be distributed to those who did not have the luxury of obtaining these things. Alms boxes would be placed in churches where congregants would donate money to be divided amongst the needy in their midst. Wealthy landlords would give their household servants bonuses, gifts, and the opportunity to visit their families as an act of gratitude for their hard work.

It is tempting to become self-absorbed during the Christmas season. With all the celebrations, gifts, and presents, it is easy to simply bask in the blessings of possessing material wealth. In all these things however, God has called His children to consider the poor. To aid the destitute is mandated in Scripture and is close to the heart of God for He has created all in His image. But we are mistaken if we think we can fulfill this mandate on our own strength and capabilities. Human tendency is to be selfish and to seek ways to glorify the self, even in our charity. Only when we have allowed the Spirit of Christ to conduct His redemptive work in our lives and yield our selfishness to Him, will He fill us with His selfless love. When we do this, we will be fulfilling His mandate not because of any counterfeit benevolence of our own, but solely by the love and compassion of Christ overflowing from within us. By allowing our hearts to be molded by Him, our ears will be open to His voice and He will move us to act with genuine concern towards those around us; bearing witness to who He is and what He intends to do for all of humanity.

December 27

WHO'S THE REAL CRIMINAL?

"You, therefore, have no excuse, you who pass judgment on someone else, for at whatever point you judge the other, you are condemning yourself, because you who pass judgment do the same things." -Romans 2:1 (NIV)

Crime has become something characteristic of life in this fallen world. In every society, in every culture, and in every age, we are made aware of the prevalence of criminal activity. Whether it is through historical documents, popular movies, or even today's news, we cannot escape the reality that deviance exists and will continue to exist as long as humans populate this world. Yet when we see images of thieves and murderers we become inflated by self-righteousness. Though we may acknowledge the depravity of their actions and look down upon them in disgust, we blind ourselves to our own innate wickedness. How many of us, in envy and jealousy, have desired to take that which was not ours to take? How many of us, in our rage, have wanted to act in violence toward another person? Sin according to Christ is not defined by sole outward action, but by the very thought, and under that definition we are all criminals.

To redeem us from our sinful nature, Christ came so that by His death and resurrection we may be free from the bondage of sin and clothed with His righteousness. But we often forget to put on these clothes which He has given us. While we may think that we are wearing these clothes and are standing up for the holy standards of Christ, we are actually naked if we have done so in a judgmental spirit. Usually we end up using our self-proclaimed righteousness as weapon to slander others and boost our own pride. Truly wearing the garments of purity Christ has given us means humbling ourselves knowing that while we were bound as sinners and still chose to indulge in sin, Christ has forgiven us in His love. Nothing will be able to snatch us from the love of God and He will continue to remain faithful to the redemptive work He wants to carry out in our lives. When we have submitted ourselves to Christ's Spirit and have allowed His righteousness to be made manifest in our lives, we will remain unapologetic in His view of sin while at the same time displaying His love. He will prompt us to remember that just as He has forgiven us of much, we are to show mercy and love by His enabling; drawing others into the hope of being restored by Him.

December 28

HE ALREADY KNOWS!

"Before they call I will answer; while they are still speaking I will hear." -Isaiah 65:24 (NIV)

Often times, a good doctor can tell what is wrong with a patient even before the patient himself utters a word. Outward signs, such as overall complexion and severity of coughing for example, can often be enough information for doctors to understand the situation and recommend prescriptions accordingly. But doctors usually do not do this right away. They first wait for the patient to tell them what is ailing them. Only after the patient requests to undergo treatment does the doctor act. Doctors cannot simply force treatment on someone, but are required to wait until the patient willingly submits himself to the doctor's expertise. When this happens, doctors are required to act towards the restoration of the health of the patient; doing all that is within their power to bring healing.

In His infinite wisdom God knows exactly what we need. He has created us and knows us intimately well; even better than we know ourselves! As the embodiment of love and righteousness He wants to provide for us in our time of need. Yet He will not act if we have not submitted ourselves to Christ and His perfect will for our lives. If we in our pride have rejected Him by clinging onto our flawed wisdom and understanding, we cannot assume that He will grant us what we need. Only when we have come with humble hearts to Him in prayer, making that choice to trust in His flawless guidance and allowing Him to direct our steps, will He unveil the wonderful plan He has in store for us according to His faultless timing. By abandoning our pride and fear; running instead into the arms of Christ and acknowledging that His ways are better than ours, we will be able to find rest in His promise that He already knows what we need in our situations and will lovingly provide for us when we ask.

December 29

A REVOLUTIONARY LOVE

> *"But I tell you who hear me: Love your enemies, do good to those who hate you, bless those who curse you, pray for those who mistreat you."* -Luke 6:27-28 (NIV)

When we have been the victim of injustice and insult, the command to love our enemies seems ludicrous. Human tendency is to seek retribution for wrongs through our own wisdom and might. If someone strikes us, our instant reaction is to strike them ten times as hard. If we have become the subject of torment and ridicule, our most treasured desire is the day when we can inflict the same misery upon our oppressors. Yet this is how the cycle of hatred and violence begins; by a simple yearning to get even. The moment we let vengeance to invade our hearts, we will be consumed by an insatiable rage. Revenge will distort our image of people and propel us to take pleasure in committing horrible acts that we thought we would never carry out. Though we may think that we are able to master these unbridled emotions, in actuality we become slaves to our hate and bitterness.

Our unwillingness to love our enemies and to do good to those who hate us often stems from the misconception that to do so is a sign of timidity and weakness, along with an acceptance of the wrongs that have been exacted upon us.

But this is far from the truth. Christ never acknowledged that the injustices committed against Him were inherently virtuous. While suffering on the cross He cried out to God in Luke 23:24, "Father forgive them, for they do not know what they are doing." Yet while He was omnipotent and could have easily overpowered His persecutors, He loved them. Redemption and restoration would not come through violence, but by a love that has no earthly parallel.

Christ went to the cross for the Pharisees who accused Him, for the soldiers who clubbed and tortured Him, for men who nailed Him, and for the crowd who hurled insult after insult while He endured the agony of crucifixion. He did this so that through His death and resurrection they may no longer be slaves to wickedness, but free under His righteousness. As children of Christ we are called to emulate the selfless love shown by Him. But as long as we have made vengeance and hatred our idol, we will never be capable of displaying this love. Only when we have allowed Christ to invade our hearts and have submitted ourselves to His Spirit will His love overflow from our lives. His sweetness is more effective than any weapon and when we make that choice to have it made manifest in ourselves, it will bear witness to those around us of the beauty and freedom that is available through the power of Christ.

December 30

STUDY YOUR HISTORY!

"For everything that was written in the past was written to teach us, so that through endurance and the encouragement of the Scriptures we might have hope." -Romans 15:4 (NIV)

I often cringe when I hear people say that studying history is boring and irrelevant. While historians are sometimes accused of having immersed themselves in the past to the point that they have disconnected themselves from the present, history itself is meant to be a guide. A good scholar of history knows how to take the lessons of the past and apply them to the present in the hopes of constructing a better future. To work to prevent the horrors of the past from occurring again, we must first understand how and why they came about. Conversely, what was good and noble of the past should be reclaimed and appropriately implemented within the context of the modern age. An understanding of history will help us make sense of the world around us; where it has been and where it is going.

The Word of God, is the best history textbook available to man. Its pages bear witness to the story of humanity from the time God created us and our descent into wickedness, to Christ's redemptive sacrifice on the cross and the hope we have through Him by identifying with His death and resurrection. Its characters are real people living in real places at real points in human history. Even historians outside the Christian tradition attest to the veracity of the Scriptures! Throughout the Bible we are provided with examples of people who chose to remain within the will of God and those who chose to remain outside; along with the consequences of their respective decisions. But unless we have personally chosen to apply the truths of the Bible to our lives, then our knowledge of the Scriptures is meaningless. Only when we have allowed the Spirit of Christ to reside in our hearts and have submitted our understanding to His perfect wisdom will He be able to teach us through His Word. With Him as our Guide, we will know how to live according to His righteousness and dwell in the hope of being ultimately restored through Him.

December 31

IT CAME AT A PRICE

"...you were bought at a price. Therefore honor God with your body." -1 Corinthians 6:20 (NIV)

Two summers ago I had the wonderful privilege of visiting Washington D.C. One of the places we visited was Arlington Cemetery; where the remains of American soldiers killed in battle are buried. Seeing rows upon rows of white gravestones was a truly sobering experience. But what left an impression on me was what our tour guide left us with. He alluded to the fact that freedom is not really free, but always comes at a price. I then remembered America's especially vital contributions to the Second World War. Faced with the scourges of fascism and ultra-nationalism, it sent its soldiers to fight in order to preserve not only its own freedom, but the freedom of many other nations as well. Those who enjoy liberty today are indebted to those who saw and continue to see to its maintenance.

When we allow Christ's Spirit to reside in us, we are no longer bound by our sinful nature, but are able to choose to follow Him. However, this freedom came at the cost of His blood. Since God is holy, He cannot tolerate sin and the appropriate punishment for sin is death. But He did not want His creation to suffer such a fate and wants to reconcile us with Him. For this reason, Christ became the one sacrificial Lamb for all who desire forgiveness and to be made right with God. By His death the penalty for our wickedness is paid, and through the resurrection of Christ we have conquered the power sin and death held over us. Yet why do we voluntarily return to our wickedness? Christ's sacrifice is not a license to indulge in vice, but it is to be treated with respect knowing that our freedom came at the cost of His life. What should our response be to His selfless and unwavering love? When we submit ourselves to His Spirit and walk in obedience to Him, we will know of the joys of living in the freedom He has given to us. This means seeking to honor Christ in whatever we do, be it in mind, body, soul, or spirit; allowing Him to aid us living according to His righteousness.

www.ingramcontent.com/pod-product-compliance
Lightning Source LLC
Chambersburg PA
CBHW022111080426
42734CB00006B/87